mjf

ASPECTS OF THE MASCULINE

Translation by R. F. C. Hull

Introduction by John Beebe

ASPECTS OF THE FEMININE

Translation by R. F. C. Hull

MJF BOOKS
NEW YORK

Published by MJF Books
Fine Communications
Two Lincoln Square
60 West 66th Street
New York, NY 10023

Library of Congress Catalog Card Number 96-78808
ISBN 1-56731-137-7

This edition published by arrangement with Princeton University Press.

Manufactured in the United States of America on acid-free paper

10 9 8 7 6 5 4 3 2 1

ASPECTS OF THE MASCULINE

C. G. JUNG

TRANSLATED BY R.F.C. HULL
INTRODUCTION AND HEADNOTES BY JOHN BEEBE

TABLE OF CONTENTS

EDITOR'S INTRODUCTION

To understand what C. G. Jung means by "the masculine" is to gain access to the ground of his entire approach to psychology, for his psychology, as he liked to admit, was his "personal confession"—the confession of a man seeking to understand human psychology in the patriarchal context of a private practice in a western European country in the first half of the twentieth century. Not even the demonstrable universality of the archetypal world that he uncovered in this endeavor could eliminate the human standpoint of the pioneer, who remained a man telling us what *his* experience had been. Therefore the present collection of excerpts from his writings affords an opportunity to discover what Jung himself understood of the contribution that gender made to his "personal equation," a chance to look at the lens of the telescope through which he made his famous and far-reaching observations of the major psychological constellations.

Surprisingly, with the exception of the very early essay, "On the Significance of the Father in the Destiny of the Individual," written when he was still a Freudian psychoanalyst, there is no single published work in which Jung devotes himself exclusively to either the psychology of men or the broader unconscious psychology of the masculine. There is neither a monograph detailing a man's process of psychological development nor an essay devoted to the animus, the masculine archetype that Jung interpreted for women as their soul-image. One has to pick one's way through many essays to uncover the thread of meaning that conveys Jung's own masculine path through the labyrinth of the unconscious. The present selection, though far from the only one possible, is an attempt to reveal this thread to the reader who wants to follow Jung's track.

The path unfolds from Jung's own childhood experiences in a vicarage as the son of a pastor who was losing his faith and the confidence of his wife and son. Paul Jung was both blocked and incapable of the kind of self-reflection that could have unlocked his spirit; for the child Jung, with his enormous potential for psychological development, this father was an unsatisfactory figure with whom to identify. In his extraordinary imaginal autobiography, *Memories, Dreams, Reflections,* Jung gives us a glimpse of the degree to which he had to found his own identity upon a private vision of the numinous power of the masculine. This vision of archetypal masculinity was of the kind that comes to a child who has at hand no human role model to incarnate the archetypal image and mediate its power and meaning:

> . . . I had the earliest dream I can remember, a dream which was to preoccupy me all my life . . . (when) I was . . . between three and four years old.
>
> The vicarage stood quite alone near Laufen castle, and there was a big meadow stretching back from the sexton's farm. In the dream I was in this meadow. Suddenly I discovered a dark, rectangular, stone-lined hole in the ground. I had never seen it before. I ran forward curiously and peered down into it. Then I saw a stone stairway leading down. Hesitantly and fearfully, I descended. At the bottom was a doorway with a round arch, closed off by a green curtain. It was a big, heavy curtain of worked stuff like brocade, and it looked very sumptuous. Curious to see what might be hidden behind, I pushed it aside. I saw before me in the dim light a rectangular chamber about thirty feet long. The ceiling was arched and of hewn stone. The floor was laid with flagstones, and in the center a red carpet ran from the entrance to a low platform. On this platform stood a wonderfully rich golden throne. I am not certain, but perhaps a red cushion lay on the seat. It was a magnificent throne, a real king's throne in a fairy tale. Something was standing on it which I thought at first was a tree trunk twelve to fifteen feet high and about one and a half to two feet thick. It was a huge thing, reaching almost to the ceiling. But it was of a curious composition: it was made of skin and naked flesh, and on top there was something like a rounded head with no face and no hair. On the very top of the head was a single eye, gazing motionlessly upward.
>
> It was fairly light in the room, although there were no windows and no apparent source of light. Above the head, however, was an aura of brightness. The thing did not move, yet I

had the feeling that it might at any moment crawl off the throne like a worm and creep toward me. I was paralyzed with terror. At that moment I heard from outside and above my mother's voice. She called out, "Yes, just look at him. That is the man-eater!" That intensified my terror still more, and I awoke sweating and scared to death. For many nights afterward I was afraid to go to sleep, because I feared I might have another dream like that.

This dream haunted me for years. Only much later did I realize that what I had seen was a phallus, and it was decades before I understood that it was a ritual phallus. . . .

The abstract significance of the phallus is shown by the fact that it was enthroned by itself, "ithyphallically" ('ιφυς, "upright"). The hole in the meadow probably represented a grave. The grave itself was an underground temple whose green curtain symbolized the meadow, in other words the mystery of earth with her covering of green vegetation. The carpet was *blood-red.* What about the vault? Perhaps I had already been to the Munot, the citadel of Schaffhausen? This is not likely, since no one would take a three-year-old child up there. So it cannot be a memory trace. Equally, I do not know where the anatomically correct phallus can have come from. The interpretation of the *orificium urethrae* as an eye, with the source of light apparently above it, points to the etymology of the word phallus (φαλος, shining, bright).

At all events, the phallus of this dream seems to be a subterranean God "not to be named," and such it remained throughout my youth, reappearing when anyone spoke too loudly about Lord Jesus. Lord Jesus never became quite real for me, never quite acceptable, never quite lovable, for again and again I would think of his underground counterpart, a frightful revelation which had been accorded me without my seeking it.[1]

How the atmosphere of the nineteenth-century Swiss parsonage emerges from Jung's recounting of this dream and his much later associations to it! We are returned to a now-vanished late Refor-

[1] C. G. Jung, *Memories, Dreams, Reflections,* recorded and ed. Aniela Jaffé, trans. Richard and Clara Winston (New York: Pantheon, 1963), pp. 11-13.

mation world in which the bodies of the parents were never seen, and the anatomical fact of the erect penis with its urethral orifice was a religious secret, a delicate matter to be broached only in the church languages of Greek and Latin, with their mythological overtones. Growing up in this repressive atmosphere, Jung was destined to meet his masculinity archetypally, and the energy with which the archetype presented itself led him to a healing understanding of what it means to be a man that is unparalleled in the psychological literature. But because Jung's approach to the masculine was so archetypal (so underground, in the language of this dream), it is easy for its relevance to the psychology of everyday men and women to remain buried. Therefore some introduction is needed to the contents of this volume to make Jung's important insights more accessible.

The most important of these insights is the association of masculinity with the process of becoming conscious, in the Socratic sense of seeing one's existence for what it is. The equation of masculinity with consciousness is implied in the etymological linkage of phallus to brightness, and the creative child's association of the phallic opening with an eye. This early intuition was one-sided in that it left out the feminine contribution to consciousness; but its peculiarly monocular insight into the phallic nature of the psyche was essential for the development of Jung's thought. It became the basis of Jung's first attempt to find a different metaphor for the psyche's drama than the Oedipus mythologem that Freud offered. Oedipus implied the doctrine of repression, an eventual self-blinding of the human in the face of the intolerable imposed upon him by the gods. From Oedipus's story had come notions of the dream as a necessarily disguised revelation and of the psyche as something to be unmasked by a technically skilled analyst against formidable resistances. This mythologem left out the pressure from within to become conscious, which for Jung was the strongest drive of the psyche, stronger than sex or the will to power. Jung's image of the developing ego in *Wandlungen und Symbole der Libido* was not of a guilt-ridden executive bent on repressing his knowledge of shameful libidinal experience, but rather of a determined solar hero whose quest through the night sea was to maintain and increase his light against the deep instinctual forces threatening to extinguish his consciousness. (Ironically, Jung found this masculine image in the unconscious material of a woman on the brink of a psychosis.) That his hero was, like Oedipus, inflated, with a dangerous masculine arrogance in the face of the dark and lunar feminine, was anything but apparent to the thirty-six-year-old Jung who had dared to challenge Freud with his own more optimistic view of the evolutionary possibilities of ego-consciousness.

Freud's rejection of these ideas (and of the self-important way in which Jung chose to present them to the psychoanalytic world) and the concurrent uncertainty of a marital crisis brought Jung out of his youthful identification with the archetype of the heroic deliverer. The problem of his marriage was resolved (at cost to all concerned) only after a difficult decision had been reached to submit concretely and literally to the power of the feminine by accepting an open liaison with Toni Wolff. Jung's involvement with his former patient, now his colleague, occurred with the full knowledge of his wife, whom he continued to love and honor. This still-controversial solution was never touted by the mature Jung as an example to others; rather it represented the best he could do against, and finally with, the power of the anima archetype, which he discovered by having to live it out. Toni Wolff helped Jung to see theoretically as well as personally that in the deep psyche the hero delivers himself from the mother archetype (and from the infantile unconsciousness that the hero's bondage to her authority represents for the conscious personality) only to encounter the demands of the anima. Like all mythic images, the anima is a root metaphor for an unconscious style of thought and behavior that underlies conscious choices. This archetype, usually symbolized by a woman closer in age to the man than his mother, but not invariably depicted as one figure, or even always as a woman, will become in her many guises his lifelong partner in the struggle for perspective, an indispensable source of the psychological complexities and ethical quandaries that will shape his consciousness and in no small measure his fate.

The anima was Jung's central discovery in the field of masculine psychology, for, as he learned, only the anima can deliver a man into a consciousness that is based, not on heroic self-mastery, but rather on empathic participation in life. Understanding the part of the psyche Jung called the anima is less an insight of the mind than an initiatory experience, a mystery to be lived until its core of meaningfulness for personality development is at last revealed. Jung solved the psychologist's problem, of formulating what can only be experienced, by resurrecting the ancient lore of initiation, with its rich symbolic descriptions of processes through which individuals get from one stage in life to another along a journey that begins with separation from the mother. The idea of initiation was the base from which Jung interpreted dreams and the progress of the psychological pilgrims with whom he worked analytically.

It was this discovery of initiation—the painful submission of the hero to the greater authority of archetypal forces with the power to mediate the development of consciousness—that marks Jung's mature understanding of masculine process and his radical departure from other depth psychologists of the modern era. As Jung's pupil (and analysand) Joseph Henderson was able to make clear in *Thresholds of Initiation,*[2] the hero role is an archetypal stage in the unconscious, denoting the formation of a strong ego-identity, which *precedes* the stage of the true initiate. This is a subtle point that Erik Erikson and other Freudian authors who have followed Jung's idea of "the stages of life" with their own models of ego development throughout the life-cycle seem to have missed. For Jung, as for no other psychological writer, the essence of genuine psychological development involves a giving up of the hero. When heroic consciousness dominates, one thinks one knows better than the unconscious who one is and feels one should therefore be in control of one's life. The hero is the mythologem of ego psychology and of the countless self-help books that keep appearing in this age of those who would "develop" the unconscious.

Obviously, the hero stage is a step forward for people at risk of drowning in the unconscious. The appearance of a hero in the unconscious of a young man who is not grounded enough to master such real-life heroic tasks as the completion of a college education or the overcoming of an addiction is a momentous event. Too often the archetypal basis of consciousness in youth is an unreal fantasy of greatness supplied by the *puer aeternus,* the god whose name means eternal boy. The shadow side of this archetype is the trickster, who seems to exist only to test psychosocial limits. These precursors of the hero archetype, as Henderson demonstrates in his book, are hard to disidentify with, and for many men in our culture their mastery is the work of the first half of life. It usually

[2] Joseph Henderson, *Thresholds of Initiation* (Middletown, Conn.: Wesleyan University Press, 1967).

requires educational experiences of the right kind to achieve the firm ego-grounding that the stage of the hero represents.

Among these educational experiences are the early love relationships described by Jung in "The Love Problem of a Student." Jung was ahead of his time in realizing that homosexual relationships, if the erotic expression is bounded by the faithfulness of the more mature person, can sometimes offer the right initiatory grounding at the preheroic stage. It is not clear, however, from his published writings whether he could see any value for individuation in love relationships between members of the same sex beyond this stage. A concretism in his understanding of the importance of the anima took hold here. Jung knew that the full psychological potential of being a man is possible only when the hero finally bows his own head and submits to initiation, not at the hands of an outer man or woman but according to the dictates of his own anima. Then a certain development of his eros from within (and not infrequently of his feeling for his place in the lives of others) will take place; so that he is at once better related to himself and to his fellow human beings. In Jung's own life, the development of the anima was intimately associated with events in his own heterosexual life. I have found, in the experience of my own practice, that while the stage of anima acceptance in men is almost always accompanied by an improvement in the quality and depth of relationships with women, the more or less permanent sexual orientation that appears at this time may be either homosexual or heterosexual, determined solely by the essential nature of the individual as mediated by the anima.

Acceptance of the anima is almost invariably difficult. The anima, as Jung points out, is the root word in animosity, and the anima (as moods) can be another name for resentment. Initiation by the anima means submitting to painful experiences of betrayal and disappointment when the projections she creates with her capacity for illusion fail to produce happiness. Accepting the pain of one's affects toward those experiences is a critical part of integrating the anima. Jung sometimes called the anima the "archetype of life," and he saw the individual as forced to suffer at the hands of life until life's power is sufficiently impressed upon him: the resultant conscious attitude, truly "a pearl of great price," is a sense of soul, which is also a respect for life's autonomy, the sort of wisdom personified by the Taoist sage Lao Tzu, whose name means "the old one." The wise old man stands behind the anima as an archetype of meaning, the masculine purpose and masculine result of this initiatory acceptance and integration of the feminine. Many contemporary analysts have questioned whether the anima may not also be an archetype that can mediate a woman's experience of herself. If so, the deep inner self revealed will be a feminine figure of wisdom, a personification of the goddess.

Jung was not ready to emphasize the anima for women. He felt that the women of his time had a special duty to realize their unconscious masculinity, which in his day was particularly in danger of being projected onto men. He understood the animus, only in some ways an analogue of the anima, to have its own particular character, as an archetype neither of life nor of meaning, but of spirit. Spirit was for Jung characteristically masculine, in contrast to soul, which he conceived as feminine. Even when he spoke of the animus as the women's soul-image, he meant that a woman has an unconscious masculine spirit where a man has an unconscious soul. Jung recognized that spirit and soul can figure in the development of both men and women, and he did speak of their *syzygy* or conjunction in the psyche of individuals. Nevertheless, with his women patients he concentrated on the recognition and integration of the spirit as their urgent psychological work. This therapeutic focus on the animus comes through clearly in what he says in the second selection from *Two Essays on Analytical Psychology* about the woman with a father transference to him and in his comments to his analysand and colleague Esther Harding as recorded in her personal notebook. When the spirit was an unconscious animus, projected onto men, he had to be freed up enough to function as an inner figure with whose help the woman could approach her own nature. Only then could she discriminate accurately who she was.

A man, by contrast, needed to learn with the help of a freed-up anima to relate to his nature with the right emotional attitude. Jung observed that among the men he saw, eros—defined as relatedness—tended to be more unconscious than in women. Logos—defined as discrimination—tended to be more unconscious in women. At times he went so far as to assert that eros was the woman's principle and logos the man's, which often sounds in our present cultural context like a sexist rigidity. Yet the unconscious vulnerability to eros in men and to logos in women seems to me to be a human fact, illustrating the everyday usefulness of Jung's gender psychology when applied to the area of his real expertise, the *unconscious* behavior of men and women. My own practice has taught me that, although neither women nor men have a monopoly on good judgment or good capacity for relationship, the unconscious of a woman reacts far more violently to opinions that threaten her world-concept while the unconscious of a man is more easily upset by feelings that violate his emotional equilibrium. Women seem, that is, to have a greater tolerance than men for feelings that challenge their prevailing patterns of relationship and men for ideas they disagree with. This notable difference seems to imply a more differentiated eros in women and a more differentiated logos in men.

On the other hand, Jung's idea of logos as the masculine principle and eros as the feminine principle has led to premature dogmatizing by some Jungian analysts as to the essential psychological character of men and of women and a storm of protest by other analysts, who have argued rightly for the complexity of individual experience. It is important to recognize that logos and eros are styles of consciousness available ultimately to both sexes, and that they represented opposites within Jung's own masculine nature. For (as the excerpts from the *Dream Analysis* seminar and Esther Harding's notebooks illustrate) it is precisely a masculine eros that anima development brings to consciousness in a man, and a feminine logos that animus development brings to a woman. In *Mysterium Coniunctionis,* Jung devoted far more space to his descriptions of the character of Sol and of Luna as personifications of these paradoxical opposites than to his earlier intuitive concepts of logos and eros. It is to this late masterwork that the reader should turn for a sense of Jung's mature thinking as to the nature of the psychological difference between men and women and between the masculine and feminine in both natures. A careful reading of that late work will enable one to dispense with the notion that Jung thought of the feminine as simply relatedness and the masculine as simply conscious discrimination. Indeed, there is a certain unrelatedness to the deep feminine spirit symbolized by Luna, with her dark cold moistness, that gives her a reflective depth; and there is an indiscriminate relatedness to Sol, with his bright warmth, that gives him a penetrating force.

In reading Jung's alchemical writings, one discovers the tradition into which his self-contradictory style of psychological explication falls. As others have observed, his is a hermetic style, one that conceals as much as it reveals, and expresses home truths in alchemical parables that seem to cancel out one another. Such a style is loyal only to nature. Jung's work on Western alchemy began to appear in print after he was sixty years old, and it is deeply grounded in the experience of masculine individuation after midlife. The process of incubating wisdom that the alchemical essays reflect and obliquely describe is one whose specific character and contents will be known only to those who are privy to the reflections of psychologically maturing individuals.

As he was putting his alchemical opus together, Jung gradually understood that even the masculine and feminine principles are not given; they are built up through experience, although the conditions for their creation follow archetypal laws. I have often observed that the building up of the feminine principle in a man during midlife obeys the following alchemical recipe, one that is only implied in Jung but is mentioned by other writers: salt conjoined with mercury produces Luna. Luna, the developed feminine principle, corresponds to an anima who is no longer naive; who has suffered enough (salt: bitterness, tears) and is capable of tricky ruthlessness in her own defense (mercury: trickster, the capacity to turn the tables on an aggressor). Men have the special task in midlife of making sure that Luna is well-enough integrated. (The brief excerpt from the difficult essay on salt speaks specifically to this inner work.) Luna is an initiated unconscious that is ready to interact with the initiated heroic consciousness that is Sol to produce an integration of personality. This is Jung's ultimate image of personality development, and it is obtained through his own masculine perspective.

"The Spirit Mercurius," source of the final selections in this volume, deserves special mention because it gives us our best glimpse into the archetypal ground of that perspective. This is probably the most personal of Jung's great essays on archetypes in that it is a description of Jung's own characteristic spirit and of the consciousness that governed the writing of his psychology. That Mercurius was for Jung the archetype of the unconscious tells us finally how masculine Jung's approach to the unconscious was. Despite his androgyny, Mercurius is a quintessentially masculine god, although not every masculinity will be grounded in this mythologem. So, not even this penetrating essay can be the last word on the masculine. Mercurius is, however, the archetype through which Jung came to understand his own psychological style. This piece stands among Jung's other writings like an ancient *herm,* an erect phallus placed by the Greeks at the gateways to new territories in honor of Hermes, who became the Roman Mercurius and the patron saint of alchemy. The phallic energy that was underground in Jung's childhood dream finds its way fully into the open with this essay. In the attributes of this god one can find Jung's own seminal ideas—the unconscious as an autonomous, creative being continually in motion between sets of opposites; the shifting shapes of the unconscious spirit as signals of its arrival at the gates of different gods; the trend of the unconscious toward stable wholeness within a contained intrapsychic life. Mercurius was the patron of Jung's alchemical effort at self-unification, Jung's ultimate father-figure and masculine way through the psyche. His is the restless masculine spirit that informs the contents of this volume.

John Beebe
San Francisco, September 1988

The editor would like to acknowledge the help of Cathie Brettschneider, Adam Frey, Joseph Henderson, Loren Hoekzema, John Levy, Daniel C. Noel, William McGuire, and Mary Webster.

I. THE HERO*

THE ORIGIN OF THE HERO

251 The finest of all symbols of the libido is the human figure, conceived as a demon or hero. Here the symbolism leaves the objective, material realm of astral and meteorological images and takes on human form, changing into a figure who passes from joy to sorrow, from sorrow to joy, and, like the sun, now stands high at the zenith and now is plunged into darkest night, only to rise again in new splendour.[1] Just as the sun, by its own motion and in accordance with its own inner law, climbs from morn till noon, crosses the meridian and goes its downward way towards evening, leaving its radiance behind it, and finally plunges into all-enveloping night, so man sets his course by immutable laws and, his journey over, sinks into darkness, to rise again in his children and begin the cycle anew.

. . . .

297 The psychic life-force, the libido, symbolizes itself in the sun [59] or personifies itself in figures of heroes with solar attributes. At the same time it expresses itself through phallic symbols. Both possibilities are found on a late Babylonian gem from Lajard's collection (fig. 19). In the middle stands an androgynous deity. On the masculine side there is a snake with a sun halo round its head; on the feminine side another snake with a sickle moon above it. This picture has a symbolic sexual nuance: on the masculine side there is a lozenge, a favourite symbol of the female genitals, and on the feminine side a wheel without its rim. The spokes are thickened at the ends into

1 Hence the beautiful name of the sun-hero Gilgamesh, "The Man of Joy and Sorrow," in Jensen, *Das Gilgamesch-Epos.*

59 Among the elements composing man, the Mithraic liturgy lays particular stress on fire as the divine element, describing it as τὸ εἰς ἐμὴν κρᾶσιν θεοδώρητον (the divine gift in my composition). Dieterich, *Mithrasliturgie,* p. 58.

* [Ed. Note. Plates cited in the text from *Symbols of Transformation* have been omitted.]

knobs, which, like the fingers we mentioned earlier, have a phallic meaning. It seems to be a phallic wheel such as was not unknown in antiquity. There are obscene gems on which Cupid is shown turning a wheel consisting entirely of phalli.[60] As to what the sun signifies, I discovered in the collection of antiquities at Verona a late Roman inscription with the following symbols: [61]

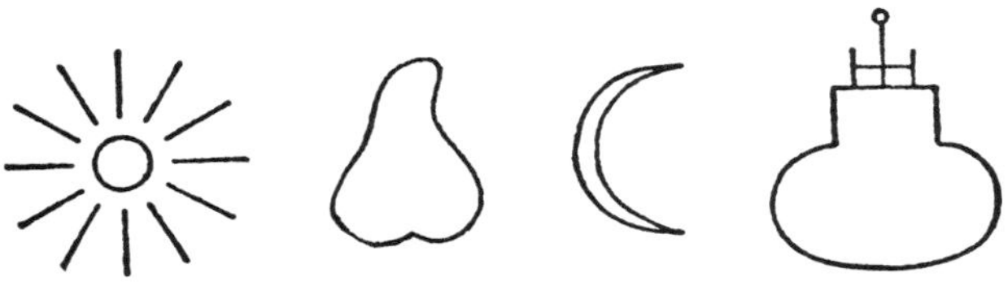

298 The symbolism is plain: sun = phallus, moon = vessel (uterus). This interpretation is confirmed by another monument from the same collection. The symbols are the same, except that the vessel [62] has been replaced by the figure of a woman. Certain symbols on coins can probably be interpreted in a similar manner. In Lajard's *Recherches sur la culte de Vénus* there is a coin from Perga, showing Artemis as a conical stone flanked by a masculine figure (alleged to be the deity Men) and a female figure (alleged to be Artemis). Men (otherwise called Lunus) appears on an Attic bas-relief with a spear, flanked by Pan with a club, and a female figure.[63] From this it is clear that sexuality as well as the sun can be used to symbolize the libido.

299 One further point deserves mention here. The dadophor Cautopates is often represented with a cock [64] and pine-cones. These are the attributes of the Phrygian god Men (pl. xxi*a*), whose cult was very widespread. He was shown with the pileus [65] (or "Phrygian cap") and pine-cones, riding on the cock, and also

60 An illustration of the periodicity or rhythm expressed in sexuality.

61 Reproduced not from a photograph, but from a drawing I myself made.

62 In a myth of the Bakairi Indians, of Brazil, a woman appears who sprang from a corn mortar. A Zulu myth tells a woman to catch a drop of blood in a pot, then close the pot, put it aside for eight months, and open it again in the ninth month. She follows this advice, opens the pot in the ninth month, and finds a child inside it. (Frobenius, I, p. 237.)

63 Roscher, *Lexikon*, II, 2733/4, s.v. "Men."

64 A well-known sun-animal.

65 Like Mithras and the dadophors.

in the form of a boy, just as the dadophors were boyish figures. (This latter characteristic relates both them and Men to the Cabiri and Dactyls.) Now Men has affinities with Attis, the son and lover of Cybele. In Imperial times Men and Attis merged into one. Attis also wears the pileus like Men, Mithras, and the dadophors. As the son and lover of his mother he raises the incest problem. Incest leads logically to ritual castration in the Attis-Cybele cult; for according to legend the hero, driven mad by his mother, mutilates himself. I must refrain from going into

Fig. 19. Androgynous divinity
Late Babylonian gem

Fig. 20. Cybele and her son-lover Attis
Roman coin

this question more deeply at present, as I would prefer to discuss the incest problem at the end of this book. Here I would only point out that the incest motif is bound to arise, because when the regressing libido is introverted for internal or external reasons it always reactivates the parental imagos and thus apparently re-establishes the infantile relationship. But this relationship cannot be re-established, because the libido is an adult libido which is already bound to sexuality and inevitably imports an incompatible, incestuous character into the reactivated relationship to the parents.[66] It is this sexual character that now gives rise to the incest symbolism. Since incest must be avoided at all costs, the result is either the death of the son-lover or his self-castration as punishment for the incest he has

66 This explanation is not satisfactory, because I found it impossible to go into the archetypal incest problem and all its complications here. I have dealt with it at some length in my "Psychology of the Transference."

committed, or else the sacrifice of instinctuality, and especially of sexuality, as a means of preventing or expiating the incestuous longing. (Cf. fig. 20.) Sex being one of the most obvious examples of instinctuality, it is sex which is liable to be most affected by these sacrificial measures, i.e., through abstinence. The heroes are usually wanderers,[67] and wandering is a symbol of longing,[68] of the restless urge which never finds its object, of nostalgia for the lost mother. The sun comparison can easily be taken in this sense: the heroes are like the wandering sun, from which it is concluded that the myth of the hero is a solar myth. It seems to us, rather, that he is first and foremost a self-representation of the longing of the unconscious, of its unquenched and unquenchable desire for the light of consciousness. But consciousness, continually in danger of being led astray by its own light and of becoming a rootless will o' the wisp, longs for the healing power of nature, for the deep wells of being and for unconscious communion with life in all its countless forms. Here I must make way for the master, who has plumbed to the root of these Faustian longings:

MEPHISTOPHELES: This lofty mystery I must now unfold.
Goddesses throned in solitude, sublime,
Set in no place, still less in any time,
At the mere thought of them my blood runs cold.
They are the Mothers!

. . . .

Goddesses, unknown to mortal mind,
And named indeed with dread among our kind.
To reach them you must plumb earth's deepest vault;
That we have need of them is your own fault.

FAUST: Where leads the way?

MEPHISTOPHELES: There's none! To the untrodden,
Untreadable regions—the unforgotten
And unforgettable—for which prepare!
There are no bolts, no hatches to be lifted,
Through endless solitudes you shall be drifted.
Can you imagine Nothing everywhere?

. . . .

67 Like Gilgamesh, Dionysus, Heracles, Mithras, etc.

68 Cf. Graf, *Richard Wagner im Fliegenden Holländer.*

Supposing you had swum across the ocean
And gazed upon the immensity of space,
Still you would see wave after wave in motion,
And even though you feared the world should cease,
You'd still see something—in the limpid green
Of the calm deep are gliding dolphins seen,
The flying clouds above, sun, moon, and star.
But blank is that eternal Void afar.
You do not hear your footfall, and you meet
No solid ground on which to set your feet.

. . . .

Here, take this key.

. . . .

The key will smell the right place from all others:
Follow it down, it leads you to the Mothers.

. . . .

Then to the depths!—I could as well say height:
It's all the same. From the Existent fleeing,
Take the free world of forms for your delight,
Rejoice in things that long have ceased from being.
The busy brood will weave like coiling cloud,
But swing your key to keep away the crowd!

. . . .

A fiery tripod warns you to beware,
This is the nethermost place where now you are.
You shall behold the Mothers by its light,
Some of them sit, some walk, some stand upright,
Just as they please. Formation, transformation,
Eternal Mind's eternal recreation.
Thronged round with images of things to be,
They see you not, shadows are all they see.
Then pluck up heart, the danger here is great,
Approach the tripod, do not hesitate,
And touch it with the key.[69]

69 Trans. based on MacNeice, pp. 175ff. Cf. also trans. by Wayne, Part II, pp. 76ff.

THE BATTLE FOR DELIVERANCE FROM THE MOTHER

For Jung, the hero is a symbol of the developing ego's libido. By libido, Jung means not simply desire or psychological energy but psychological *purpose* as well. For him, the hero myth expresses the ego's desire to replace dependency upon the unconscious with self-direction—a purpose that necessitates an ambivalent struggle with the mother, who symbolizes the unconscious.

---

441 Once again we recognize the typical elements of a libido myth: original bisexuality, immortality (invulnerability) through entry into the mother (splitting the mother with the foot), resurrection as a soul-bird, and production of fertility (rain). When a hero of this type causes his lance to be worshipped, he probably does so because he thinks it a valid equivalent of himself.

442 From this standpoint the passage in Job, which we quoted in Part I, appears in a new light:

> He hath set me up for his mark.
> His archers compass me round about,
> He cleaveth my reins asunder, and doth not spare;
> He poureth out my gall upon the ground.
> He breaketh me with breach upon breach,
> He runneth upon me like a giant.[50]

443 Here Job is voicing the torment of soul caused by the onslaught of unconscious desires; the libido festers in his flesh, a cruel God has overpowered him and pierced him through with barbed thoughts that agonize his whole being.

[50] Job 16: 12ff.

444 The same image occurs in Nietzsche:

Stretched out, shivering,
Like one half dead whose feet are warmed,
Shaken by unknown fevers,
Shuddering from the icy pointed arrows of frost,
Hunted by thee, O thought,
Unutterable! veiled! horrible one!
Thou huntsman behind the clouds.
Struck to the ground by thee,
Thou mocking eye that gazeth at me from the dark:
Thus do I lie,
Twisting, writhing, tortured
With eternal tortures,
Smitten
By thee, cruel huntsman,
Thou unknown—God!

Smite deeper!
Smite once more!
Pierce, rend my heart!
What meaneth this torturing
With blunt-toothed arrows?
Why gazest thou again,
Never weary of human agony,
With sardonic gods'-eyes, flashing lightning?
Why wilt thou not kill,
Only torture, torture? [51]

445 No long-drawn explanations are needed to see in this comparison the martyred and sacrificed god whom we have already met in the Aztec crucifixions and in the sacrifice of Odin.[52] We meet the same image in depictions of the martyrdom of St. Sebastian, where the glowing, girlishly tender flesh of the young saint betrays all the pain of renunciation which the sensibility of the artist projected into it. An artist cannot prevent his work from being coloured by the psychology of his time. This is true in even higher degree of the Christian symbol, the Crucified pierced by the lance. It is a true symbol of the man of the Christian era, tormented by his desires and crucified in Christ.

51 *Thus Spake Zarathustra.* (*Werke,* VI, pp. 367f.) [Cf. trans. by Common, p. 293.]
52 Spielrein's patient said that she too had been shot by God three times—"then came a resurrection of the spirit."

446 That the torment which afflicts mankind does not come from outside, but that man is his own huntsman, his own sacrificer, his own sacrificial knife, is clear from another poem of Nietzsche's, where the dualism is resolved into a psychic conflict through the same symbolism:

O Zarathustra,
Most cruel Nimrod!
Erstwhile hunter of God,
Snare of all virtue,
Arrow of evil!
And now
Self-hunted,
Thine own quarry,
Thyself pierced through . . .

Now
Alone with thyself,
Split in thine own knowledge,
Amidst a hundred mirrors
To thine own self false,
Amidst a hundred memories
Uncertain,
Languishing with each wound,
Shivering with each frost,
Strangled in thine own snares,
Self-knower!
Self-hangman!

Why didst thou hang thyself
With the noose of thy wisdom?
Why hast thou enticed thyself
Into the old serpent's Paradise?
Why hast thou stolen
Into thyself, thyself? [53]

447 The deadly arrows do not strike the hero from without; it is himself who hunts, fights, and tortures himself. In him, instinct wars with instinct; therefore the poet says, "Thyself pierced through," which means that he is wounded by his own arrow. As we know that the arrow is a libido-symbol, the mean-

53 "Between Birds of Prey." (*Werke*, VIII, p. 414.) [Cf. trans. in *Ecce Homo and Poetry* by Ludovici, Cohn, et al., p. 179.]

ing of this "piercing" is clear: it is the act of union with oneself, a sort of self-fertilization, and also a self-violation, a self-murder, so that Zarathustra can justly call himself his own hangman (like Odin, who sacrifices himself to Odin). One should not of course take this psychologem in too voluntaristic a sense: nobody deliberately inflicts such tortures on himself, they just happen to him. If a man reckons the unconscious as part of his personality, then one must admit that he is in fact raging against himself. But, in so far as the symbolism thrown up by his suffering is archetypal and collective, it can be taken as a sign that he is no longer suffering from himself, but rather from the spirit of the age. He is suffering from an objective, impersonal cause, from his collective unconscious which he has in common with all men.

448 Being wounded by one's own arrow signifies, therefore, a state of introversion. What this means we already know: the libido sinks "into its own depths" (a favourite image of Nietzsche's), and discovers in the darkness a substitute for the upper world it has abandoned—the world of memories ("Amidst a hundred memories"), the strongest and most influential of which are the earliest ones. It is the world of the child, the paradisal state of early infancy, from which we are driven out by the relentless law of time. In this subterranean kingdom slumber sweet feelings of home and the hopes of all that is to be. As Heinrich says of his miraculous work in Gerhart Hauptmann's *The Sunken Bell:*

> It sings a song, long lost and long forgotten,
> A song of home, a childlike song of love,
> Born in the waters of some fairy well,
> Known to all mortals, and yet heard of none.[54]

449 Yet "the danger is great," [55] as Mephistopheles says, for these depths fascinate. When the libido leaves the bright upper world, whether from choice, or from inertia, or from fate, it sinks back into its own depths, into the source from which it originally flowed, and returns to the point of cleavage, the navel, where it first entered the body. This point of cleavage is called the mother, because from her the current of life reached us. Whenever some great work is to be accomplished, before which a man

[54] Trans. by Meltzner, p. 75.

[55] *Faust,* Part II, "The Mothers."

recoils, doubtful of his strength, his libido streams back to the fountainhead—and that is the dangerous moment when the issue hangs between annihilation and new life. For if the libido gets stuck in the wonderland of this inner world,[56] then for the upper world man is nothing but a shadow, he is already moribund or at least seriously ill. But if the libido manages to tear itself loose and force its way up again, something like a miracle happens: the journey to the underworld was a plunge into the fountain of youth, and the libido, apparently dead, wakes to renewed fruitfulness. This idea is illustrated in an Indian myth: Vishnu sank into a profound trance, and in his slumber brought forth Brahma, who, enthroned on a lotus, rose out of Vishnu's navel, bringing with him the Vedas (pl. XLVI*a*), which he diligently read. (Birth of creative thought from introversion.) But through Vishnu's ecstatic absentmindedness a mighty flood came upon the world. (Devouring and destruction of the world through introversion.) Taking advantage of the general confusion, a demon stole the Vedas and hid them in the depths. Brahma then roused Vishnu, who, changing himself into a fish (pl. XLVII), plunged into the flood, fought the demon, conquered him, and recaptured the Vedas.

450 This is a primitive way of describing the libido's entry into the interior world of the psyche, the unconscious. There, through its introversion and regression, contents are constellated which till now were latent. These are the primordial images, the archetypes, which have been so enriched with individual memories through the introversion of libido as to become perceptible to the conscious mind, in much the same way as the crystalline structure latent in the saturated solution takes visible shape from the aggregation of molecules. Since these introversions and regressions only occur at moments when a new orientation and a new adaptation are necessary, the constellated archetype is always the primordial image of the need of the

[56] This is mythologically represented in the legend of Theseus and Peirithous, who wanted to abduct Persephone from the underworld. They entered a chasm in the grove of Colonus and descended into the bowels of the earth. When they got down below they wished to rest a little, but found they had grown fast to the rocks and could not rise. In other words, they remained stuck in the mother and were lost to the upper world. Later Theseus was rescued by Heracles, who appeared in the role of the death-conquering hero. The Theseus myth is therefore a representation of the individuation process.

moment. Although the changing situations of life must appear infinitely various to our way of thinking, their possible number never exceeds certain natural limits; they fall into more or less typical patterns that repeat themselves over and over again. The archetypal structure of the unconscious corresponds to the average run of events. The changes that may befall a man are not infinitely variable; they are variations of certain typical occurrences which are limited in number. When therefore a distressing situation arises, the corresponding archetype will be constellated in the unconscious. Since this archetype is numinous, i.e., possesses a specific energy, it will attract to itself the contents of consciousness—conscious ideas that render it perceptible and hence capable of conscious realization. Its passing over into consciousness is felt as an illumination, a revelation, or a "saving idea." Repeated experience of this process has had the general result that, whenever a critical situation arises, the mechanism of introversion is made to function artificially by means of ritual actions which bring about a spiritual preparation, e.g., magical ceremonies, sacrifices, invocations, prayers, and suchlike. The aim of these ritual actions is to direct the libido towards the unconscious and compel it to introvert. If the libido connects with the unconscious, it is as though it were connecting with the mother, and this raises the incest-taboo. But as the unconscious is infinitely greater than the mother and is only symbolized by her, the fear of incest must be conquered if one is to gain possession of those "saving" contents—the treasure hard to attain. Since the son is not conscious of his incest tendency, it is projected upon the mother or her symbol. But the symbol of the mother is not the mother herself, so in reality there is not the slightest possibility of incest, and the taboo can therefore be ruled out as a reason for resistance. In so far as the mother represents the unconscious, the incest tendency, particularly when it appears as the amorous desire of the mother (e.g., Ishtar and Gilgamesh) or of the anima (e.g., Chryse and Philoctetes), is really only the desire of the unconscious to be taken notice of. The rejection of the unconscious usually has unfortunate results; its instinctive forces, if persistently disregarded, rise up in opposition: Chryse changes into a venomous serpent. The more negative the attitude of the conscious towards the unconscious, the more dangerous does the latter become.[57] Chryse's curse was fulfilled so completely that Philoctetes, on approaching her altar, wounded himself in the foot with his own poison-tipped arrow, or, according to other versions[58] which are in fact better attested, was bitten in the foot by a poisonous snake,[59] and fell into a decline.[60]

451 This very typical injury also destroyed Ra, and is described as follows in an Egyptian hymn:

The mouth of the god twitched with age,
So that he dropped his spittle on the earth,
And what he spat fell on the ground.
Isis then kneaded it with her hands
Together with the earth which was there;
She fashioned from it a noble worm
And made it like a spear.

57 When the Greeks set out on their expedition to Troy, they wished, like the Argonauts and Heracles before them, to offer sacrifice on the altar of Chryse, a nymph who lived on an island of the same name, in order to secure a happy end to their voyage. Philoctetes was the only one among them who knew the way to her hidden shrine. But there the disaster befell him which is described above. Sophocles treats of this episode in his *Philoctetes.* We learn from a scholiast that Chryse offered the hero her love, but, on being scorned, cursed him. Philoctetes, like his forerunner Heracles, is the prototype of the wounded and ailing king, a motif that is continued in the legend of the Grail and in alchemical symbolism (cf. *Psychology and Alchemy,* pars. 491ff. and fig. 149).

58 Roscher, *Lexikon,* 2318, 15ff., s.v. "Philoctetes."

59 When the Russian sun-hero Oleg approached the skull of the slain horse, a snake darted out and bit him in the foot, so that he fell sick and died. And when Indra, in the form of Shyena the falcon, stole the soma drink, Krishanu the herdsman wounded him in the foot with an arrow. De Gubernatis, *Zoological Mythology,* II, pp. 181–82.

60 Like the Grail king who guards the chalice, symbol of the mother. The myth of Philoctetes comes from the wider context of the Heracles cycle. Heracles had two mothers, the helpful Alcmene and the vengeful Hera, from whose breast he drank the milk of immortality. Heracles conquered Hera's serpents while yet in the cradle; that is, he freed himself from the grip of the unconscious. But from time to time Hera sent him fits of madness, in one of which he killed his own children. This is indirect proof that she was a lamia. According to one tradition, Heracles perpetrated this deed after refusing to perform the labours for his task-master Eurystheus. As a consequence of his hanging back, the libido that was ready for the work regressed to the unconscious mother-imago, and this resulted in madness. In this state he identified with the lamia and killed his own children. The Delphic oracle told him that he was named Heracles because he owed his immortal fame to Hera, who through her persecutions drove him to his great deeds. It is evident that the great deed really means overcoming the mother and thus winning immortality. His characteristic weapon, the club, he cut from the

She did not wind it living about her face,
But threw it in a coil upon the path
Upon which the great god was wont to walk
At pleasure through his two countries.
The noble god stepped forth in his splendour,
The gods who served Pharaoh accompanied him,
And he walked as he did each day.
Then the noble worm stung him . . .
The divine god opened his mouth,
And the voice of his majesty rang through the heavens.
And the gods cried: Behold! Behold!
He could not answer them,
His jawbones chattered,
All his limbs trembled,
And the poison invaded his flesh
As the Nile invades his territory.[61]

452 In this hymn Egypt has preserved for us a primitive version of the snake-sting motif. The aging of the autumn sun as a symbol of human senility is traced back to poisoning by a serpent. The mother is blamed for causing the death of the sun-god with her mischievous arts. The serpent symbolizes the mysterious numen of the "mother" (and of other daimonia) who kills, but who is at the same time man's only security against death, as she is the source of life.[62] Accordingly, only the mother can cure him who is sick unto death, and the hymn goes on to describe how the gods were called together to take counsel:

Then came Isis with her wisdom,
Whose mouth is full of the breath of life,
Whose decree banishes pain,
And whose word gives life to those who no longer breathe.

maternal olive-tree. Like the sun, he possessed the arrows of Apollo. He conquered the Nemean lion in its cave, whose meaning is the "grave in the mother's womb" (see the end of this chapter). Then follows the fight with the Hydra (cf. also fig. 17) and his other deeds, which were all wished on him by Hera. All of them symbolize the fight with the unconscious. At the end of his career, however, he became the slave of Omphale (ὀμφαλός = 'navel') as the oracle prophesied: that is, he had to submit after all to the unconscious.

61 This and the following passages trans. from Erman, pp. 265–67, modified.

62 How concretely this mythologem is taken on the primitive level can be seen from the description in Gatti, *South of the Sahara* (pp. 226ff.), of a medicine-woman in Natal who had a twenty-foot boa constrictor as her familiar.

She said: What is it, what is it, divine Father?
Behold, a worm hath done thee this wrong.

Tell me thy name, divine Father,
For he whose name is spoken shall live.

453 Ra answers:

I am he who created heaven and earth, and piled up the mountains,
And made all living things.
I am he who made the water and caused the great flood,
Who made the Bull of his Mother,
Who is the Begetter.

The poison did not depart, it went further,
The great god was not healed.
Then said Isis to Ra:
That is not thy name which thou tellest me.
Tell me thy name, that the poison may depart,
For he whose name is spoken shall live.

454 Finally Ra decides to utter his true name. He was only partially cured, just as Osiris was only incompletely reconstituted, and in addition he lost his power and finally had to retire on the back of the heavenly cow.

455 The poisonous worm is a deadly instead of an animating form of libido. The "true name" is Ra's soul and magic power (his libido). What Isis demands is the transference of libido to the mother. This request is fulfilled to the letter, for the aging god returns to the heavenly cow, the symbol of the mother.

456 The meaning of this symbolism becomes clear in the light of what we said earlier: the forward-striving libido which rules the conscious mind of the son demands separation from the mother, but his childish longing for her prevents this by setting up a psychic resistance that manifests itself in all kinds of neurotic fears—that is to say, in a general fear of life. The more a person shrinks from adapting himself to reality, the greater becomes the fear which increasingly besets his path at every point. Thus a vicious circle is formed: fear of life and people causes more shrinking back, and this in turn leads to infantilism and finally "into the mother." The reasons for this are generally projected outside oneself: the fault lies with external circumstances, or else the parents are made responsible. And indeed, it remains

to be found out how much the mother is to blame for not letting the son go. The son will naturally try to explain everything by the wrong attitude of the mother, but he would do better to refrain from all such futile attempts to excuse his own ineptitude by laying the blame on his parents.

457 This fear of life is not just an imaginary bogy, but a very real panic, which seems disproportionate only because its real source is unconscious and therefore projected: the young, growing part of the personality, if prevented from living or kept in check, generates fear and changes into fear. The fear seems to come from the mother, but actually it is the deadly fear of the instinctive, unconscious, inner man who is cut off from life by the continual shrinking back from reality. If the mother is felt as the obstacle, she then becomes the vengeful pursuer. Naturally it is not the real mother, although she too may seriously injure her child by the morbid tenderness with which she pursues it into adult life, thus prolonging the infantile attitude beyond the proper time. It is rather the mother-imago that has turned into a lamia.[63] (Cf. pls. XXXVIII*a*, XLVIII.) The mother-imago, however, represents the unconscious, and it is as much a vital necessity for the unconscious to be joined to the conscious as it is for the latter not to lose contact with the unconscious. Nothing endangers this connection more in a man than a successful life; it makes him forget his dependence on the unconscious. The case of Gilgamesh is instructive in this respect: he was so successful that the gods, the representatives of the unconscious, saw themselves compelled to deliberate how they could best bring about his downfall. Their efforts were unavailing at first, but when the hero had won the herb of immortality (cf. pl. XIX) and was almost at his goal, a serpent stole the elixir of life from him while he slept.

458 The demands of the unconscious act at first like a paralysing poison on a man's energy and resourcefulness, so that it may well be compared to the bite of a poisonous snake. (Cf. fig. 30.)

[63] The myth of Hippolytus has similar ingredients: His step-mother Phaedra falls in love with him, he repulses her, she accuses him of violation before her husband, who calls upon Poseidon to punish Hippolytus. Whereupon a monster comes out of the sea; Hippolytus' horses take fright and drag him to death. But he is restored to life by Aesculapius, and the gods convey him to the grove of the wise nymph Egeria, the counsellor of Numa Pompilius.

Apparently it is a hostile demon who robs him of energy, but in actual fact it is his own unconscious whose alien tendencies are beginning to check the forward striving of the

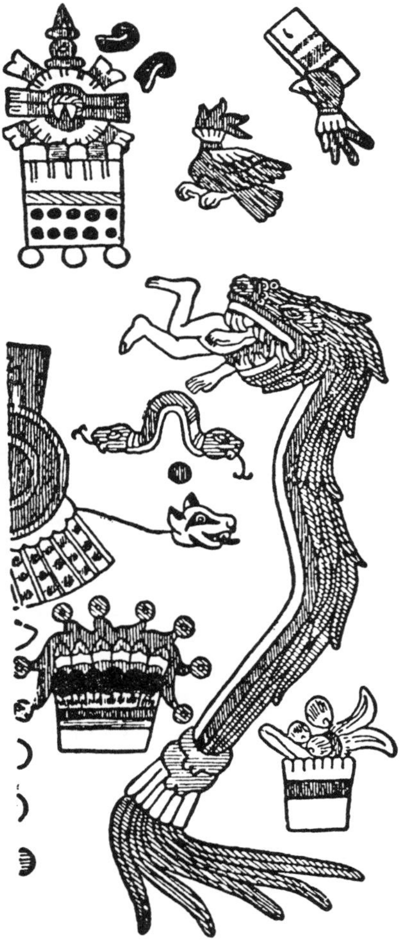

Fig. 30. Quetzalcoatl devouring a man
From the Codex Borbonicus, Aztec 16th century

conscious mind. The cause of this process is often extremely obscure, the more so as it is complicated by all kinds of external factors and subsidiary causes, such as difficulties in work, disappointments, failures, reduced efficiency due to age, depressing family problems, and so on and so forth. According to the myths it is the woman who secretly enslaves a man, so that he can no longer free himself from her and becomes a child again.[64] It is also significant that Isis, the sister-wife of the sun-god, creates the poisonous serpent from his spittle, which, like all bodily secretions, has a magical significance, being a libido equivalent. She creates the serpent from the libido of the god, and by this means weakens him and makes him dependent on her. Delilah acts in the same way with Samson: by cutting off his hair, the sun's rays, she robs him of his strength. This demon-woman of mythology is in truth the "sister-wife-mother," the woman in the man, who unexpectedly turns up during the second half of life and tries to effect a forcible change of personality. I have dealt with certain aspects of this change in my essay on "The Stages of Life." It consists in a partial feminization of the man and a corresponding masculinization of the woman. Often it takes place under very dramatic circumstances: the man's strongest quality, his Logos principle, turns against him and as it were betrays him. The same thing happens with the Eros of the woman. The man becomes rigidly set in his previous attitude, while the woman remains caught in her emotional ties and fails to develop her reason and understanding, whose place is then taken by equally obstinate and inept "animus" opinions. The fossilization of the man shrouds itself in a smoke-screen of moods, ridiculous irritability, feelings of distrust and resentment, which are meant to justify his rigid attitude. A perfect example of this type of psychology is Schreber's account of his own psychosis, *Memoirs of My Nervous Illness*.[65]

459 The paralysis of progressive energy has in truth some very disagreeable aspects. It seems like an unwelcome accident or a positive catastrophe, which one would naturally rather avoid. In most cases the conscious personality rises up against the assault of the unconscious and resists its demands, which, it is clearly felt, are directed not only against all the weak spots in the man's character, but also against his chief virtue (the differentiated function and the ideal). It is evident from the myths of Heracles and Gilgamesh that this assault can become the

64 Cf. Heracles and Omphale.

65 The case was written up at the time by Freud in a very unsatisfactory way after I had drawn his attention to the book. See "Psycho-Analytical Notes upon an Autobiographical Account of a Case of Paranoia."

source of energy for an heroic conflict; indeed, so obvious is this impression that one has to ask oneself whether the apparent enmity of the maternal archetype is not a ruse on the part of Mater Natura for spurring on her favoured child to his highest achievement. The vengeful Hera would then appear as the stern "Mistress Soul," who imposes the most difficult labours on her hero and threatens him with destruction unless he plucks up courage for the supreme deed and actually becomes what he always potentially was. The hero's victory over the "mother," or over her daemonic representative (dragon, etc.), is never anything but temporary. What must be regarded as regression in a young person—feminization of the man (partial identity with the mother) and masculinization of the woman (partial identity with the father)—acquires a different meaning in the second half of life. The assimilation of contrasexual tendencies then becomes a task that must be fulfilled in order to keep the libido in a state of progression. The task consists in integrating the unconscious, in bringing together "conscious" and "unconscious." I have called this the individuation process, and for further details must refer the reader to my later works.[65a] At this stage the mother-symbol no longer connects back to the beginnings, but points towards the unconscious as the creative matrix of the future. "Entry into the mother" then means establishing a relationship between the ego and the unconscious. Nietzsche probably means something of the kind in his poem:

Why hast thou enticed thyself
Into the old serpent's Paradise?
Why hast thou stolen
Into thyself, thyself?

A sick man now,
Sick of the serpent's poison;[66]
A captive now
Who drew the hardest lot:
Bent double
Working in thine own pit,

65a [Cf. especially "A Study in the Process of Individuation."—EDITORS.]

66 Spielrein's patient was also sick from "snake poison" (p. 385). Schreber said he was infected by "corpse poison," that "soul murder" had been committed on him, etc. (pp. 54ff.).

Encaved within thyself,
Burrowing into thyself,
Heavy-handed,
Stiff,
A corpse—
Piled with a hundred burdens,
Loaded to death with thyself,
A knower!
Self-knower!
The wise Zarathustra!
You sought the heaviest burden
And found yourself.[67]

460 Sunk in his own depths, he is like one buried in the earth; a dead man who has crawled back into the mother; [68] a Kaineus "piled with a hundred burdens" and pressed down to death, groaning beneath the intolerable weight of his own self and his own destiny. Who does not think here of Mithras, who, in the Taurophoria, took his bull (or, as the Egyptian hymn says, "the bull of his mother"), namely his love for his Mater Natura, on his back, and with this heaviest burden set forth on the *via dolorosa* of the Transitus? [69] The way of this passion leads to the cave in which the bull is sacrificed. So, too, Christ had to bear the Cross [70] to the place of sacrifice, where, according to the Christian version, the Lamb was slain in the form of the

67 "Between Birds of Prey." (*Werke,* VIII, p. 414.) [Cf. trans. in *Ecce Homo and Poetry,* by Ludovici et al., p. 179.]

68 Spielrein's patient (p. 336) uses the same images; she speaks of the "rigidity of the soul on the cross," of "stone figures" who must be "melted."

69 Gurlitt says: "The carrying of the bull [pl. XLIX*a*] is one of the difficult ἆθλα which Mithras performed for the redemption of mankind; it corresponds roughly —if we may compare small things with great—to Christ carrying the cross." ("Vorbericht über Ausgrabungen in Pettau"; cited in Cumont, *Textes,* I, p. 172.)

70 Robertson (*Christianity and Mythology,* p. 401) makes an interesting contribution to the symbol of carrying the cross: Samson carried the gate-posts of the city of Gaza, and died between the pillars of the temple of the Philistines. Heracles carried his pillars to Gades (Cadiz), where, according to the Syrian version of the legend, he died. The Pillars of Hercules mark the point in the west where the sun sinks into the sea. "In ancient art," says Robertson, "he was actually represented carrying the two pillars in such a way under his arms that they form exactly a cross. Here, probably, we have the origin of the myth of Jesus carrying his own cross to the place of execution. Singularly enough, the three Synoptics substitute for Jesus as cross-bearer one Simon, a man of Cyrene. Cyrene is in Libya, the legendary scene, as we saw, of the pillar-carrying exploit of Heracles;

god, and was then laid to earth in the sepulchre.[71] The cross, or whatever other heavy burden the hero carries, is *himself*, or rather *the* self, his wholeness, which is both God and animal—not merely the empirical man, but the totality of his being, which is rooted in his animal nature and reaches out beyond the merely human towards the divine. His wholeness implies a tremendous tension of opposites paradoxically at one with themselves, as in the cross, their most perfect symbol. What seems like a poetic figure of speech in Nietzsche is really an age-old myth. It is as if the poet could still sense, beneath the words of contemporary speech and in the images that crowd in upon his imagination, the ghostly presence of bygone spiritual worlds, and possessed the capacity to make them come alive again. As Gerhart Hauptmann says: "Poetry is the art of letting the primordial word resound through the common word." [72]

---

and Simon (Simeon) is the nearest Greek name-form to Samson. . . . In Palestine, Simon, or Sem, was actually a god-name, representing the ancient sun-god Shemesh, identified with Baal, from whose mythus that of Samson unquestionably arose; and the God Simon was especially worshipped in Samaria." I give Robertson's words here, but must emphasize that the etymological connection between Simon and Samson is exceedingly questionable. The cross of Heracles may well be the sun-wheel, for which the Greeks used the symbol of the cross. The sun-wheel on the bas-relief of the Little Metropolis in Athens actually contains a cross which looks very like the Maltese cross. (Cf. Thiele, *Antike Himmelsbilder*, p. 59.) Here I must refer the reader to the mandala symbolism in *Psychology and Alchemy* and in *The Secret of the Golden Flower*.

71 The legend of Ixion (pl. XLVI*b*), who was "crucified on the four-spoked wheel" (Pindar), says the same thing. Ixion first murdered his father-in-law but was afterwards absolved from guilt by Zeus and blessed with his favour. Ixion, with gross ingratitude, then tried to seduce Hera, but Zeus tricked him by getting the cloud-goddess Nephele to assume Hera's shape. From this union the centaurs are said to have sprung. Ixion boasted of his deed, but as a punishment for his crimes Zeus cast him into the underworld, where he was bound on a wheel that turned forever in the wind.

72 Cited from the *Zentralblatt für Psychoanalyse*, II (1912), p. 365 [in a note by W. Stekel, quoting extracts from Hauptmann's published diary.—EDITORS].

II. INITIATION AND THE DEVELOPMENT OF MASCULINITY

THE STAGES OF LIFE

Jung's notion of the stages of life implies a lifelong series of initiations. The developing individual struggles successively with problems typical of each time of life, and these problems are never fully solved. Rather, they serve the purpose of promoting consciousness. When Jung conceives this development in masculine, transcendental terms as fulfillment of an inner demand for the progress of consciousness, he continues the German Romantic tradition of Schopenhauer and Nietzsche. Schopenhauer had postulated a *principium individuationis,* which Jung reads as the psychological drive to be the self that one truly is. Nietzsche supplied the idea of the life-task, which in Jung becomes the moral imperative to accomplish one's mission of individuation. Yet Jung sees clearly that genuine development will force the individual to give up all pretensions to heroic mastery. Using the metaphor of the sun's daily journey, he envisioned the psychology of the individual as an ascent to bright consciousness in the first half of life, followed by a sacrifice of that brightness in a descent to the unconscious in life's second half. In a man, this loss of ego was compensated by the emergence of the anima.

---

759 And here we come to our real theme—the problem of the stages of life. First of all we must deal with the period of youth. It extends roughly from the years just after puberty to middle life, which itself begins between the thirty-fifth and fortieth year.

760 I might well be asked why I begin with the second stage, as though there were no problems connected with childhood. The

complex psychic life of the child is, of course, a problem of the first magnitude to parents, educators, and doctors, but when normal the child has no real problems of its own. It is only the adult human being who can have doubts about himself and be at variance with himself.

761 We are all familiar with the sources of the problems that arise in the period of youth. For most people it is the demands of life which harshly put an end to the dream of childhood. If the individual is sufficiently well prepared, the transition to a profession or career can take place smoothly. But if he clings to illusions that are contrary to reality, then problems will surely arise. No one can take the step into life without making certain assumptions, and occasionally these assumptions are false—that is, they do not fit the conditions into which one is thrown. Often it is a question of exaggerated expectations, underestimation of difficulties, unjustified optimism, or a negative attitude. One could compile quite a list of the false assumptions that give rise to the first conscious problems.

762 But it is not always the contradiction between subjective assumptions and external facts that gives rise to problems; it may just as often be inner, psychic difficulties. They may exist even when things run smoothly in the outside world. Very often it is the disturbance of psychic equilibrium caused by the sexual instinct; equally often it is the feeling of inferiority which springs from an unbearable sensitivity. These inner conflicts may exist even when adaptation to the outer world has been achieved without apparent effort. It even seems as if young people who have had a hard struggle for existence are spared inner problems, while those who for some reason or other have no difficulty with adaptation run into problems of sex or conflicts arising from a sense of inferiority.

763 People whose own temperaments offer problems are often neurotic, but it would be a serious misunderstanding to confuse the existence of problems with neurosis. There is a marked difference between the two in that the neurotic is ill because he is unconscious of his problems, while the person with a difficult temperament suffers from his conscious problems without being ill.

764 If we try to extract the common and essential factors from the almost inexhaustible variety of individual problems found

in the period of youth, we meet in all cases with one particular feature: a more or less patent clinging to the childhood level of consciousness, a resistance to the fateful forces in and around us which would involve us in the world. Something in us wishes to remain a child, to be unconscious or. at most, conscious only of the ego; to reject everything strange, or else subject it to our will; to do nothing, or else indulge our own craving for pleasure or power. In all this there is something of the inertia of matter; it is a persistence in the previous state whose range of consciousness is smaller, narrower, and more egoistic than that of the dualistic phase. For here the individual is faced with the necessity of recognizing and accepting what is different and strange as a part of his own life, as a kind of "also-I."

765 The essential feature of the dualistic phase is the widening of the horizon of life, and it is this that is so vigorously resisted. To be sure, this expansion—or diastole, as Goethe called it—had started long before this. It begins at birth, when the child abandons the narrow confinement of the mother's body; and from then on it steadily increases until it reaches a climax in the problematical state, when the individual begins to struggle against it.

766 What would happen to him if he simply changed himself into that foreign-seeming "also-I" and allowed the earlier ego to vanish into the past? We might suppose this to be a quite practical course. The very aim of religious education, from the exhortation to put off the old Adam right back to the rebirth rituals of primitive races, is to transform the human being into the new, future man, and to allow the old to die away.

767 Psychology teaches us that, in a certain sense, there is nothing in the psyche that is old; nothing that can really, finally die away. Even Paul was left with a thorn in the flesh. Whoever protects himself against what is new and strange and regresses to the past falls into the same neurotic condition as the man who identifies himself with the new and runs away from the past. The only difference is that the one has estranged himself from the past and the other from the future. In principle both are doing the same thing: they are reinforcing their narrow range of consciousness instead of shattering it in the tension of opposites and building up a state of wider and higher consciousness.

768 This outcome would be ideal if it could be brought about in the second stage of life—but there's the rub. For one thing, nature cares nothing whatsoever about a higher level of consciousness; quite the contrary. And then society does not value these feats of the psyche very highly; its prizes are always given for achievement and not for personality, the latter being rewarded for the most part posthumously. These facts compel us towards a particular solution: we are forced to limit ourselves to the attainable, and to differentiate particular aptitudes in which the socially effective individual discovers his true self.

769 Achievement, usefulness and so forth are the ideals that seem to point the way out of the confusions of the problematical state. They are the lodestars that guide us in the adventure of broadening and consolidating our physical existence; they help us to strike our roots in the world, but they cannot guide us in the development of that wider consciousness to which we give the name of culture. In the period of youth, however, this course is the normal one and in all circumstances preferable to merely tossing about in a welter of problems.

770 The dilemma is often solved, therefore, in this way: whatever is given to us by the past is adapted to the possibilities and demands of the future. We limit ourselves to the attainable, and this means renouncing all our other psychic potentialities. One man loses a valuable piece of his past, another a valuable piece of his future. Everyone can call to mind friends or schoolmates who were promising and idealistic youngsters, but who, when we meet them again years later, seem to have grown dry and cramped in a narrow mould. These are examples of the solution mentioned above.

771 The serious problems in life, however, are never fully solved. If ever they should appear to be so it is a sure sign that something has been lost. The meaning and purpose of a problem seem to lie not in its solution but in our working at it incessantly. This alone preserves us from stultification and petrifaction. So also the solution of the problems of youth by restricting ourselves to the attainable is only temporarily valid and not lasting in a deeper sense. Of course, to win for oneself a place in society and to transform one's nature so that it is more or less fitted to this kind of existence is in all cases a considerable achievement. It is a fight waged within oneself as well as out-

side, comparable to the struggle of the child for an ego. That struggle is for the most part unobserved because it happens in the dark; but when we see how stubbornly childish illusions and assumptions and egoistic habits are still clung to in later years we can gain some idea of the energies that were needed to form them. And so it is with the ideals, convictions, guiding ideas and attitudes which in the period of youth lead us out into life, for which we struggle, suffer, and win victories: they grow together with our own being, we apparently change into them, we seek to perpetuate them indefinitely and as a matter of course, just as the young person asserts his ego in spite of the world and often in spite of himself.

772 The nearer we approach to the middle of life, and the better we have succeeded in entrenching ourselves in our personal attitudes and social positions, the more it appears as if we had discovered the right course and the right ideals and principles of behaviour. For this reason we suppose them to be eternally valid, and make a virtue of unchangeably clinging to them. We overlook the essential fact that the social goal is attained only at the cost of a diminution of personality. Many—far too many—aspects of life which should also have been experienced lie in the lumber-room among dusty memories; but sometimes, too, they are glowing coals under grey ashes.

773 Statistics show a rise in the frequency of mental depressions in men about forty. In women the neurotic difficulties generally begin somewhat earlier. We see that in this phase of life—between thirty-five and forty—an important change in the human psyche is in preparation. At first it is not a conscious and striking change; it is rather a matter of indirect signs of a change which seems to take its rise in the unconscious. Often it is something like a slow change in a person's character; in another case certain traits may come to light which had disappeared since childhood; or again, one's previous inclinations and interests begin to weaken and others take their place. Conversely—and this happens very frequently—one's cherished convictions and principles, especially the moral ones, begin to harden and to grow increasingly rigid until, somewhere around the age of fifty, a period of intolerance and fanaticism is reached. It is as if the existence of these principles were endangered and it were therefore necessary to emphasize them all the more.

774 The wine of youth does not always clear with advancing years; sometimes it grows turbid. All the phenomena mentioned above can best be seen in rather one-sided people, turning up sometimes sooner and sometimes later. Their appearance, it seems to me, is often delayed by the fact that the parents of the person in question are still alive. It is then as if the period of youth were being unduly drawn out. I have seen this especially in the case of men whose fathers were long-lived. The death of the father then has the effect of a precipitate and almost catastrophic ripening.

775 I know of a pious man who was a churchwarden and who, from the age of forty onward, showed a growing and finally unbearable intolerance in matters of morality and religion. At the same time his moods grew visibly worse. At last he was nothing more than a darkly lowering pillar of the Church. In this way he got along until the age of fifty-five, when suddenly, sitting up in bed in the middle of the night, he said to his wife: "Now at last I've got it! I'm just a plain rascal." Nor did this realization remain without results. He spent his declining years in riotous living and squandered a goodly part of his fortune. Obviously quite a likable fellow, capable of both extremes!

776 The very frequent neurotic disturbances of adult years all have one thing in common: they want to carry the psychology of the youthful phase over the threshold of the so-called years of discretion. Who does not know those touching old gentlemen who must always warm up the dish of their student days, who can fan the flame of life only by reminiscences of their heroic youth, but who, for the rest, are stuck in a hopelessly wooden Philistinism? As a rule, to be sure, they have this one merit which it would be wrong to undervalue: they are not neurotic, but only boring and stereotyped. The neurotic is rather a person who can never have things as he would like them in the present, and who can therefore never enjoy the past either.

777 As formerly the neurotic could not escape from childhood, so now he cannot part with his youth. He shrinks from the grey thoughts of approaching age, and, feeling the prospect before him unbearable, is always straining to look behind him. Just as the childish person shrinks back from the unknown in the world and in human existence, so the grown man shrinks back from the second half of life. It is as if unknown and dangerous tasks

awaited him, or as if he were threatened with sacrifices and losses which he does not wish to accept, or as if his life up to now seemed to him so fair and precious that he could not relinquish it.

778 Is it perhaps at bottom the fear of death? That does not seem to me very probable, because as a rule death is still far in the distance and therefore somewhat abstract. Experience shows us, rather, that the basic cause of all the difficulties of this transition is to be found in a deep-seated and peculiar change within the psyche. In order to characterize it I must take for comparison the daily course of the sun—but a sun that is endowed with human feeling and man's limited consciousness. In the morning it rises from the nocturnal sea of unconsciousness and looks upon the wide, bright world which lies before it in an expanse that steadily widens the higher it climbs in the firmament. In this extension of its field of action caused by its own rising, the sun will discover its significance; it will see the attainment of the greatest possible height, and the widest possible dissemination of its blessings, as its goal. In this conviction the sun pursues its course to the unforeseen zenith—unforeseen, because its career is unique and individual, and the culminating point could not be calculated in advance. At the stroke of noon the descent begins. And the descent means the reversal of all the ideals and values that were cherished in the morning. The sun falls into contradiction with itself. It is as though it should draw in its rays instead of emitting them. Light and warmth decline and are at last extinguished.

779 All comparisons are lame, but this simile is at least not lamer than others. A French aphorism sums it up with cynical resignation: *Si jeunesse savait, si vieillesse pouvait.*

780 Fortunately we are not rising and setting suns, for then it would fare badly with our cultural values. But there is something sunlike within us, and to speak of the morning and spring, of the evening and autumn of life is not mere sentimental jargon. We thus give expression to psychological truths and, even more, to physiological facts, for the reversal of the sun at noon changes even bodily characteristics. Especially among southern races one can observe that older women develop deep, rough voices, incipient moustaches, rather hard features and other masculine traits. On the other hand the masculine physique is

toned down by feminine features, such as adiposity and softer facial expressions.

781 There is an interesting report in the ethnological literature about an Indian warrior chief to whom in middle life the Great Spirit appeared in a dream. The spirit announced to him that from then on he must sit among the women and children, wear women's clothes, and eat the food of women. He obeyed the dream without suffering a loss of prestige. This vision is a true expression of the psychic revolution of life's noon, of the beginning of life's decline. Man's values, and even his body, do tend to change into their opposites.

782 We might compare masculinity and femininity and their psychic components to a definite store of substances of which, in the first half of life, unequal use is made. A man consumes his large supply of masculine substance and has left over only the smaller amount of feminine substance, which must now be put to use. Conversely, the woman allows her hitherto unused supply of masculinity to become active.

783 This change is even more noticeable in the psychic realm than in the physical. How often it happens that a man of forty-five or fifty winds up his business, and the wife then dons the trousers and opens a little shop where he perhaps performs the duties of a handyman. There are many women who only awaken to social responsibility and to social consciousness after their fortieth year. In modern business life, especially in America, nervous breakdowns in the forties are a very common occurrence. If one examines the victims one finds that what has broken down is the masculine style of life which held the field up to now, and that what is left over is an effeminate man. Contrariwise, one can observe women in these self-same business spheres who have developed in the second half of life an uncommonly masculine tough-mindedness which thrusts the feelings and the heart aside. Very often these changes are accompanied by all sorts of catastrophes in marriage, for it is not hard to imagine what will happen when the husband discovers his tender feelings and the wife her sharpness of mind.

784 The worst of it all is that intelligent and cultivated people live their lives without even knowing of the possibility of such transformations. Wholly unprepared, they embark upon the second half of life. Or are there perhaps colleges for forty-year-

olds which prepare them for their coming life and its demands as the ordinary colleges introduce our young people to a knowledge of the world? No, thoroughly unprepared we take the step into the afternoon of life; worse still, we take this step with the false assumption that our truths and ideals will serve us as hitherto. But we cannot live the afternoon of life according to the programme of life's morning; for what was great in the morning will be little at evening, and what in the morning was true will at evening have become a lie. I have given psychological treatment to too many people of advancing years, and have looked too often into the secret chambers of their souls, not to be moved by this fundamental truth.

785 Ageing people should know that their lives are not mounting and expanding, but that an inexorable inner process enforces the contraction of life. For a young person it is almost a sin, or at least a danger, to be too preoccupied with himself; but for the ageing person it is a duty and a necessity to devote serious attention to himself. After having lavished its light upon the world, the sun withdraws its rays in order to illuminate itself. Instead of doing likewise, many old people prefer to be hypochondriacs, niggards, pedants, applauders of the past or else eternal adolescents—all lamentable substitutes for the illumination of the self, but inevitable consequences of the delusion that the second half of life must be governed by the principles of the first.

786 I said just now that we have no schools for forty-year-olds. That is not quite true. Our religions were always such schools in the past, but how many people regard them like that today? How many of us older ones have been brought up in such a school and really prepared for the second half of life, for old age, death and eternity?

787 A human being would certainly not grow to be seventy or eighty years old if this longevity had no meaning for the species. The afternoon of human life must also have a significance of its own and cannot be merely a pitiful appendage to life's morning. The significance of the morning undoubtedly lies in the development of the individual, our entrenchment in the outer world, the propagation of our kind, and the care of our children. This is the obvious purpose of nature. But when this purpose has been attained—and more than attained—shall the

earning of money, the extension of conquests, and the expansion of life go steadily on beyond the bounds of all reason and sense? Whoever carries over into the afternoon the law of the morning, or the natural aim, must pay for it with damage to his soul, just as surely as a growing youth who tries to carry over his childish egoism into adult life must pay for this mistake with social failure. Money-making, social achievement, family and posterity are nothing but plain nature, not culture. Culture lies outside the purpose of nature. Could by any chance culture be the meaning and purpose of the second half of life?

788 In primitive tribes we observe that the old people are almost always the guardians of the mysteries and the laws, and it is in these that the cultural heritage of the tribe is expressed. How does the matter stand with us? Where is the wisdom of our old people, where are their precious secrets and their visions? For the most part our old people try to compete with the young. In the United States it is almost an ideal for a father to be the brother of his sons, and for the mother to be if possible the younger sister of her daughter.

789 I do not know how much of this confusion is a reaction against an earlier exaggeration of the dignity of age, and how much is to be charged to false ideals. These undoubtedly exist, and the goal of those who hold them lies behind, and not ahead. Therefore they are always striving to turn back. We have to grant these people that it is hard to see what other goal the second half of life can offer than the well-known aims of the first. Expansion of life, usefulness, efficiency, the cutting of a figure in society, the shrewd steering of offspring into suitable marriages and good positions—are not these purposes enough? Unfortunately not enough meaning and purpose for those who see in the approach of old age a mere diminution of life and can feel their earlier ideals only as something faded and worn out. Of course, if these persons had filled up the beaker of life earlier and emptied it to the lees, they would feel quite differently about everything now; they would have kept nothing back, everything that wanted to catch fire would have been consumed, and the quiet of old age would be very welcome to them. But we must not forget that only a very few people are artists in life; that the art of life is the most distinguished and rarest of all the arts. Who ever succeeded in draining the whole cup with grace?

So for many people all too much unlived life remains over—sometimes potentialities which they could never have lived with the best of wills, so that they approach the threshold of old age with unsatisfied demands which inevitably turn their glances backward.

790 It is particularly fatal for such people to look back. For them a prospect and a goal in the future are absolutely necessary. That is why all great religions hold out the promise of a life beyond, of a supramundane goal which makes it possible for mortal man to live the second half of life with as much purpose and aim as the first. For the man of today the expansion of life and its culmination are plausible goals, but the idea of life after death seems to him questionable or beyond belief. Life's cessation, that is, death, can only be accepted as a reasonable goal either when existence is so wretched that we are only too glad for it to end, or when we are convinced that the sun strives to its setting "to illuminate distant races" with the same logical consistency it showed in rising to the zenith. But to believe has become such a difficult art today that it is beyond the capacity of most people, particularly the educated part of humanity. They have become too accustomed to the thought that, with regard to immortality and such questions, there are innumerable contradictory opinions and no convincing proofs. And since "science" is the catchword that seems to carry the weight of absolute conviction in the temporary world, we ask for "scientific" proofs. But educated people who can think know very well that proof of this kind is a philosophical impossibility. We simply cannot know anything whatever about such things.

. . . .

Jung's description of childhood and old age as periods "without any conscious problems" is of course overstated, but his image of our lives as beginning and ending in submersion in the unconscious explains the different tasks of the hero in the first and second halves of life. At the beginning of life, it takes a hero's effort to mount a consciousness; at the end of life, the hero must be sacrificed in order to accept the unconscious as the final arbiter of the individual's fate.

---

795 In conclusion I would like to come back for a moment to the comparison with the sun. The one hundred and eighty degrees of the arc of life are divisible into four parts. The first quarter, lying to the east, is childhood, that state in which we are a problem for others but are not yet conscious of any problems of our own. Conscious problems fill out the second and third quarters; while in the last, in extreme old age, we descend again into that condition where, regardless of our state of consciousness, we once more become something of a problem for others. Childhood and extreme old age are, of course, utterly different, and yet they have one thing in common: submersion in unconscious psychic happenings. Since the mind of a child grows out of the unconscious its psychic processes, though not easily accessible, are not as difficult to discern as those of a very old person who is sinking again into the unconscious, and who progressively vanishes within it. Childhood and old age are the stages of life without any conscious problems, for which reason I have not taken them into consideration here.

Jung realized that the initiation of young men with mother complexes does not mean separation from everything maternal in favor of everything masculine. Often a deepened connection with positive aspects of the mother archetype could help to heal a damaged masculine spirit. Here (in terms somewhat marred by the medical thinking of his time that equated homosexuality with arrested development) Jung describes a young man whose dreams urged this feminine initiatory route in favor of sexual relations with a fraternity brother.

---

167 First I must acquaint the reader in some measure with the personality of the dreamer, for without this acquaintance he will hardly be able to transport himself into the peculiar atmosphere of the dreams. There are dreams that are pure poems and can therefore only be understood through the mood they convey as a whole. The dreamer is a youth of a little over twenty, still entirely boyish in appearance. There is even a touch of girlishness in his looks and manner of expression. The latter betrays a very good education and upbringing. He is intelligent, with pronounced intellectual and aesthetic interests. His aestheticism is very much in evidence: we are made instantly aware of his good taste and his fine appreciation of all forms of art. His feelings are tender and soft, given to the enthusiasms typical of puberty, but somewhat effeminate. There is no trace of adolescent callowness. Undoubtedly he is too young for his age, a clear case of retarded development. It is quite in keeping with this that he should have come to me on account of his homosexuality. The

night preceding his first visit he had the following dream: "*I am in a lofty cathedral filled with mysterious twilight. They tell me that it is the cathedral at Lourdes. In the centre there is a deep dark well, into which I have to descend.*"

168 The dream is clearly a coherent expression of mood. The dreamer's comments are as follows: "Lourdes is the mystic fount of healing. Naturally I remembered yesterday that I was going to you for treatment and was in search of a cure. There is said to be a well like this at Lourdes. It would be rather unpleasant to go down into this water. The well in the church was ever so deep."

169 Now what does dream tell us? On the surface it seems clear enough, and we might be content to take it as a kind of poetic formulation of the mood of the day before. But we should never stop there, for experience shows that dreams are much deeper and more significant. One might almost suppose that the dreamer came to the doctor in a highly poetic mood and was entering upon the treatment as though it were a sacred religious act to be performed in the mystical half-light of some awe-inspiring sanctuary. But this does not fit the facts at all. The patient merely came to the doctor to be treated for that unpleasant matter, his homosexuality, which is anything but poetic. At any rate we cannot see from the mood of the preceding day why he should dream so poetically, if we were to accept so direct a causation for the origin of the dream. But we might conjecture, perhaps, that the dream was stimulated precisely by the dreamer's impressions of that highly unpoetical affair which impelled him to come to me for treatment. We might even suppose that he dreamed in such an intensely poetical manner just because of the unpoeticalness of his mood on the day before, much as a man who has fasted by day dreams of delicious meals at night. It cannot be denied that the thought of treatment, of the cure and its unpleasant procedure, recurs in the dream, but poetically transfigured, in a guise which meets most effectively the lively aesthetic and emotional needs of the dreamer. He will be drawn on irresistibly by this inviting picture, despite the fact that the well is dark, deep, and cold. Something of the dream-mood will persist after sleep and will even linger on into the morning of the day on which he has to submit to the unpleasant and unpoetical duty of visiting me. Perhaps the drab reality will be

touched by the bright, golden after-glow of the dream feeling.

70 Is this, perhaps, the purpose of the dream? That would not be impossible, for in my experience the vast majority of dreams are compensatory.[11] They always stress the other side in order to maintain the psychic equilibrium. But the compensation of mood is not the only purpose of the dream picture. The dream also provides a *mental corrective.* The patient had of course nothing like an adequate understanding of the treatment to which he was about to submit himself. But the dream gives him a picture which describes in poetic metaphors the nature of the treatment before him. This becomes immediately apparent if we follow up his associations and comments on the image of the cathedral: "Cathedral," he says, "makes me think of Cologne Cathedral. Even as a child I was fascinated by it. I remember my mother telling me of it for the first time, and I also remember how, whenever I saw a village church, I used to ask if that were Cologne Cathedral. I wanted to be a priest in a cathedral like that."

71 In these associations the patient is describing a very important experience of his childhood. As in nearly all cases of this kind, he had a particularly close tie with his mother. By this we are not to understand a particularly good or intense *conscious* relationship, but something in the nature of a secret, subterranean tie which expresses itself consciously, perhaps, only in the retarded development of character, i.e., in a relative infantilism. The developing personality naturally veers away from such an unconscious infantile bond; for nothing is more obstructive to development than persistence in an unconscious—we could also say, a psychically embryonic—state. For this reason instinct seizes on the first opportunity to replace the mother by another object. If it is to be a real mother-substitute, this object must be, in some sense, an analogy of her. This is entirely the case with our patient. The intensity with which his childish fantasy seized upon the symbol of Cologne Cathedral corresponds to the strength of his unconscious need to find a substitute for the mother. The unconscious need is heightened still further in a case where the infantile bond could become harmful. Hence the enthusiasm with which his childish imagination took up the idea

11 The idea of compensation has already been extensively used by Alfred Adler.

of the Church; for the Church is, in the fullest sense, a mother. We speak not only of Mother Church, but even of the Church's womb. In the ceremony known as the *benedictio fontis,* the baptismal font is apostrophized as "immaculatus divini fontis uterus"—the immaculate womb of the divine font. We naturally think that a man must have known this meaning consciously before it could get to work in his fantasy, and that an unknowing child could not possibly be affected by these significations. Such analogies certainly do not work by way of the conscious mind, but in quite another manner.

172 The Church represents a higher spiritual substitute for the purely natural, or "carnal," tie to the parents. Consequently it frees the individual from an unconscious natural relationship which, strictly speaking, is not a relationship at all but simply a condition of inchoate, unconscious identity. This, just because it is unconscious, possesses a tremendous inertia and offers the utmost resistance to any kind of spiritual development. It would be hard to say what the essential difference is between this state and the soul of an animal. Now, it is by no means the special prerogative of the Christian Church to try to make it possible for the individual to detach himself from his original, animal-like condition; the Church is simply the latest, and specifically Western, form of an instinctive striving that is probably as old as mankind itself. It is a striving that can be found in the most varied forms among all primitive peoples who are in any way developed and have not yet become degenerate: I mean the institution or rite of initiation into manhood. When he has reached puberty the young man is conducted to the "men's house," or some other place of consecration, where he is systematically alienated from his family. At the same time he is initiated into the religious mysteries, and in this way is ushered not only into a wholly new set of relationships, but, as a renewed and changed personality, into a new world, like one reborn (*quasimodo genitus*). The initiation is often attended by all kinds of tortures, sometimes including such things as circumcision and the like. These practices are undoubtedly very old. They have almost become instinctive mechanisms, with the result that they continue to repeat themselves without external compulsion, as in the "baptisms" of German students or the

even more wildly extravagant initiations in American students' fraternities. They are engraved on the unconscious as a primordial image.

173 When his mother told him as a little boy about Cologne Cathedral, this primordial image was stirred and awakened to life. But there was no priestly instructor to develop it further, so the child remained in his mother's hands. Yet the longing for a man's leadership continued to grow in the boy, taking the form of homosexual leanings—a faulty development that might never have come about had a man been there to educate his childish fantasies. The deviation towards homosexuality has, to be sure, numerous historical precedents. In ancient Greece, as also in certain primitive communities, homosexuality and education were practically synonymous. Viewed in this light, the homosexuality of adolescence is only a misunderstanding of the otherwise very appropriate need for masculine guidance. One might also say that the fear of incest which is based on the mother-complex extends to women in general; but in my opinion an immature man is quite right to be afraid of women, because his relations with women are generally disastrous.

174 According to the dream, then, what the initiation of the treatment signifies for the patient is the fulfilment of the true meaning of his homosexuality, i.e., his entry into the world of the adult man. All that we have been forced to discuss here in such tedious and long-winded detail, in order to understand it properly, the dream has condensed into a few vivid metaphors, thus creating a picture which works far more effectively on the imagination, feeling, and understanding of the dreamer than any learned discourse. Consequently the patient was better and more intelligently prepared for the treatment than if he had been overwhelmed with medical and pedagogical maxims. (For this reason I regard dreams not only as a valuable source of information but as an extraordinarily effective instrument of education.)

175 We come now to the second dream. I must explain in advance that in the first consultation I did not refer in any way to the dream we have just been discussing. It was not even mentioned. Nor was there a word said that was even remotely connected with the foregoing. This is the second dream: "*I am in a great Gothic cathedral. At the altar stands a priest. I stand be-*

fore him with my friend, holding in my hand a little Japanese ivory figure, with the feeling that it is going to be baptized. Suddenly an elderly woman appears, takes the fraternity ring from my friend's finger, and puts it on her own. My friend is afraid that this may bind him in some way. But at the same moment there is a sound of wonderful organ music."

176 Here I will only bring out briefly those points which continue and supplement the dream of the preceding day. The second dream is unmistakably connected with the first: once more the dreamer is in church, that is, in the state of initiation into manhood. But a new figure has been added: the priest, whose absence in the previous situation we have already noted. The dream therefore confirms that the unconscious meaning of his homosexuality has been fulfilled and that a further development can be started. The actual initiation ceremony, namely the baptism, may now begin. The dream symbolism corroborates what I said before, namely that it is not the prerogative of the Christian Church to bring about such transitions and psychic transformations, but that behind the Church there is a living primordial image which in certain conditions is capable of enforcing them.

177 What, according to the dream, is to be baptized is a little Japanese ivory figure. The patient says of this: "It was a tiny, grotesque little manikin that reminded me of the male organ. It was certainly odd that this member was to be baptized. But after all, with the Jews circumcision is a sort of baptism. That must be a reference to my homosexuality, because the friend standing with me before the altar is the one with whom I have sexual relations. We belong to the same fraternity. The fraternity ring obviously stands for our relationship."

178 We know that in common usage the ring is the token of a bond or relationship, as for example the wedding ring. We can therefore safely take the fraternity ring in this case as symbolizing the homosexual relationship, and the fact that the dreamer appears together with his friend points in the same direction.

179 The complaint to be remedied is homosexuality. The dreamer is to be led out of this relatively childish condition and initiated into the adult state by means of a kind of circumcision ceremony under the supervision of a priest. These ideas correspond exactly to my analysis of the previous dream. Thus far the development has proceeded logically and consistently with the

aid of archetypal images. But now a disturbing factor comes on the scene. An elderly woman suddenly takes possession of the fraternity ring; in other words, she draws to herself what has hitherto been a homosexual relationship, thus causing the dreamer to fear that he is getting involved in a new relationship with obligations of its own. Since the ring is now on the hand of a woman, a marriage of sorts has been contracted, i.e., the homosexual relationship seems to have passed over into a heterosexual one, but a heterosexual relationship of a peculiar kind since it concerns an elderly woman. "She is a friend of my mother's," says the patient. "I am very fond of her, in fact she is like a mother to me."

180 From this remark we can see what has happened in the dream: as a result of the initiation the homosexual tie has been cut and a heterosexual relationship substituted for it, a platonic friendship with a motherly type of woman. In spite of her resemblance to his mother, this woman is not his mother any longer, so the relationship with her signifies a step beyond the mother towards masculinity, and hence a partial conquest of his adolescent homosexuality.

181 The fear of the new tie can easily be understood, firstly as fear which the woman's resemblance to his mother might naturally arouse—it might be that the dissolution of the homosexual tie has led to a complete regression to the mother—and secondly as fear of the new and unknown factors in the adult heterosexual state with its possible obligations, such as marriage, etc. That we are in fact concerned here not with a regression but with a progression seems to be confirmed by the music that now peals forth. The patient is musical and especially susceptible to solemn organ music. Therefore music signifies for him a very positive feeling, so in this case it forms a harmonious conclusion to the dream, which in its turn is well qualified to leave behind a beautiful, holy feeling for the following morning.

182 If you consider the fact that up to now the patient had seen me for only one consultation, in which little more was discussed than a general anamnesis, you will doubtless agree with me when I say that both dreams make astonishing anticipations. They show the patient's situation in a highly remarkable light, and one that is very strange to the conscious mind, while at the same time lending to the banal medical situation an aspect that

is uniquely attuned to the mental peculiarities of the dreamer, and thus capable of stringing his aesthetic, intellectual, and religious interests to concert pitch. No better conditions for treatment could possibly be imagined. One is almost persuaded, from the meaning of these dreams, that the patient entered upon the treatment with the utmost readiness and hopefulness, quite prepared to cast aside his boyishness and become a man. In reality, however, this was not the case at all. Consciously he was full of hesitation and resistance; moreover, as the treatment progressed, he constantly showed himself antagonistic and difficult, ever ready to slip back into his previous infantilism. Consequently the dreams stand in strict contrast to his conscious behaviour. They move along a progressive line and take the part of the educator. They clearly reveal their special function. This function I have called compensation. The unconscious progressiveness and the conscious regressiveness together form a pair of opposites which, as it were, keeps the scales balanced. The influence of the educator tilts the balance in favour of progression.

183 In the case of this young man the images of the collective unconscious play an entirely positive role, which comes from the fact that he has no really dangerous tendency to fall back on a fantasy-substitute for reality and to entrench himself behind it against life. The effect of these unconscious images has something fateful about it. Perhaps—who knows?—these eternal images are what men mean by fate.

LECTURE VIII, 13 March 1929

In the following transcription from his 1929 English Seminar on dreams, Jung discusses the masculine archetype of the *puer aeternus,* the eternal boy who is so often a personification of the immature eros of a man. Jung saw the immaturity of eros as characteristic of the masculine nature. The inner recognition of this problem, as in the dream that is discussed here, was the first step to its solution.

Next dream [12], *the same night:* There is an extraordinary difference between the next dream and the last, with a most remarkable compensation. "I am in a bedroom with my wife, and I see a door which leads into another room slowly open. I immediately go to the door, push it open, and in the other room I find a little boy completely naked. I carry him into the bedroom and I am convinced in the dream that he is not a natural boy. In order to prevent his getting away (he is struggling in my arms) I press him against me, and he gives me the most remarkable feeling (not at all a sexual feeling) of satisfaction as if this true thing were satisfactory to the longings of my feelings. Then my wife brings in a variety of food for the child. I see black bread and white bread. The child does not want to eat the black bread but eats the white. Then suddenly he flies out of the window and beckons to us from the air."

Associations: Door slowly opening: An allusion to a passage in the second part of *Faust* when Faust is getting old and has been trying to live a rational life. There is a monologue about the fact that he likes to think along the rational lines of the day and be scientific; then night comes and all is different, the door opens and no one comes in! We cannot do without magic. In the man's dream the door opens and no one comes in.[6] That means something supernatural. He has studied occultism, and he uses the word exteriorization, the theory of what formerly was attributed to spirits, table-tipping, rapping, noises in the wall. His theory is that it is not done by a ghost but by something in ourselves, the exteriorizing of psychological contents, and the dreamer is convinced of the reality of such facts. In the dream he has the feeling that the door is opening in a queer way. So he goes to see and finds the little naked boy in the other room.

The boy: The only association he had is the traditional representation of Eros, the naked baby boy. It gives a peculiar satisfaction to his feelings when he presses the boy against him.

Bread: The black bread is more nourishing than the white because it contains a protein in the silver skin of the grain. "The little amourette has not been fed in the right way by my wife, therefore he flies away and is beckoning from afar." Here you get a precious piece of masculine psychology. I am giving the whole sex away! That dream needs some mending. It is a good dream, an intimate, personal dream. How do you explain it after such an objective dream?

Dr. Binger: The contents are much the same. He sees himself as a child, Eros his infantile self. In the other dream he projected himself into his father, so he himself was a child.

Dr. Jung: Well, that needs discussion. I think we had better begin with the text to be sure that we are going right. The dreamer is in the bedroom with his wife, therefore it means in an intimate situation with his wife. That statement in the dream before, that he has to deal with his highest values and not with his lowest, leads

[6] *Faust*, Part II, Act V, in the tr. of Louis MacNeice (*Goethe's Faust*, London, 1951), p. 281:

"But now such spectredom so throngs the air
That none knows how to dodge it, none knows where.
Though one day greet us with a rational gleam,
The night entangles us in webs of dream.
We come back happy from the fields of spring—
And a bird croaks. Croaks what? Some evil thing.
Enmeshed in superstition night and morn,
It forms and shows itself and comes to warn.
And we, so scared, stand without friend or kin,
And the door creaks—and nobody comes in."

him to his intimate problem with his wife. Something in the business does not work, something in his relation to his wife does not work. The man who leads a provisional life does not deal with Eros. His father knows all about that, so he does not have to bother about it. He can close his eyes to the whole Eros side, and he is not adapted to his wife at all. You cannot deal with a woman with mere objectivity, so it is quite natural that in this dream the obstacle appears. The dream leads him right into the bedroom, for it is also a sexual trouble, sex being the strongest and clearest expression of relatedness. In this situation, certain contents of the unconscious seem to be exteriorized. As far as my knowledge reaches, those contents of the unconscious that are so near, so close that they are almost conscious, have a tendency to get exteriorized. They are almost ready to burst into consciousness, but certain obstacles are in the way and they are exteriorized. Here we have a little miracle. I have no prejudice against these little miracles. Such peculiar things take place occasionally, but how they are connected with our psychology God knows, I don't. Only fools think that everything can be explained. The true substance of the world is inexplicable. In this case it should dawn upon the dreamer that the thing lacking in his relation to his wife is Eros. It is almost a miracle that he has not seen it. It is Eros that ought to come in. He opens the door but no one comes in, then he finds the little boy in the other room and he holds him in his arms for a minute, feeling a peculiar satisfaction when he presses the child against him, and he thinks it is odd that it is not a sexual feeling. That is one of the foolish ideas which men have. They think that Eros is sex, but not at all, Eros is relatedness. Woman has something to say to that! He likes to think that it is a sexual problem, but it is not, it is an Eros problem.

Bread: Black bread would be more nourishing, yet the child refuses it and eats the white bread.

Dr. Shaw: Does the black bread stand for his thinking, his superior function?

Dr. Jung: There is no sign of that.

Miss Bianchi: He stresses the difference between the white and the black, the contrast. Can one assume that it has something to do with the nature of the two people?

Dr, Jung: I am not so sure of that. I would say that bread suggests food. Our mind, heart, body, every function must have its specific food, to continue living, so Eros cannot live without being fed. The food given to Eros is here called bread. Black and white is the ordinary symbolism for moral values. White is innocence, purity; black is earth dirt, night, Hell. The very black bread (pumpernickel) is very heavy and not easy to digest. They have a very primitive way of grinding the grain, so that all the husks are left in. It makes moist and heavy bread, but it is very nourishing. The boy refuses the black bread and accepts the white. What does that mean?

Mr. Gibb: He accepts the more idealistic.

Dr. Jung: The dreamer is much concerned with the kind of food he eats himself. He has a complex about food, and if you study such complexes you always find something interesting behind them. White bread is made from the very heart of the grain and the husks are thrown away, or given to the swine, so white bread gives the idea of luxury, nobility, or soul. It is made from the "soul" of the grain. The people who eat only white bread are noble, fine people, and those who eat black bread are coarse, vulgar, plebeian, earthy. Now, the question is whether the child is fed with heavy substantial food of the earth. To our Christian conscience that means food of devils and Hell. What is of the earth, earthy? Sexuality! But the general assumption that Eros is fed on sexuality is wrong. Curiously enough, he is fed only on white bread, on the very heart of the grain, by something hidden within sexuality, that is the *feeling,* the *relatedness.* If I should say to the patient, "Having sexual intercourse with your wife does not prove that you are related to her," he would not understand, for he thinks it would. You have relatedness by your feeling, by your rapport, and that is what feeds Eros. One expects that after sexual intercourse the soul should not be sad, but often the worst fights and misunderstandings in marriage happen after sexual intercourse, because sexuality does not feed Eros. This is often the direct cause of quarrels and separations.

The dream so far is a very important realization. Eros comes in a miraculous way and disappears in a miraculous way. He flies out of the window. What does that mean?

Dr. Binger: The man is not ready for a feeling relation.

Dr. Jung: We don't know what Eros would do if he stayed long enough. He might feed on the black bread too after a while, but he does not stay long enough. He just says, "Nothing doing; goodbye!" It is a good joke and a terrible truth. It is the promised land, but only for a moment is the fleeting vision clear; then he flies away before he can feed on the black bread. This is often the way in analysis. Just for a moment you see the way ahead quite clearly, then the vision vanishes, the mist gathers, and again you are in confusion. It is a sudden vision of the truth that appears and vanishes again without concretization. Eating the bread in his house is an archaic symbol for hospitality. But Eros does not eat all the bread, only the white, then he disappears, beckoning from afar, "Au revoir, nice to have seen you, perhaps I will see you again, it's not quite certain."

Mrs. Sigg: I have some doubt about the boy being only Eros. In *Faust*, the boy had something to do with poetry and imagination. He was something else.

Dr. Jung: True, he may not be Eros alone. I have my doubts too. But I kept to Eros as the dreamer was unaware of the general quality of his dream. One could say that the fact that he associated with Faust in the beginning points to the charioteer, Homunculus, and Euphorion,[7] the three forms of that element which I technically term the Puer Aeternus symbol in dreams. To my mind it refers to this symbolism. After the father complex, the infantile complex necessarily appears, where he is the son. First he turned his eyes to the father, now he is the son, still in the psychology of a boy of eight or ten years, so the Eros figure would be the infantile side of the dreamer. But if you say that, then the infantile side is to come into relation with his wife, and he isn't quite up to that situation yet. You could say that his natural unsophisticated feeling had better come into relation with his wife. It is quite true that the child is the infantile side of the dreamer, but it is also the promising thing in him. The things which one has developed are finished, but the undeveloped things are still a promise for the future. So the boy represents what may be developed, the self-renewing thing in man, and a good term to give to this figure is the Puer Aeternus. The old idea was that the Puer Aeternus was a Divine Child who eternally appeared and disappeared in a miraculous way. The Etruscan boy Tages,[8] a little naked boy, appears in the furrow

[7] *Faust*, Part II, Act II. A summary of the fates of these three figures is given at the beginning of the lecture of 27 March 1929, below.

[8] For Tages, the legendary founder of Etruscan augural lore, and Oannes, mentioned a few lines further, see CW 5, pars. 291-2. Adonis was a Phoenician vegetation god and Tammuz his Babylonian equivalent.

where the peasant is ploughing, and he teaches the people laws, arts, and culture. Adonis was such a boy. Tammuz appears to the women every spring. The Babylonian fish-god Oannes comes out of the water as a fish, appears at sunrise, and teaches the people agriculture, laws, etc., during the day, disappearing at night into the sea again. Meister Eckhart had a vision of a little naked boy who visited him.[9] Then there are some English fairy stories of the radiant boy, in which the vision of the boy is always unlucky, sometimes absolutely fatal. There must be some reason for this, I do not know what it may be. The Puer Aeternus[10] is simply the personification of the infantile side of our character, repressed because it is infantile. If the dreamer allows that element to come in, it is as though he himself had disappeared and come back as a little naked boy. Then if his wife could accept him as such, everything would be all right. The little boy ought to be brought up, educated, perhaps spanked. If the inferior element can enter life, then there is a promise of future life, things can develop, there can be progress. In mythology, the figure of this little naked boy has an almost divine creative character. As the Puer Aeternus he appears in a miraculous way and then disappears in the same way. In *Faust* he has three forms: Boy Charioteer, Homunculus, Euphorion. They were all destroyed by fire, which meant in Goethe's case that the Pueri Aeterni all disappeared in a passionate outbreak. Fire puts an end to everything, even an end to the world. Fire that is the sap of culture can burst forth and destroy everything. This happens from time to time, as for instance in the Bolshevist Revolution, when the cultural form could not hold the tension of energy any more, and the fire broke forth and destroyed the Russian civilization.

[9] For further details see below, p. 188.

[10] Jung was to develop this theme later in "The Psychology of the Child Archetype" (1941), CW 9 i.

THE LOVE PROBLEM OF A STUDENT

Jung saw the early love-relationships, whether homosexual or heterosexual, as places where eros could be cultivated.

---

216 As to whether student marriages are premature, we must take note of a fact that applies to all early marriages, namely, that a girl of twenty is usually older than a man of twenty-five, as far as maturity of judgment is concerned. With many men of twenty-five the period of psychological puberty is not yet over. Puberty is a period of illusion and only partial responsibility. The psychological difference is due to the fact that a boy, up to the time of sexual maturity, is as a rule quite childish, whereas a girl develops much earlier than he does the psychological subtleties that go hand in hand with adolescence. Into this childishness sexuality often breaks with brutal force, while, despite the onset of puberty, it often goes on slumbering in a girl until the passion of love awakens it. There are a surprising number of women whose real sexuality, even though they are married, remains virginal for years; they become conscious of it only when they fall in love with another man. That is the reason why very many women have no understanding at all of masculine sexuality—they are completely unconscious of their own. With men it is different. Sexuality bursts on them like a tempest, filling them with brute desires and needs, and there is scarcely one of them who escapes the painful problem of masturbation. But a girl can masturbate for years without knowing what she is doing.

217 The onrush of sexuality in a boy brings about a powerful

change in his psychology. He now has the sexuality of a grown man with the soul of a child. Often the flood of obscene fantasies and smutty talk with schoolfellows pours like a torrent of dirty water over all his delicate and childish feelings, sometimes smothering them for ever. Unexpected moral conflicts arise, temptations of every description lie in wait for him and weave themselves into his fantasies. The psychic assimilation of the sexual complex causes him the greatest difficulties even though he may not be conscious of its existence. The onset of puberty also brings about considerable changes in his metabolism, as can be seen from the pimples and acne that so often afflict adolescents. The psyche is disturbed in a similar manner and thrown off its balance. At this age the young man is full of illusions, which are always a sign of psychic disequilibrium. They make stability and maturity of judgment impossible. His tastes, his interests, his plans alter fitfully. He can suddenly fall head over heels in love with a girl, and a fortnight later he cannot conceive how anything of the sort could have happened to him. He is so riddled with illusions that he actually needs these mistakes to make him conscious of his own taste and individual judgment. He is still experimenting with life, and *must* experiment with it in order to learn how to judge things correctly. Hence there are very few men who have not had sexual experience of some kind before they are married. During puberty it is mostly homosexual experiences, and these are much more common than is generally admitted. Heterosexual experiences come later, not always of a very beautiful kind. For the less the sexual complex is assimilated to the whole of the personality, the more autonomous and instinctive it will be. Sexuality is then purely animal and recognizes no psychological distinctions. The most inferior woman will do; it is enough if she has the typical secondary sexual characteristics. A false step of this kind does not entitle us to draw conclusions about a man's character, as the act can easily occur at a time when the sexual complex is still split off from the psyche's influence. Nevertheless, too many experiences of this nature have a bad effect on the formation of the personality, as by force of habit they fix sexuality on too low a level and make it unacceptable to moral judgment. The result is that though the man in question is outwardly a respectable citizen, inwardly he is prey to sexual fantasies of the lowest kind, or else he represses them and on some festive occasion they come leaping to the surface in their primitive form, much to the astonishment of his unsuspecting wife—assuming, of course, that she notices what is going on. A frequent accompaniment is premature coldness towards the wife. Women are often frigid from the first day of marriage because their sensation function does not respond to this kind of sexuality in their husbands. The weakness of a man's judgment at the time of psychological puberty should prompt him to reflect very deeply on the premature choice of a wife.

218 Let us now turn to other forms of relationship between the sexes that are customary during the student period. There are, as you know, characteristic liaisons between students, chiefly in the great universities of other countries. These relationships are sometimes fairly stable and may even have a psychological value, as they do not consist entirely of sexuality but also, in part, of love. Occasionally the liaison is continued into marriage. The relationship stands, therefore, considerably higher than prostitution. But as a rule it is limited to those students who were careful in the choice of their parents. It is usually a question of money, for most of the girls are dependent on their lovers for financial help, though they could not be said to sell their love for money. Very often the relationship is a beautiful episode in the girl's life, otherwise poor and empty, while for the man it may be his first intimate acquaintance with a woman, and in later life a memory on which he looks back with emotion. Often, again, there is nothing valuable in these affairs, partly owing to the man's crude sensuality, thoughtlessness, and lack of feeling, and partly owing to the frivolity and fickleness of the girl.

219 Over all these relationships hangs the Damoclean sword of their transitoriness, which prevents the formation of real values. They are passing episodes, experiments of very limited validity. Their injurious effect on the personality is due to the fact that the man gets the girl too easily, so that the value of the love-object is depreciated. It is convenient for him to dispose of his sexual problem in such a simple and irresponsible way. He becomes spoilt. But even more, the fact that he is sexually satisfied robs him of a driving-force which no young man can do without. He becomes blasé and can afford to wait. Meanwhile he

can calmly review the massed femininity passing before him until the right party turns up. Then the wedding comes along and the latest date is thrown over. This procedure adds little of advantage to his character. The low level of relationship tends to keep sexuality on a correspondingly low level of development, and this can easily lead to difficulties in marriage. Or if his sexual fantasies are repressed, the result is only too likely to be a neurotic or, worse still, a moral zealot.

220 Homosexual relations between students of either sex are by no means uncommon. So far as I can judge of this phenomenon, I would say that these relationships are less common with us, and on the continent generally, than in certain other countries where boy and girl college students live in strict segregation. I am speaking here not of pathological homosexuals who are incapable of real friendship and meet with little sympathy among normal individuals, but of more or less normal youngsters who enjoy such a rapturous friendship that they also express their feelings in sexual form. With them it is not just a matter of mutual masturbation, which in all school and college life is the order of the day among the younger age groups, but of a higher and more spiritual form which deserves the name "friendship" in the classical sense of the word. When such a friendship exists between an older man and a younger its educative significance is undeniable. A slightly homosexual teacher, for example, often owes his brilliant educational gifts to his homosexual disposition. The homosexual relation between an older and a younger man can thus be of advantage to both sides and have a lasting value. An indispensable condition for the value of such a relation is the steadfastness of the friendship and their loyalty to it. But only too often this condition is lacking. The more homosexual a man is, the more prone he is to disloyalty and to the seduction of boys. Even when loyalty and true friendship prevail the results may be undesirable for the development of personality. A friendship of this kind naturally involves a special cult of feeling, of the feminine element in a man. He becomes gushing, soulful, aesthetic, over-sensitive, etc. —in a word, effeminate, and this womanish behaviour is detrimental to his character.

221 Similar advantages and disadvantages can be pointed out in friendships between women, only here the difference in age

and the educative factor are not so important. The main value lies in the exchange of tender feelings on the one hand and of intimate thoughts on the other. Generally they are high-spirited, intellectual, and rather masculine women who are seeking to maintain their superiority and to defend themselves against men. Their attitude to men is therefore one of disconcerting self-assurance, with a trace of defiance. Its effect on their character is to reinforce their masculine traits and to destroy their feminine charm. Often a man discovers their homosexuality only when he notices that these women leave him stone-cold.

222 Normally, the practice of homosexuality is not prejudicial to later heterosexual activity. Indeed, the two can even exist side by side. I know a very intelligent woman who spent her whole life as a homosexual and then at fifty entered into a normal relationship with a man.

223 Among the sexual relations of the student period we must mention yet another, which is quite normal even if rather peculiar. This is the attachment of a young man to an older woman, possibly married or at any rate widowed. You will perhaps remember Jean Jacques Rousseau and his connection with Mme de Warens; this is the kind of relationship I have in mind. The man is usually rather shy, unsure of himself, inwardly afraid, sometimes infantile. He naturally seeks a mother, perhaps because he has had too much or too little love in his own family. Many women like nothing better than a man who is rather helpless, especially when they are considerably older than he is; they do not love a man's strength, his virtues and his merits, but his weaknesses. They find his infantilisms charming. If he stammers a little, he is enchanting; or perhaps he has a limp, and this excites maternal compassion and a little more besides. As a rule the woman seduces him, and he willingly submits to her mothering.

224 Not always, however, does a timid youth remain half a child. It may be that this surfeit of maternal solicitude was just what was needed to bring his undeveloped masculinity to the surface. In this way the woman educates his feeling and brings it to full consciousness. He learns to understand a woman who has experience of life and the world, is sure of herself, and thus he has a rare opportunity for a glimpse behind the scenes. But he

can take advantage of it only if he quickly outgrows this relationship, for should he get stuck in it her mothering would ruin him. Maternal tenderness is the most pernicious poison for anyone who has to equip himself for the hard and pitiless struggle of life. If he cannot let go of her apron-strings he will become a spineless parasite—for most of these women have money—and sink to the level of a lap-dog or a pet cat.

225 We must now discuss those forms of relationship which offer no solution of the sexual question for the reason that they are asexual or "platonic." If there were any reliable statistics on this subject, I believe they would show that in Switzerland the majority of students prefer a platonic relationship. Naturally, this raises the question of sexual abstinence. One often hears that abstaining from sexual intercouse is injurious to health. This view is incorrect, at least for people of the student age. Abstinence is injurious to health only when a man has reached the age when he could win a woman for himself, and should do so according to his individual inclinations. The extraordinary intensification of the sexual need that is so often felt at this time has the biological aim of forcibly eliminating the man's scruples, misgivings, doubts, and hesitations. This is very necessary, because the very idea of marriage, with all its doubtful possibilities, often makes a man panicky. It is only to be expected, therefore, that nature will push him over the obstacle. Abstention from sexual intercourse may certainly have injurious effects under these conditions, but not when there is no urgent physical or psychological need for it.

226 This brings us to the very similar question concerning the injurious effects of masturbation. When for physical or psychological reasons normal intercouse is impossible, masturbation as a safety-valve has no ill effects. Young people who come to the doctor suffering from the harmful effects of masturbation are not by any means excessive masturbationists—these usually have no need of a doctor because they are not in any sense ill—rather, their masturbation has harmful effects because it shows psychic complications and is attended by pangs of conscience or by a riot of sexual fantasies. The latter are particularly common among women. Masturbation with psychic complications is harmful, but not the ordinary, uncomplicated kind. If, however, it is continued up to the age when normal intercourse

becomes physically, psychologically, and socially possible, and is indulged in merely in order to avoid the necessary tasks of life, then it is harmful.

227 Platonic relationships are very important during the student period. The form they most commonly take is flirting. Flirting is the expression of an experimental attitude which is altogether appropriate at this age. It is a voluntary activity which, by tacit agreement, puts neither side under an obligation. This is an advantage and at the same time a disadvantage. The experimental attitude enables both parties to get to know each other without any immediately undesirable results. Both exercise their judgment and their skill in self-expression, adaptation, and defence. An enormous variety of experiences which are uncommonly valuable in later life can be picked up from flirting. On the other hand, the absence of any obligation can easily lead to one's becoming an habitual flirt, shallow, frivolous, and heartless. The man turns into a drawing-room hero and professional heart-breaker, never dreaming what a boring figure he cuts; the girl a coquette, and a serious man instinctively feels that she is not to be taken seriously.

228 A phenomenon that is as rare as flirting is common is the conscious cultivation of a serious love. We might call this simply the ideal, without, however, identifying it with traditional romanticism. For the development of personality, there can be no doubt that the timely awakening and conscious cultivation of deeply serious and responsible feelings are of the utmost value. A relationship of this kind can be the most effective shield against the temptations that beset a young man, as well as being a powerful incentive to hard work, loyalty, and reliability. However, there is no value so great that it does not have its unfavourable side. A relationship that is too ideal easily becomes exclusive. Through his love the young man is too much cut off from the acquaintance of other women, and the girl does not learn the art of erotic conquest because she has got her man already. Woman's instinct for possession is a dangerous thing, and it may easily happen that the man will regret all the experiences he never had with women before marriage and will make up for them afterwards.

229 Hence it must not be concluded that every relationship of this kind is ideal. There are cases where the exact opposite is

true—when, for instance, a man or girl trails round with a school sweetheart for no intelligible reason, from mere force of habit. Whether from inertia, or lack of spirit, or helplessness they simply cannot get rid of each other. Perhaps the parents on both sides find the match suitable, and the affair, begun in a moment of thoughtlessness and prolonged by habit, is passively accepted as a *fait accompli*. Here the disadvantages pile up without a single advantage. For the development of personality, acquiescence and passivity are harmful because they are an obstacle to valuable experience and to the exercise of one's specific gifts and virtues. Moral qualities are won only in freedom and prove their worth only in morally dangerous situations. The thief who refrains from stealing merely because he is in prison is not a moral personality. Though the parents may gaze benignly on this touching marriage and add their children's respectability to the tale of their own virtues, it is all a sham and a delusion, lacking real strength, and sapped by moral inertia.

230 After this brief survey of the problems as we meet them in actual life, I will, in conclusion, turn to the land of heart's desire and utopian possibilities.

231 Nowadays we can hardly discuss the love problem without speaking of the utopia of free love, including trial marriage. I regard this idea as a wishful fantasy and an attempt to make light of a problem which in actual life is invariably very difficult. It is no more possible to make life easy than it is to grow a herb of immortality. The force of gravity can be overcome only by the requisite application of energy. Similarly, the solution of the love problem challenges all our resources. Anything else would be useless patchwork. Free love would be conceivable only if everyone were capable of the highest moral achievement. The idea of free love was not invented with this aim in view, but merely to make something difficult appear easy. Love requires depth and loyalty of feeling; without them it is not love but mere caprice. True love will always commit itself and engage in lasting ties; it needs freedom only to effect its choice, not for its accomplishment. Every true and deep love is a sacrifice. The lover sacrifices all other possibilities, or rather, the illusion that such possibilities exist. If this sacrifice is not made, his illusions prevent the growth of any deep and responsible

feeling, so that the very possibility of experiencing real love is denied him.

232 Love has more than one thing in common with religious faith. It demands unconditional trust and expects absolute surrender. Just as nobody but the believer who surrenders himself wholly to God can partake of divine grace, so love reveals its highest mysteries and its wonder only to those who are capable of unqualified devotion and loyalty of feeling. And because this is so difficult, few mortals can boast of such an achievement. But, precisely because the truest and most devoted love is also the most beautiful, let no man seek to make it easy. He is a sorry knight who shrinks from the difficulty of loving his lady. Love is like God: both give themselves only to their bravest knights.

233 I would offer the same criticism of trial marriages. The very fact that a man enters into a marriage on trial means that he is making a reservation; he wants to be sure of not burning his fingers, to risk nothing. But that is the most effective way of forestalling any real experience. You do not experience the terrors of the Polar ice by perusing a travel-book, or climb the Himalayas in a cinema.

234 Love is not cheap—let us therefore beware of cheapening it! All our bad qualities, our egotism, our cowardice, our worldly wisdom, our cupidity—all these would persuade us not to take love seriously. But love will reward us only when we do. I must even regard it as a misfortune that nowadays the sexual question is spoken of as something distinct from love. The two questions should not be separated, for when there is a sexual problem it can be solved only by love. Any other solution would be a harmful substitute. Sexuality dished out as sexuality is brutish; but sexuality as an expression of love is hallowed. Therefore, never ask what a man does, but how he does it. If he does it from love or in the spirit of love, then he serves a god; and whatever he may do is not ours to judge, for it is ennobled.

235 I trust that these remarks will have made it clear to you that I pass no sort of moral judgment on sexuality as a natural phenomenon, but prefer to make its moral evaluation dependent on the way it is expressed.

III. THE FATHER

THE SIGNIFICANCE OF THE FATHER IN THE DESTINY OF THE INDIVIDUAL

Case 2

707 A man of thirty-four, of small build, with a clever, kindly expression. He was easily embarrassed, blushed often. He had come for treatment on account of "nervousness." He said he was very irritable, readily fatigued, had nervous stomach-trouble, was often so deeply depressed that he sometimes thought of suicide.

708 Before coming to me for treatment he had sent me a circumstantial autobiography, or rather a history of his illness, in order to prepare me for his visit. His story began: "My father was a very big and strong man." This sentence awakened my curiosity; I turned over a page and there read: "When I was fifteen a big lad of nineteen took me into a wood and indecently assaulted me."

709 The numerous gaps in the patient's story induced me to obtain a more exact anamnesis from him, which led to the following disclosures: The patient was the youngest of three brothers. His father, a big, red-haired man, was formerly a soldier in the Swiss Guard at the Vatican; later he became a policeman. He was a stern, gruff old soldier, who brought up his sons with military discipline; he issued commands, did not call them by name, but whistled for them. He had spent his youth in Rome, and during his gay life there had contracted syphilis, from the consequences of which he still suffered in old age. He was fond of talking about his adventures in early life. His eldest son (considerably older than the patient) was exactly like him, a big, strong man with red hair. The mother was an ailing woman, prematurely aged. Exhausted and tired of life, she died at forty when the patient was eight years old. He preserved a tender and beautiful memory of his mother.

710 At school he was always the whipping-boy and always the object of his schoolfellows' mockery. He thought his peculiar dialect might be to blame. Later he was apprenticed to a strict and unkind master, with whom he stuck it out for over two years, under conditions so trying that all the other apprentices ran away. At fifteen the assault already mentioned took place, together with several other, milder homosexual experiences. Then fate packed him off to France. There he made the acquaintance of a man from the south, a great boaster and Don Juan. He dragged the patient to a brothel; he went unwillingly and out of fear, and found he was impotent. Later he went to Paris, where his eldest brother, a master-mason and the replica of his father, was leading a dissolute life. The patient stayed there a long time, badly paid and helping his sister-in-law out of pity. The brother often took him along to a brothel, but he was always impotent.

711 One day his brother asked him to make over to him his inheritance, 6,000 francs. The patient consulted his second brother, who was also in Paris, and who urgently tried to dissuade him from handing over the money, because it would only be squandered. Nevertheless the patient went and gave his inheritance to his brother, who naturally ran through it in the shortest possible time. And the second brother, who would have dissuaded him, was also let in for 500 francs. To my astonished question why he had so light-heartedly given the money to his brother without any guarantee he replied: well, he asked for it. He was not a bit sorry about the money, he would give him another 6,000 francs if he had it. The eldest brother afterwards went to the bad altogether and his wife divorced him.

712 The patient returned to Switzerland and remained for a year without regular employment, often suffering from hunger. During this time he made the acquaintance of a family and became a frequent visitor. The husband belonged to some peculiar sect, was a hypocrite, and neglected his family. The wife was elderly, ill, and weak, and moreover pregnant. There were six children, all living in great poverty. For this woman the patient developed a warm affection and shared with her the little he possessed. She told him her troubles, saying she felt sure she would die in childbed. He promised her (although he possessed nothing) that he would take charge of the children and bring them up. The

woman did die in childbed, but the orphanage interfered and allowed him only one child. So now he had a child but no family, and naturally could not bring it up by himself. He thus came to think of marrying. But as he had never yet fallen in love with a girl he was in great perplexity.

713 It then occurred to him that his elder brother was divorced from his wife, and he resolved to marry her. He wrote to her in Paris, saying what he intended. She was seventeen years older than he, but not averse to his plan. She invited him to come to Paris to talk matters over. But on the eve of the journey fate willed that he should run an iron nail into his foot, so that he could not travel. After a while, when the wound was healed, he went to Paris and found that he had imagined his sister-in-law, now his fiancée, to be younger and prettier than she really was. The wedding took place, however, and three months later the first coitus, on his wife's initiative. He himself had no desire for it. They brought up the child together, he in the Swiss and she in the Parisian fashion, as she was a French woman. At the age of nine the child was run over and killed by a cyclist. The patient then felt very lonely and dismal at home. He proposed to his wife that they should adopt a young girl, whereupon she broke out into a fury of jealousy. Then, for the first time in his life, he fell in love with a young girl, and simultaneously the neurosis started with deep depression and nervous exhaustion, for meanwhile his life at home had become a hell.

714 My suggestion that he should separate from his wife was dismissed out of hand, on the ground that he could not take it upon himself to make the old woman unhappy on his account. He obviously preferred to go on being tormented, for the memories of his youth seemed to him more precious than any present joys.

715 This patient, too, moved all through his life in the magic circle of the family constellation. The strongest and most fateful factor was the relationship to the father; its masochistic-homosexual colouring is clearly apparent in everything he did. Even the unfortunate marriage was determined by the father, for the patient married the divorced wife of his elder brother, which amounted to marrying his mother. At the same time, his wife was the mother-substitute for the woman who died in childbed. The neurosis set in the moment the libido was withdrawn from

the infantile relationship and for the first time came a bit nearer to an individually determined goal. In this as in the previous case, the family constellation proved to be by far the stronger, so that the narrow field of neurosis was all that was left over for the struggling individuality.

. . . .

Jung revised this early essay forty years after its first publication.* It shows an evolution of his understanding from a time when the father complex seemed to him entirely an effect of the personal father to his mature years when he had come to appreciate the ambivalent archetype to which experiences of a father are assimilated. All archetypes contain positive and negative features, but where the mother archetype tends to split into positive and negative images, the father archetype tends to combine its opposites into a single ambiguous image of seductive and paralyzing power.

Case 4

731 An eight-year-old boy, intelligent, rather delicate-looking, brought to me by his mother on account of enuresis. During the consultation the child clung all the time to his mother, a pretty, youthful woman. The marriage was a happy one, but the father was strict, and the boy (the eldest child) was rather afraid of him. The mother compensated for the father's strictness by a corresponding tenderness, to which the boy responded so much that he never got away from his mother's apron-strings. He never played with his school-fellows, never went alone into the street unless he had to go to school. He feared the boys' roughness and violence and played thoughtful games at home or helped his mother with the housework. He was extremely jealous of his father, and could not bear it when the father showed tenderness to the mother.

* [Ed. Note. Passages added to the 1949 version are given in angle brackets, and passages replaced or omitted from the 1909 version are given in square brackets in the footnotes.]

732 I took the boy aside and asked him about his dreams. Very often he dreamt of a *black snake that wanted to bite his face.* Then he would cry out, and his mother had to come to him from the next room and stay by his bedside.

733 In the evening he would go quietly to bed. But when falling asleep it seemed to him that a *wicked black man with a sword or a gun was lying on his bed, a tall thin man who wanted to kill him.* The parents slept in the next room. The boy often dreamt that something dreadful was going on in there, as if there were *great black snakes or evil men who wanted to kill Mama.* Then he would cry out, and Mama came to comfort him. Every time he wet his bed he called his mother, who would then have to change the bedclothes.

734 The father was a tall thin man. Every morning he stood naked at the wash-stand in full view of the boy, to perform a thorough ablution. The boy also told me that at night he often started up from sleep at the sound of strange noises in the next room; then he was always horribly afraid that something dreadful was going on in there, a struggle of some kind, but his mother would quiet him and say it was nothing.

735 It is not difficult to see what was happening in the next room. It is equally easy to understand the boy's aim in calling out for his mother: he was jealous and was separating her from the father. He did this also in the daytime whenever he saw his father caressing her. Thus far the boy was simply the father's rival for his mother's love.

736 But now comes the fact that the snake and the wicked man threaten him as well: the same thing happens to him as happens to his mother in the next room. To that extent he identifies with his mother and thus puts himself in a similar relationship to the father. This is due to his homosexual component, which feels feminine towards the father. ⟨The bed-wetting is in this case a substitute for sexuality. Pressure of urine in dreams and also in the waking state is often an expression of some other pressure, for instance of fear, expectation, suppressed excitement, inability to speak, the need to express an unconscious content, etc. In our case the substitute for sexuality has the significance of a premature masculinity which is meant to compensate the inferiority of the child.

737 ⟨Although I do not intend to go into the psychology of

dreams in this connection, the motif of the black snake and of the black man should not pass unmentioned. Both these terrifying spectres threaten the dreamer as well as his mother. "Black" indicates something dark, the unconscious. The dream shows that the mother-child relationship is menaced by unconsciousness. The threatening agency is represented by the mythological motif of the "father animal"; in other words the father appears as threatening. This is in keeping with the tendency of the child to remain unconscious and infantile, which is decidedly dangerous. For the boy, the father is an anticipation of his own masculinity, conflicting with his wish to remain infantile. The snake's attack on the boy's face, the part that "sees," represents the danger to consciousness (blinding).⟩ [20]

738 This little example shows what goes on in the psyche of an eight-year-old child who is over-dependent on his parents, the blame for this lying partly on the too strict father and the too tender mother. ⟨The boy's identification with his mother and fear of his father are in this individual instance an infantile neurosis, but they represent at the same time the original human situation, the clinging of primitive consciousness to the unconscious, and the compensating impulse which strives to tear consciousness away from the embrace of the darkness. Because man has a dim premonition of this original situation behind his individual experience, he has always tried to give it generally valid expression through the universal motif of the divine hero's fight with the mother dragon, whose purpose is to deliver man from the power of darkness. This myth has a "saving," i.e., therapeutic significance, since it gives adequate expression to the dynamism underlying the individual entanglement. The myth is not to be causally explained as the consequence of a personal father-complex, but should be understood teleologically, as an attempt of the unconscious itself to rescue consciousness from the danger of regression. The ideas of "salvation" are not subsequent rationalizations of a father-complex; they are, rather,

20 [*Orig.:* It is not difficult to see, from the Freudian standpoint, what the bed-wetting means in this case. Micturition dreams give us the clue. Here I would refer the reader to an analysis of this kind in my paper "The Analysis of Dreams" (cf. supra, pars. 82f.). Bed-wetting must be regarded as an infantile sexual substitute, and even in the dream-life of adults it is easily used as a cloak for the pressure of sexual desire.]

archetypally preformed mechanisms for the development of consciousness.⟩ [21]

739 What we see enacted on the stage of world-history happens also in the individual. The child is guided by the power of the parents as by a higher destiny. But as he grows up, the struggle between his infantile attitude and his increasing consciousness begins. The parental influence, dating from the early infantile period, is repressed and sinks into the unconscious, but is not eliminated; by invisible threads it directs the apparently individual workings of the maturing mind. Like everything that has fallen into the unconscious, the infantile situation still sends up dim, premonitory feelings, feelings of being secretly guided by otherworldly influences. ⟨Normally these feelings are not referred back to the father, but to a positive or negative

21 [*Orig.:* The infantile attitude, it is evident, is nothing but infantile sexuality. If we now survey all the far-reaching possibilities of the infantile constellation, we are obliged to say that *in essence our life's fate is identical with the fate of our sexuality*. If Freud and his school devote themselves first and foremost to tracing out the individual's sexuality, it is certainly not in order to excite piquant sensations but to gain a deeper insight into the driving forces that determine the individual's fate. In this we are not saying too much, but rather understating the case. For, when we strip off the veils shrouding the problems of individual destiny, we at once widen our field of vision from the history of the individual to the history of nations. We can take a look, first of all, at the history of religion, at the history of the fantasy systems of whole peoples and epochs. The religion of the Old Testament exalted the paterfamilias into the Jehovah of the Jews, whom the people had to obey in fear and dread. The patriarchs were a stepping-stone to the Deity. The neurotic fear in Judaism, an imperfect or at any rate unsuccessful attempt at sublimation by a still too barbarous people, gave rise to the excessive severity of Mosaic law, the compulsive ceremonial of the neurotic.* Only the prophets were able to free themselves from it; for them the identification with Jehovah, complete sublimation, was successful. They became the fathers of the people. Christ, the fulfiller of their prophecies, put an end to this fear of God and taught mankind that the true relation to the Deity is love. Thus he destroyed the compulsive ceremonial of the law and was himself the exponent of the personal loving relationship to God. Later, the imperfect sublimations of the Christian Mass resulted once again in the ceremonial of the Church, from which only those of the numerous saints and reformers who were really capable of sublimation were able to break free. Not without cause, therefore, does modern theology speak of the liberating effect of "inner" or "personal" experience, for always the ardour of love transmutes fear and compulsion into a higher, freer type of feeling.

[* *Orig. footnote:* Cf. Freud, *Zeitschrift für Religionspsychologie* (1907).] [I.e., "Obsessive Acts and Religious Practices."—EDITORS.]

deity. This change is accomplished partly under the influence of education, partly spontaneously. It is universal. Also, it resists conscious criticism with the force of an instinct, for which reason the soul (*anima*) may fittingly be described as *naturaliter religiosa.* The reason for this development, indeed its very possibility, is to be found in the fact that the child possesses an inherited system that anticipates the existence of parents and their influence upon him. In other words, behind the father stands the archetype of the father, and in this pre-existent archetype lies the secret of the father's power, just as the power which forces the bird to migrate is not produced by the bird itself but derives from its ancestors.

740 It will not have escaped the reader that the role which falls to the father-imago in our case is an ambiguous one. The threat it represents has a dual aspect: fear of the father may drive the boy out of his identification with the mother, but on the other hand it is possible that his fear will make him cling still more closely to her. A typically neurotic situation then arises: he wants and yet does not want, saying yes and no at the same time.

741 This double aspect of the father-imago is characteristic of the archetype in general: it is capable of diametrically opposite effects and acts on consciousness rather as Yahweh acted towards Job—ambivalently. And, as in the Book of Job, man is left to take the consequences. We cannot say with certainty that the archetype always acts in this way, for there are experiences which prove the contrary. But they do not appear to be the rule.〉[22]

742 An instructive and well-known example of the ambivalent behaviour of the father-imago is the love-episode in the Book of Tobit.[23] Sara, the daughter of Raguel, of Ecbatana, desires to marry. But her evil fate wills it that seven times, one after the

22 [*Orig.:* These are the roots of the first religious sublimations. In the place of the father with his constellating virtues and faults there appears on the one hand an altogether sublime deity, and on the other hand the devil, who in modern times has been largely whittled away by the realization of one's own moral responsibility. Sublime love is attributed to the former, low sexuality to the latter. As soon as we enter the field of neurosis, this antithesis is stretched to the limit. God becomes the symbol of the most complete sexual repression, the devil the symbol of sexual lust. Thus it is that the conscious expression of the father-constellation, like every expression of an unconscious complex when it appears in consciousness, acquires its Janus face, its positive and its negative components.]

23 Chs. 3 : 7ff. and 8 : 1ff.

other, she chooses a husband who dies on the wedding-night. It is the evil spirit Asmodeus, by whom she is persecuted, that kills these men. She prays to Yahweh to let her die rather than suffer this shame again, for she is despised even by her father's maid-servants. The eighth bridegroom, her cousin Tobias, the son of Tobit, is sent to her by God. He too is led into the bridal chamber. Then old Raguel, who had only pretended to go to bed, goes out and thoughtfully digs his son-in-law's grave, and in the morning sends a maid to the bridal chamber to make sure that he is dead. But this time Asmodeus' role is played out, for Tobias is alive.

743 ⟨The story shows father Raguel in his two roles, as the inconsolable father of the bride and the provident digger of his son-in-law's grave. Humanly speaking he seems beyond reproach, and it is highly probable that he was. But there is still the evil spirit Asmodeus and his presence needs explaining. If we suspect old Raguel personally of playing a double role, this malicious insinuation would apply only to his sentiments; there is no evidence that he committed murder. These wicked deeds transcend the old man's daughter-complex as well as Sara's father-complex, for which reason the legend fittingly ascribes them to a demon. Asmodeus plays the role of a jealous father who will not give up his beloved daughter and only relents when he remembers his own positive aspect, and in that capacity at last gives Sara a pleasing bridegroom. He, significantly enough, is the eighth: the last and highest stage.[24] Asmodeus stands for the negative aspect of the father archetype, for the archetype is the genius and daemon of the personal human being, "the god of human nature, changeful of countenance, white and black." [25] The legend offers a psychologically correct explanation: it does not attribute superhuman evil to Raguel, it distinguishes between man and daemon, just as psychology must distinguish between what the human individual is and can do and what must be ascribed to the congenital, instinctual system, which the individual has not made but finds within him. We would be doing the gravest injustice to Raguel if we held

24 ⟨Cf. the axiom of Maria and the discussion of 3 and 4, 7 and 8, in *Psychology and Alchemy*, pars. 201ff. and 209.⟩

25 ⟨Horace, *Epistles*, II, 2, 187–89.⟩

him responsible for the fateful power of this system, that is, of the archetype.

744 ⟨The potentialities of the archetype, for good and evil alike, transcend our human capacities many times, and a man can appropriate its power only by identifying with the daemon, by letting himself be possessed by it, thus forfeiting his own humanity. The fateful power of the father complex comes from the archetype, and this is the real reason why the *consensus gentium* puts a divine or daemonic figure in place of the father. The personal father inevitably embodies the archetype, which is what endows his figure with its fascinating power. The archetype acts as an amplifier, enhancing beyond measure the effects that proceed from the father, so far as these conform to the inherited pattern.⟩ [26]

26 [*Orig.:* Unfortunately medical etiquette forbids me to report a case of hysteria which fits this pattern exactly, except that there were not seven husbands but only three, unluckily chosen under all the ominous signs of an infantile constellation. Our first case, too, belongs to this category, and in our third case we see the old peasant at work, preparing to dedicate his daughter to a like fate.

[As a pious and dutiful daughter (cf. her prayer in Tobit, ch. 3), Sara has brought about the usual sublimation and splitting of the father-complex, on the one hand elevating her infantile love into the worship of God, and on the other turning the obsessive power of the father into the persecuting demon Asmodeus. The story is beautifully worked out and shows father Raguel in his two roles, as the inconsolable father of the bride and the provident digger of his son-in-law's grave, whose fate he foresees.

[This pretty fable has become a classic example in my analytical work, for we frequently meet with cases where the father-demon has laid his hand upon his daughter, so that her whole life long, even when she does marry, there is never a true inward union, because her husband's image never succeeds in obliterating the unconscious and continually operative infantile father-ideal. This is true not only of daughters, but also of sons. An excellent example of this kind of father-constellation can be found in Brill's recently published "Psychological Factors in Dementia Praecox" (1908).

[In my experience it is usually the father who is the decisive and dangerous object of the child's fantasy, and if ever it happened to be the mother I was able to discover behind her a grandfather to whom she belonged in her heart.

[I must leave this question open, because my findings are not sufficient to warrant a decision. It is to be hoped that experience in the years to come will sink deeper shafts into this obscure territory, on which I have been able to shed but a fleeting light, and will discover more about the secret workshop of the demon who shapes our fate, of whom Horace says:

"Scit Genius natale comes qui temperat astrum,
Naturae deus humanae, mortalis in unum,
Quodque caput, vultu mutabilis, albus et ater."]

THE PERSONAL AND THE COLLECTIVE UNCONSCIOUS

Jung's idea that an archetypal image of masculine spirit lies at the core of an individual's father complex is given a convincing clinical demonstration in his account of a case.

---

202 In Freud's view, as most people know, the contents of the unconscious are reducible to infantile tendencies which are repressed because of their incompatible character. Repression is a process that begins in early childhood under the moral influence of the environment and continues throughout life. By means of analysis the repressions are removed and the repressed wishes made conscious.

203 According to this theory, the unconscious contains only those parts of the personality which could just as well be conscious, and have been suppressed only through the process of education. Although from one point of view the infantile tendencies of the unconscious are the most conspicuous, it would nonetheless be a mistake to define or evaluate the unconscious entirely in these terms. The unconscious has still another side to it: it includes not only repressed contents, but all psychic material that lies below the threshold of consciousness. It is impossible to explain the subliminal nature of all this material on the principle of repression, for in that case the removal of repression ought to endow a person with a prodigious memory which would thenceforth forget nothing.

204 We therefore emphatically affirm that in addition to the repressed material the unconscious contains all those psychic components that have fallen below the threshold, as well as sub-

liminal sense-perceptions. Moreover we know, from abundant experience as well as for theoretical reasons, that the unconscious also contains all the material that has *not yet* reached the threshold of consciousness. These are the seeds of future conscious contents. Equally we have reason to suppose that the unconscious is never quiescent in the sense of being inactive, but is ceaselessly engaged in grouping and regrouping its contents. This activity should be thought of as completely autonomous only in pathological cases; normally it is co-ordinated with the conscious mind in a compensatory relationship.

205 It is to be assumed that all these contents are of a personal nature in so far as they are acquired during the individual's life. Since this life is limited, the number of acquired contents in the unconscious must also be limited. This being so, it might be thought possible to empty the unconscious either by analysis or by making a complete inventory of the unconscious contents, on the ground that the unconscious cannot produce anything more than what is already known and assimilated into consciousness. We should also have to suppose, as already said, that if one could arrest the descent of conscious contents into the unconscious by doing away with repression, unconscious productivity would be paralysed. This is possible only to a very limited extent, as we know from experience. We urge our patients to hold fast to repressed contents that have been re-associated with consciousness, and to assimilate them into their plan of life. But this procedure, as we may daily convince ourselves, makes no impression on the unconscious, since it calmly goes on producing dreams and fantasies which, according to Freud's original theory, must arise from personal repressions. If in such cases we pursue our observations systematically and without prejudice, we shall find material which, although similar in form to the previous personal contents, yet seems to contain allusions that go far beyond the personal sphere.

206 Casting about in my mind for an example to illustrate what I have just said, I have a particularly vivid memory of a woman patient with a mild hysterical neurosis which, as we expressed it in those days [about 1910], had its principal cause in a "father-complex." By this we wanted to denote the fact that the patient's peculiar relationship to her father stood in her way. She had been on very good terms with her father, who had since

died. It was a relationship chiefly of feeling. In such cases it is usually the intellectual function that is developed, and this later becomes the bridge to the world. Accordingly our patient became a student of philosophy. Her energetic pursuit of knowledge was motivated by her need to extricate herself from the emotional entanglement with her father. This operation may succeed if her feelings can find an outlet on the new intellectual level, perhaps in the formation of an emotional tie with a suitable man, equivalent to the former tie. In this particular case, however, the transition refused to take place, because the patient's feelings remained suspended, oscillating between her father and a man who was not altogether suitable. The progress of her life was thus held up, and that inner disunity so characteristic of a neurosis promptly made its appearance. The so-called normal person would probably be able to break the emotional bond in one or the other direction by a powerful act of will, or else—and this is perhaps the more usual thing—he would come through the difficulty unconsciously, on the smooth path of instinct, without ever being aware of the sort of conflict that lay behind his headaches or other physical discomforts. But any weakness of instinct (which may have many causes) is enough to hinder a smooth unconscious transition. Then all progress is delayed by conflict, and the resulting stasis of life is equivalent to a neurosis. In consequence of the standstill, psychic energy flows off in every conceivable direction, apparently quite uselessly. For instance, there are excessive innervations of the sympathetic system, which lead to nervous disorders of the stomach and intestines; or the vagus (and consequently the heart) is stimulated; or fantasies and memories, uninteresting enough in themselves, become overvalued and prey on the conscious mind (mountains out of molehills). In this state a new motive is needed to put an end to the morbid suspension. Nature herself paves the way for this, unconsciously and indirectly, through the phenomenon of the transference (Freud). In the course of treatment the patient transfers the father-imago to the doctor, thus making him, in a sense, the father, and in the sense that he is *not* the father, also making him a substitute for the man she cannot reach. The doctor therefore becomes both a father and a kind of lover—in other words, an object of conflict. In him the opposites are united, and for this reason he stands for a quasi-ideal solution of the conflict. Without in the least wishing it, he draws upon himself an over-valuation that is almost incredible to the outsider, for to the patient he seems like a saviour or a god. This way of speaking is not altogether so laughable as it sounds. It is indeed a bit much to be a father and lover at once. Nobody could possibly stand up to it in the long run, precisely because it is too much of a good thing. One would have to be a demigod at least to sustain such a role without a break, for all the time one would have to be the giver. To the patient in the state of transference, this provisional solution naturally seems ideal, but only at first; in the end she comes to a standstill that is just as bad as the neurotic conflict was. Fundamentally, nothing has yet happened that might lead to a real solution. The conflict has merely been transferred. Nevertheless a successful transference can—at least temporarily—cause the whole neurosis to disappear, and for this reason it has been very rightly recognized by Freud as a healing factor of first-rate importance, but, at the same time, as a provisional state only, for although it holds out the possibility of a cure, it is far from being the cure itself.

207 This somewhat lengthy discussion seemed to me essential if my example was to be understood, for my patient had arrived at the state of transference and had already reached the upper limit where the standstill begins to make itself disagreeable. The question now arose: what next? I had of course become the complete saviour, and the thought of having to give me up was not only exceedingly distasteful to the patient, but positively terrifying. In such a situation "sound common sense" generally comes out with a whole repertory of admonitions: "you simply must," "you really ought," "you just cannot," etc. So far as sound common sense is, happily, not too rare and not entirely without effect (pessimists, I know, exist), a rational motive can, in the exuberant feeling of buoyancy you get from the transference, release so much enthusiasm that a painful sacrifice can be risked with a mighty effort of will. If successful—and these things sometimes are—the sacrifice bears blessed fruit, and the erstwhile patient leaps at one bound into the state of being practically cured. The doctor is generally so delighted that he fails to tackle the theoretical difficulties connected with this little miracle.

208 If the leap does not succeed—and it did not succeed with my patient—one is then faced with the problem of resolving the

transference. Here "psychoanalytic" theory shrouds itself in a thick darkness. Apparently we are to fall back on some nebulous trust in fate: somehow or other the matter will settle itself. "The transference stops automatically when the patient runs out of money," as a slightly cynical colleague once remarked to me. Or the ineluctable demands of life make it impossible for the patient to linger on in the transference—demands which compel the involuntary sacrifice, sometimes with a more or less complete relapse as a result. (One may look in vain for accounts of such cases in the books that sing the praises of psychoanalysis!)

209 To be sure, there are hopeless cases where nothing helps; but there are also cases that do not get stuck and do not inevitably leave the transference situation with bitter hearts and sore heads. I told myself, at this juncture with my patient, that there must be a clear and respectable way out of the impasse. My patient had long since run out of money—if indeed she ever possessed any—but I was curious to know what means nature would devise for a satisfactory way out of the transference deadlock. Since I never imagined that I was blessed with that "sound common sense" which always knows exactly what to do in every quandary, and since my patient knew as little as I, I suggested to her that we could at least keep an eye open for any movements coming from a sphere of the psyche uncontaminated by our superior wisdom and our conscious plannings. That meant first and foremost her dreams.

210 Dreams contain images and thought-associations which we do not create with conscious intent. They arise spontaneously without our assistance and are representatives of a psychic activity withdrawn from our arbitrary will. Therefore the dream is, properly speaking, a highly objective, natural product of the psyche, from which we might expect indications, or at least hints, about certain basic trends in the psychic process. Now, since the psychic process, like any other life-process, is not just a causal sequence, but is also a process with a teleological orientation, we might expect dreams to give us certain *indicia* about the objective causality as well as about the objective tendencies, precisely because dreams are nothing less than self-representations of the psychic life-process.

211 On the basis of these reflections, then, we subjected the dreams to a careful examination. It would lead too far to quote

word for word all the dreams that now followed. Let it suffice to sketch their main character: the majority referred to the person of the doctor, that is to say, the actors were unmistakably the dreamer herself and her doctor. The latter, however, seldom appeared in his natural shape, but was generally distorted in a remarkable way. Sometimes his figure was of supernatural size, sometimes he seemed to be extremely aged, then again he resembled her father, but was at the same time curiously woven into nature, as in the following dream: *Her father (who in reality was of small stature) was standing with her on a hill that was covered with wheat-fields. She was quite tiny beside him, and he seemed to her like a giant. He lifted her up from the ground and held her in his arms like a little child. The wind swept over the wheat-fields, and as the wheat swayed in the wind, he rocked her in his arms.*

212 From this dream and from others like it I could discern various things. Above all I got the impression that her unconscious was holding unshakably to the idea of my being the father-lover, so that the fatal tie we were trying to undo appeared to be doubly strengthened. Moreover one could hardly avoid seeing that the unconscious placed a special emphasis on the supernatural, almost "divine" nature of the father-lover, thus accentuating still further the over-valuation occasioned by the transference. I therefore asked myself whether the patient had still not understood the wholly fantastic character of her transference, or whether perhaps the unconscious could never be reached by understanding at all, but must blindly and idiotically pursue some nonsensical chimera. Freud's idea that the unconscious can "do nothing but wish," Schopenhauer's blind and aimless Will, the gnostic demiurge who in his vanity deems himself perfect and then in the blindness of his limitation creates something lamentably imperfect—all these pessimistic suspicions of an essentially negative background to the world and the soul came threateningly near. And there would indeed be nothing to set against this except a well-meaning "you ought," reinforced by a stroke of the axe that would cut down the whole phantasmagoria for good and all.

213 But, as I turned the dreams over and over in my mind, there dawned on me another possibility. I said to myself: it cannot be denied that the dreams continue to speak in the same old meta-

phors with which our conversations have made the patient as well as myself sickeningly familiar. But the patient has an undoubted understanding of her transference fantasy. She knows that I appear to her as a semi-divine father-lover, and she can, at least intellectually, distinguish this from my factual reality. Therefore the dreams are obviously reiterating the conscious standpoint minus the conscious criticism, which they completely ignore. They reiterate the conscious contents, not *in toto,* but insist on the fantastic standpoint as opposed to "sound common sense."

214 I naturally asked myself what was the source of this obstinacy and what was its purpose? That it must have some purposive meaning I was convinced, for there is no truly living thing that does not have a final meaning, that can in other words be explained as a mere left-over from antecedent facts. But the energy of the transference is so strong that it gives one the impression of a vital instinct. That being so, what is the purpose of such fantasies? A careful examination and analysis of the dreams, especially of the one just quoted, revealed a very marked tendency—in contrast to conscious criticism, which always seeks to reduce things to human proportions—to endow the person of the doctor with superhuman attributes. He had to be gigantic, primordial, huger than the father, like the wind that sweeps over the earth—was he then to be made into a god? Or, I said to myself, was it rather the case that the unconscious was trying to *create* a god out of the person of the doctor, as it were to free a vision of God from the veils of the personal, so that the transference to the person of the doctor was no more than a misunderstanding on the part of the conscious mind, a stupid trick played by "sound common sense"? Was the urge of the unconscious perhaps only apparently reaching out towards the person, but in a deeper sense towards a god? Could the longing for a god be a *passion* welling up from our darkest, instinctual nature, a passion unswayed by any outside influences, deeper and stronger perhaps than the love for a human person? Or was it perhaps the highest and truest meaning of that inappropriate love we call "transference," a little bit of real *Gottesminne,* that has been lost to consciousness ever since the fifteenth century?

215 No one will doubt the reality of a passionate longing for a human person; but that a fragment of religious psychology, an

historical anachronism, indeed something of a medieval curiosity—we are reminded of Mechtild of Magdeburg—should come to light as an immediate living reality in the middle of the consulting-room, and be expressed in the prosaic figure of the doctor, seems almost too fantastic to be taken seriously.

216 A genuinely scientific attitude must be unprejudiced. The sole criterion for the validity of an hypothesis is whether or not it possesses an heuristic—i.e., explanatory—value. The question now is, can we regard the possibilities set forth above as a valid hypothesis? There is no *a priori* reason why it should not be just as possible that the unconscious tendencies have a goal beyond the human person, as that the unconscious can "do nothing but wish." Experience alone can decide which is the more suitable hypothesis. This new hypothesis was not entirely plausible to my very critical patient. The earlier view that I was the father-lover, and as such presented an ideal solution of the conflict, was incomparably more attractive to her way of feeling. Nevertheless her intellect was sufficiently keen to appreciate the theoretical possibility of the new hypothesis. Meanwhile the dreams continued to disintegrate the person of the doctor and swell him to ever vaster proportions. Concurrently with this there now occurred something which at first I alone perceived, and with the utmost astonishment, namely a kind of subterranean undermining of the transference. Her relations with a certain friend deepened perceptibly, notwithstanding the fact that consciously she still clung to the transference. So that when the time came for leaving me, it was no catastrophe, but a perfectly reasonable parting. I had the privilege of being the only witness during the process of severance. I saw how the transpersonal control-point developed—I cannot call it anything else—a *guiding function* and step by step gathered to itself all the former personal over-valuations; how, with this afflux of energy, it gained influence over the resisting conscious mind without the patient's consciously noticing what was happening. From this I realized that the dreams were not just fantasies, but self-representations of unconscious developments which allowed the psyche of the patient gradually to grow out of the pointless personal tie.[1]

217 This change took place, as I showed, through the unconscious development of a transpersonal control-point; a virtual

1 Cf. the "transcendent function" in *Psychological Types*, Def. 51, "Symbol."

goal, as it were, that expressed itself symbolically in a form which can only be described as a vision of God. The dreams swelled the human person of the doctor to superhuman proportions, making him a gigantic primordial father who is at the same time the wind, and in whose protecting arms the dreamer rests like an infant. If we try to make the patient's conscious, and traditionally Christian, idea of God responsible for the divine image in the dreams, we would still have to lay stress on the distortion. In religious matters the patient had a critical and agnostic attitude, and her idea of a possible deity had long since passed into the realm of the inconceivable, i.e., had dwindled into a complete abstraction. In contrast to this, the god-image of the dreams corresponded to the archaic conception of a nature-daemon, something like Wotan. Θεὸς τὸ πνεῦμα, 'God is spirit,' is here translated back into its original form where πνεῦμα means 'wind': God is the wind, stronger and mightier than man, an invisible breath-spirit. As in Hebrew *ruah*, so in Arabic *ruh* means breath and spirit.[2] Out of the purely personal form the dreams develop an archaic god-image that is infinitely far from the conscious idea of God. It might be objected that this is simply an infantile image, a childhood memory. I would have no quarrel with this assumption if we were dealing with an old man sitting on a golden throne in heaven. But there is no trace of any sentimentality of that kind; instead, we have a primordial idea that can correspond only to an archaic mentality.

218 These primordial ideas, of which I have given a great many examples in my *Symbols of Transformation*, oblige one to make, in regard to unconscious material, a distinction of quite a different character from that between "preconscious" and "unconscious" or "subconscious" and "unconscious." The justification for these distinctions need not be discussed here. They have their specific value and are worth elaborating further as points of view. The fundamental distinction which experience has forced upon me claims to be no more than that. It should be evident from the foregoing that we have to distinguish in the unconscious a layer which we may call the *personal unconscious*. The materials contained in this layer are of a personal nature in so far as they have the character partly of acquisitions derived

2 For a fuller elaboration of this theme see *Symbols of Transformation*, index, s.v. "wind."

from the individual's life and partly of psychological factors which could just as well be conscious. It can readily be understood that incompatible psychological elements are liable to repression and therefore become unconscious. But on the other hand this implies the possibility of making and keeping the repressed contents conscious once they have been recognized. We recognize them as personal contents because their effects, or their partial manifestation, or their source can be discovered in our personal past. They are the integral components of the personality, they belong to its inventory, and their loss to consciousness produces an inferiority in one respect or another—an inferiority, moreover, that has the psychological character not so much of an organic lesion or an inborn defect as of a lack which gives rise to a feeling of moral resentment. The sense of moral inferiority always indicates that the missing element is something which, to judge by this feeling about it, really ought not be missing, or which could be made conscious if only one took sufficient trouble. The moral inferiority does not come from a collision with the generally accepted and, in a sense, arbitrary moral law, but from the conflict with one's own self which, for reasons of psychic equilibrium, demands that the deficit be redressed. Whenever a sense of moral inferiority appears, it indicates not only a need to assimilate an unconscious component, but also the possibility of such assimilation. In the last resort it is a man's moral qualities which force him, either through direct recognition of the need or indirectly through a painful neurosis, to assimilate his unconscious self and to keep himself fully conscious. Whoever progresses along this road of self-realization must inevitably bring into consciousness the contents of the personal unconscious, thus enlarging the scope of his personality. I should add at once that this enlargement has to do primarily with one's moral consciousness, one's knowledge of oneself, for the unconscious contents that are released and brought into consciousness by analysis are usually unpleasant—which is precisely why these wishes, memories, tendencies, plans, etc. were repressed. These are the contents that are brought to light in much the same way by a thorough confession, though to a much more limited extent. The rest comes out as a rule in dream analysis. It is often very interesting to watch how the dreams fetch up the essential points, bit by bit and with the nicest choice.

The total material that is added to consciousness causes a considerable widening of the horizon, a deepened self-knowledge which, more than anything else, one would think, is calculated to humanize a man and make him modest. But even self-knowledge, assumed by all wise men to be the best and most efficacious, has different effects on different characters. We make very remarkable discoveries in this respect in practical analysis, but I shall deal with this question in the next chapter.

219 As my example of the archaic idea of God shows, the unconscious seems to contain other things besides personal acquisitions and belongings. My patient was quite unconscious of the derivation of "spirit" from "wind," or of the parallelism between the two. This content was not the product of her thinking, nor had she ever been taught it. The critical passage in the New Testament was inaccessible to her—*τὸ πνεῦμα πνεῖ ὅπου θέλει*—since she knew no Greek. If we must take it as a wholly personal acquisition, it might be a case of so-called cryptomnesia,[3] the unconscious recollection of a thought which the dreamer had once read somewhere. I have nothing against such a possibility in this particular case; but I have seen a sufficient number of other cases—many of them are to be found in the book mentioned above—where cryptomnesia can be excluded with certainty. Even if it were a case of cryptomnesia, which seems to me very improbable, we should still have to explain what the predisposition was that caused just this image to be retained and later, as Semon puts it, "ecphorated" (*ἐκφορεῖν*, Latin *efferre*, 'to produce'). In any case, cryptomnesia or no cryptomnesia, we are dealing with a genuine and thoroughly primitive god-image that grew up in the unconscious of a civilized person and produced a living effect—an effect which might well give the psychologist of religion food for reflection. There is nothing about this image that could be called personal: it is a wholly collective image, the ethnic origin of which has long been known to us. Here is an historical image of world-wide distribution that has come into existence again through a natural psychic function. This is not so very surprising, since my patient was born into the

3 Cf. Flournoy, *Des Indes à la planète Mars: Étude sur un cas de somnambulisme avec glossolalie* (trans. by D. B. Vermilye as *From India to the Planet Mars*), and Jung, "Psychology and Pathology of So-called Occult Phenomena," pars. 138ff.

world with a human brain which presumably still functions to-day much as it did of old. We are dealing with a reactivated *archetype,* as I have elsewhere called these primordial images.[4] These ancient images are restored to life by the primitive, analogical mode of thinking peculiar to dreams. It is not a question of inherited ideas, but of inherited thought-patterns.[5]

220 In view of these facts we must assume that the unconscious contains not only personal, but also impersonal collective components in the form of inherited categories[6] or archetypes. I have therefore advanced the hypothesis that at its deeper levels the unconscious possesses collective contents in a relatively active state. That is why I speak of a collective unconscious.

4 Cf. *Psychological Types,* Def. 26.

5 Consequently, the accusation of "fanciful mysticism" levelled at my ideas is lacking in foundation.

6 Hubert and Mauss, *Mélanges d'histoire des religions,* p. xxix.

IV. LOGOS AND EROS; SOL AND LUNA

THE PERSONIFICATION OF THE OPPOSITES
THE MOON NATURE

Jung's attempt to equate Logos and Eros, his intuitive conceptions of masculine and feminine consciousness, with the alchemical Sol and Luna is only partly successful; there is more than "discrimination, judgement and insight" to Sol and more, certainly, than "the capacity to relate" to Luna. These stereotyped conceptions are of most use when applied to the unconscious of men and women, where the character of the opposite sex appears in a caricatured, archetypal way. Jung comments wryly that in a man the lunar anima and in a woman the solar animus has the greatest influence upon consciousness.

---

224 For purely psychological reasons I have, in other of my writings, tried to equate the masculine consciousness with the concept of Logos and the feminine with that of Eros. By Logos I meant discrimination, judgment, insight, and by Eros I meant the capacity to relate. I regarded both concepts as intuitive ideas which cannot be defined accurately or exhaustively. From the scientific point of view this is regrettable, but from a practical one it has its value, since the two concepts mark out a field of experience which it is equally difficult to define.

225 As we can hardly ever make a psychological proposition without immediately having to reverse it, instances to the contrary leap to the eye at once: men who care nothing for discrimination, judgment, and insight, and women who display an almost excessively masculine proficiency in this respect. I would like to describe such cases as the regular exceptions. They demonstrate, to my mind, the common occurrence of a psychically predomi-

nant contrasexuality. Wherever this exists we find a forcible intrusion of the unconscious, a corresponding exclusion of the consciousness specific to either sex, predominance of the shadow and of contrasexuality, and to a certain extent even the presence of symptoms of possession (such as compulsions, phobias, obsessions, automatisms, exaggerated affects, etc.). This inversion of roles is probably the chief psychological source for the alchemical concept of the hermaphrodite. In a man it is the lunar anima, in a woman the solar animus, that influences consciousness in the highest degree. Even if a man is often unaware of his own anima-possession, he has, understandably enough, all the more vivid an impression of the animus-possession of his wife, and vice versa.

226 Logos and Eros are intellectually formulated intuitive equivalents of the archetypal images of Sol and Luna. In my view the two luminaries are so descriptive and so superlatively graphic in their implications that I would prefer them to the more pedestrian terms Logos and Eros, although the latter do pin down certain psychological peculiarities more aptly than the rather indefinite "Sol and Luna." The use of these images requires at any rate an alert and lively fantasy, and this is not an attribute of those who are inclined by temperament to purely intellectual concepts. These offer us something finished and complete, whereas an archetypal image has nothing but its naked fullness, which seems inapprehensible by the intellect. Concepts are coined and negotiable values; images are life.

THE PERSONIFICATION OF THE OPPOSITES

1. INTRODUCTION

104 The alchemist's endeavours to unite the opposites culminate in the "chymical marriage," the supreme act of union in which the work reaches its consummation. After the hostility of the four elements has been overcome, there still remains the last and most formidable opposition, which the alchemist expressed very aptly as the relationship between male and female. We are inclined to think of this primarily as the power of love, of passion, which drives the two opposite poles together, forgetting that such a vehement attraction is needed only when an equally strong resistance keeps them apart. Although enmity was put only between the serpent and the woman (Genesis 3 : 15), this curse nevertheless fell upon the relationship of the sexes in general. Eve was told: "Thy desire shall be to thy husband, and he shall rule over thee." And Adam was told: "Cursed is the ground for thy sake . . . because thou hast hearkened unto the voice of thy wife" (3 : 16f.). Primal guilt lies between them, an *interrupted state of enmity,* and this appears unreasonable only to our rational mind but not to our psychic nature. Our reason is often influenced far too much by purely physical considerations, so that the union of the sexes seems to it the only sensible thing and the urge for union the most sensible instinct of all. But if we conceive of nature in the higher sense as the totality of all phenomena, then the physical is only one of her aspects, the other is pneumatic or spiritual. The first has always been regarded as feminine, the second as masculine. The goal of the one is union, the goal of the other is discrimination. Because it overvalues the physical, our contemporary reason lacks spiritual orientation, that is, pneuma. The alchemists seem to have had an inkling of this, for how otherwise could they have come upon that strange myth of the country of the King of the Sea, where

only like pairs with like and the land is unfruitful?[1] It was obviously a realm of innocent friendship, a kind of paradise or golden age, to which the "Philosophers," the representatives of the physical, felt obliged to put an end with their good advice. But what happened was not by any means a natural union of the sexes; on the contrary it was a "royal" incest, a sinful deed that immediately led to imprisonment and death and only afterwards restored the fertility of the country. As a parable the myth is certainly ambiguous; like alchemy in general, it can be understood spiritually as well as physically, "tam moralis quam chymica."[2] The physical goal of alchemy was gold, the panacea, the elixir of life; the spiritual one was the rebirth of the (spiritual) light from the darkness of Physis: healing self-knowledge and the deliverance of the pneumatic body from the corruption of the flesh.

105 A subtle feature of the "Visio Arislei" is that the very one who is meditating a pairing of the sexes is king of the land of innocence. Thus the *rex marinus* says: "Truly I have a son and a daughter, and therefore I am king over my subjects, because they possess nothing of these things. Yet I have borne a son and a daughter in my brain."[3] Hence the king is a potential traitor to the paradisal state of innocence because he can generate "in his head," and he is king precisely because he is capable of this sin against the previous state of innocence. Since he can be different from them he is *more* than any of his subjects and therefore rightly their king, although, from the physical standpoint, he is counted a bad ruler.[4]

106 Here again we see the contrast between alchemy and the prevailing Christian ideal of attempting to restore the original state of innocence by monasticism and, later, by the celibacy of the priesthood. The conflict between worldliness and spirituality, latent in the love-myth of Mother and Son, was elevated by Christianity to the mystic marriage of sponsus (Christ) and sponsa (Church), whereas the alchemists transposed it to the physical plane as the coniunctio of Sol and Luna. The Christian solution of the conflict is purely pneumatic, the physical rela-

1 "Visio Arislei," *Art. aurif.*, I, pp. 146ff.

2 Maier, *Symb. aur. mensae*, p. 156.

3 "Visio Arislei," p. 147.

4 The philosophers say to him: "Lord, king you may be, but you rule and govern badly." *

tions of the sexes being turned into an allegory or—quite illegitimately—into a sin that perpetuates and even intensifies the original one in the Garden. Alchemy, on the other hand, exalted the most heinous transgression of the law, namely incest, into a symbol of the union of opposites, hoping in this way to bring back the golden age. For both trends the solution lay in extrapolating the union of sexes into another medium: the one projected it into the spirit, the other into matter. But neither of them located the problem in the place where it arose—the soul of man.

107 No doubt it would be tempting to assume that it was more convenient to shift such a supremely difficult question on to another plane and then represent it as having been solved. But this explanation is too facile, and is psychologically false because it supposes that the problem was asked consciously, found to be painful, and consequently moved on to another plane. This stratagem accords with our modern way of thinking but not with the spirit of the past, and there are no historical proofs of any such neurotic operation. Rather does all the evidence suggest that the problem has always seemed to lie outside the psyche as known to us. Incest was the hierosgamos of the gods, the mystic prerogative of kings, a priestly rite, etc. In all these cases we are dealing with an archetype of the collective unconscious which, as consciousness increased, exerted an ever greater influence on conscious life. It certainly seems today as if the ecclesiastical allegories of the bridegroom and bride, not to mention the now completely obsolete alchemical coniunctio, had become so faded that one meets with incest only in criminology and the psychopathology of sex. Freud's discovery of the Oedipus complex, a special instance of the incest problem in general, and its universal incidence have, however, reactivated this ancient problem, though mostly only for doctors interested in psychology. Even though laymen know very little about certain medical anomalies or have a wrong idea of them, this does not alter the facts any more than does the layman's ignorance of the actual percentage of cases of tuberculosis or psychosis.

108 Today the medical man knows that the incest problem is practically universal and that it immediately comes to the surface when the customary illusions are cleared away from the foreground. But mostly he knows only its pathological side and

leaves it steeped in the odium of its name, without learning the lesson of history that the painful secret of the consulting-room is merely the embryonic form of a perennial problem which, in the suprapersonal sphere of ecclesiastical allegory and in the early phases of natural science, created a symbolism of the utmost importance. Generally he sees only the "materia vilis et in via eiecta" from the pathological side and has no idea of its spiritual implications. If he saw this, he could also perceive how the spirit that has disappeared returns in each of us in unseemly, indeed reprehensible guise, and in certain predisposed cases causes endless confusion and destruction in great things as in small. The psychopathological problem of incest is the aberrant, natural form of the union of opposites, a union which has either never been made conscious at all as a psychic task or, if it was conscious, has once more disappeared from view.

109 The persons who enact the drama of this problem are man and woman, in alchemy King and Queen, Sol and Luna. In what follows I shall give an account of the way in which alchemy describes the symbolic protagonists of the supreme opposition.

2. SOL

110 In alchemy, the sun signifies first of all gold, whose sign it shares. But just as the "philosophical" gold is not the "common" gold,[5] so the sun is neither just the metallic gold [6] nor the heavenly orb.[7] Sometimes the sun is an active substance hidden in the gold and is extracted as the *tinctura rubea* (red tincture). Sometimes, as the heavenly body, it is the possessor of magically effective and transformative rays. As gold and a heavenly body [8]

5 Senior, *De chemia*, p. 92.*

6 "Gold and silver in their metallic form are not the matter of our stone." * "Tractatus aureus," *Mus. herm.*, p. 32 (Waite, I, p. 33).

7 Because gold is not subject to oxidization, Sol is an arcanum described in the "Consilium coniugii" as follows: "A substance equal, permanent, fixed for the length of eternity" * (*Ars chemica*, p. 58). "For Sol is the root of incorruption." * "Verily there is no other foundation of the Art than the sun and its shadow" * (ibid., p. 138).

8 Rupescissa, *La Vertu et la propriété de la quinte essence*, p. 19: "Jceluy soleil est vray or. . . . L'or de Dieu est appelé par les Philosophes, Soleil; car il est fils du Soleil du Ciel, et est engendré par les influences du Soleil ès entrailles et veines de la terre."

it contains an active sulphur of a red colour, hot and dry.[9] Because of this red sulphur the alchemical sun, like the corresponding gold, is red.[10] As every alchemist knew, gold owes its red colour to the admixture of Cu (copper), which he interpreted as Kypris (the Cyprian, Venus), mentioned in Greek alchemy as the transformative substance.[11] Redness, heat, and dryness are the classical qualities of the Egyptian Set (Gk. Typhon), the evil principle which, like the alchemical sulphur, is closely connected with the devil. And just as Typhon has his kingdom in the forbidden sea, so the sun, as *sol centralis,* has its sea, its "crude perceptible water," and as *sol coelestis* its "subtle imperceptible water." This sea water (*aqua pontica*) is extracted from sun and moon. Unlike the Typhonian sea, the life-giving power of this water is praised, though this does not mean that it is invariably good.[12] It is the equivalent of the two-faced Mercurius, whose poisonous nature is often mentioned. The Typhonian aspect of the active sun-substance, of the red sulphur, of the water "that does not make the hands wet," [13] and of the "sea water" should not be left out of account. The author of the "Novum lumen chemicum" cannot suppress a reference to the latter's paradoxical nature: "Do not be disturbed because you sometimes find contradictions in my treatises, after the custom of the philosophers; these are necessary, if you understand that no rose is found without thorns." [14]

111 The active sun-substance also has favourable effects. As the so-called "balsam" it drips from the sun and produces lemons, oranges, wine, and, in the mineral kingdom, gold.[15] In man the

9 Sulphur is even identical with fire. Cf. "Consil. coniugii" (*Ars chemica,* p. 217): "Know therefore that sulphur is fire, that is, Sol." * In Mylius (*Phil. ref.,* p. 185) Sol is identical with sulphur, i.e., the alchemical Sol signifies the active substance of the sun or of the gold.

10 "Our Sol is ruddy and burning." * (Zacharius, "Opusculum," *Theatr. chem.,* I, p. 840.) Bernardus Trevisanus goes so far as to say: "Sol is nothing other than sulphur and quicksilver." * (Ibid., Flamel's annotations, p. 860.)

11 Olympiodorus (Berthelot, *Alch. grecs,* II, iv, 43): "Smear [with it] the leaves of the shining goddess, the red Cyprian."

12 Cf. the sulphur parable (infra par. 144), where the water is "most dangerous."

13 Hoghelande, *Theatr. chem.,* I, p. 181.

14 *Mus. herm.,* pp. 581f. (Waite, II, p. 107).

15 Steeb, *Coelum sephiroticum,* p. 50. Paracelsus, in "De natura rerum" (Sudhoff, XI, p. 330), says: "Now the life of man is none other than an astral balsam, a balsamic impression, a heavenly and invisible fire, an enclosed air." *De Vita longa*

balsam forms the "radical moisture, from the sphere of the supracelestial waters"; it is the "shining" or "lucent body" which "from man's birth enkindles the inner warmth, and from which come all the motions of the will and the principle of all appetition." It is a "vital spirit," and it has "its seat in the brain and its governance in the heart." [16]

112 In the "Liber Platonis Quartorum," a Sabaean treatise, the *spiritus animalis* or solar sulphur is still a *πνεῦμα πάρεδρον*, a ministering spirit or familiar who can be conjured up by magical invocations to help with the work.[17]

113 From what has been said about the active sun-substance it should be clear that Sol in alchemy is much less a definite chemical substance than a "virtus," a mysterious power [18] believed to have a generative [19] and transformative effect. Just as the physical sun lightens and warms the universe, so, in the human body, there is in the heart a sunlike arcanum from which life and warmth stream forth.[20] "Therefore Sol," says Dorn, "is rightly named the first after God, and the father and begetter of all,[21] because in him the seminal and formal virtue of all things whatsoever lies hid." [22] This power is called "sulphur." [23] It is a hot, daemonic principle of life, having the closest affinities with the sun in the earth, the "central fire" or "ignis gehennalis" (fire of

(ed. Bodenstein, fol. c 7v): "(Treating of a certain invisible virtue) he calls it balsam, surpassing all bodily nature, which preserves the two bodies by conjunction, and upholds the celestial body together with the four elements." *

16 Steeb, p. 117. The moon draws "universal form and natural life" from the sun. (Dorn, "Physica genesis," *Theatr. chem.*, I, p. 397.)

17 *Theatr. chem.*, V. p. 130.

18 "It were vain to believe, as many do, that the sun is merely a heavenly fire." * (Dorn, "Physica Trismegisti," *Theatr. chem.*, I, p. 423.)

19 The alchemists still believed with Proclus that the sun generates the gold. Cf. Proclus, *Commentaries on the Timaeus of Plato* 18 B (trans. by Taylor), I, p. 36.

20 Dorn ("Phys. Trismeg.," p. 423) says: "As the fount of life of the human body, it is the centre of man's heart, or rather that secret thing which lies hid within it, wherein the natural heat is active." *

21 Zosimos (Berthelot, *Alch. grecs*, III, xxi, 3) cites the saying of Hermes: "The sun is the maker of all things." *

22 "Phys. Trismeg.," p. 423.* The Codex Berol. Lat. 532 (fol. 154v) says of the germ-cell of the egg: "The sun-point, that is, the germ of the egg, which is in the yolk." *

23 "The first and most powerful male and universal seed is, by its nature, sulphur, the first and most powerful cause of all generation. Wherefore Paracelsus says that the sun and man through man generate man." * (Dorn, ibid.)

hell). Hence there is also a *Sol niger,* a black sun, which coincides with the *nigredo* and *putrefactio,* the state of death.[24] Like Mercurius, Sol in alchemy is ambivalent.

114 The miraculous power of the sun, says Dorn, is due to the fact that "all the simple elements are contained in it, as they are in heaven and in the other heavenly bodies." "We say that the sun is a single element," he continues, tacitly identifying it with the quintessence. This view is explained by a remarkable passage from the "Consilium coniugii": "The Philosophers maintained that the father of the gold and silver is the animating principle [*animal*] of earth and water, or man or part of a man, such as hair, blood, menstruum, etc." [25] The idea at the back of this is that primitive conception of a universal power of growth, healing, magic, and prestige,[26] which is to be found as much in the sun as in men and plants, so that not only the sun but man too, and especially the enlightened man, the adept, can generate the gold by virtue of this universal power. It was clear to Dorn (and to other alchemists as well) that the gold was not made by the usual chemical procedures,[27] for which reason he called gold-making (chrysopoeia) a "miracle." The miracle was performed by a *natura abscondita* (hidden nature), a metaphysical entity "perceived not with the outward eyes, but solely by the mind." [28] It was "infused from heaven,[29] provided that the adept had approached as closely as possible to things divine and

24 Cf. infra, p. 98. The alchemical sun also rises out of the darkness of the earth, as in *Aurora Consurgens,* pp. 125f.: "This earth made the moon . . . then the sun arose . . . after the darkness which thou hast appointed therein before the sunrise." *

25 *Ars chemica,* p. 158. On a primitive level, blood is the seat of the soul. Hair signifies strength and divine power. (Judges 13 : 5 and 16 : 17ff.)

26 Cf. the works of Lehmann, Preuss, and Röhr. A collection of mana-concepts can be found in my "On Psychic Energy," pars. 114ff.

27 Cf. Bonus, "Pretiosa margarita novella," *Theatr. chem.,* V, p. 648: "And in this wise Alchemy is supernatural, and is divine. And in this stone is all the difficulty of the Art, nor can any sufficient natural reason be adduced why this should be so. And thus it is when the intellect cannot comprehend this nor satisfy itself, but must yet believe it, as in miraculous divine matters; even as the foundation of the Christian faith, being supernatural, must first be taken as true by unbelievers, because its end is attained miraculously and supernaturally. Therefore God alone is the operator, nature taking no part in the work." *

28 "Spec. phil.," *Theatr. chem.,* I, p. 298; also "Phil. chemica," p. 497.

29 Cf. *Aurora Consurgens,* p. 111: "For I could not wonder enough at the great virtue of the thing, which is bestowed upon and infused into it from heaven." *

at the same time had extracted from the substances the subtlest powers "fit for the miraculous act." "There is in the human body a certain aethereal substance, which preserves its other elemental parts and causes them to continue," [30] he says. This substance or virtue is hindered in its operations by the "corruption of the body"; but "the Philosophers, through a kind of divine inspiration, knew that this virtue and heavenly vigour can be freed from its fetters, not by its contrary . . . but by its like." [31] Dorn calls it "veritas." "It is the supreme power, an unconquerable fortress, which hath but very few friends, and is besieged by innumerable enemies." It is "defended by the immaculate Lamb," and signifies the heavenly Jerusalem in the inner man. "In this fortress is the true and indubitable treasure, which is not eaten into by moths, nor dug out by thieves, but remaineth for ever, and is taken hence after death." [32]

115 For Dorn, then, the spark of divine fire implanted in man becomes what Goethe in his original version of *Faust* called Faust's "entelechy," which was carried away by the angels. This supreme treasure "the animal man understandeth not. . . . We are made like stones, having eyes and seeing not." [33]

116 After all this, we can say that the alchemical Sol, as a "certain luminosity" (*quaedam luminositas*), is in many respects equal to the *lumen naturae*. This was the real source of illumination in alchemy, and from alchemy Paracelsus borrowed this same source in order to illuminate the art of medicine. Thus the concept of Sol has not a little to do with the growth of modern consciousness, which in the last two centuries has relied more and more on the observation and experience of natural objects. Sol therefore seems to denote an important psychological fact. Consequently, it is well worth while delineating its peculiarities in greater detail on the basis of the very extensive literature.

117 Generally Sol is regarded as the masculine and active half of Mercurius, a supraordinate concept whose psychology I have discussed in a separate study.[34] Since, in his alchemical form,

30 "Phil. meditativa," *Theatr. chem.*, I, p. 456. There is a similar passage on p. 457: "Further, in the human body is concealed a certain substance of heavenly nature, known to very few, which needeth no medicament, being itself the incorrupt medicament." * 31 P. 457.

32 P. 458. See also "Spec. phil.," p. 266.

33 P. 459.*

34 "The Spirit Mercurius."

Mercurius does not exist in reality, he must be an unconscious projection, and because he is an absolutely fundamental concept in alchemy he must signify the unconscious itself. He is by his very nature the unconscious, where nothing can be differentiated; but, as a *spiritus vegetativus* (living spirit), he is an active principle and so must always appear in reality in differentiated form. He is therefore fittingly called "duplex," both active and passive. The "ascending," active part of him is called Sol, and it is only through this that the passive part can be perceived. The passive part therefore bears the name of Luna, because she borrows her light from the sun.[35] Mercurius demonstrably corresponds to the cosmic Nous of the classical philosophers. The human mind is a derivative of this and so, likewise, is the diurnal life of the psyche, which we call consciousness.[36] Consciousness requires as its necessary counterpart a dark, latent, non-manifest side, the unconscious, whose presence can be known only by the light of consciousness.[37] Just as the day-star rises out of the nocturnal sea, so, ontogenetically and phylogenetically, consciousness is born of unconsciousness and sinks back every night to this primal condition. This duality of our psychic life is the prototype and archetype of the Sol-Luna symbolism. So much did the alchemist sense the duality of his unconscious assumptions that, in the face of all astronomical evidence, he equipped the sun with a shadow: "The sun and its shadow bring the work to perfection." [38] Michael Maier, from whom this saying is taken, avoids the onus of explanation by substituting the shadow of the earth for the shadow of the sun in the forty-fifth discourse of his *Scrutinium*. Evidently he could

35 Cf. the ancient idea that the sun corresponds to the right eye and the moon to the left. (Olympiodorus in Berthelot, *Alch. grecs*, II, iv, 51.)

36 Just as for the natural philosophers of the Middle Ages the sun was the god of the physical world, so the "little god of the world" is consciousness.

37 Consciousness, like the sun, is an "eye of the world." (Cf. Pico della Mirandola, "Disputationes adversus astrologos," lib. III, cap. X, p. 88r.) In his *Heptaplus* (Expositio 7, cap. IV, p. 11r) he says: "Since Plato calls the Sun . . . the visible son of God, why do we not understand that we are the image of the invisible son? And if he is the true light enlightening every mind, he hath as his most express image this Sun, which is the light of the image enlightening every body." *

38 This idea occurs already in the *Turba* (ed. by Ruska, p. 130): "But he who hath tinged the poison of the sages with the sun and its shadow, hath attained to the greatest secret." * Mylius (*Phil. ref.*, p. 22) says: "In the shadow of the sun is the heat of the moon." *

not wholly shut his eyes to astronomical reality. But then he cites the classical saying of Hermes: "Son, extract from the ray its shadow," [39] thus giving us clearly to understand that the shadow is contained in the sun's rays and hence could be extracted from them (whatever that might mean). Closely related to this saying is the alchemical idea of a black sun, often mentioned in the literature.[40] This notion is supported by the self-evident fact that without light there is no shadow, so that, in a sense, the shadow too is emitted by the sun. For this physics requires a dark object interposed between the sun and the observer, a condition that does not apply to the alchemical Sol, since occasionally it appears as black itself. It contains both light and darkness. "For what, in the end," asks Maier, "is this sun without a shadow? The same as a bell without a clapper." While Sol is the most precious thing, its shadow is *res vilissima* or *quid vilius alga* (more worthless than seaweed). The antinomian thinking of alchemy counters every position with a negation and vice versa. "Outwardly they are bodily things, but inwardly they are spiritual," says Senior.[41] This view is true of all alchemical qualities, and each thing bears in itself its opposite.[42]

118 To the alchemical way of thinking the shadow is no mere *privatio lucis;* just as the bell and its clapper are of a tangible substantiality, so too are light and shadow. Only thus can the saying of Hermes be understood. In its entirety it runs: "Son,

39 From ch. II of the "Tractatus aureus," *Ars chemica,* p. 15.*

40 Cf. Mylius, *Phil. ref.,* p. 19. Here the *sol niger* is synonymous with the *caput corvi* and denotes the *anima media natura* in the state of *nigredo,* which appears when the "earth of the gold is dissolved by its own proper spirit." * Psychologically, this means a provisional extinction of the conscious standpoint owing to an invasion from the unconscious. Mylius refers to the "ancient philosophers" as a source for the *sol niger.* A similar passage occurs on p. 118: "The sun is obscured at its birth. And this denigration is the beginning of the work, the sign of putrefaction, and the sure beginning of the commixture." * This *nigredo* is the "changing darkness of purgatory." Ripley (*Chymische Schrifften,* p. 51) speaks of a "dark" sun, adding: "You must go through the gate of the blackness if you would gain the light of Paradise in the whiteness." Cf. *Turba,* p. 145: "nigredo solis."

41 *De chemia,* p. 91.*

42 The *sol niger* is a "counter-sun," just as there is an invisible sun enclosed in the centre of the earth. (See Agnostus, *Prodromus Rhodostauroticus,* 1620, Vr.) A similar idea is found in Ventura (*Theatr. chem.,* II, p. 276): "And as at the beginning the sun is hidden in the Moon, so, hidden at the end, it is extracted from the moon." *

extract from the ray its shadow, and the corruption that arises from the mists which gather about it, befoul it and veil its light; for it is consumed by necessity and by its redness." [43] Here the shadow is thought of quite concretely; it is a mist that is capable not only of obscuring the sun but of befouling it ("coinquinare" —a strong expression). The redness (*rubedo*) of the sun's light is a reference to the red sulphur in it, the active burning principle, destructive in its effects. In man the "natural sulphur," Dorn says, is identical with an "elemental fire" which is the "cause of corruption," and this fire is "enkindled by an invisible sun unknown to many, that is, the sun of the Philosophers." The natural sulphur tends to revert to its first nature, so that the body becomes "sulphurous" and fitted to receive the fire that "corrupts man back to his first essence." [44] The sun is evidently an instrument in the physiological and psychological drama of return to the prima materia, the death that must be undergone if man is to get back to the original condition of the simple elements and attain the incorrupt nature of the pre-worldly paradise. For Dorn this process was spiritual and moral as well as physical.

119 Sol appears here in a dubious, indeed a "sulphurous" light: it corrupts, obviously because of the sulphur it contains.[45]

120 Accordingly, Sol is the transformative substance, the prima materia as well as the gold tincture. The anonymous treatise "De arte chymica" distinguishes two parts or stages of the lapis. The first part is called the *sol terrenus* (earthly sun). "Without

43 "Tractatus aureus," *Ars chemica*, p. 15.

44 Dorn, "Spec. phil.," *Theatr. chem.*, I, p. 308. He conceives it in the first place as a physiologically destructive action which turns the salts in the body into chalk, so that the body becomes "sulphurous." But this medical observation is introduced by the remark: "Because man is engendered in corruption, his own substance pursues him with hatred." By this he means original sin and the corruption resulting therefrom.

45 I am not forgetting that the dangerous quality of Sol may also be due to the fact that his rays contain the miraculous water "which by the power of the magnet is extracted from the rays of the sun and moon." * This water is a putrefying agent, because "before it is properly cooked it is a deadly poison." Mylius, *Phil. ref.*, p. 314. This aqua permanens is the *ὕδωρ θεῖον* (divine water), the "divinity" being sulphur. It was called "sulphur water" (*τὸ θεῖον* also means sulphur) and is the same as mercury. Θεῖον or *θήϊον* in Homer was believed to possess apotropaic powers, and this may be the reason why it was called "divine."

the earthly sun, the work is not perfected." [46] In the second part of the work Sol is joined with Mercurius.

On earth these stones are dead, and they do nothing unless the activity of man is applied to them. [Consider] [47] the profound analogy of the gold: the aethereal heaven was locked to all men, so that all men had to descend into the underworld, where they were imprisoned for ever. But Christ Jesus unlocked the gate of the heavenly Olympus and threw open the realm of Pluto, that the souls might be freed, when the Virgin Mary, with the cooperation of the Holy Ghost in an unutterable mystery and deepest sacrament, conceived in her virgin womb that which was most excellent in heaven and upon earth, and finally bore for us the Redeemer of the whole world, who by his overflowing goodness shall save all who are given up to sin, if only the sinner shall turn to him. But the Virgin remained incorrupt and inviolate: therefore not without good reason is Mercurius made equal [*aequiparatur*] to the most glorious and worshipful Virgin Mary.[48]

It is evident from this that the coniunctio of Sol and Mercurius is a hierosgamos, with Mercurius playing the role of bride. If one does not find this analogy too offensive, one may ask oneself with equanimity whether the arcanum of the opus alchymicum, as understood by the old masters, may not indeed be considered an equivalent of the dogmatic mystery. For the psychologist the decisive thing here is the subjective attitude of the alchemist. As I have shown in *Psychology and Alchemy,* such a profession of faith is by no means unique.[49]

121 The metaphorical designation of Christ as Sol [50] in the language of the Church Fathers was taken quite literally by the alchemists and applied to their *sol terrenus.* When we remember that the alchemical Sol corresponds psychologically to consciousness, the diurnal side of the psyche, we must add the Christ analogy to this symbolism. Christ appears essentially as the *son*—the son of his mother-bride. The role of the son does in fact devolve upon ego-consciousness since it is the offspring of the maternal

[46] *Art. aurif.,* I, p. 58ff.*

[47] The text only has "auri similitudinem profundam," without a verb.

[48] *Art. aurif.,* I, pp. 580ff.

[49] "The Lapis-Christ Parallel."

[50] Especially as "sol iustitiae" (sun of justice), Malachi 4 : 2. Cf. Honorius of Autun, *Speculum de mysteriis Ecclesiae* (Migne, *P.L.,* vol. 172, col. 921): "For, like to the sun beneath a cloud, so did the sun of justice lie concealed under human flesh." * Correspondingly, the Gnostic Anthropos is identical with the sun. (Cf. Reitzenstein, *Poimandres,* p. 280.)

unconscious. Now according to the arch authority, the "Tabula smaragdina," Sol is the father of Mercurius, who in the above quotation appears as feminine and as the mother-bride. In that capacity Mercurius is identical with Luna, and—via the Luna-Mary-Ecclesia symbolism—is equated with the Virgin. Thus the treatise "Exercitationes in Turbam" says: "As blood is the origin of flesh, so is Mercurius the origin of Sol . . . and thus Mercurius is Sol and Sol is Mercurius."[51] Sol is therefore father and son at once, and his feminine counterpart is mother and daughter in one person; furthermore, Sol and Luna are merely aspects of the same substance that is simultaneously the cause and the product of both, namely Mercurius duplex, of whom the philosophers say that he contains everything that is sought by the wise. This train of thought is based on a quaternity:

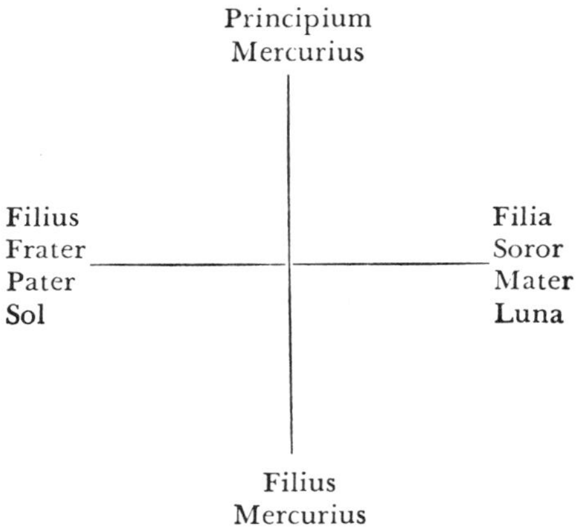

122 Although the Sol symbolism is reminiscent of the dogmatic models, its basic schema is very different; for the dogmatic schema is a Trinity embracing only the Deity but not the universe.[52] The alchemical schema appears to embrace only the material world, yet, on account of its quaternary character, it comes near to being a representation of totality as exemplified in the symbol of the cross erected between heaven and earth. The cross is by implication the Christian totality symbol: as an instrument of torture it expresses the sufferings on earth of the

[51] *Art. aurif.*, I, p. 155.

[52] The alchemical equivalent of the Trinity is the three-headed serpent (Mercurius). See *Psychology and Alchemy*, fig. 54.

incarnate God, and as a quaternity it expresses the universe, which also includes the material world. If we now add to this cruciform schema the four protagonists of the divine world-drama—the Father as *auctor rerum,* the Son, his counterpart the Devil (to fight whom he became man), and the Holy Ghost, we get the following quaternity:

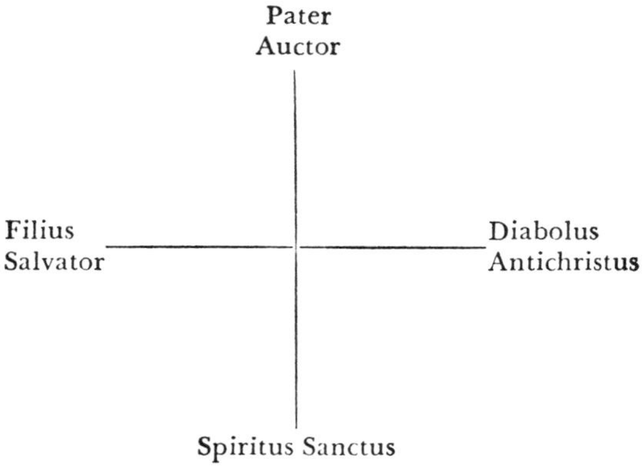

123 I will not discuss the various aspects of this quaternity more closely here, as I have already done so in a separate study.[53] I mention it only for comparison with the alchemical one. Quaternities such as these are logical characteristics of Gnostic thinking, which Koepgen has aptly called "circular." [54] We have

[53] Cf. my "Psychological Approach to the Dogma of the Trinity," pars. 243ff. Though some may find it objectionable, the opposition between Christ and the devil in the above schema presupposes an inner relationship (regarded by the Ebionites, says Epiphanius, as that between two brothers). Angelus Silesius seems to have felt something of the sort, too:

"Were from the Devil all his His-ness gone,
You'd see the Devil sitting in God's throne."

Cherubinischer Wandersmann, I, No. 143 (Cf. Flitch version, p. 144). By "His-ness" Angelus Silesius means the "selfhood which damns," as is incontestably true of all selfhood that does not acknowledge its identity with God.

[54] The thinking in the Psalms and of the prophets is "circular. Even the Apocalypse consists of spiral images . . . One of the main characteristics of Gnostic thinking is circularity." (Koepgen, *Gnosis des Christentums,* p. 149.) Koepgen gives an example from Ephraem Syrus: "Make glad the body through the soul, but give the soul back to the body, that both may be glad that after the separation they are joined again" (p. 151). An alchemist could have said the same of the uroboros, since this is the primal symbol of alchemical truth. Koepgen also describes dogma as "circular": it is "round in the sense of a living reality. . . . Dogmas are con-

already met similar figures in our account of the opposites, which were often arranged in quaternities. The rhythm of both schemas is divided into three steps:

Alchemical:	Beginning Origin Mercurius	—	Development Sol Luna	—	Goal Filius Mercurius
Christian:	Auctor Pater	—	Development of Conflict Salvator Diabolus	—	Paraclete Holy Ghost Church or Kingdom of God

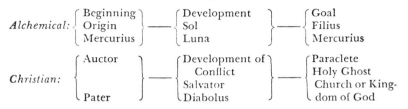

24 The alchemical drama leads from below upwards, from the darkness of the earth to the winged, spiritual *filius macrocosmi* and to the *lux moderna;* the Christian drama, on the other hand, represents the descent of the Kingdom of Heaven to earth. One has the impression of a mirror-world, as if the God-man coming down from above—as in the Gnostic legend—were reflected in the dark waters of Physis. The relation of the unconscious to the conscious mind is to a certain extent complementary, as elementary psychogenic symptoms and dreams caused by simple somatic stimuli prove.[55] (Hence the strange idea, taught for instance by Rudolf Steiner, that the Hereafter possesses qualities complementary to those of this world.) Careful observation and analysis show, however, that not all dreams can be regarded mechanically as mere complementary devices but must be interpreted rather as attempts at *compensation,* though this does not prevent very many dreams from having, on a superficial view, a distinct complementary character. Similarly, we could regard the alchemical movement as a reflection of the Christian one.[56]

cerned with the religious reality, and this is circular" (p. 52). He calls attention to the "fact of not knowing and not recognizing, which lies at the core of the dogma itself" (p. 51). This remark indicates the reason or one of the reasons for the "roundness": dogmas are approximative concepts for a fact that exists yet cannot be described, and can only be approached by circumambulation. At the same time, these facts are "spheres" of indeterminable extent, since they represent *principles.* Psychologically they correspond to the archetypes. Overlapping and interpenetration are an essential part of their nature. "Roundness" is a peculiarity not only of dogmas, but, in especial degree, of alchemical thought.

55 Particularly dreams about hunger, thirst, pain, and sex. Another complementary factor is the feminine nature of the unconscious in a man.

56 For the compensatory aspect of this "reflection" see *Psychology and Alchemy,* pars. 26ff.

Koepgen makes a significant distinction between two aspects of Christ: the descending, incarnate God, and the ascending, Gnostic Christ who returns to the Father. We cannot regard the latter as the same as the alchemical *filius regius,* although Koepgen's schema offers an exact parallel to the alchemical situation.[57] The redeemer figure of alchemy is not commensurable with Christ. Whereas Christ is God and is begotten by the Father, the *filius regius* is the soul of nature, born of the world-creating Logos, of the Sapientia Dei sunk in matter. The *filius regius* is also a son of God, though of more distant descent and not begotten in the womb of the Virgin Mary but in the womb of Mother Nature: he is a "third sonship" in the Basilidian sense.[58] No traditional influences should be invoked in considering the conceptual structure of this filius; he is more an autochthonous product deriving from an unconscious, logical development of trends which had already reached the field of consciousness in the early Christian era, impelled by the same unconscious necessity as produced the later development of ideas. For, as our modern experience has shown, the collective unconscious is a living process that follows its own inner laws and gushes up like a spring at the appointed time. That it did so in alchemy in such an obscure and complicated way was due essentially to the great psychological difficulties of antinomian thinking, which continually came up against the demand for the logical consistency of the metaphysical figures, and for their emotional absoluteness. The "bonum superexcedens" of God allows no integration of evil. Although Nicholas Cusanus ventured the bold thought of the *coincidentia oppositorum,* its logical consequence—the relativity of the God-concept—proved disastrous for

57 Koepgen, p. 112.

58 Cf. "The Spirit Mercurius," pars. 282f. In another respect, also, the *filius philosophorum* is a "third" when we consider the development in the concept of the devil among the Ebionites (Epiphanius, *Panarium,* XXX). They spoke of two figures begotten by God, one of them Christ, the other the devil. The latter, according to Psellus, was called by the Euchites Satanaël, the elder brother of Christ. (Cf. *Aion,* par. 229, and "The Spirit Mercurius," pars. 271f. In relation to these two the *filius regius*—as *donum Spiritus Sancti* and son of the prima materia—is a "third sonship," which, in common with the prima materia, can trace its descent—though a more distant one—from God. For the threefold sonship see Hippolytus, *Elenchos,* VII, 22, 7f. (Legge, II, pp. 71f.) and *Aion,* pars. 118f. The "sonships" come from the "true light" (John 1 : 9), from the Logos, the *sapientia Patris.* Hippolytus, VII, 22, 4 (Legge, II, pp. 68f.).

Angelus Silesius, and only the withered laurels of the poet lie on his grave. He had drunk with Jacob Boehme at the fount of Mater Alchimia. The alchemists, too, became choked in their own confusions.

125 Once again, therefore, it is the medical investigators of nature who, equipped with new means of knowledge, have rescued these tangled problems from projection by making them the proper subject of psychology. This could never have happened before, for the simple reason that there was no psychology of the unconscious. But the medical investigator, thanks to his knowledge of archetypal processes, is in the fortunate position of being able to recognize in the abstruse and grotesque-looking symbolisms of alchemy the nearest relatives of those serial fantasies which underlie the delusions of paranoid schizophrenia as well as the healing processes at work in the psychogenic neuroses. The overweening contempt which other departments of science have for the apparently negligible psychic processes of "pathological individuals" should not deter the doctor in his task of helping and healing the sick. But he can help the sick psyche only when he meets it as the unique psyche of that particular individual, and when he knows its earthly and unearthly darknesses. He should also consider it just as important a task to defend the standpoint of consciousness, clarity, "reason," and an acknowledged and proven good against the raging torrent that flows for all eternity in the darkness of the psyche—a *πάντα ῥεῖ* that leaves nothing unaltered and ceaselessly creates a past that can never be retrieved. He knows that there is nothing purely good in the realm of human experience, but also that for many people it is better to be convinced of an absolute good and to listen to the voice of those who espouse the superiority of consciousness and unambiguous thinking. He may solace himself with the thought that one who can join the shadow to the light is the possessor of the greater riches. But he will not fall into the temptation of playing the law-giver, nor will he pretend to be a prophet of the truth: for he knows that the sick, suffering, or helpless patient standing before him is not the public but is Mr or Mrs X, and that the doctor has to put something tangible and helpful on the table or he is no doctor. His duty is always to the individual, and he is persuaded that nothing has happened if this individual has not been helped. He is answerable

to the individual in the first place and to society only in the second. If he therefore prefers individual treatment to collective ameliorations, this accords with the experience that social and collective influences usually produce only a mass intoxication, and that only man's action upon man can bring about a real transformation.[59]

126 It cannot have escaped the alchemists that their Sol had something to do with man. Thus Dorn says: "From the beginning man was sulphur." Sulphur is a destructive fire "enkindled by the invisible sun," and this sun is the Sol Philosophorum,[60] which is the much sought-after and highly praised philosophic gold, indeed the goal of the whole work.[61] In spite of the fact that Dorn regards the sun and its sulphur as a kind of physiological component of the human body, it is clear that we are dealing with a piece of physiological mythology, i.e., a projection.

127 In the course of our inquiry we have often seen that, despite the complete absence of any psychology, the alchemical projections sketch a picture of certain fundamental psychological facts and, as it were, reflect them in matter. One of these fundamental facts is the primary pair of opposites, consciousness and unconsciousness, whose symbols are Sol and Luna.

128 We know well enough that the unconscious appears personified: mostly it is the anima[62] who in singular or plural form represents the collective unconscious. The personal unconscious is personified by the shadow.[63] More rarely, the collective unconscious is personified as a Wise Old Man.[64] (I am speaking here

59 In psychotherapy the situation is no different from what it is in somatic medicine, where surgery is performed on the *individual.* I mention this fact because of the modern tendency to treat the psyche by group analysis, as if it were a collective phenomenon. The psyche as an individual factor is thereby eliminated.

60 "Spec. phil.," *Theatr. chem.,* I, p. 308.

61 Ripley, *Chymische Schrifften,* p. 34: "For then your Work will obtain the perfect whiteness. Then turn from the East towards midday, there it should rest at a fiery place, for that is the harvest or end of the Work. . . . Thereupon the sun will shine pure red in its circle and will triumph after the darkness."

62 Cf. "Concerning the Archetypes, with Special Reference to the Anima Concept." An example of the anima in plural form is given in *Psychology and Alchemy,* pars. 58ff.

63 Examples of both archetypes are to be found ibid., Part II. Cf. also *Aion,* chs. 2 and 3. Another problem is the *shadow of the self,* which is not considered here.

64 Cf. *Psychology and Alchemy,* par. 159.

only of masculine psychology, which alone can be compared with that of the alchemists.) It is still rarer for Luna to represent the nocturnal side of the psyche in dreams. But in the products of active imagination the symbol of the moon appears much more often, as also does the sun, which represents the luminous realm of the psyche and our diurnal consciousness. The modern unconscious has little use for sun and moon as dream-symbols.[65] Illumination ("a light dawns," "it is becoming clear," etc.) can be expressed just as well or even better in modern dreams by switching on the electric light.

29 It is therefore not surprising if the unconscious appears in projected and symbolized form, as there is no other way by which it might be perceived. But this is apparently not the case with consciousness. Consciousness, as the essence of all conscious contents, seems to lack the basic requirements for a projection. Properly understood, projection is not a voluntary happening; it is something that approaches the conscious mind from "outside," a kind of sheen on the object, while all the time the subject remains unaware that he himself is the source of light which causes the cat's eye of the projection to shine. Luna is therefore conceivable as a projection; but Sol as a projection, since it symbolizes consciousness, seems at first glance a contradiction in terms, yet Sol is no less a projection than Luna. For just as we perceive nothing of the real sun but light and heat and, apart from that, can know its physical constitution only by inference, so our consciousness issues from a dark body, the ego, which is the indispensable condition for all consciousness, the latter being nothing but the association of an object or a content with the ego. The ego, ostensibly the thing we know most about, is in fact a highly complex affair full of unfathomable obscurities. Indeed, one could even define it as a *relatively constant personification of the unconscious itself,* or as the Schopenhauerian mirror in which the unconscious becomes aware of its own face.[66] All the worlds that have ever existed before man were

65 Examples of the sun and moon dreams are given ibid., p. 135.

66 Here the concept of the *self* can be mentioned only in passing. (For a detailed discussion see *Aion,* ch. 4.) The self is the hypothetical summation of an indescribable totality, one half of which is constituted by ego-consciousness, the other by the shadow. The latter, so far as it can be established empirically, usually presents itself as the inferior or negative personality. It comprises that part of the collective unconscious which intrudes into the personal sphere, there forming the so-called

physically *there*. But they were a nameless happening, not a definite actuality, for there did not yet exist that minimal concentration of the psychic factor, which was also present, to speak the word that outweighed the whole of Creation: That is the world, and this is I! That was the first morning of the world, the first sunrise after the primal darkness, when that inchoately conscious complex, the ego, the son of the darkness, knowingly sundered subject and object, and thus precipitated the world and itself into definite existence,[67] giving it and itself a voice and a name. The refulgent body of the sun is the ego and its field of consciousness—*Sol et eius umbra:* light without and darkness within. In the source of light there is darkness enough for any amount of projections, for the ego grows out of the darkness of the psyche.

130 In view of the supreme importance of the ego in bringing reality to light, we can understand why this infinitesimal speck in the universe was personified as the sun, with all the attributes that this image implies. As the medieval mind was incomparably more alive than ours to the divine quality of the sun, we may assume that the totality character of the sun-image was implicit in all its allegorical or symbolic applications. Among the sig-

---

personal unconscious. The shadow forms, as it were, the bridge to the figure of the anima, who is only partly personal, and through her to the impersonal figures of the collective unconscious. The concept of the self is essentially intuitive and embraces ego-consciousness, shadow, anima, and collective unconscious in indeterminable extension. As a totality, the self is a coincidentia oppositorum; it is therefore bright and dark and yet neither.

If we hypostatize the self and derive from it (as from a kind of pre-existent personality) the ego and the shadow, then these would appear as the empirical aspects of the opposites that are preformed in the self. Since I have no wish to construct a world of speculative concepts, which leads merely to the barren hair-splitting of philosophical discussion, I set no particular store by these reflections. If such concepts provisionally serve to put the empirical material in order, they will have fulfilled their purpose. The empiricist has nothing to say about the concepts self and God in themselves, and how they are related to one another.

67 Genesis 1 : 1–7 is a projection of this process. The coming of consciousness is described as an objective event, the active subject of which is not the ego but Elohim. Since primitive people very often do not feel themselves the subject of their thinking, it is possible that in the distant past consciousness appeared as an outside event that happened to the ego, and that it was integrated with the subject only in later times. Illumination and inspiration, which in reality are sudden expansions of consciousness, still seem to have, even for us, a subject that is not the ego. Cf. Neumann, *The Origins and History of Consciousness,* pp. 102ff.

nifications of the sun as totality the most important was its frequent use as a God-image, not only in pagan times but in the sphere of Christianity as well.

131 Although the alchemists came very close to realizing that the ego was the mysteriously elusive arcane substance and the longed-for lapis, they were not aware that with their sun symbol they were establishing an intimate connection between God and the ego. As already remarked, projection is not a voluntary act; it is a natural phenomenon beyond the interference of the conscious mind and peculiar to the nature of the human psyche. If, therefore, it is this nature that produces the sun symbol, nature herself is expressing an identity of God and ego. In that case only unconscious nature can be accused of blasphemy, but not the man who is its victim. It is the rooted conviction of the West that God and the ego are worlds apart. In India, on the other hand, their identity was taken as self-evident. It was the nature of the Indian mind to become aware of the world-creating significance of the consciousness [68] manifested in man.[69] The West, on the contrary, has always emphasized the littleness, weakness, and sinfulness of the ego, despite the fact that it elevated one man to the status of divinity. The alchemists at least suspected man's hidden godlikeness, and the intuition of Angelus Silesius finally expressed it without disguise.

132 The East resolves these confusing and contradictory aspects by merging the ego, the personal atman, with the universal atman and thus explaining the ego as the veil of Maya. The Western alchemist was not consciously aware of these problems. But when his unspoken assumptions and his symbols reached the plane of conscious gnosis, as was the case with Angelus

68 I use the word "consciousness" here as being equivalent to "ego," since in my view they are aspects of the same phenomenon. Surely there can be no consciousness without a knowing subject, and vice versa.

69 Cf. Rig-Veda, X, 31, 6 (trans. from Deussen, *Geschichte der Philosophie,* I, 1, p. 140):

> "And this prayer of the singer, continually expanding,
> Became a cow that was there before the world was,
> The gods are foster-children of the same brood,
> Dwelling together in the womb of this god."

Vajasaneyi-samhita, 34, 3 (trans. from Deussen, *Die Geheimlehre des Veda,* p. 17):

> "He who as consciousness, thought, decision,
> Dwells as immortal light within man."

Silesius, it was precisely the littleness and lowliness of the ego [70] that impelled him to recognize its identity with its extreme opposite.[71] It was not the arbitrary opinions of deranged minds that gave rise to such insights, but rather the nature of the psyche itself, which, in East and West alike, expresses these truths either directly or clothed in transparent metaphors. This is understandable when we realize that a world-creating quality attaches to human consciousness as such. In saying this we violate no religious convictions, for the religious believer is at liberty to regard man's consciousness (through which, as it were, a second world-creation was enacted) as a divine instrument.

133 I must point out to the reader that these remarks on the significance of the ego might easily prompt him to charge me with grossly contradicting myself. He will perhaps remember that he has come across a very similar argument in my other writings. Only there it was not a question of ego but of the *self,* or rather, of the personal atman in contradistinction and in relation to the suprapersonal atman. I have defined the self as the totality of the conscious and the unconscious psyche, and the ego as the central reference-point of consciousness. It is an essential part of the self, and can be used *pars pro toto* when the significance of consciousness is borne in mind. But when we want to lay emphasis on the psychic totality it is better to use the term "self." There is no question of a contradictory definition, but merely of a difference of standpoint.

70 "Save as a child, one goes not in where all
God's children are: the door is much too small."
Cherubinischer Wandersmann, I, No. 153.

71 "I am God's child and son, and he is mine.
How comes it that we both can both combine?" (I, 256)
"God is my centre when I close him in;
And my circumference when I melt in him." (III, 148)
"God, infinite, more present is in me
Than if a sponge should soak up all the sea." (IV, 156)
"The hen contains the egg, the egg the hen,
The twain in one, and yet the one in twain." (IV, 163)
"God becomes 'I' and takes my manhood on:
Because I was before him was that done!" (IV, 259)

V. THE MASCULINE IN WOMEN

Anonymous

[ORIGINAL IN ENGLISH]

Dear Dr. N., 12 November 1957

What you told me is a typical story of what I call the projection of the anima into a woman and of the animus into a man. Anima is the soul-image of a man, represented in dreams or fantasies by a feminine figure. It symbolizes the function of relationship. The animus is the image of spiritual forces in a woman, symbolized by a masculine figure. If a man or a woman is unconscious of these inner forces, they appear in a projection.

The psychiatrist calls you "his equal," and that feeling of relationship shows that you carry the image of his soul. Since he is unable to see you as a real woman behind his projection, you seem to be a "sphinx." In reality his soul is his sphinx, and he should try to solve the riddle.

You are wrong in assuming that he alone needs help. You need help as well. You call yourself a woman of a "very ordinary intellectual capacity" who has "never delved very deep into any metaphysical subject." As your story shows, the projection of the animus into a "psychiatrist of international repute" happened because you should get more psychological knowledge. Knowing more about the soul and its mysteries you could free yourself from the fascination which makes you suffer. In the second half of life one should begin to get acquainted with the inner world. That is a general problem.

Your world seemed to be a happy one. But the strange happenings showed that something ought to be changed.

The projection of anima and animus causes mutual fascination. Phenomena which you describe as "telepathic" happen when one gets emotional, i.e., when the unconscious has an opportunity to enter consciousness. You really ought to know a bit more about the psychology of the unconscious. It would help you to understand the situation, which—by the way—should be understood. There is a little book by Frieda Fordham: *Introduction to Jung's Psychology* (Pelican Books), which I recommend to you.

Faithfully yours, C. G. JUNG

☐ A woman, M.D., in England.

So you see, when you have lived in primitive conditions, in the primeval forest among primitive people, you know that phenomenon. You are seized by a spell, and then you do something that is unexpected. Several times when I was in Africa I got into such situations and afterwards I was amazed. One day I was in the Sudan, and it was really a very dangerous situation which I didn't recognize at the moment at all. But I was seized by a spell, and I did something I wouldn't have expected, I couldn't have invented it. The archetype is a force. It has an autonomy and it can suddenly seize you. It is like a seizure. Falling in love at first sight is something like that. You see, you have a certain image in yourself, without knowing it, of woman, of *the* woman. Then you see that girl, or at least a good imitation of your type, and instantly you get a seizure and you are gone. And afterwards you may discover that it was a hell of a mistake. A man is quite able, he is intelligent enough, to see that the woman of his "choice," as one says, was no choice, he has been caught! He sees that she is no good at all, that she is a hell of a business, and he tells me so. He says, "For God's sake, doctor, help me to get rid of that woman!" He can't, though, he is like clay in her fingers. That is the archetype, the archetype of the anima.[9] And he thinks it is all his soul, you know! It's the same with the girls. When a man sings very high, a girl thinks he must have a very wonderful spiritual character because he can sing the high C, and she is badly disappointed when she marries that particular number. Well, that's the archetype of the animus.

[9] For the anima see *Two Essays on Analytical Psychology,* CW 7, pars. 296ff.; "Concerning the Archetypes, with Special Reference to the Anima Concept," CW 9 i; *Aion,* CW 9 ii, ch. III.

FROM ESTHER HARDING'S NOTEBOOKS: 1922, 1925

4 July

I began by describing how I always had so much to say before I got into the room, so that I had to edit my thoughts because of the many undertones of meaning. Jung agreed that my language was scanty, and yet he felt it to be full of allusion. Extraverts' language is thin and poor, but profuse, so that although what they want to say may be very slight, at least when they have finished they have said what they set out to say. He went on to say that when speaking to an extravert he has to cut down his thoughts; also when he is speaking to an introvert he has to cut down, for the thought of an introvert, even if expanded into a book, would not be fully expressed. . . .

I had been trying to find out the meaning of my [slip of the tongue] and thought it was in protest against the extra difficulty of the feminine position regarding searching for the anima. This he denied. He said a man must take up a feminine attitude, while a woman must fight her animus, a masculine attitude. I asked, "Is this why I always want to fight you?" And he replied, "In so far as I am your animus. As far as you are identified to your animus, so far will you project him to me. And then, if you battle me with him who is demonic, I call *my* demon, my anima, to my aid, and it is two married couples fighting. Then you have a hell of a row." He said this is what happens when you get a reciprocal transference. But that as he is not [word illegible], I need not fear that would happen to him.

Then he began talking about how it happens that a professional woman lives her animus. The professional situation is new for woman and needs a new adaptation, and this, as always, is readily supplied by the animus. On the other hand, analysis requires a new adaptation from a man, for to sit still and patiently try to understand a woman's mind is far from a masculine attitude. The only time he does it is as lover to his mistress; he will not do so for his wife, for she is only his wife. In love, his anima shows him how. He then takes on a feminine tenderness and uses the baby talk he learned from his mother; he calls on the eternal image of the feminine in himself. But [in analysis] that won't do. [The male analyst] has got to learn the feminineness of a man, which is not the anima. He must not let his masculinity be overwhelmed, or his weakness calls out the animus in the woman patient.

Similarly, the professional woman takes on the animus, the prototype of the father, and develops a god-almightiness, [an imitation of] the hero, instead of developing the masculinity of the female. This animus is *primitive* man, and men want to react to it with their fists. But, as this is a woman, that way is barred to them; so they shun her—just as a man who lives his anima is shunned by all really womanly women.

Dr. Jung went on to speak of the strength of womanhood, how it is stronger than any [imitation of the] male adaptation, and how a woman who is woman from the crown of her head to the tip of her toe can afford to be masculine, just as a man who is sure of his masculinity can afford to be tender and patient like a woman. . . .

Next he spoke of the Self and how it can be separated off from the demons. He reiterated that words in the realm of the spirit are creative and full of power. I said "You mean as *Logos*?" He replied, "Yes. God spake and created from the chaos—and here we are all gods for ourselves. But use few words here, words that you are sure of. Do not make a long theory or you will entangle yourself in a net, in a trap."

Next he spoke of fear. He said, "Be afraid of the world, for it is big and strong; and fear the demons within, for they are many and brutal; but do not fear yourself, for that is your Self." I said I feared to open the door for fear the demons would come out and destroy. He said, "If you lock them up they will as surely destroy. The only way of delimiting the Self is by experiment. Go as far as your desire goes, and you will presently find that you have gone as far as your own laws allow. If you feel afraid, be brave enough to run away. Find a hole to hide in, for this is the action of a brave man, and by so doing you are exercising courage. Presently the swing of cowardice will be over, and courage will take its place." I said, "But how hopelessly unstable and changeable you will appear!" He replied, "Then be unstable. A new stability will reassert itself. Does one live for other people or for oneself? Here is the place where one must learn true unselfishness."

The law was made by man. We made it. It is therefore below us, and we can be above it. As St. Paul said, "I am redeemed and am freed from the law." He realized that, as man, he had made it. So also a contract cannot bind us, for we who made it can break it.

Thus, vice too, if entered into sincerely as a means of finding and expressing the Self, is not vice, for the fearless honesty cuts that out. But when we are bound by an artificial barrier, or by laws and moralities that have entered into us, then we are prevented from finding, or even from seeing, that there is a real barrier of the Self outside this artificial barrier. We fear that if we break through this artificial barrier we shall find ourselves in limitless space. But within each of us is the *self-regulating Self.*

5 July

I began the hour by telling Jung how something wonderful had happened to me yesterday, that his talk on the animus relationship had cleared things up, so that much had clicked into place, and that now I felt quite different. I said that yesterday we were dealing with the negative relationship to the animus, but there must also be a positive relationship. He replied that there certainly must—but that the important part of analysis was to get that negative point cleared, for that is the growing point of differentiation from the unconscious. Until that is clear, the voice of the animus is as the voice of God within us; in any case, we respond to it as if it were. When we are not aware of the negative aspect of the animus, we are still animal, still connected to nature, therefore unconscious and less than human. We need to reach a higher degree of consciousness, which must be sought at *that* point. Then we discover a new country. And it is our responsibility to cultivate it. ("To him that knoweth to do good and doeth it not, to him it is sin.") Also the legend of Christ and the man working on the Sabbath, to whom he said, "If thou knowest what thou doest, blessed art thou! But if thou knowest not what thou doest, cursed art thou!" If we are conscious, morality no longer exists. If we are not conscious, we are still slaves, and we are accursed if we obey not the law. He said that if we belong to the secret church, then we belong, and we need not worry about it, but can go our own way. If we do not belong, no amount of teaching or organization can bring us there.

Then I asked him about a single animus figure, and he said, "Many souls are young; they are promiscuous; they are prostitutes in the unconscious and sell themselves cheaply. They are like flowers that bloom and die and come again. Other souls are older, like trees or palms. They find, or must seek, one complete animus, who shall perhaps be many in one. And when they find him, it is like the closing of an electric circuit. Then they know the meaning of life.

"But to have an animus like an archimandrite[2] is as if to say, You are a priest of the Mysteries. And this needs a great humility to counterbalance it. You need to go down to the level of the mice. And as a tree, so great as the height of its branches, so deep must be the depths of its roots. And the meaning of the tree is neither in the roots, nor in the uplifted crown, but in the life in between them."

Then I asked him how to get the mean between the two worlds, between the world of the unconscious and that of reality. He replied, "You are the mediator. It is in your immediate life that they meet. In the pleroma they are merged—in nature they are one—and the primitive is always striving up against its oneness. The glacier is always there. Our civilization finds an adaptation that will satisfy these things for a while, and they are quiet. Then they begin to come up again, and again we find a new adaptation, and they are quiet once more. Today we are in a period of great transition, and they come up again. Eventually they will swallow man, but it will not be the same again, for he has attained the union of the opposites through their separation. Possibly, after man will come a period of the animal and then again the plant—who knows?—and who or what will carry on the lamp of consciousness? Who knows?"

[2] Dr. Harding had dreamed of an abbot, an archimandrite.—E.F.E.

VI. THE ANIMA

CONCERNING THE ARCHETYPES WITH SPECIAL REFERENCE TO THE ANIMA CONCEPT

134 These few examples may suffice to characterize the experience of projection and those features of it which are independent of tradition. We can hardly get round the hypothesis that an emotionally charged content is lying ready in the unconscious and springs into projection at a certain moment. This content is the syzygy motif, and it expresses the fact that a masculine element is always paired with a feminine one. The wide distribution and extraordinary emotionality of this motif prove that it is a fundamental psychic factor of great practical importance, no matter whether the individual psychotherapist or psychologist understands where and in what way it influences his special field of work. Microbes, as we know, played their dangerous role long before they were discovered.

135 As I have said, it is natural to suspect the parental pair in all syzygies. The feminine part, the mother, corresponds to the anima. But since, for the reasons discussed above, consciousness of the object prevents its projection, there is nothing for it but to assume that parents are also the least known of all human beings, and consequently that an unconscious reflection of the parental pair exists which is as unlike them, as utterly alien and incommensurable, as a man compared with a god. It would be conceivable, and has as we know been asserted, that the unconscious reflection is none other than the image of father and mother that was acquired in early childhood, overvalued, and later repressed on account of the incest-fantasy associated with it. This hypothesis presupposes that the image was once *conscious,* otherwise it could not have been "repressed." It also presupposes that the act of moral repression has itself become unconscious, for otherwise the act would remain preserved in

consciousness together with the memory of the repressive moral reaction, from which the nature of the thing repressed could easily be recognized. I do not want to enlarge on these misgivings, but would merely like to emphasize that there is general agreement on one point: that the parental imago comes into existence not in the pre-puberal period or at a time when consciousness is more or less developed, but in the initial stages between the first and fourth year, when consciousness does not show any real continuity and is characterized by a kind of island-like discontinuity. The ego-relationship that is required for continuity of consciousness is present only in part, so that a large proportion of psychic life at this stage runs on in a state which can only be described as relatively unconscious. At all events it is a state which would give the impression of a somnambulistic, dream, or twilight state if observed in an adult. These states, as we know from the observation of small children, are always characterized by an apperception of reality filled with fantasies. The fantasy-images outweigh the influence of sensory stimuli and mould them into conformity with a *pre-existing psychic image.*

136 It is in my view a great mistake to suppose that the psyche of a new-born child is a *tabula rasa* in the sense that there is absolutely nothing in it. In so far as the child is born with a differentiated brain that is predetermined by heredity and therefore individualized, it meets sensory stimuli coming from outside not with *any* aptitudes, but with *specific* ones, and this necessarily results in a particular, individual choice and pattern of apperception. These aptitudes can be shown to be inherited instincts and preformed patterns, the latter being the *a priori* and formal conditions of apperception that are based on instinct. Their presence gives the world of the child and the dreamer its anthropomorphic stamp. They are the archetypes, which direct all fantasy activity into its appointed paths and in this way produce, in the fantasy-images of children's dreams as well as in the delusions of schizophrenia, astonishing mythological parallels such as can also be found, though in lesser degree, in the dreams of normal persons and neurotics. It is not, therefore, a question of inherited *ideas* but of inherited *possibilities* of ideas. Nor are they individual acquisitions but, in the main,

common to all, as can be seen from the universal occurrence of the archetypes.[25]

137 Just as the archetypes occur on the ethnological level as myths, so also they are found in every individual, and their effect is always strongest, that is, they anthropomorphize reality most, where consciousness is weakest and most restricted, and where fantasy can overrun the facts of the outer world. This condition is undoubtedly present in the child during the first years of its life. It therefore seems to me more probable that the archetypal form of the divine syzygy first covers up and assimilates the image of the real parents until, with increasing consciousness, the real figures of the parents are perceived—often to the child's disappointment. Nobody knows better than the psychotherapist that the mythologizing of the parents is often pursued far into adulthood and is given up only with the greatest resistance.

138 I remember a case that was presented to me as the victim of a high-grade mother and castration complex, which had still not been overcome in spite of psychoanalysis. Without any hint from me, the man had made some drawings which showed the mother first as a superhuman being, and then as a figure of woe, with bloody mutilations. I was especially struck by the fact that a castration had obviously been performed on the mother, for in front of her gory genitals lay the cut-off male sexual organs. The drawings clearly represented a diminishing climax: first the mother was a divine hermaphrodite, who then, through the son's disappointing experience of reality, was robbed of its androgynous, Platonic perfection and changed into the woeful figure of an ordinary old woman. Thus from the very beginning, from the son's earliest childhood, the mother was assimilated to the archetypal idea of the syzygy, or conjunction of male and female, and for this reason appeared perfect and super-

25 Hubert and Mauss (*Mélanges d'histoire des religions,* preface, p. xxix) call these *a priori* thought-forms "categories," presumably with reference to Kant: "They exist ordinarily as habits which govern consciousness, but are themselves unconscious." The authors conjecture that the primordial images are conditioned by language. This conjecture may be correct in certain cases, but in general it is contradicted by the fact that a great many archetypal images and associations are brought to light by dream psychology and psychopathology which would be absolutely incommunicable through language.

human.[26] The latter quality invariably attaches to the archetype and explains why the archetype appears strange and as if not belonging to consciousness, and also why, if the subject identifies with it, it often causes a devastating change of personality, generally in the form of megalomania or its opposite.

139 The son's disappointment effected a castration of the hermaphroditic mother: this was the patient's so-called castration complex. He had tumbled down from his childhood Olympus and was no longer the son-hero of a divine mother. His so-called fear of castration was fear of real life, which refused to come up to his erstwhile childish expectations, and everywhere lacked that mythological meaning which he still dimly remembered from his earliest youth. His life was, in the truest sense of the word, "godless." And that, for him—though he did not realize it—meant a dire loss of hope and energy. He thought of himself as "castrated," which is a very plausible neurotic misunderstanding—so plausible that it could even be turned into a theory of neurosis.

140 Because people have always feared that the connection with the instinctive, archetypal stage of consciousness might get lost in the course of life, the custom has long since been adopted of giving the new-born child, in addition to his bodily parents, two godparents, a "godfather" and a "godmother," who are supposed to be responsible for the spiritual welfare of their godchild. They represent the pair of gods who appear at its birth, thus illustrating the "dual birth" motif.[27]

26 Conforming to the bisexual Original Man in Plato, *Symposium*, XIV, and to the hermaphroditic Primal Beings in general.

27 The "dual birth" refers to the motif, well known from hero mythology, which makes the hero descend from divine as well as from human parents. In most mysteries and religions it plays an important role as a baptism or rebirth motif. It was this motif that misled Freud in his study of Leonardo da Vinci. Without taking account of the fact that Leonardo was by no means the only artist to paint the motif of St. Anne, Mary, and the Christ-child, Freud tried to reduce Anne and Mary, the grandmother and mother, to the mother and stepmother of Leonardo; in other words, to assimilate the painting to his theory. But did the other painters all have stepmothers?! What prompted Freud to this violent interpretation was obviously the fantasy of dual descent suggested by Leonardo's biography. This fantasy covered up the inconvenient reality that St. Anne was the grandmother, and prevented Freud from inquiring into the biographies of other artists who also painted St. Anne. The "religious inhibition of thought" mentioned on p. 79 (1957 edn.) proved true of the author himself. Similarly, the incest theory on

141 The anima image, which lends the mother such superhuman glamour in the eyes of the son, gradually becomes tarnished by commonplace reality and sinks back into the unconscious, but without in any way losing its original tension and instinctivity. It is ready to spring out and project itself at the first opportunity, the moment a woman makes an impression that is out of the ordinary. We then have Goethe's experience with Frau von Stein, and its repercussions in the figures of Mignon and Gretchen, all over again. In the case of Gretchen, Goethe also showed us the whole underlying "metaphysic." The love life of a man reveals the psychology of this archetype in the form either of boundless fascination, overvaluation, and infatuation, or of misogyny in all its gradations and variants, none of which can be explained by the real nature of the "object" in question, but only by a transference of the mother complex. The complex, however, was caused in the first place by the assimilation of the mother (in itself a normal and ubiquitous phenomenon) to the pre-existent, feminine side of an archetypal "male-female" pair of opposites, and secondly by an abnormal delay in detaching from the primordial image of the mother. Actually, nobody can stand the total loss of the archetype. When that happens, it gives rise to that frightful "discontent in our culture," where nobody feels at home because a "father" and "mother" are missing. Everyone knows the provisions that religion has always made in this respect. Unfortunately there are very many people who thoughtlessly go on asking whether these provisions are "true," when it is really a question of a psychological need. Nothing is achieved by explaining them away rationalistically.

142 When projected, the anima always has a feminine form with definite characteristics. This empirical finding does not mean

which he lays so much stress is based on another archetype, the well-known incest motif frequently met with in hero myths. It is logically derived from the original hermaphrodite type, which seems to go far back into prehistory. Whenever a psychological theory is forcibly applied, we have reason to suspect that an archetypal fantasy-image is trying to distort reality, thus bearing out Freud's own idea of the "religious inhibition of thought." But to explain the genesis of archetypes by means of the incest theory is about as useful as ladling water from one kettle into another kettle standing beside it, which is connected with the first by a pipe. You cannot explain one archetype by another; that is, it is impossible to say where the archetype comes from, because there is no Archimedean point outside the *a priori* conditions it represents.

that the archetype is constituted like that *in itself*. The male-female syzygy is only one among the possible pairs of opposites, albeit the most important one in practice and the commonest. It has numerous connections with other pairs which do not display any sex differences at all and can therefore be put into the sexual category only by main force. These connections, with their manifold shades of meaning, are found more particularly in Kundalini yoga,[28] in Gnosticism,[29] and above all in alchemical philosophy,[30] quite apart from the spontaneous fantasy-products in neurotic and psychotic case material. When one carefully considers this accumulation of data, it begins to seem probable that an archetype in its quiescent, unprojected state has no exactly determinable form but is in itself an indefinite structure which can assume definite forms only in projection.

143 This seems to contradict the concept of a "type." If I am not mistaken, it not only seems but actually *is* a contradiction. Empirically speaking, we are dealing all the time with "types," definite forms that can be named and distinguished. But as soon as you divest these types of the phenomenology presented by the case material, and try to examine them in relation to other archetypal forms, they branch out into such far-reaching ramifications in the history of symbols that one comes to the conclusion that the basic psychic elements are infinitely varied and ever changing, so as utterly to defy our powers of imagination. The empiricist must therefore content himself with a theoretical "as if." In this respect he is no worse off than the atomic physicist, even though his method is not based on quantitative measurement but is a morphologically descriptive one.

144 The anima is a factor of the utmost importance in the psychology of a man wherever emotions and affects are at work. She intensifies, exaggerates, falsifies, and mythologizes all emotional relations with his work and with other people of both sexes. The resultant fantasies and entanglements are all her doing. When the anima is strongly constellated, she softens the man's character and makes him touchy, irritable, moody, jealous, vain, and unadjusted. He is then in a state of "discontent" and spreads

28 Cf. Avalon, *The Serpent Power; Shrī-Chakra-Sambhara Tantra;* Woodroffe, *Shakti and Shakta.*

29 Schultz, *Dokumente der Gnosis,* especially the lists in Irenaeus, *Adversus haereses.*

30 Cf. *Psychology and Alchemy.*

discontent all around him. Sometimes the man's relationship to the woman who has caught his anima accounts for the existence of this syndrome.

145 The anima, as I have remarked elsewhere,[31] has not escaped the attentions of the poets. There are excellent descriptions of her, which at the same time tell us about the symbolic context in which the archetype is usually embedded. I give first place to Rider Haggard's novels *She, The Return of She,* and *Wisdom's Daughter,* and Benoît's *L'Atlantide.* Benoît was accused of plagiarizing Rider Haggard, because the two accounts are disconcertingly alike. But it seems he was able to acquit himself of this charge. Spitteler's *Prometheus* contains some very subtle observations, too, and his novel *Imago* gives an admirable description of projection.

146 The question of *therapy* is a problem that cannot be disposed of in a few words. It was not my intention to deal with it here, but I would like to outline my point of view. Younger people, who have not yet reached the middle of life (around the age of 35), can bear even the total loss of the anima without injury. The important thing at this stage is for a man to be a man. The growing youth must be able to free himself from the anima fascination of his mother. There are exceptions, notably artists, where the problem often takes a different turn; also homosexuality, which is usually characterized by identity with the anima. In view of the recognized frequency of this phenomenon, its interpretation as a pathological perversion is very dubious. The psychological findings show that it is rather a matter of incomplete detachment from the hermaphroditic archetype, coupled with a distinct resistance to identify with the role of a one-sided sexual being. Such a disposition should not be adjudged negative in all circumstances, in so far as it preserves the archetype of the Original Man, which a one-sided sexual being has, up to a point, lost.

147 After the middle of life, however, permanent loss of the anima means a diminution of vitality, of flexibility, and of human kindness. The result, as a rule, is premature rigidity, crustiness, stereotypy, fanatical one-sidedness, obstinacy, pedantry, or else resignation, weariness, sloppiness, irresponsibility, and finally a childish *ramollissement* with a tendency to alcohol. After

31 Cf. the first paper in this volume.

middle life, therefore, the connection with the archetypal sphere of experience should if possible be re-established.[32]

[32] The most important problems for therapy are discussed in my essay "The Relations between the Ego and the Unconscious" and also in the "Psychology of the Transference." For the mythological aspects of the anima, the reader is referred to another paper in this volume, "The Psychological Aspects of the Kore."

THE PERSONIFICATION OF THE OPPOSITES INTERPRETATION AND MEANING OF SALT

Jung's alchemical writings are exercises in hermeneutics, interpretations grounded in his intuition that in their philosophic treatises on the nature of chemical materials, the alchemists projected psychological processes onto matter. Much of the unconscious masculine nature was the substance sulphur, which contributed to the fiery character of Sol. But in the formation of the man's lunar unconscious, which had a feminine character, the root substance appeared to be salt, associated throughout human history with tears. Jung's understanding of the importance of experiences of bitter disappointment in the development of the anima reaches beyond the traditional Christian emphasis on suffering and sacrifice embodied in the Virgin Mary to the more seasoned femininity of the Gnostic Sophia, who personifies earth wisdom.

---

330 Apart from its lunar wetness and its terrestrial nature, the most outstanding properties of salt are bitterness and wisdom. As in the double quaternio of the elements and qualities, earth and water have coldness in common, so bitterness and wisdom would form a pair of opposites with a third thing between. (See diagram on facing page.) The factor common to both, however incommensurable the two ideas may seem, is, psychologically, the function of *feeling*. Tears, sorrow, and disappointment are bitter, but wisdom is the comforter in all psychic suffering. Indeed, bitterness and wisdom form a pair of alternatives: where there is bitterness wisdom is lacking, and where wisdom is there can be no bitterness. Salt, as the carrier of this fateful alternative,

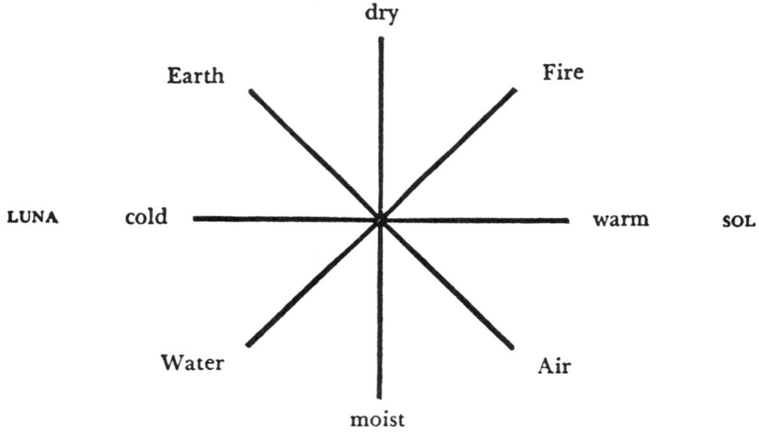

is co-ordinated with the nature of woman. The masculine, solar nature in the right half of the quaternio knows neither coldness, nor a shadow, nor heaviness, melancholy, etc., because, so long as all goes well, it identifies as closely as possible with consciousness, and that as a rule is the idea which one has of oneself. In this idea the shadow is usually missing: first because nobody likes to admit to any inferiority, and second because logic forbids something white to be called black. A good man has good qualities, and only the bad man has bad qualities. For reasons of prestige we pass over the shadow in complete silence. A famous example of masculine prejudice is Nietzsche's Superman, who scorns compassion and fights against the "Ugliest Man"—the ordinary man that everyone is. The shadow must not be seen, it must be denied, repressed, or twisted into something quite extraordinary. The sun is always shining and everything smiles back. There is no room for any prestige-diminishing weakness, so the *sol niger* is never seen. Only in solitary hours is its presence feared.

331 Things are different with Luna: every month she is darkened and extinguished; she cannot hide this from anybody, not even from herself. She knows that this same Luna is now bright and now dark—but who has ever heard of a dark sun? We call this quality of Luna "woman's closeness to nature," and the fiery brilliance and hot air that plays round the surface of things we like to call "the masculine mind."

332 Despite all attempts at denial and obfuscation there is an

unconscious factor, a black sun, which is responsible for the surprisingly common phenomenon of masculine split-mindedness, when the right hand mustn't know what the left is doing. This split in the masculine psyche and the regular darkening of the moon in woman together explain the remarkable fact that the woman is accused of all the darkness in a man, while he himself basks in the thought that he is a veritable fount of vitality and illumination for all the females in his environment. Actually, he would be better advised to shroud the brilliance of his mind in the profoundest doubt. It is not difficult for this type of mind (which besides other things is a great trickster like Mercurius) to admit a host of sins in the most convincing way, and even to combine it with a spurious feeling of ethical superiority without in the least approximating to a genuine insight. This can never be achieved without the participation of feeling; but the intellect admits feeling only when it is convenient. The novilunium of woman is a source of countless disappointments for man which easily turn to bitterness, though they could equally well be a source of wisdom if they were understood. Naturally this is possible only if he is prepared to acknowledge his black sun, that is, his shadow.

33 Confirmation of our interpretation of salt as Eros (i.e., as a feeling relationship) is found in the fact that the bitterness is the origin of the *colours* (par. 245). We have only to look at the drawings and paintings of patients who supplement their analysis by active imagination to see that colours are feeling-values. Mostly, to begin with, only a pencil or pen is used to make rapid sketches of dreams, sudden ideas, and fantasies. But from a certain moment on the patients begin to make use of colour, and this is generally the moment when merely intellectual interest gives way to emotional participation. Occasionally the same phenomenon can be observed in dreams, which at such moments are dreamt in colour, or a particularly vivid colour is insisted upon.

To Jolande Jacobi

Dear Dr. Jacobi, Bollingen, 26 August 1943

. . .

The mistake you are making consists in your being drawn too much into X.'s neurotic problem. This is evident from the fact, for instance, that your animus is trying like mad to interpret when there is nothing to be interpreted. *Why* does he say he has other relationships? Why indeed! As though anyone knew. He just says it. That is very nice of him, inconsiderate, truthful, tactless, unpremeditated, confiding, etc., etc. If you knew the *real* reason you would also know who X. was at his birth and at his death. But we shall only find that out in the Hereafter. He has absolutely no reason he can state, it has simply happened and can be interpreted quite superflously in a hundred different ways, and no single interpretation holds water, being merely an insistence which, once made, only has the effect of driving him into further whimsical and uninterpretable reactions. In reality his irrational behaviour represents the conscious and unconscious sides of the anima, and is absolutely necessary in order to gain insight into her, just as in general he needs a bevy of women in order to grasp the essence of this glamorous figure. Of course he is still too naïve to notice this. But you, just as naïvely, have intruded yourself as an anima figure into this witches' sabbath and are therefore caught up in the dance as though you were nothing but an anima. Wherever you stick a finger in out of "love" or involuntary participation you will burn it, for it is not involvement that is expected of you, but objective, disincarnate observation, and if you want to snatch something out of it for the heart—and no reasonable objection can be made to this—you must pay for it in blood, as was always so and always will be. At least one must keep one's head out of it so as not to be eaten up entirely by emotional ape-men. Where there are emotional ties one is always the disappointed disappointer. This one has to know if one wants, or is forced, to participate correctly.

. . .

With cordial greetings,

Yours sincerely, C. G. JUNG

LECTURE V

19 February 1930

Dr. Jung:

I have brought you today the picture[1] of which I spoke last week, the reproduction of the Tibetan mandala. It is a *yantra,* used for the purpose of concentration upon the most philosophical thought of the Tibetan Lamas. It shows in the innermost circle the diamond wedge or thunderbolt, that symbol of potential energy, and the white light symbolizing absolute truth. And here are the four functions, the four fields of colour, and then the four gates to the world. Then comes the gazelle garden, and finally the ring of the fire of desirousness outside. You will notice that it is embedded in the earth region exactly to the middle, with the upper part reaching to the celestial world. The figures above are three great teachers, the living Buddhas or Bodhisattvas, two yellow and one red. That has to do with the Tibetan Lamaistic doctrine. They correspond to the mountains on the earth below. What the mountain is on earth the great teacher is among men. I have another mandala where, instead of a thunderbolt in the centre, there is the god Mahasukha, one form of the Indian god Shiva, in the embrace of his wife Shakti. Today I think we will continue our dreams.

Dream [23]

Our patient says that he is at a sort of festival celebration in a Protestant church, in which the benches are not all arranged in the

[1] Jung published the yantra as a frontispiece to *The Secret of the Golden Flower* (in orig., 1929, and tr., 1931) and again in *Psychology and Alchemy* (1944), CW 12, fig. 43 (described there as a Tibetan painted banner, formerly in the China Institute, Frankfurt, and destroyed in World War II). He published it again with "Concerning Mandala Symbolism" (1950), CW 9 i, fig. 1, analyzed in pars. 630-38.

same direction but in the form of a square, so that they all face the pulpit, which is in the middle of one of the long walls of the church. A hymn is being sung, a very well-known one, typical of our Christmas festivals: "O du fröhliche, O du selige Weihnachtszeit."[2] (One hears it everywhere at that time of the year.) He joins in the singing of the hymn and suddenly hears somebody behind him singing the same words in a peculiar soprano voice, exceedingly loud and the melody quite different, so that everyone around that person gets completely out of tune. Our dreamer immediately stops and looks back to see who the singer can be. It is a man sitting on a bench at right angles to his own and wearing, strangely enough, a sort of woman's garment, so that he feels unable to make out positively whether it is a man or a woman. Then the service comes to an end, and on going out, he finds he has left his hat and overcoat in the wardrobe. (He was thinking naturally not of the word "wardrobe," but of "garde-robe" which is of course really a French word, but in French one would say "vestiaire". "Garde-robe" is used in German, taken over from the old French word, which originally meant the man who takes care of the wraps.) On the way back to the wardrobe, he wonders whether the word "garde-robe" in French is a masculine or feminine noun, and he comes to the conclusion that one should say "le garde-robe," and not, as it is used in German as a feminine noun, "die Garde-robe." While thinking of that, he suddenly hears the singer talking to a man who is with him, saying that today he has shown for once that he too can sing. Our dreamer again turns back to look at him and has to restrain himself from making a disagreeable remark to him. He notices that he appears more masculine this time and that he has a Jewish type of face, and then seems to know who he is and remembers that his son is a friend of his. Then the son suddenly appears and violently reproaches his father because he upset the hymn.

Associations: As a child he had been *forced to go to church* every Sunday. On account of that compulsion, he developed an antipathy to churches and parsons, which is the reason that he almost never goes to church except on special festivals. The church in which the benches are arranged as he described, all facing the pulpit, is the church to which he had been made to go as a boy.

[2] Sung to the tune "Sanctissima," usually with the English words "O thou joyful day, O thou blessed day, Holy, peaceful Christmastide."

Concerning the *hymn* he says, "When I think of that hymn, I think of the end, the refrain, 'Freue dich O Christenheit,' meaning 'Rejoice, O Christendom.' "

Then he associates with his joining in the hymn the fact that he *cannot sing*. He is quite unmusical, and if he tried he would probably upset the melody as much as the man who sang an entirely different melody in a high woman's soprano.

With the peculiar *singer, whose sex is uncertain,* he associates the fact that he, as a boy, read a book called *Der Golem* by Meyrink.[3] (That is quite a remarkable book; I think it has now been translated into English.) You remember that in a former seminar he dreamed of a square building where he climbed over a fence. We spoke especially of his associations with the end of that book, *Der Golem,* where the hero comes to the locked gates. Here again he associates just that last scene, where the hero arrives at the supreme moment when he really should find the answer to all riddles, the supreme solution of the whole problem, but then comes to the locked gate upon which is the symbol of the hermaphrodite. The dreamer says that this symbol of the hermaphrodite means, as he would interpret it, the alchemical nuptial, that is, the blending of the male and female in one indivisible whole. He says that he can't help feeling that that song would sound very different from the hymn in the Protestant church—in other words, that such ideas would not fit in with the ideas of the Protestant church and would prove most disturbing. Obviously!

Concerning the word "garde-robe," the uncertainty whether it is masculine or feminine refers naturally to the same thing as the dubious sex of the man, and again he associates the hermaphrodite symbol.

As to the discovery that the *singer is Jewish,* he says that he thinks Meyrink must be a Jew; he is convinced that even if he does not confess to it, his creed would be Judaic, he would be reserving in the secret room of his soul the Judaic conviction. That would explain, he says, why Meyrink in his book *The Green Face*[4] sends the hero to Brazil to save him when the continent of Europe collapses. You see, that book has a somewhat unsatisfactory ending. Apparently Meyrink got very involved in a complicated plot and did not

[3] See above, 19 June 1929, n. 6, and text following.

[4] Gustav Meyrink, *Das grüne Gesicht* (Leipzig, 1916).

know how to find his way out of the tangle; then by divine providence, a great storm came up and devastated the whole Occident and got him out of the difficulty of a satisfactory solution. His hero, Sephardi, the Jewish scholar, having foreseen it, had collected his family and friends and emigrated to Brazil unharmed, as it is a local storm in Europe only. Obviously the dreamer means that Meyrink, being a Jew, saves his tribesmen in the fatal moment and nobody else, a sort of exodus out of the cursed land.

You probably would not have expected such a dream after the ones before, I certainly would not have guessed it. That is the wonderful irrationality of the unconscious which always beats us. I would not have foreseen it—except in one respect: that last mandala dream would upset certain Occidental convictions, and as this man has had a definite religious education of a narrow kind, he cannot help preserving certain prejudices which would be cruelly hurt by the ideas of the mandala psychology, because that brings a new ethical orientation. It is a point of view that does not fit into the Christian standpoint, which divides the world into good and evil and does not allow any reconciliation. The whole of Christian eschatology follows this line of thought in teaching about the ultimate things—that at the end of the world there will be a Last Judgment where good and evil are divided definitely and forever by those two remarkable institutions Heaven and Hell. All the evil ones will be cast into hell and will cook there forever, and the good ones will attain that blissful condition where they are allowed to make music during all eternity. This is a dogmatic statement of the irreconcilability of good and evil. Nothing to be done about it, just give up, no choice. But the mandala psychology is of a very different kind: an endless chain of lives moving on through good and evil, through all aspects of things. The eternally revolving wheel of existence, now in the shadow, now in the light. This is an extraordinary relativation of the ethical problem—that having been high you will be low, having been low you will be high. Out of the darkness comes the light, and after the light comes again the darkness, so evil is not so bad and good is not so good because they are related and only together by a mistake which remains inexplicable. Why, after all, is it not perfect since it is the work of a perfect Master? The Occidental answer is: because the devil put some dirt into it, or man was such an ass that he spoiled it somehow, this work of an omnipotent and omniscient Being. The fact of evil was the cause of the invention of the devil, who double-crossed the good intentions of the perfect Master.

In the Eastern mandala psychology, all this takes on an entirely different aspect. Relativity is rather shocking to a Westerner. It intimates a certain indulgence even, and to a puritanical mind that is almost unbearable. That is the case with this man. It would not be so much so in theory. He does not go to church, he does not follow the traditional creed; but when it comes to practical life it is a bit awkward, because our church views are all linked up with our real god, which is respectability, the eyes of the community. When he comes to that, the real god, and his fear of those eyes, he collapses into a terrible conflict.

Now, if he has really understood the meaning of the last dream, that the machine is now going to function, it would indicate that he is about to enter life in a new way, where every wheel is in place and where the machine will yield the all-around life which it is meant to yield, a complete life, with light and shadow. But no sooner is he at that point than he hurts himself against traditional convictions, and this next dream contains obviously the problem of the offended Western values. Therefore he is brought instantly back to his childhood, when he was forced to go to church. It is as if a voice from within said, "Remember the days when you were still in the church and believed these things. How can you get away from that? You are still there singing the same song as the whole Christian community." And then comes the first disturbance, that soprano voice. Now where does that soprano voice come from?

Miss Howells: It is the feminine side of himself, the anima.

Dr. Jung: Sure! It is Madame Anima who suddenly begins to sing too. He was singing the song of the community as if he were a perfectly respectable member of that church, and then the anima breaks in with an entirely unsuitable song. And what does that melody express? Not the words, but the melody. What is the value of that?

Answer: Feeling.

Dr. Jung: Yes, nothing is more impressive than an organ. When you are reminded of a Protestant church you just yawn, a terrible bore, but when you hear the music, you cannot help having feeling, it stirs you. Perhaps not if you go regularly, but a man like myself, who has not been to church for an eternity, will naturally have a sentimental feeling—a beautiful remembrance which appeals to one's feeling. It is wrong not to acknowledge it. A sermon is tedious, while music pulls at the heart. So it is very typical that the dream speaks of feelings, which are really dangerous in a man's case. In his thinking these ideas have no hold on him any longer; he is firm in his convictions. But the music gets him, and he is ground under. He is drawn in and cannot help singing, so he gets into a situation or mood that is quite opposed to the intention mentioned in the dream before. Then the conflict arises in his feeling sphere, and that is why his anima begins to sing. The anima is always connected with the inferior function. As he is an intellectual, his feelings are somewhat inferior, and she is like a personification of his inferior feeling function. Why does the anima not sing the church song? Why an entirely different melody?

Mrs. Baynes: To tell him she is there.

Dr. Jung: But what for?

Mrs. Baynes: Because she wants to make trouble.

Dr. Jung: That would be almost a depreciation of the anima.

Mrs. Baynes: He does not appreciate her, so she wants to make herself felt.

Dr. Jung: But if she only wants to make herself felt or to make trouble, she could just as well be a dog that barks, or an automobile that begins whooping outside the church.

Mrs. Sigg: The anima has a different taste. It is not the taste of the Church, it would perhaps be more like the Indian style.

Dr. Jung: You mean more in favour of the mandala psychology? That is exceedingly probable, because the anima has to be excluded from the Christian frame. She is eternally a heretic and does not fit in at all, a perfect pagan, in more or less open revolt against the Christian point of view. Perhaps you are astonished that I speak of her in such a personal way, but that has forever been the way of taking her, that figure has always been expressed by poets in a personal form. Usually she is projected into a real woman, who thereby becomes more imaginary, like the Lady of the Troubadours and the Knights of the Cours d'Amour,[5] slightly divine. Then you know how Rider Haggard speaks of "She who must be obeyed";[6] he makes her a very definite figure. So to give her the right quality we must describe her as a personality and not as a scientific ab-

[5] These concepts belong to the chivalric tradition of medieval Western Europe.
[6] See above, 12 Dec. 1928, n. 8.

straction. In zoology you can speak of the species, the *whale*. But there are many different kinds of whales, you must say *which* whale, and then it has a specific value. The anima represents the primitive layer of man's psychology, and primitive psychology shuns abstractions. There are practically no concepts in primitive languages. In Arabic, there are sixty words for types of camel and no word for camel in the abstract. Ask an Arab the word for camel and he does not know. It is either an old, or a young, or a female camel, etc., each called by a different name. In a language more primitive still there are thirty different words for cutting—cutting with a knife, a sword, string, etc.—and no word for the act of cutting.

My particular friend Steiner[7] supposes that there were pre-stages of the earth, one a globe of fire, another a globe of gases, and on one of them, he says, there could even be observed some sensations of taste. Now, whose were the sensations of taste? There is no such thing as abstract sensation, some sensation suspended in space to the Big Dipper or Sirius. In one Negro language there are fifty expressions for walking, but not one for the act of walking; one cannot say, "I am walking." Nor is there a word for *man*. We have all these abstract concepts, and in a way they are misleading, or rather, not informing. We can say a man or a woman or, even more indefinite, a person wants to speak to you, and how little we know—whether he or she is outside, inside, standing up, alive or dead. A primitive telling you the same thing by the very nature of his language would inform you, for instance, that an alive, erect man was standing outside your door. There are no words in their language for a man without an almost complete description. They have the most curious expressions for walking which describe exactly how it is done, each specific case of walking, with knees bent, on his heels, etc., so if you hear of him at all you can fairly see that man moving. It is an almost grotesque description of each subject. This absence of collective notions is absolutely characteristic of the primitive mind.

Now, concerning my concept of the anima, I have been reproached occasionally by scholars for using an almost mythological term to express a scientific fact. They expect me to translate her

[7] Rudolf Steiner (1861-1925), German occultist, first a Theosophist, then the founder of Anthroposophy, an offshoot of Theosophy. The reference here is perhaps to his book *Wie erlangt man Erkenntnisse der höheren Welten?* (1922) (= "How does one attain knowledge of higher worlds?"), a copy of which Jung owned.

into scientific terminology, which would deprive the figure of its—or her—specific life. If you say, for instance, that the anima is a function of connection or relationship between the conscious and unconscious, that is a very pale thing. It is as if you should show a picture of a great philosopher and call it simply *Homo sapiens*; of course a picture of a criminal or an idiot would be *Homo sapiens* just as well. The scientific term conveys nothing, and the merely abstract notion of the anima conveys nothing, but when you say the anima is almost personal, a complex that behaves exactly as if she were a little person, or at times as if she were a very important person, then you get it about right. Therefore, chiefly for practical purposes, I leave the anima in her personified form, just as I would in describing President Wilson, or Bismarck, or Mussolini. I would not say they were specimens of *Homo sapiens*, I deal with them specifically as they are. And so the anima is personal and specific. Otherwise it is just a function, as intuition or thinking are functions. But that does not cover the actual facts, nor does it express the extraordinary personality of the anima, the absolutely recognizable personality, so that one can easily point it out anywhere. Therefore I quite intentionally keep to the very personal term, meaning that she is a personal factor, almost as good as a person.

Naturally there is danger on the other side that people think she is a sort of ghost. Sure enough, to the primitive mind she is a ghost. She is a definite entity, and, if you are in a very primitive mood, you might see her in the form of a ghost—a smoke figure or a breath figure. She may become an hallucination. One sees that, for instance, in lunatics when they are possessed by the anima. Not very long ago I was called in as consulting physician to see an insane boy in a clinic in Zurich. When I came into the room he greeted me very politely and said, "You will probably not believe it, but I am my sister and I am a Buddhist." He has actually a married sister, but she plays no role in his life. He thought it was just a mistake that people took him for a man, and even declared that it was a malevolent invention on the part of his mother. To him that anima sister was absolutely real, more real than himself, he was identical with her. She was a Buddhist and therefore initiated into the mysteries of the East, and she had an Indian name, which was an extraordinarily clever contrivance. I don't remember it exactly, but it consisted of three syllables, and the middle syllable was *dava*, which is a Hindu word for divine. It was half Italian and half Hindu or Sanskrit and a bit of Greek. It was a typical designation, and the meaning was divine-mistress-sister. I have known many other cases where men have felt the anima as an extraordinary reality. I am quite certain that Rider Haggard could not possibly have written such an interminable series of novels if the anima had not been extremely real to him. That is the reason why I stress the personal character so much. We have to deal with the figure in a form that is entirely different from the usual because it designates a living factor, despite the fact that this factor, under certain conditions of development, may lose all that personal character and transform into a mere function. But that can only be the case when the conscious attitude is such that it loses the quality and characteristics of a human being—that is the mandala psychology.

Miss Howells: Is it common for her to take on the quality of the Orient or an older civilization? Here she is a Jewess.

Dr. Jung: It would seem so. In *She* the anima is an Oriental being, and in Pierre Bênoit's *Atlantide.*[8] The animus also. But we had better not talk of the animus now. It just scares me, it is much more difficult to deal with. The anima is definite and the animus is indefinite.

Question: Is the anima definitely a part of every man and every woman?

Dr. Jung: No, she is the female part of a man's psychology, so she would not naturally exist in a woman. When she does, she is absolutely identical with the woman's conscious principle, and then I would call it Eros. The same is true of a man reversed. Animus in a man is not a person, it is his conscious principle, and then I call it Logos.

In Chinese philosophy they speak of the masculine and feminine souls of a man. Therefore Wilhelm uses animus and anima exactly as I would. The terms animus and anima correspond to the Chinese *hun* and *kwei*,[9] but always they apply to a man. The Chinese were not concerned with women's psychology—as I unfortunately am! Even in the Middle Ages women were said to have no souls worth

[8] The novel *L'Atlantide* (1919), another work often cited by Jung, as early as March 1920; see letter quoted in *C. G. Jung: Word and Image* (1979), p. 151.

[9] In Wilhelm's discussion of the Chinese text (*Golden Flower*, 1962 edn., pp. 14f.) and in Jung's commentary (ibid., pp. 115ff.; CW 13, pars. 57-60), the Chinese word for anima is *p'o*; *kwei* is said to mean "demon" or "ghost of the departed one." Cary Baynes's footnote to Wilhelm (loc. cit.) aims to clarify the use of the terms.

mentioning, or only "little souls," like the story of the penguins in *L'île des pingouins*, by Anatole France.[10] Since St. Maël had baptized them, it became a question whether they had souls or not, and they at last called in St. Catherine of Alexandria to decide. "Well," she said, giving the final word in the celestial discussion, "Donnez-leur une âme immortelle, mais petite!" So in the Middle Ages women's psychology was *chose inconnue*, and similarly the old Chinese philosophers had the concept that the masculine animus was meant for heaven, while the female soul would become only a spectre, a phantom, who sinks into the earth after death. One goes on into Eternity and the other becomes a sort of haunting ghost, a demon. Therefore the Chinese meant by the animus in man what we mean by the Logos principle, or the conscious principle.

But since I have to deal with women's psychology as well as men's, I have found it better to call the conscious principle in man Logos, and the principle of relatedness in women Eros. The inferior Eros in man I designate as anima and the inferior Logos in woman as animus. These concepts, Logos and Eros, correspond roughly with the Christian idea of the soul. And the thing that does not fit in, the thing that sings the wrong tune, would be in a man the anima representing the Eros principle, and in a woman the animus representing the Logos principle, but in a sort of inferior form, a minor position. The reason why the anima is here playing that role of *diabolos in musica* is that the exclusive Logos principle in man does not allow for the Eros principle. He must discriminate, see things in their separateness, otherwise he is unable to recognize them. But that is against the principle of relatedness. A woman does not want to have things segregated, she wants to see them almost synchronized. A man who is possessed by his anima gets into the most awful difficulties, for he cannot discriminate, especially among women. While a woman under the law of the animus cannot relate, she becomes nothing but discrimination, surrounded by a wall of spiky cactus laws. She tells a man what he is up to and that chills him to the bone and he cannot get at her.

Now in regard to the particular role of the anima in this dream, that she is feminine is probably quite clear to you, but why is she masculine too? This is a very unusual case. And mind you, after-

[10] Jung relates the story in *Mysterium Coniunctionis* (1955), CW 14, par. 227, and briefly in his commentary on the *Tibetan Book of the Dead* (1935), CW 11, par. 835. Concerning Anatole France's novel *Penguin Island*, see above, 23 Jan. 1929, n. 2.

wards she becomes a man, a Jew. What do you think of the conditions under which a man's anima would be either male or hermaphroditic?

Answer: Homosexuality.

Dr. Jung: That is true. One often encounters anima figures of very doubtful sex, or quite indubitably masculine, when the conscious mind is feminine. But in the case of our dreamer there is no question of homosexuality. He is perhaps not quite free of perversions, everybody has the statistical amount; we all have that percentage of murder in our being, the whole population. But in him there is no trace of anything like repressed homosexuality. So why has he a masculine anima?

Mrs. Fierz: The anima is so incapable of making the man accept her that she has to play that role, use a sort of mimicry, to do so. It is the unconscious approaching the conscious.

Mrs. Sawyer: Isn't he identified with her and therefore she is masculine?

Dr. Jung: You mean since he cannot approach her he has to identify? Mrs. Fierz takes it from the unconscious side, that the unconscious is trying to make itself heard. Mrs. Sawyer sees it as the conscious trying to connect with the unconscious—his conscious possessed by the anima and so hermaphroditic. In either point of view one must detach her in order to establish a connection.

Mrs. Henley: Might it in this case simply express lack of development, because homosexuality is an attribute of youth?

Dr. Jung: That is also true, since he is undeveloped on the side of religion; from that point of view he could be expressed as a sort of homosexual boy about ten or twelve years old. That would be symbolic homosexuality. It is a fact that certain apparent sex perversions are merely symbolical; expressing an undeveloped state. In this case, there was no conscious manifestation of homosexuality that could be pointed out, so we may assume that this is symbolical homosexuality and not a disturbance of the normal. There have been traces of this feeling in some of his former dreams, in the dream of the Puer Aeternus, for instance, where he called the boy Eros and had a decided feeling of tenderness towards him.[11] And again in a dream which he had during our last seminar, that case

[11] Above, 13 Mar. 1929, p. 170.

of synchronicity, where he was worshipping the boy Telesphoros[12] and had doubts then also whether there was something homosexual about it. But it was merely symbolical, a certain immaturity, like the twelve-year-old condition. Such mental immaturity may be very local, it may refer to a specific expression of it, or it may go so far that a man is capable of believing that he actually is homosexual, in spite of the fact that he never had the experience. I have had men come to me complaining that they were homosexual, but when I say to such a man, "How was it? Did you get into trouble with boys," he exclaims indignantly that he would not touch a boy. "Men then?" "No." "Then why the devil do you call yourself homosexual?" And then he explains that a doctor said he was because he had had dreams where something homosexual happened. This simply means that the man in certain respects is not mature, and his immaturity may express itself in different ways—that he is not up to women, or not up to life, or not up to spiritual things. That must be the case here: that he is definitely immature in certain respects is expressed in the dream by his being brought back to his boyhood. Now in regard to what is he immature? Where is he unconscious?

Mrs. Deady: He can't manage his sexuality.

Dr. Jung: But you must keep in mind that he is a man who has allowed himself all sorts of things with fast women and who is not at all unaware of sexuality. His sex is wrong but not concretely. Now what is the trouble with him?

Dr. Deady: He has the sex of a boy of sixteen without feeling.

Dr. Jung: That is the point, no feeling. His sex is perfectly normal but it is unrelated sex, a sort of auto-eroticism, a kind of masturbation. There is no relation to the object, and that is probably the reason for the frigidity of his wife, and the reason of his other adventures. Eros is undeveloped, not his sexuality. That is by no means undeveloped, but his relationship to sexuality is wrong. In the last dream he was going to set his machine in motion, and the question came up whether the parts of the machine were properly related to the central part. All these functions, particularly his sexuality, have to be worked into the total mechanism. If unrelated, he naturally cannot function as a total personality. His sexuality must come into complete consideration, and he must have feelings

[12] Above, 11 Dec. 1929, p. 431.

about it. In other words, the Eros principle must be recognized. The reason why the anima appears is that she *is* Eros. And when he has the old point of view, singing the old song, Eros is repressed forever and the very devil. Therefore she comes up in church and disturbs the church hymn. His immaturity is expressed by the fact that he is back in his childhood and also by his symbolic homosexuality. If a man's anima is masculine, he is absolutely possessed—obsessed—by her, and he cannot establish a relationship with her until she is feminine. To say he is effeminate means the same thing—that she has power over him. The fact that the dream expresses is: you are effeminate, you are possessed by your anima.

VII. THE SPIRIT

THE PHENOMENOLOGY OF THE SPIRIT IN FAIRYTALES

The wise old man, subject of the excerpts that follow, is one of the easiest of all archetypes to recognize. In stories, he comes frequently to the aid of the *puer aeternus,* who derives support and counsel from his apparent maturity. When wisdom is a male rather than a female figure, a preexisting sagacity in the unconscious is indicated, rather than the archetypal wisdom that can only be won through bitter experience. Divinatory systems tap this faculty of omniscience in the psyche, which is an attribute of the archetypal Self. In every dream, this "wise" aspect of the self can be found, making its point about every life experience, assigning a meaning to it. This inner guide can be seductive. There is a tendency for the individual who comes in touch with this masculine source of wisdom to become isolated, identified, and inflated with him. Often this inflation leads to foolish and irresponsible acts. Jung's essay on Mercurius, some of which follows these excerpts, dissolves any simple notion of the unconscious as wise father by emphasizing the essential ambivalence of all psychic spirituality.

---

401 The frequency with which the spirit-type appears as an old man is about the same in fairytales as in dreams.[12] The old man always appears when the hero is in a hopeless and desperate situation from which only profound reflection or a lucky idea —in other words, a spiritual function or an endopsychic autom-

12 I am indebted to Mrs. H. von Roques and Dr. Marie-Louise von Franz for the fairytale material used here.

atism of some kind—can extricate him. But since, for internal and external reasons, the hero cannot accomplish this himself, the knowledge needed to compensate the deficiency comes in the form of a personified thought, i.e., in the shape of this sagacious and helpful old man. An Estonian fairytale,[13] for instance, tells how an ill-treated little orphan boy who had let a cow escape was afraid to return home again for fear of more punishment. So he ran away, chancing to luck. He naturally got himself into a hopeless situation, with no visible way out. Exhausted, he fell into a deep sleep. When he awoke, "it seemed to him that he had something liquid in his mouth, and he saw a little old man with a long grey beard standing before him, who was in the act of replacing the stopper in his little milk-flask. 'Give me some more to drink,' begged the boy. 'You have had enough for today,' replied the old man. 'If my path had not chanced to lead me to you, that would assuredly have been your last sleep, for when I found you, you were half dead.' Then the old man asked the boy who he was and where he wanted to go. The boy recounted everything he could remember happening to him up to the beating he had received the previous evening. 'My dear child,' said the old man, 'you are no better and no worse off than many others whose dear protectors and comforters rest in their coffins under the earth. You can no longer turn back. Now that you have run away, you must seek a new fortune in the world. As I have neither house nor home, nor wife nor child, I cannot take further care of you, but I will give you some good advice for nothing.' "

402 So far the old man has been expressing no more than what the boy, the hero of the tale, could have thought out for himself. Having given way to the stress of emotion and simply run off like that into the blue, he would at least have had to reflect that he needed food. It would also have been necessary, at such a moment, to consider his position. The whole story of his life up to the recent past would then have passed before his mind, as is usual in such cases. An anamnesis of this kind is a purpose-

13 *Finnische und estnische Volksmärchen,* No. 68, p. 208 ["How an Orphan Boy Unexpectedly Found His Luck"]. [All German collections of tales here cited are listed under "Folktales" in the bibliography, q.v. English titles of tales are given in brackets, though no attempt has been made to locate published translations. —EDITORS.]

ful process whose aim is to gather the assets of the whole personality together at the critical moment, when all one's spiritual and physical forces are challenged, and with this united strength to fling open the door of the future. No one can help the boy to do this; he has to rely entirely on himself. There is no going back. This realization will give the necessary resolution to his actions. By forcing him to face the issue, the old man saves him the trouble of making up his mind. Indeed the old man is himself this purposeful reflection and concentration of moral and physical forces that comes about spontaneously in the psychic space outside consciousness when conscious thought is not yet—or is no longer—possible. The concentration and tension of psychic forces have something about them that always looks like magic: they develop an unexpected power of endurance which is often superior to the conscious effort of will. One can observe this experimentally in the artificial concentration induced by hypnosis: in my demonstrations I used regularly to put an hysteric, of weak bodily build, into a deep hypnotic sleep and then get her to lie with the back of her head on one chair and her heels resting on another, stiff as a board, and leave her there for about a minute. Her pulse would gradually go up to 90. A husky young athlete among the students tried in vain to imitate this feat with a conscious effort of will. He collapsed in the middle with his pulse racing at 120.

403 When the clever old man had brought the boy to this point he could begin his good advice, i.e., the situation no longer looked hopeless. He advised him to continue his wanderings, always to the eastward, where after seven years he would reach the great mountain that betokened his good fortune. The bigness and tallness of the mountain are allusions to his adult personality.[14] Concentration of his powers brings assurance and is therefore the best guarantee of success.[15] From now on he will

14 The mountain stands for the goal of the pilgrimage and ascent, hence it often has the psychological meaning of the self. The *I Ching* describes the goal thus: "The king introduces him / To the Western Mountain" (Wilhelm/Baynes trans., 1967, p. 74—Hexagram 17, *Sui,* "Following"). Cf. Honorius of Autun (*Expositio in Cantica canticorum,* col. 389): "The mountains are prophets." Richard of St. Victor says: "Vis videre Christum transfiguratum? Ascende in montem istum, disce cognoscere te ipsum" (Do you wish to see the transfigured Christ? Ascend that mountain and learn to know yourself). (*Benjamin minor,* cols. 53–56.)

15 In this respect we would call attention to the phenomenology of yoga.

lack for nothing. "Take my scrip and my flask," says the old man, "and each day you will find in them all the food and drink you need." At the same time he gave him a burdock leaf that could change into a boat whenever the boy had to cross water.

404 Often the old man in fairytales asks questions like who? why? whence? and whither?[16] for the purpose of inducing self-reflection and mobilizing the moral forces, and more often still he gives the necessary magical talisman,[17] the unexpected and improbable power to succeed, which is one of the peculiarities of the unified personality in good or bad alike. But the intervention of the old man—the spontaneous objectivation of the archetype—would seem to be equally indispensable, since the conscious will by itself is hardly ever capable of uniting the personality to the point where it acquires this extraordinary power to succeed. For that, not only in fairytales but in life generally, the objective intervention of the archetype is needed, which checks the purely affective reactions with a chain of inner confrontations and realizations. These cause the who? where? how? why? to emerge clearly and in this wise bring knowledge of the immediate situation as well as of the goal. The resultant enlightenment and untying of the fatal tangle often has something positively magical about it—an experience not unknown to the psychotherapist.

405 The tendency of the old man to set one thinking also takes the form of urging people to "sleep on it." Thus he says to the girl who is searching for her lost brothers: "Lie down:

16 There are numerous examples of this: *Spanische und Portugiesische Volksmärchen,* pp. 158, 199 ["The White Parrot" and "Queen Rose, or Little Tom"]; *Russische Volksmärchen,* p. 149 ["The Girl with No Hands"]; *Balkanmärchen,* p. 64 ["The Shepherd and the Three Samovilas (Nymphs)"]; *Märchen aus Iran,* pp. 150ff. ["The Secret of the Bath of Windburg"]; *Nordische Volksmärchen,* I, p. 231 ["The Werewolf"].

17 To the girl looking for her brothers he gives a ball of thread that rolls towards them (*Finnische und Estnische Volksmärchen,* p. 260 ["The Contending Brothers"]). The prince who is searching for the kingdom of heaven is given a boat that goes by itself (*Deutsche Märchen seit Grimm,* pp. 381f. ["The Iron Boots"]). Other gifts are a flute that sets everybody dancing (*Balkanmärchen,* p. 173 ["The Twelve Crumbs"]), or the path-finding ball, the staff of invisibility (*Nordische Volksmärchen,* I, p. 97 ["The Princess with Twelve Pairs of Golden Shoes"]), miraculous dogs (ibid., p. 287 ["The Three Dogs"]), or a book of secret wisdom (*Chinesische Volksmärchen,* p. 258 ["Jang Liang"]).

morning is cleverer than evening." [18] He also sees through the gloomy situation of the hero who has got himself into trouble, or at least can give him such information as will help him on his journey. To this end he makes ready use of animals, particularly birds. To the prince who has gone in search of the kingdom of heaven the old hermit says: "I have lived here for three hundred years, but never yet has anybody asked me about the kingdom of heaven. I cannot tell you myself; but up there, on another floor of the house, live all kinds of birds, and they can surely tell you." [19] The old man knows what roads lead to the goal and points them out to the hero.[20] He warns of dangers to come and supplies the means of meeting them effectively. For instance, he tells the boy who has gone to fetch the silver water that the well is guarded by a lion who has the deceptive trick of sleeping with his eyes open and watching with his eyes shut;[21] or he counsels the youth who is riding to a magic fountain in order to fetch the healing draught for the king, only to draw the water at a trot because of the lurking witches who lasso everybody that comes to the fountain.[22] He charges the princess whose lover has been changed into a werewolf to make a fire and put a cauldron of tar over it. Then she must plunge her beloved white lily into the boiling tar, and when the werewolf comes, she must empty the cauldron over its head, which will release her lover from the spell.[23] Occasionally the old man is a very critical old man, as in the Caucasian tale of the youngest prince who wanted to build a flawless church for his father, so as to inherit the kingdom. This he does, and nobody can discover a single flaw, but then an old man comes along and says, "That's a fine church you've built, to be sure! What a pity the main wall is a bit crooked!" The prince has the church pulled down again

18 *Finnische und estnische Volksmärchen,* loc. cit.

19 *Deutsche Märchen seit Grimm,* p. 382 [op. cit.]. In one Balkan tale (*Balkanmärchen,* p. 65 ["The Shepherd and the Three Samovilas"]) the old man is called the "Czar of all the birds." Here the magpie knows all the answers. Cf. the mysterious "master of the dovecot" in Gustav Meyrink's novel *Der weisse Dominikaner.*

20 *Märchen aus Iran,* p. 152 [op. cit.].

21 *Spanische und Portugiesische Märchen,* p. 158 ["The White Parrot"].

22 Ibid., p. 199 ["Queen Rose, or Little Tom"].

23 *Nordische Volksmärchen,* Vol. I, p. 231f. ["The Werewolf"].

and builds a new one, but here too the old man discovers a flaw, and so on for the third time.[24]

406 The old man thus represents knowledge, reflection, insight, wisdom, cleverness, and intuition on the one hand, and on the other, moral qualities such as goodwill and readiness to help, which make his "spiritual" character sufficiently plain. Since the archetype is an autonomous content of the unconscious, the fairytale, which usually concretizes the archetypes, can cause the old man to appear in a dream in much the same way as happens in modern dreams. In a Balkan tale the old man appears to the hard-pressed hero in a dream and gives him good advice about accomplishing the impossible tasks that have been imposed upon him.[25] His relation to the unconscious is clearly expressed in one Russian fairytale, where he is called the "King of the Forest." As the peasant sat down wearily on a tree stump, a little old man crept out: "all wrinkled he was and a green beard hung down to his knees." "Who are you?" asked the peasant. "I am Och, King of the Forest," said the manikin. The peasant hired out his profligate son to him, "and the King of the Forest departed with the young man, and conducted him to that other world under the earth and brought him to a green hut. . . . In the hut everything was green: the walls were green and the benches, Och's wife was green and the children were green . . . and the little water-women who waited on him were as green as rue." Even the food was green. The King of the Forest is here a vegetation or tree numen who reigns in the woods and, through the nixies, also has connections with water, which clearly shows his relation to the unconscious since the latter is frequently expressed through wood and water symbols.

407 There is equally a connection with the unconscious when the old man appears as a dwarf. The fairytale about the princess who was searching for her lover says: "Night came and the darkness, and still the princess sat in the same place and wept. As she sat there lost in thought, she heard a voice greeting her: 'Good evening, pretty maid! Why are you sitting here so lonely and sad?' She sprang up hastily and felt very confused, and that was no wonder. But when she looked round there was only a tiny little old man standing before her, who nodded his head at her

24 *Kaukasische Märchen,* pp. 35f. ["The False and the True Nightingale"].
25 *Balkanmärchen,* p. 217 ["The Lubi (She-Devil) and the Fair of the Earth"].

and looked so kind and simple." In a Swiss fairytale, the peasant's son who wants to bring the king's daughter a basket of apples encounters "es chlis isigs Männdli, das frogt-ne, was er do i dem Chratte häig?" (a little iron man who asked what he had there in the basket). In another passage the "Männdli" has "es isigs Chlaidli a" (iron clothes on). By "isig" presumably "eisern" (iron) is meant, which is more probable than "eisig" (icy). In the latter case it would have to be "es Chlaidli vo Is" (clothes of ice).[26] There are indeed little ice men, and little metal men too; in fact, in a modern dream I have even come across a little black iron man who appeared at a critical juncture, like the one in this fairytale of the country bumpkin who wanted to marry the princess.

408 In a modern series of visions in which the figure of the wise old man occurred several times, he was on one occasion of normal size and appeared at the very bottom of a crater surrounded by high rocky walls; on another occasion he was a tiny figure on the top of a mountain, inside a low, stony enclosure. We find the same motif in Goethe's tale of the dwarf princess who lived in a casket.[27] In this connection we might also mention the Anthroparion, the little leaden man of the Zosimos vision,[28] as well as the metallic men who dwell in the mines, the crafty dactyls of antiquity, the homunculi of the alchemists, and the gnomic throng of hobgoblins, brownies, gremlins, etc. How "real" such conceptions are became clear to me on the occasion of a serious mountaineering accident: after the catastrophe two of the climbers had the collective vision, in broad daylight, of a little hooded man who scrambled out of an inaccessible crevasse in the ice face and passed across the glacier, creating a regular panic in the two beholders. I have often encountered motifs which made me think that the unconscious must be the world of the infinitesimally small. Such an idea could be derived rationalistically from the obscure feeling that in all these visions we are dealing with something endopsychic, the inference being that a thing must be exceedingly small in order to fit

26 This occurs in the tale of the griffin, No. 84 in the volume of children's fairytales collected by the brothers Grimm (1912), II, pp. 84ff. The text swarms with phonetic mistakes. [The English text (trans. by Margaret Hunt, rev. by James Stern, no. 165) has "hoary."—TRANS.]

27 Goethe, "Die neue Melusine."

28 Cf. "The Visions of Zosimos," par. 87 (III, i, 2–3).

inside the head. I am no friend of any such "rational" conjectures, though I would not say that they are all beside the mark. It seems to me more probable that this liking for diminutives on the one hand and for superlatives—giants, etc.—on the other is connected with the queer uncertainty of spatial and temporal relations in the unconscious.[29] Man's sense of proportion, his rational conception of big and small, is distinctly anthropomorphic, and it loses its validity not only in the realm of physical phenomena but also in those parts of the collective unconscious beyond the range of the specifically human. The atman is "smaller than small and bigger than big," he is "the size of a thumb" yet he "encompasses the earth on every side and rules over the ten-finger space." And of the Cabiri Goethe says: "little in length / mighty in strength." In the same way, the archetype of the wise old man is quite tiny, almost imperceptible, and yet it possesses a fateful potency, as anyone can see when he gets down to fundamentals. The archetypes have this peculiarity in common with the atomic world, which is demonstrating before our eyes that the more deeply the investigator penetrates into the universe of microphysics the more devastating are the explosive forces he finds enchained there. That the greatest effects come from the smallest causes has become patently clear not only in physics but in the field of psychological research as well. How often in the critical moments of life everything hangs on what appears to be a mere nothing!

409 In certain primitive fairytales, the illuminating quality of our archetype is expressed by the fact that the old man is identified with the sun. He brings a firebrand with him which he uses for roasting a pumpkin. After he has eaten, he takes the fire away again, which causes mankind to steal it from him.[30] In a North American Indian tale, the old man is a witch-doctor who owns the fire.[31] Spirit too has a fiery aspect, as we know from the language of the Old Testament and from the story of the Pentecostal miracle.

29 In one Siberian fairytale (*Märchen aus Sibirien,* no. 13 ["The Man Turned to Stone"]) the old man is a white shape towering up to heaven.

30 *Indianermärchen aus Südamerika,* p. 285 ["The End of the World and the Theft of Fire"—Bolivian].

31 *Indianermärchen aus Nordamerika,* p. 74 [Tales of Manabos: "The Theft of Fire"].

THE SPIRIT MERCURIUS

Part I

1. THE SPIRIT IN THE BOTTLE

39 In my contribution[1] to the symposium on Hermes I will try to show that this many-hued and wily god did not by any means die with the decline of the classical era, but on the contrary has gone on living in strange guises through the centuries, even into recent times, and has kept the mind of man busy with his deceptive arts and healing gifts. Children are still told Grimm's fairytale of "The Spirit in the Bottle," which is ever-living like all fairytales, and moreover contains the quintessence and deepest meaning of the Hermetic mystery as it has come down to us today:

Once upon a time there was a poor woodcutter. He had an only son, whom he wished to send to a high school. However, since he could give him only a little money to take with him, it was used up long before the time for the examinations. So the son went home and helped his father with the work in the forest. Once, during the midday rest, he roamed the woods and came to an immense old oak. There he heard a voice calling from the ground, "Let me out, let me out!" He dug down among the roots of the tree and found a well-sealed glass bottle from which, clearly, the voice had come. He opened it and instantly a spirit rushed out and soon became half as high as the tree. The spirit cried in an awful voice: "I have had my punishment and I will be revenged! I am the great and mighty spirit Mercurius, and now you shall have your reward. Whoso releases me, him I must strangle." This made the boy uneasy and, quickly thinking up a trick, he said, "First, I must be sure that you are the same spirit that was shut up in that little bottle." To prove this, the spirit crept back into the bottle. Then the boy made haste to seal it and the spirit was caught again. But now the spirit promised to reward him richly if the boy would let

[1] I give only a general survey of the Mercurius concept in alchemy and by no means an exhaustive exposition of it. The illustrative material cited should therefore be taken only as examples and makes no claim to completeness. [For the "symposium on Hermes" see the editorial note on p. 191.—EDITORS.]

him out. So he let him out and received as a reward a small piece of rag. Quoth the spirit: "If you spread one end of this over a wound it will heal, and if you rub steel or iron with the other end it will turn into silver." Thereupon the boy rubbed his damaged axe with the rag, and the axe turned to silver and he was able to sell it for four hundred thaler. Thus father and son were freed from all worries. The young man could return to his studies, and later, thanks to his rag, he became a famous doctor.[2]

240 Now, what insight can we gain from this fairytale? As you know, we can treat fairytales as fantasy products, like dreams, conceiving them to be spontaneous statements of the unconscious about itself.

241 As at the beginning of many dreams something is said about the scene of the dream action, so the fairytale mentions the forest as the place of the magic happening. The forest, dark and impenetrable to the eye, like deep water and the sea, is the container of the unknown and the mysterious. It is an appropriate synonym for the unconscious. Among the many trees—the living elements that make up the forest—one tree is especially conspicuous for its great size. Trees, like fishes in the water, represent the living contents of the unconscious. Among these contents one of special significance is characterized as an "oak." Trees have individuality. A tree, therefore, is often a symbol of personality.[3] Ludwig II of Bavaria is said to have honoured certain particularly impressive trees in his park by having them saluted. The mighty old oak is proverbially the king of the forest. Hence it represents a central figure among the contents of the unconscious, possessing personality in the most marked degree. It is the prototype of the *self*, a symbol of the source and goal of the individuation process. The oak stands for the still unconscious core of the personality, the plant symbolism indicating a state of deep unconsciousness. From this it may be concluded that the hero of the fairytale is profoundly unconscious of himself. He is one of the "sleepers," the "blind" or "blindfolded," whom we

2 [Author's paraphrase. Cf. "The Spirit in the Bottle," *Grimm's Fairy Tales* (trans. Hunt, rev. Stern), pp. 458–62.—EDITORS.]

3 Concerning personification of trees, see Frazer, *The Magic Art,* II, ch. 9. Trees are also the dwelling places of spirits of the dead or are identical with the life of the newborn child (ibid., I, p. 184).

encounter in the illustrations of certain alchemical treatises.[4] They are the unawakened who are still unconscious of themselves, who have not yet integrated their future, more extensive personality, their "wholeness," or, in the language of the mystics, the ones who are not yet "enlightened." For our hero, therefore, the tree conceals a great secret.[5]

242 The secret is hidden not in the top but in the roots of the tree;[6] and since it is, or has, a personality it also possesses the most striking marks of personality—voice, speech, and conscious purpose, and it demands to be set free by the hero. It is caught and imprisoned against its will, down there in the earth among the roots of the tree. The roots extend into the inorganic realm, into the mineral kingdom. In psychological terms, this would mean that the self has its roots in the body, indeed in the body's chemical elements. Whatever this remarkable statement of the fairytale may mean in itself, it is in no way stranger than the miracle of the living plant rooted in the inanimate earth. The alchemists described their four elements as *radices,* corresponding to the Empedoclean *rhizomata,* and in them they saw the constituents of the most significant and central symbol of alchemy, the *lapis philosophorum,* which represents the goal of the individuation process.

243 The secret hidden in the roots is a spirit sealed inside a bottle. Naturally it was not hidden away among the roots to start with, but was first confined in a bottle, which was then hidden. Presumably a magician, that is, an alchemist, caught and imprisoned it. As we shall see later, this spirit is something like the numen of the tree, its *spiritus vegetativus,* which is one

4 Cf. the title-page of *Mutus liber,* showing an angel waking the sleeper with a trumpet ("The Psychology of the Transference," Fig. 11). Also the illustration in Michelspacher's *Cabala, speculum artis et naturae* (*Psychology and Alchemy,* Fig. 93). In the foreground, before a mountain upon which is a temple of the initiates, stands a blindfolded man, while further back another man runs after a fox which is disappearing into a hole in the mountain. The "helpful animal" shows the way to the temple. The fox or hare is itself the "evasive" Mercurius as guide (ὁδηγός).

5 For additional material on the tree symbol, see infra, "The Philosophical Tree," Part II.

6 This motif was used in the same sense by the Gnostics. Cf. Hippolytus, *Elenchos,* V, 9, 15, where the many-named and thousand-eyed "Word of God" is "hidden in the root of All."

definition of Mercurius. As the life principle of the tree, it is a sort of spiritual quintessence abstracted from it, and could also be described as the *principium individuationis.* The tree would then be the outward and visible sign of the realization of the self. The alchemists appear to have held a similar view. Thus the "Aurelia occulta" says: "The philosophers have sought most eagerly for the centre of the tree which stands in the midst of the earthly paradise." [7] According to the same source, Christ himself is this tree.[8] The tree comparison occurs as early as Eulogius of Alexandria (*c.* A.D. 600), who says: "Behold in the Father the root, in the Son the branch, and in the Spirit the fruit: for the substance [*οὐσία*] in the three is one." [9] Mercurius, too, is *trinus et unus.*

244 So if we translate it into psychological language, the fairytale tells us that the mercurial essence, the *principium individuationis,* would have developed freely under natural conditions, but was robbed of its freedom by deliberate intervention from outside, and was artfully confined and banished like an evil spirit. (Only evil spirits have to be confined, and the wickedness of this spirit was shown by its murderous intent.) Supposing the fairytale is right and the spirit was really as wicked as it relates, we would have to conclude that the Master who imprisoned the *principium individuationis* had a good end in view. But who is this well-intentioned Master who has the power to banish the principle of man's individuation? Such power is given only to a ruler of souls in the spiritual realm. The idea that the principle of individuation is the source of all evil is found in Schopenhauer and still more in Buddhism. In Christianity, too, human nature is tainted with original sin and is redeemed from this stain by Christ's self-sacrifice. Man in his "natural" condition is neither good nor pure, and if he should develop in the natural way the result would be a product not essentially different from an animal. Sheer instinctuality and naïve unconsciousness untroubled by a sense of guilt would prevail if the Master had not interrupted the free development of the natural being by introducing a distinction between good and evil and outlawing the evil. Since without guilt there is no moral consciousness and

7 *Theatrum chemicum,* IV (1659), p. 500.

8 Ibid., p. 478: "(Christ), who is the tree of life both spiritual and bodily."

9 Krueger, *Das Dogma von der Dreieinigkeit und Gottmenschheit,* p. 207.

without awareness of differences no consciousness at all, we must concede that the strange intervention of the master of souls was absolutely necessary for the development of any kind of consciousness and in this sense was for the good. According to our religious beliefs, God himself is this Master—and the alchemist, in his small way, competes with the Creator in so far as he strives to do work analogous to the work of creation, and therefore he likens his microcosmic opus to the work of the world creator.[10]

245 In our fairytale the natural evil is banished to the "roots," that is, to the earth, in other words the body. This statement agrees with the historical fact that Christian thought in general has held the body in contempt, without bothering much about the finer doctrinal distinctions.[11] For, according to doctrine, neither the body nor nature in general is evil *per se:* as the work of God, or as the actual form in which he manifests himself, nature cannot be identical with evil. Correspondingly, the evil spirit in the fairytale is not simply banished to the earth and allowed to roam about at will, but is only hidden there in a safe and special container, so that he cannot call attention to himself anywhere except right under the oak. The bottle is an artificial human product and thus signifies the intellectual purposefulness and artificiality of the procedure, whose obvious aim is to isolate the spirit from the surrounding medium. As the *vas Hermeticum* of alchemy, it was "hermetically" sealed (i.e., sealed with the sign of Hermes);[12] it had to be made of glass, and had also to be as round as possible, since it was meant to represent the cosmos in which the earth was created.[13] Transparent glass is something like solidified water or air, both of which are synonyms for spirit. The alchemical retort is therefore equivalent to the *anima mundi,* which according to an old alchemical conception surrounds the cosmos. Caesarius of Heisterbach (thirteenth century) mentions a vision in which the soul appeared as a

10 In the "Dicta Belini" Mercurius even says: "Out of me is made the bread from which comes the whole world, and the world is formed from my mercy, and it fails not, because it is the gift of God" (Distinctio XXVIII, in *Theatr. chem.,* V, 1660, p. 87).

11 Cf. the doctrine of the *status iustitiae originalis* and *status naturae integrae.*

12 Cf. Rev. 20 : 3: "and set a seal upon him."

13 "The Fift is of Concord and of Love, / Betweene your Warkes and the Spheare above."—Norton's "Ordinall of Alchimy," *Theatrum chemicum Britannicum,* ch. 6, p. 92.

spherical glass vessel.[14] Likewise the "spiritual" or "ethereal" (*aethereus*) philosophers' stone is a precious *vitrum* (sometimes described as *malleabile*) which was often equated with the gold glass (*aurum vitreum*) of the heavenly Jerusalem (Rev. 21 : 21).

246 It is worth noting that the German fairytale calls the spirit confined in the bottle by the name of the pagan god, Mercurius, who was considered identical with the German national god, Wotan. The mention of Mercurius stamps the fairytale as an alchemical folk legend, closely related on the one hand to the allegorical tales used in teaching alchemy, and on the other to the well-known group of folktales that cluster round the motif of the "spellbound spirit." Our fairytale thus interprets the evil spirit as a pagan god, forced under the influence of Christianity to descend into the dark underworld and be morally disqualified. Hermes becomes the demon of the mysteries celebrated by all *tenebriones* (obscurantists), and Wotan the demon of forest and storm; Mercurius becomes the soul of the metals, the metallic man (*homunculus*), the dragon (*serpens mercurialis*), the roaring fiery lion, the night raven (*nycticorax*), and the black eagle—the last four being synonyms for the devil. In fact the spirit in the bottle behaves just as the devil does in many other fairytales: he bestows wealth by changing base metal into gold; and like the devil, he also gets tricked.

14 *Dialogus miraculorum,* trans. by Scott and Bland, I, pp. 42, 236.

2. THE CONNECTION BETWEEN SPIRIT AND TREE

247 Before continuing our discussion of the spirit Mercurius, I should like to point out a not unimportant fact. The place where he lies confined is not just any place but a very essential one—namely, under the oak, the king of the forest. In psychological terms, this means that the evil spirit is imprisoned in the roots of the self, as the secret hidden in the principle of individuation. He is not identical with the tree, nor with its roots, but has been put there by artificial means. The fairytale gives us no reason to think that the oak, which represents the self, has grown out of the spirit in the bottle; we may rather conjecture that the oak presented a suitable place for concealing a secret. A treasure, for instance, is preferably buried near some kind of landmark, or else such a mark is put up afterwards. The tree of paradise serves as a prototype for this and similar tales: it, too, is not identical with the voice of the serpent which issued from it.[1] However, it must not be forgotten that these mythical motifs have a significant connection with certain psychological phenomena observed among primitive peoples. In all such cases there is a notable analogy with primitive animism: certain trees are animated by souls—have the character of personality, we would say—and possess a voice that gives commands to human beings. Amaury Talbot[2] reports one such case from Nigeria, where a native soldier heard an *oji* tree calling to him, and tried desperately to break out of the barracks and hasten to the tree. Under cross-examination he alleged that all those who bore the name of the tree now and then heard its voice. Here the voice is undoubtedly identical with the tree. These psychic phenomena

1 Mercurius, in the form of Lilith or Melusina, appears in the tree in the Ripley *Scrowle*. To this context belongs also the hamadryad as an interpretation of the so-called "Aenigma Bononiense." Cf. *Mysterium Coniunctionis*, pp. 68f.

2 *In the Shadow of the Bush*, pp. 31f.

suggest that originally the tree and the daemon were one and the same, and that their separation is a secondary phenomenon corresponding to a higher level of culture and consciousness. The original phenomenon was nothing less than a nature deity, a *tremendum* pure and simple, which is morally neutral. But the secondary phenomenon implies an act of discrimination which splits man off from nature and thus testifies to the existence of a more highly differentiated consciousness. To this is added, as a tertiary phenomenon testifying to a still higher level, the moral qualification which declares the voice to be an evil spirit under a ban. It goes without saying that this third level is marked by a belief in a "higher" and "good" God who, though he has not finally disposed of his adversary, has nevertheless rendered him harmless for some time to come by imprisonment (Rev. 20 : 1–3).

248 Since at the present level of consciousness we cannot suppose that tree daemons exist, we are forced to assert that the primitive suffers from hallucinations, that he hears his own unconscious which has projected itself into the tree. If this theory is correct—and I do not know how we could formulate it otherwise today—then the second level of consciousness has effected a differentiation between the object "tree" and the unconscious content projected into it, thereby achieving an act of enlightenment. The third level rises still higher and attributes "evil" to the psychic content which has been separated from the object. Finally a fourth level, the level reached by our consciousness today, carries the enlightenment a stage further by denying the objective existence of the "spirit" and declaring that the primitive has heard nothing at all, but merely had an auditory hallucination. Consequently the whole phenomenon vanishes into thin air—with the great advantage that the evil spirit becomes obviously non-existent and sinks into ridiculous insignificance. A fifth level, however, which is bound to take a quintessential view of the matter, wonders about this conjuring trick that turns what began as a miracle into a senseless self-deception—only to come full circle. Like the boy who told his father a made-up story about sixty stags in the forest, it asks: "But what, then, was all the rustling in the woods?" The fifth level is of the opinion that something did happen after all: even though the psychic content was not the tree, nor a spirit in the tree, nor indeed any spirit at

all, it was nevertheless a phenomenon thrusting up from the unconscious, the existence of which cannot be denied if one is minded to grant the psyche any kind of reality. If one did not do that, one would have to extend God's *creatio ex nihilo*—which seems so obnoxious to the modern intellect—very much further to include steam engines, automobiles, radios, and every library on earth, all of which would presumably have arisen from unimaginably fortuitous conglomerations of atoms. The only thing that would have happened is that the Creator would have been renamed Conglomeratio.

49 The fifth level assumes that the unconscious exists and has a reality just like any other existent. However odious it may be, this means that the "spirit" is also a reality, and the "evil" spirit at that. What is even worse, the distinction between "good" and "evil" is suddenly no longer obsolete, but highly topical and necessary. The crucial point is that so long as the evil spirit cannot be proved to be a subjective psychic experience, then even trees and other suitable objects would have, once again, to be seriously considered as its lodging places.

3. THE PROBLEM OF FREEING MERCURIUS

250 We will not pursue the paradoxical reality of the unconscious any further now, but will return to the fairytale of the spirit in the bottle. As we have seen, the spirit Mercurius bears some resemblance to the "cheated devil." The analogy, however, is only a superficial one, since, unlike the gifts of the devil, the gold of Mercurius does not turn to horse droppings but remains good metal, and the magic rag does not turn to ashes by morning but retains its healing power. Nor is Mercurius tricked out of a soul that he wanted to steal. He is only tricked into his own better nature, one might say, in that the boy succeeds in bottling him up again in order to cure his bad mood and make him tractable. Mercurius becomes polite, gives the young fellow a useful ransom and is accordingly set free. We now hear about the student's good fortune and how he became a wonder-working doctor, but—strangely enough—nothing about the doings of the liberated spirit, though these might be of some interest in view of the web of meanings in which Mercurius, with his many-sided associations, entangles us. What happens when this pagan god, Hermes-Mercurius-Wotan, is let loose again? Being a god of magicians, a *spiritus vegetativus,* and a storm daemon, he will hardly have returned to captivity, and the fairytale gives us no reason to suppose that the episode of imprisonment has finally changed his nature to the pink of perfection. The bird of Hermes has escaped from the glass cage, and in consequence something has happened which the experienced alchemist wished at all costs to avoid. That is why he always sealed the stopper of his bottle with magic signs and set it for a very long time over the lowest fire, so that "he who is within may not fly out." For if he escapes, the whole laborious opus comes to nothing and has to be started all over again. Our lad was a Sunday's child and possibly one of the poor in spirit, on whom was bestowed a bit of the Kingdom of Heaven in the shape of the self-

renewing tincture, with reference to which it was said that the opus needed to be performed only once.[1] But if he had lost the magic rag he would certainly never have been able to produce it a second time, by himself. It looks as though some Master had succeeded in capturing the mercurial spirit and then hid him in a safe place, like a treasure—perhaps putting him aside for some future use. He may even have planned to tame the wild Mercurius to serve him as a willing "familiar," like Mephisto—such trains of thought are not strange to alchemy. Perhaps he was disagreeably surprised when he returned to the oak tree and found that his bird had flown. At any rate, it might have been better not to have left the fate of the bottle to chance.

51 Be that as it may, the behaviour of the boy—successfully as it worked out for him—must be described as alchemically incorrect. Apart from the fact that he may have infringed upon the legitimate claims of an unknown Master by setting Mercurius free, he was also totally unconscious of what might follow if this turbulent spirit were let loose upon the world. The golden age of alchemy was the sixteenth and the first half of the seventeenth century. At that time a storm bird did indeed escape from a spiritual vessel which the daemons must have felt was a prison. As I have said, the alchemists were all for not letting Mercurius escape. They wanted to keep him in the bottle in order to transform him: for they believed, like Petasios, that lead (another arcane substance) was "so bedevilled and shameless that all who wish to investigate it fall into madness through ignorance."[2] The same was said of the elusive Mercurius who evades every grasp—a real trickster who drove the alchemists to despair.[3]

1 "For he that shall end it once for certeyne, / Shall never have neede to begin againe."—Norton's "Ordinall of Alchimy," *Theatr. chem. Brit.*, ch. 4, p. 48.

2 Olympiodorus in Berthelot, *Alchimistes grecs,* II, iv, 43.

3 Cf. the entertaining "Dialogus Mercurii alchymistae et naturae," in *Theatr. chem.*, IV (1659), pp. 449ff.

10. SUMMARY

284 The multiple aspects of Mercurius may be summarized as follows:

(1) Mercurius consists of all conceivable opposites. He is thus quite obviously a duality, but is named a unity in spite of the fact that his innumerable inner contradictions can dramatically fly apart into an equal number of disparate and apparently independent figures.

(2) He is both material and spiritual.

(3) He is the process by which the lower and material is transformed into the higher and spiritual, and vice versa.

(4) He is the devil, a redeeming psychopomp, an evasive trickster, and God's reflection in physical nature.

(5) He is also the reflection of a mystical experience of the artifex that coincides with the *opus alchymicum*.

(6) As such, he represents on the one hand the self and on the other the individuation process and, because of the limitless number of his names, also the collective unconscious.[1]

* * *

285 Certainly goldmaking, as also chemical research in general, was of great concern to alchemy. But a still greater, more impassioned concern appears to have been—one cannot very well say the "investigation"—but rather the *experience* of the unconscious. That this side of alchemy—the μυστικά—was for so long misunderstood is due solely to the fact that nothing was known of psychology, let alone of the suprapersonal, collective unconscious. So long as one knows nothing of psychic actuality, it will be projected, if it appears at all. Thus the first knowledge of psychic law and order was found in the stars, and was later extended by projections into unknown matter. These two realms of experience branched off into sciences: astrology became astron-

1 Hence the designation of Mercurius as *mare nostrum*.

omy, and alchemy chemistry. On the other hand, the peculiar connection between character and the astronomical determination of time has only very recently begun to turn into something approaching an empirical science. The really important psychic facts can neither be measured, weighed, nor seen in a test tube or under a microscope. They are therefore supposedly indeterminable, in other words they must be left to people who have an inner sense for them, just as colours must be shown to the seeing and not to the blind.

86 The store of projections found in alchemy is, if possible, even less known, and there is a further drawback which makes closer investigation extremely difficult. For, unlike the astrological constituents of character which, if negative, are at most unpleasant for the individual, though amusing to his neighbour, the alchemical projections represent collective contents that stand in painful contrast—or rather, in compensatory relation—to our highest rational convictions and values. They give the strange answers of the natural psyche to the ultimate questions which reason has left untouched. Contrary to all progress and belief in a future that will deliver us from the sorrowful present, they point back to something primeval, to the apparently hopelessly static, eternal sway of matter that makes our fondly believed-in world look like a phantasmagoria of shifting scenes. They show us, as the redemptive goal of our active, desirous life, a symbol of the inorganic—the stone—something that does not live but merely exists or "becomes," the passive subject of a limitless and unfathomable play of opposites. "Soul," that bodiless abstraction of the rational intellect, and "spirit," that two-dimensional metaphor of dry-as-dust philosophical dialectic, appear in alchemical projection in almost physical, plastic form, like tangible breath-bodies, and refuse to function as component parts of our rational consciousness. The hope for a psychology without the soul is brought to nothing, and the illusion that the unconscious has only just been discovered vanishes: in a somewhat peculiar form, admittedly, it has been known for close on two thousand years. Let us, however, not delude ourselves: no more than we can separate the constituents of character from the astronomical determinants of time are we able to separate that unruly and evasive Mercurius from the autonomy of matter. Something of the projection-carrier always clings to the projec-

tion, and even if we succeed to some degree in integrating into our consciousness the part we recognize as psychic, we shall integrate along with it something of the cosmos and its materiality; or rather, since the cosmos is infinitely greater than we are, we shall have been assimilated by the inorganic. "Transform yourselves into living philosophical stones!" cries an alchemist, but he did not know how infinitely slowly the stone "becomes." Anyone who gives serious thought to the "natural light" that emanates from the projections of alchemy will certainly agree with the Master who spoke of the "wearisomeness of the interminable meditation" demanded by the work. In these projections we encounter the phenomenology of an "objective" spirit, a true matrix of psychic experience, the most appropriate symbol for which is matter. Nowhere and never has man controlled matter without closely observing its behaviour and paying heed to its laws, and only to the extent that he did so could he control it. The same is true of that objective spirit which today we call the unconscious: it is refractory like matter, mysterious and elusive, and obeys laws which are so non-human or suprahuman that they seem to us like a *crimen laesae majestatis humanae*. If a man puts his hand to the opus, he repeats, as the alchemists say, God's work of creation. The struggle with the unformed, with the chaos of Tiamat, is in truth a primordial experience.

287 Since the psyche, when directly experienced, confronts us in the "living" substance it has animated and appears to be one with it, Mercurius is called *argentum vivum*. Conscious discrimination, or consciousness itself, effects that world-shattering intervention which separates body from soul and divides the spirit Mercurius from the *hydrargyrum,* as if drawing off the spirit into the bottle, to speak in terms of our fairytale. But since body and soul, in spite of the artificial separation, are united in the mystery of life, the mercurial spirit, though imprisoned in the bottle, is yet found in the roots of the tree, as its quintessence and living numen. In the language of the Upanishads, he is the personal atman of the tree. Isolated in the bottle, he corresponds to the ego and the principle of individuation, which in the Indian view leads to the illusion of individual existence. Freed from his prison, Mercurius assumes the character of the suprapersonal atman. He becomes the *one* animating principle of all

created things, the *hiranyagarbha* (golden germ),[2] the supra-personal self, represented by the *filius macrocosmi,* the *one* stone of the wise. "Rosinus ad Sarratantam" cites a saying of "Malus Philosophus" [3] which attempts to formulate the psychological relation of the lapis to consciousness: "This stone is below thee, as to obedience; above thee, as to dominion; therefore from thee, as to knowledge; about thee, as to equals." [4] Applied to the self, this would mean: "The self is subordinate to you, yet on the other hand rules you. It is dependent on your own efforts and your knowledge, but transcends you and embraces all those who are of like mind." This refers to the collective nature of the self, since the self epitomizes the wholeness of the personality. By definition, wholeness includes the collective unconscious, which as experience seems to show is everywhere identical.

288 The encounter of the poor student with the spirit in the bottle portrays the spiritual adventure of a blind and unawakened human being. The same motif underlies the tale of the swineherd who climbed the world-tree,[5] and also forms the *leitmotiv* of alchemy. For what it signifies is the individuation process as it prepares itself in the unconscious and gradually enters consciousness. The commonest alchemical symbol for this is the tree, the *arbor philosophica,* which derives from the paradisal tree of knowledge. Here, as in our fairytale, a daemonic serpent, an evil spirit, prods and persuades to knowledge. In view of the Biblical precedent, it is not surprising that the spirit Mercurius has, to say the least, a great many connections with the dark side. One of his aspects is the female serpent-daemon, Lilith or Melusina, who lives in the philosophical tree. At the same time, he not only partakes of the Holy Spirit but, according to alchemy, is actually identical with it. We have no choice but to accept this shocking paradox after all we have learnt about the ambivalence of the spirit archetype. Our ambiguous Mercurius simply con-

2 Cf. Maitrayana-Brāhmana Upanishad, V, 8 (Sacred Books of the East, vol. 15, p. 311). He occurs as the *spiritus vegetativus* and collective soul in the Vedanta-Sutras (ibid., vol. 34, p. 173, and vol. 48, p. 578).

3 The treatise of Rosinus (Zosimos) is probably of Arabic origin. "Malus" might be a corruption of "Magus." The *Fihrist* of Ibn al-Nadim (A.D. 987) lists, along with writings of Rimas (Zosimos), two works by Magus one of which is entitled "The Book of the Wise Magus (?) on the Art" (Ruska, *Turba,* p. 272).

4 *Art. aurif.,* I, p. 310.

5 Cf. "The Phenomenology of the Spirit in Fairytales," pp. 231ff.

firms the rule. In any case, the paradox is no worse than the Creator's whimsical notion of enlivening his peaceful, innocent paradise with the presence of an obviously rather dangerous tree-snake, "accidentally" located on the very same tree as the forbidden apples.

289 It must be admitted that the fairytale and alchemy both show Mercurius in a predominantly unfavourable light, which is all the more striking because his positive aspect relates him not only to the Holy Spirit, but, in the form of the lapis, also to Christ and, as a triad, even to the Trinity. It looks as if it were precisely these relationships which led the alchemists to put particular stress on the dark and dubious quality of Mercurius, and this militates strongly against the assumption that by their lapis they really meant Christ. If this had been their meaning, why should they have renamed Christ the *lapis philosophorum?* The lapis is at most a counterpart or analogy of Christ in the physical world. Its symbolism, like that of Mercurius who constitutes its substance, points, psychologically speaking, to the self, as also does the symbolic figure of Christ.[6] In comparison with the purity and unity of the Christ symbol, Mercurius-lapis is ambiguous, dark, paradoxical, and thoroughly pagan. It therefore represents a part of the psyche which was certainly not moulded by Christianity and can on no account be expressed by the symbol "Christ." On the contrary, as we have seen, in many ways it points to the devil, who is known at times to disguise himself as an angel of light. The lapis formulates an aspect of the self which stands apart, bound to nature and at odds with the Christian spirit. It represents all those things which have been eliminated from the Christian model. But since they possess living reality, they cannot express themselves otherwise than in dark Hermetic symbols. The paradoxical nature of Mercurius reflects an important aspect of the self—the fact, namely, that it is essentially a *complexio oppositorum,* and indeed can be nothing else if it is to represent any kind of totality. Mercurius as *deus terrestris* has something of that *deus absconditus* (hidden god) which is an essential element of the psychological self, and the self cannot be distinguished from a God-image (except by incontestable and unprovable faith). Although I have stressed that the lapis is

6 [Cf. *Psychology and Alchemy,* ch. 5, "The Lapis-Christ Parallel," and *Aion,* ch. 5, "Christ, a Symbol of the Self."—EDITORS.]

a symbol embracing the opposites, it should not be thought of as a—so to speak—more complete symbol of the self. That would be decidedly incorrect, for actually it is an image whose form and content are largely determined by the unconscious. For this reason it is never found in the texts in finished and well-defined form; we have to combine all the scattered references to the various arcane substances, to Mercurius, to the transformation process and the end product. Although the lapis in one aspect or another is almost always the subject discussed, there is no real consensus of opinion in regard to its actual form. Almost every author has his own special allegories, synonyms, and metaphors. This makes it clear that the stone, though indeed an object of general experiment, was to an even greater extent an outcropping of the unconscious, which only sporadically crossed the borderline of subjectivity and gave rise to the vague general concept of the *lapis philosophorum.*

290 Opposed to this figure veiled in the twilight of more or less secret doctrines there stands, sharply outlined by dogma, the Son of Man and Salvator Mundi, Christ the Sol Novus, before whom the lesser stars pale. He is the affirmation of the daylight of consciousness in trinitarian form. So clear and definite is the Christ figure that whatever differs from him must appear not only inferior but perverse and vile. This is not the result of Christ's own teaching, but rather of what is taught about him, and especially of the crystal purity which dogma has bestowed upon his figure. As a result, a tension of opposites such as had never occurred before in the whole history of Christianity beginning with the Creation arose between Christ and the Antichrist, as Satan or the fallen angel. At the time of Job, Satan is still found among the sons of God. "Now there was a day," it says in Job 1 : 6, "when the sons of God came to present themselves before the Lord, and Satan came also among them." This picture of a celestial family reunion gives no hint of the New Testament "Get thee hence, Satan" (Matthew 4 : 10), nor yet of the dragon chained in the underworld for a thousand years (Rev. 20 : 2). It looks as if the superabundance of light on one side had produced an all the blacker darkness on the other. One can also see that the uncommonly great diffusion of black substance makes a sinless being almost impossible. A loving belief in such a being naturally involves cleansing one's own house of black filth. But the

filth must be dumped somewhere, and no matter where the dump lies it will plague even the best of all possible worlds with a bad smell.

291 The balance of the primordial world is upset. What I have said is not intended as a criticism, for I am deeply convinced not only of the relentless logic but of the expediency of this development. The emphatic differentiation of opposites is synonymous with sharper discrimination, and that is the *sine qua non* for any broadening or heightening of consciousness. The progressive differentiation of consciousness is the most important task of human biology and accordingly meets with the highest rewards—vastly increased chances of survival and the development of power technology. From the phylogenetic point of view, the effects of consciousness are as far-reaching as those of lung-breathing and warm-bloodedness. But clarification of consciousness necessarily entails an obscuration of those dimmer elements of the psyche which are less capable of becoming conscious, so that sooner or later a split occurs in the psychic system. Since it is not recognized as such it is projected, and appears in the form of a metaphysical split between the powers of light and the powers of darkness. The possibility of this projection is guaranteed by the presence of numerous archaic vestiges of the original daemons of light and darkness in any age. It seems likely, therefore, that the tension of opposites in Christianity is derived to a still unclarified degree from the dualism of ancient Persia, though the two are not identical.

292 There can be no doubt that the moral consequences of the Christian development represent a very considerable advance compared with the ancient Israelite religion of law. The Christianity of the synoptic gospels signifies little more than a coming to terms with issues inside Judaism, which may fairly be compared with the much earlier Buddhist reformation inside Hindu polytheism. Psychologically, both reformations resulted in a tremendous strengthening of consciousness. This is particularly evident in the maieutic method employed by Shakyamuni. But the sayings of Jesus manifest the same tendency, even if we discard as apocryphal the clearest formulation of this kind, the logion in Codex Bezae to Luke 6 : 4: "Man, if thou knowest what thou doest, thou art blessed. If thou knowest it not, thou art accursed and a transgressor of the law." At all events, the para-

ble of the unjust steward (Luke 16) has not found its way into the Apocrypha, where it would have fitted so well.

93 The rift in the metaphysical world has slowly risen into consciousness as a split in the human psyche, and the struggle between light and darkness moves to the battleground within. This shift of scene is not entirely self-evident, for which reason St. Ignatius Loyola considered it necessary to open our eyes to the conflict and impress it on our feelings by means of the most drastic spiritual exercises.[7] These efforts, for obvious reasons, had only a very limited range of application. And so, strangely enough, it was the medical men who, at the turn of the nineteenth century, were forced to intervene and get the obstructed process of conscious realization going again. Approaching the problem from a scientific angle, and innocent of any religious aim, Freud uncovered the abysmal darkness of human nature which a would-be enlightened optimism had striven to conceal. Since then psychotherapy, in one form or another, has persistently explored the extensive area of darkness which I have called the shadow. This attempt of modern science opened the eyes of only a few. However, the historic events of our time have painted a picture of man's psychic reality in indelible colours of blood and fire, and given him an object lesson which he will never be able to forget if—and this is the great question—he has today acquired enough consciousness to keep up with the furious pace of the devil within him. The only other hope is that he may learn to curb a creativity which is wasting itself in the exploitation of material power. Unfortunately, all attempts in that direction look like bloodless Utopias.

94 The figure of Christ the Logos has raised the *anima rationalis* in man to a level of importance which remains unobjectionable so long as it knows itself to be below and subject to the κύριος, the Lord of Spirits. Reason, however, has set itself free and proclaimed itself the ruler. It has sat enthroned in Notre Dame as Déesse Raison and heralded events that were to come. Our consciousness is no longer confined within a sacred temenos of otherworldly, eschatological images. It was helped to break free by a force that did not stream down from above—like the *lumen de lumine*—but came up with tremendous pressure from below and increased in strength as consciousness detached itself from the

[7] *The Spiritual Exercises* (trans. Rickaby), pp. 75ff.

darkness and climbed into the light. In accordance with the principle of compensation which runs through the whole of nature, every psychic development, whether individual or collective, possesses an optimum which, when exceeded, produces an enantiodromia, that is, turns into its opposite. Compensatory tendencies emanating from the unconscious may be noted even during the approach to the critical turning-point, though if consciousness persists in its course they are completely repressed. The stirrings in the darkness necessarily seem like a devilish betrayal of the ideal of spiritual development. Reason cannot help condemning as unreasonable everything that contradicts it or deviates from its laws, in spite of all evidence to the contrary. Morality can permit itself no capacity for change, for whatever it does not agree with is inevitably immoral and has therefore to be repressed. It is not difficult to imagine the multitude of energies which must flow off into the unconscious under such conscious domination.

295 Hesitantly, as in a dream, the introspective brooding of the centuries gradually put together the figure of Mercurius and created a symbol which, according to all the psychological rules, stands in a compensatory relation to Christ. It is not meant to take his place, nor is it identical with him, for then indeed it could replace him. It owes its existence to the law of compensation, and its object is to throw a bridge across the abyss separating the two psychological worlds by presenting a subtle compensatory counterpoint to the Christ image. The fact that in *Faust* the compensatory figure is not, as one might almost have expected from the author's classical predilections, the wily messenger of the gods, but, as the name "Mephistopheles" [8] shows, a *familiaris* risen from the cesspits of medieval magic, proves, if anything, the ingrained Christian character of Goethe's consciousness. To the Christian mentality, the dark antagonist is always the devil. As I have shown, Mercurius escapes this prejudice by only a hair's breadth. But he escapes it, thanks to the fact that he scorns to carry on opposition at all costs. The magic of his name enables him, in spite of his ambiguity and duplicity, to keep outside the split, for as an ancient pagan god he possesses a natural undividedness which is impervious to logical and moral contradictions. This gives him invulnerability and incorrupti-

[8] [From L. *mephitis,* a noxious exhalation from the earth.—TRANSLATOR.]

bility, the very qualities we so urgently need to heal the split in ourselves.

96 If one makes a synopsis of all the descriptions and alchemical pictures of Mercurius, they form a striking parallel to the symbols of the self derived from other sources. One can hardly escape the conclusion that Mercurius as the lapis is a symbolic expression for the psychological complex which I have defined as the self. Similarly, the Christ figure must be viewed as a self symbol, and for the same reasons. But this leads to an apparently insoluble contradiction, for it is not at first clear how the unconscious can shape two such different images from one and the same content, which moreover possesses the character of totality. Certainly the centuries have done their spiritual work upon these two figures, and one is inclined to assume that both have been in large measure anthropomorphized during the process of assimilation. For those who hold that both figures are inventions of the intellect, the contradiction is quickly resolved. It then merely reflects the subjective psychic situation: the two figures would stand for man and his shadow.

97 This very simple and obvious solution is, unfortunately, founded on premises that do not stand up to criticism. The figures of Christ and the devil are both based on archetypal patterns, and were never invented but rather *experienced*. Their existence preceded all cognition of them,[9] and the intellect had no hand in the matter, except to assimilate them and if possible give them a place in its philosophy. Only the most superficial intellectualism can overlook this fundamental fact. We are actually confronted with two different images of the self, which in all likelihood presented a duality even in their original form. This duality was not invented, but is an autonomous phenomenon.

98 Since we naturally think from the standpoint of consciousness, we inevitably come to the conclusion that the split between consciousness and the unconscious is the sole cause of this duality. But experience has demonstrated the existence of a preconscious psychic functioning and of corresponding autonomous factors, the archetypes. Once we can accept the fact that the voices and delusions of the insane and the phobias and obsessions of the neurotic are beyond rational control, and that the ego cannot voluntarily fabricate dreams but simply dreams what

[9] Evidence for this is the widespread motif of the two hostile brothers.

it has to, then we can also understand that the gods came first and theology later. Indeed, we must go a step further and assume that in the beginning there were two figures, one bright and one shadowy, and only afterwards did the light of consciousness detach itself from the night and the uncertain shimmer of its stars.

299 So if Christ and the dark nature-deity are autonomous images that can be directly experienced, we are obliged to reverse our rationalistic causal sequence, and instead of deriving these figures from our psychic conditions, must derive our psychic conditions from these figures. This is expecting a good deal of the modern intellect but does not alter the logic of our hypothesis. From this standpoint Christ appears as the archetype of consciousness and Mercurius as the archetype of the unconscious. As Cupid and Kyllenios, he tempts us out into the world of sense; he is the *benedicta viriditas* and the *multi flores* of early spring, a god of illusion and delusion of whom it is rightly said: "Invenitur in vena / Sanguine plena" (He is found in the vein swollen with blood). He is at the same time a Hermes Chthonios and an Eros, yet it is from him that there issues the "light surpassing all lights," the *lux moderna,* for the lapis is none other than the figure of light veiled in matter.[10] It is in this sense that St. Augustine quotes I Thessalonians 5 : 5, "Ye are all the children of light, and the children of the day: we are not of the night, nor of darkness," and distinguishes two forms of knowledge, a *cognitio vespertina* and a *cognitio matutina,* the first corresponding to the *scientia creaturae* and the second to the *scientia Creatoris.*[11] If we equate *cognitio* with consciousness, then Augustine's thought would suggest that the merely human and natural consciousness gradually darkens, as at nightfall. But just as evening gives birth to morning, so from the darkness arises a new light, the *stella matutina,* which is at once the evening and the morning star—Lucifer, the light-bringer.

300 Mercurius is by no means the Christian devil—the latter

10 Cf. the saying of Ostanes concerning the stone that has a spirit.

11 "For the knowledge of the creature, in comparison with the knowledge of the Creator, is but a twilight; and so it dawns and breaks into morning when the creature is drawn to the love and praise of the Creator. Nor is it ever darkened, save when the Creator is abandoned by the love of the creature."—*The City of God,* XI, vii.

could rather be said to be a "diabolization" of Lucifer or of Mercurius. Mercurius is an adumbration of the primordial light-bringer, who is never himself the light, but a φωσφόρος who brings the light of nature, the light of the moon and the stars which fades before the new morning light. Of this light St. Augustine says that it will never turn to darkness unless the Creator is abandoned by the love of his creatures. But this, too, belongs to the rhythm of day and night. As Hölderlin says in "Patmos";

> and shamefully
> A power wrests away the heart from us;
> For the Heavenly each demand sacrifice,
> But if it should be withheld,
> Never has that led to good.

301 When all visible lights are extinguished one finds, according to the words of the wise Yajñavalkya, the light of the self. "What then is the light of man? Self is his light. It is by the light of the self that a man rests, goes forth, does his work and returns." [12] Thus, with Augustine, the first day of creation begins with self-knowledge, *cognitio sui ipsius*,[13] by which is meant a knowledge not of the ego but of the self, that objective phenomenon of which the ego is the subject.[14] Then, following the order of the days of creation in Genesis, comes knowledge of the firmament, of the earth, the sea, the plants, the stars, the animals of the water and air, and finally, on the sixth day, knowledge of the land animals and of *ipsius hominis*, of man himself. The *cognitio matutina* is self-knowledge, but the *cognitio vespertina* is knowledge of man.[15] As Augustine describes it, the *cognitio*

12 Brihadāranyaka Upanishad, IV, 3, 6 (cf. Hume, *The Thirteen Principal Upanishads*, p. 133).

13 "And when it [the creature's knowledge] comes to the knowledge of itself, that is one day" (Et hoc cum facit in cognitione sui ipsius, dies unus est).—*The City of God*, XI, vii. This may be the source for the strange designation of the lapis as "filius unius diei." [Cf. *Mysterium Coniunctionis*, pp. 335, 504.]

14 "Since no knowledge is better than that by which man knows himself, let us examine our thoughts, words, and deeds. For what does it avail us if we are to investigate carefully and understand rightly the nature of all things, yet do not understand ourselves?"—*Liber de Spiritu et Anima*, LI (Migne, *P.L.*, vol. 40, cols. 816–17). This book is a very much later treatise falsely attributed to Augustine.

15 "Wherefore the knowledge of the creature, which is in itself evening knowledge, was in God morning knowledge; for the creature is more plainly seen in

matutina gradually grows old as it loses itself in the "ten thousand things" and finally comes to man, although one would expect this to have happened already with the onset of self-knowledge. But if this were true, Augustine's parable would have lost its meaning by contradicting itself. Such an obvious lapse cannot be ascribed to so gifted a man. His real meaning is that self-knowledge is the *scientia Creatoris,*[16] a morning light revealed after a night during which consciousness slumbered, wrapped in the darkness of the unconscious. But the knowledge arising with this first light finally and inevitably becomes the *scientia hominis,* the knowledge of man, who asks himself: "Who is it that knows and understands everything? Why, it is myself." That marks the coming of darkness,[17] out of which arises the seventh day, the day of rest: "But the rest of God signifies the rest of those who rest in God." [18] The Sabbath is therefore the day on which man returns to God and receives anew the light of the *cognitio matutina.* And this day has no evening.[19] From the symbological standpoint it may not be without significance that Augustine had in mind the pagan names of the days of the week. The growing darkness reaches its greatest intensity on the day of Venus (Friday), and changes into Lucifer on Sat-

God than it is seen in itself."—*Dialogus Quaestionum LXV,* Quaest. XXVI (Migne, *P.L.,* vol. 40, col. 741).

16 The *Liber de Spiritu et Anima* attributes very great importance to self-knowledge, as being an essential condition for union with God. "There are some who seek God through outward things, forsaking that which is in them, and in them is God. Let us therefore return to ourselves, that we may ascend to ourselves. . . . At first we ascend to ourselves from these outward and inferior things. Secondly, we ascend to the high heart. . . . In the third ascent we ascend to God" (chs. LI–LII; Migne, *P.L.,* vol. 40, col. 817). The "high heart" (*cor altum;* also "deep heart") is the mandala divided into four, the *imago Dei,* or self. The *Liber de Spiritu et Anima* is in the mainstream of Augustinian tradition. Augustine himself says (*De vera religione LXXII,* Migne, *P.L.,* vol. 34, col. 154): "Go not outside, return into yourself; truth dwells in the inner man. And if you find that you are by nature changeable, transcend yourself. But remember that when you transcend yourself, you must transcend yourself as a reasoning soul."

17 "Evening descends when the sun sets. Now the sun has set for man, that is to say, that light of justice which is the presence of God."—*Enarrationes in Ps. XXIX,* II, 16 (trans. Hobgin and Corrigan, I, p. 308). These words refer to Ps. 30 : 5 (A.V.): "Weeping may tarry for the night but joy cometh in the morning."

18 *The City of God,* XI, viii. Cf. also *Dialog. Quaest. LXV,* Quaest. XXVI.

19 *Confessions* (trans. Sheed), p. 289.

urn's day. Saturday heralds the light which appears in full strength on Sun-day. As I have shown, Mercurius is closely related not only to Venus but more especially to Saturn. As Mercurius he is *juvenis,* as Saturn *senex.*

02 It seems to me that Augustine apprehended a great truth, namely that every spiritual truth gradually turns into something material, becoming no more than a tool in the hand of man. In consequence, man can hardly avoid seeing himself as a knower, yes, even as a creator, with boundless possibilities at his command. The alchemist was basically this sort of person, but much less so than modern man. An alchemist could still pray: "Purge the horrible darknesses of our mind," but modern man is already so darkened that nothing beyond the light of his own intellect illuminates his world. "Occasus Christi, passio Christi." [20] That surely is why such strange things are happening to our much lauded civilization, more like a *Götterdämmerung* than any normal twilight.

03 Mercurius, that two-faced god, comes as the *lumen naturae,* the Servator and Salvator, only to those whose reason strives towards the highest light ever received by man, and who do not trust exclusively to the *cognitio vespertina.* For those who are unmindful of this light, the *lumen naturae* turns into a perilous *ignis fatuus,* and the psychopomp into a diabolical seducer. Lucifer, who could have brought light, becomes the father of lies whose voice in our time, supported by press and radio, revels in orgies of propaganda and leads untold millions to ruin.

20 *Enarrationes in Ps. CIII,* Sermo III, 21 (Migne, *P.L.,* vol. 37, col. 1374).

ASPECTS OF THE FEMININE

C. G. JUNG

TRANSLATED BY R.F.C. HULL

BOLLINGEN SERIES

PRINCETON UNIVERSITY PRESS

EDITORIAL NOTE

The present collection offers a range of articles and extracts from Jung's writings that convey his views on the feminine and on topics that are intrinsic or related: marriage, Eros, the mother, the maiden, and the anima/animus concept, which is a central feature of Jung's theory of personality structure. Jung did not compose a single formal statement on the psychology of women, perhaps because some of his woman colleagues—chiefly Toni Wolff, Esther Harding, and Emma Jung—were dealing separately and comprehensively with that subject.

These selections, given in chronological order, date from 1921, when Jung devoted an important section of *Psychological Types* to a discussion of the veneration of woman in poetry, to 1951, when he presented a mature discussion of the intertwined concepts of shadow, anima, and animus in a late work, *Aion*.

"Probably Jung's greatest contribution to female psychology is his concept of the animus, the contrasexual (male) archetypal component of the female psyche," Mary Ann Mattoon has recently written. "Jung tended to emphasize its negative aspects. . . . Too little has been written about the positive side of the animus. Jung mentioned its 'discriminative function,' which 'gives to woman's consciousness a capacity for reflection, deliberation, and self-knowledge,' " and its qualities of creativity, procreativity, assertiveness, and initiative. For an interpretation of approaches to the theme of the feminine by Jung and his followers, the reader is referred to Dr. Mattoon's book *Jungian Psychology in Perspective* (1981), pp. 84 ff.

W. M.

TABLE OF CONTENTS

I

THE WORSHIP OF WOMAN AND THE WORSHIP OF THE SOUL

THE LOVE PROBLEM OF A STUDENT

MARRIAGE AS A PSYCHOLOGICAL RELATIONSHIP

WOMAN IN EUROPE

ANIMA AND ANIMUS

THE WORSHIP OF WOMAN AND THE WORSHIP OF THE SOUL*

75 The Christian principle which unites the opposites is the *worship of God,* in Buddhism it is the *worship of the self* (self-development), while in Spitteler and Goethe it is the *worship of the soul* symbolized by the *worship of woman.* Implicit in this categorization is the modern individualistic principle on the one hand, and on the other a primitive poly-daemonism which assigns to every race, every tribe, every family, every individual its specific religious principle.

76 The medieval background of *Faust* has a quite special significance because there actually was a medieval element that presided over the birth of modern individualism. It began, it seems to me, with the worship of woman, which strengthened the man's soul very considerably as a psychological factor, since the worship of woman meant worship of the soul. This is nowhere more beautifully and perfectly expressed than in Dante's *Divine Comedy.*

77 Dante is the spiritual knight of his lady; for her sake he embarks on the adventure of the lower and upper worlds. In this heroic endeavour her image is exalted into the heavenly, mystical figure of the Mother of God—a figure that has detached itself from the object and become the personification of a purely psychological factor, or rather, of those unconscious contents whose personification I have termed the *anima.* Canto XXXIII of the *Paradiso* expresses this culminating point of Dante's psychic development in the prayer of St. Bernard:

*[Section 4 of "The Type Problem in Poetry: Carl Spitteler: Prometheus and Epimetheus"]

O Virgin Mother, daughter of thy Son,
Humbler and more exalted than all others,
Predestined object of the eternal will!
Thou gavest such nobility to man
That He who made mankind did not disdain
To make Himself a creature of His making.

Verses 22–27, 29–33, 37–39 also allude to this development:

This man, who from the nethermost abyss
Of all the universe, as far as here,
Has seen the spiritual existences,
Now asks thy grace, so thou wilt grant him strength
That he may with his eyes uplift himself
Still higher toward the ultimate salvation.
. . .
I . . . proffer to thee
All my prayers—and pray they may suffice—
That thou wilt scatter from him every cloud
Of his mortality, with thine own prayers,
So that the bliss supreme may be revealed.
. . .
May thy protection quell his human passions!
Lo, Beatrice and many a blessed soul
Entreat thee, with clasped hands, to grant my wish![124]

378 The very fact that Dante speaks here through the mouth of St. Bernard is an indication of the transformation and exaltation of his own being. The same transformation also happens to Faust, who ascends from Gretchen to Helen and from Helen to the Mother of God; his nature is altered by repeated figurative deaths (Boy Charioteer, homunculus, Euphorion), until finally he attains the highest goal as Doctor Marianus. In that form Faust utters his prayer to the Virgin Mother:

Pavilioned in the heaven's blue,
Queen on high of all the world,
For the holy sight I sue,
Of the mystery unfurled.
Sanction what in man may move
Feelings tender and austere,
And with glow of sacred love
Lifts him to thy presence near.

124 *The Divine Comedy* (trans. L. G. White), p. 187.

Souls unconquerable rise
If, sublime, thou will it;
Sinks that storm in peaceful wise
If thy pity still it.
Virgin, pure in heavenly sheen,
Mother, throned supernal,
Highest birth, our chosen Queen,
Godhead's peer eternal.

. . .

O contrite hearts, seek with your eyes
The visage of salvation;
Blissful in that gaze, arise,
Through glad regeneration.
Now may every pulse of good
Seek to serve before thy face,
Virgin, Queen of Motherhood,
Keep us, Goddess, in thy grace.[125]

9 We might also mention in this connection the symbolic attributes of the Virgin in the Litany of Loreto:

Mater amabilis	Lovable Mother
Mater admirabilis	Wonderful Mother
Mater boni consilii	Mother of good counsel
Speculum justitiae	Mirror of justice
Sedes sapientiae	Seat of wisdom
Causa nostrae laetitiae	Cause of our gladness
Vas spirituale	Vessel of the spirit
Vas honorabile	Vessel of honour
Vas insigne devotionis	Noble vessel of devotion
Rosa mystica	Mystical rose
Turris Davidica	Tower of David
Turris eburnea	Tower of ivory
Domus aurea	House of gold
Foederis arca	Ark of the covenant
Janua coeli	Gate of heaven
Stella matutina	Morning star[126]

0 These attributes reveal the functional significance of the Virgin Mother image: they show how the soul-image (anima) affects the conscious attitude. She appears as a vessel of devotion, a source of wisdom and renewal.

125 *Faust, Part Two* (trans. Wayne), pp. 284f., 288.

126 [From the *Rituale Romanum*, trans. here by A. S. B. Glover.]

381 We find this characteristic transition from the worship of woman to the worship of the soul in an early Christian document, the *Shepherd* of Hermas, who flourished about A.D. 140. This book, written in Greek, consists of a number of visions and revelations describing the consolidation of the new faith. The book, long regarded as canonical, was nevertheless rejected by the Muratori Canon. It begins as follows:

> The man who reared me sold me to a certain Rhoda in Rome. After many years, I made her acquaintance again and began to love her as a sister. One day I saw her bathing in the Tiber, and gave her my hand and helped her out of the water. When I saw her beauty I thought in my heart: "How happy I would be if I had a wife of such beauty and distinction." This was my only thought, and no other, no, not one.[127]

382 This experience was the starting-point for the visionary episode that followed. Hermas had apparently served Rhoda as a slave; then, as often happened, he obtained his freedom, and met her again later, when, probably as much from gratitude as from delight, a feeling of love stirred in his heart, though so far as he was aware it had merely the character of brotherly love. Hermas was a Christian, and moreover, as the text subsequently reveals, he was at that time already the father of a family, circumstances which would readily explain the repression of the erotic element. Yet the peculiar situation, doubtless provocative of many problems, was all the more likely to bring the erotic wish to consciousness. It is, in fact, expressed quite clearly in the thought that he would have liked Rhoda for a wife, though, as Hermas is at pains to emphasize, it is confined to this simple statement since anything more explicit and more direct instantly fell under a moral ban and was repressed. It is abundantly clear from what follows that this repressed libido wrought a powerful transformation in his unconscious, for it imbued the soul-image with life and brought about a spontaneous manifestation:[128]

127 [This and the following extracts were translated by an unknown hand (possibly by Baynes) from the German source used by the author. For an alternative version see *The Shepherd of Hermas* (trans. Kirsopp Lake), in *The Apostolic Fathers*, vol. 2.—TRANSLATOR.] Cf. ibid., p. 7.

128 Cf. ibid., pp. 7–9.

After a certain time, as I journeyed unto Cumae, praising God's creation in its immensity, beauty, and power, I grew heavy with sleep. And a spirit caught me up, and led me away through a pathless region where a man may not go. For it was a place full of crevices and torn by water-courses. I made my passage over the river and came upon even ground, where I threw myself upon my knees, and prayed to God, confessing my sins. While I thus prayed, the heavens opened and I beheld that lady for whom I yearned, who greeted me from heaven and said: "Hail to thee, Hermas!" While my eyes dwelt upon her, I spake, saying: "Mistress, what doest thou there?" And she answered: "I was taken up, in order to charge thee with thy sins before the Lord." I said unto her: "Dost thou now accuse me?" "No," said she, "yet hearken now unto the words I shall speak unto thee. For God, who dwelleth in heaven, and hath created the existing out of the non-existing, and hath magnified it and brought it to increase for the sake of His Holy Church, is wroth with thee, because thou has sinned against me." I answered and spake unto her: "How have I sinned against thee? When and where spake I ever an evil word unto thee? Have I not looked upon thee as a goddess? Have I not ever treated thee like a sister? Wherefore, O lady, dost thou falsely charge me with such evil and unclean things?" She smiled and said unto me: "The desire of sin arose in thy heart. Or is it not indeed a sin in thine eyes for a just man to cherish a sinful desire in his heart? Verily is it a sin," said she, "and a great one. For the just man striveth after what is just."

3 Solitary wanderings are, as we know, conducive to day-dreaming and reverie. Presumably Hermas, on his way to Cumae, was thinking of his mistress; while thus engaged, the repressed erotic fantasy gradually pulled his libido down into the unconscious. Sleep overcame him, as a result of this lowering of the intensity of consciousness, and he fell into a somnambulant or ecstatic state, which itself was nothing but a particularly intense fantasy that completely captivated his conscious mind. It is significant that what then came to him was not an erotic fantasy; instead he is transported as it were to another land, represented in fantasy as the crossing of a river and a journey through a pathless country. The unconscious appears to him as an upper world in which events take place and men move about exactly as in the real world. His mistress appears before him not in an erotic fantasy but in "divine" form, seem-

ing to him like a goddess in heaven. The repressed erotic impression has activated the latent primordial image of the goddess, i.e., the archetypal soul-image. The erotic impression has evidently become united in the collective unconscious with archaic residues which have preserved from time immemorial the imprint of vivid impressions of the nature of woman—woman as mother and woman as desirable maid. Such impressions have immense power, as they release forces, both in the child and in the adult man, which fully merit the attribute "divine" i.e., something irresistible and absolutely compelling. The recognition of these forces as daemonic powers can hardly be due to moral repression, but rather to a self-regulation of the psychic organism which seeks by this change of front to guard against loss of equilibrium. For if, in face of the overwhelming might of passion, which puts one human being wholly at the mercy of another, the psyche succeeds in building up a counterposition so that, at the height of passion, the boundlessly desired object is unveiled as an idol and man is forced to his knees before the divine image, then the psyche has delivered him from the curse of the object's spell. He is restored to himself again and, flung back on himself, finds himself once more between gods and men, following his own path and subject to his own laws. The awful fear that haunts the primitive, his terror of everything impressive, which he at once senses as magic, as though it were charged with magical power, protects him in a purposive way against that most dreaded of all possibilities, loss of soul, with its inevitable sequel of sickness and death.

384 Loss of soul amounts to a tearing loose of part of one's nature; it is the disappearance and emancipation of a complex, which thereupon becomes a tyrannical usurper of consciousness, oppressing the whole man. It throws him off course and drives him to actions whose blind one-sidedness inevitably leads to self-destruction. Primitives are notoriously subject to such phenomena as running amok, going berserk, possession, and the like. The recognition of the daemonic character of passion is an effective safeguard, for it at once deprives the object of its strongest spell, relegating its source to the world of demons, i.e., to the unconscious, whence the force of passion actually springs. Exorcistic rites, whose aim is to bring back

the soul and release it from enchantment, are similarly effective in causing the libido to flow back into the unconscious.

5 This mechanism obviously worked in the case of Hermas. The transformation of Rhoda into a divine mistress deprived the actual object of her provocative and destructive power and brought Hermas under the law of his own soul and its collective determinants. Thanks to his abilities and connections, Hermas no doubt had a considerable share in the spiritual movements of his age. At that very time his brother Pius occupied the episcopal see at Rome. Hermas, therefore, was probably qualified to collaborate in the great task of his time to a greater degree than he, as a former slave, may have consciously realized. No able mind could for long have withstood the contemporary task of spreading Christianity, unless of course the barriers and peculiarities of race assigned him a different function in the great process of spiritual transformation. Just as the external conditions of life force a man to perform a social function, so the collective determinants of the psyche impel him to socialize ideas and convictions. By transforming a possible social *faux pas* into the service of his soul after having been wounded by the dart of passion, Hermas was led to accomplish a social task of a spiritual nature, which for that time was surely of no small importance.

6 In order to fit him for this task, it was clearly necessary that his soul should destroy the last possibility of an erotic attachment to the object, as this would have meant dishonesty towards himself. By consciously denying any erotic wish, Hermas merely demonstrated that it would be more agreeable for him if the erotic wish did not exist, but it by no means proved that he actually had no erotic intentions and fantasies. Therefore his sovereign lady, the soul, mercilessly revealed to him the existence of his sin, thus releasing him from his secret bondage to the object. As a "vessel of devotion" she took over the passion that was on the point of being fruitlessly lavished upon her. The last vestige of this passion had to be eradicated if the contemporary task was to be accomplished, and this consisted in delivering man from sensual bondage, from the state of primitive *participation mystique*. For the man of that age this bondage had become intolerable. The spiritual function had to be differentiated in order to restore the psychic equi-

librium. All philosophical attempts to do this by achieving "equanimity," most of which concentrated on the Stoic doctrine, came to grief because of their rationalism. Reason can give a man equilibrium only if his reason is already an equilibrating organ. But for how many individuals and at what periods of history has it been that? As a rule, a man needs the opposite of his actual condition to force him to find his place in the middle. For the sake of mere reason he can never forgo the sensuous appeal of the immediate situation. Against the power and delight of the temporal he must set the joy of the eternal, and against the passion of the sensual the ecstasy of the spiritual. The undeniable reality of the one must be matched by the compelling power of the other.

387 Through insight into the actual existence of his erotic desire, Hermas was able to acknowledge this metaphysical reality. The sensual libido that had previously clung to the concrete object now passed to his soul-image and invested it with the reality which the object had claimed exclusively for itself. Consequently his soul could speak to good effect and successfully enforce her demands.

388 After his conversation with Rhoda, her image vanishes and the heavens close. In her stead there now appears an "old woman in shining garments," who informs Hermas that his erotic desire is a sinful and foolish defiance of a venerable spirit, but that God is angry with him not so much on that account as because he tolerates the sins of his family. In this adroit fashion the libido is drawn away entirely from the erotic desire and in a flash is directed to the social task. An especial refinement is that the soul has discarded the image of Rhoda and taken on the appearance of an old woman, thus allowing the erotic element to recede into the background. It is later revealed to Hermas that this old woman is the Church; the concrete and personal has resolved itself into an abstraction, and the idea acquires a reality it had never before possessed. The old woman then reads to him from a mysterious book attacking heathens and apostates, but whose exact meaning he is unable to grasp. Subsequently we learn that the book sets forth a mission. Thus his sovereign lady presents him with his task, which as her knight he is pledged to accomplish. Nor is the trial of virtue lacking. For, not long after, Hermas has a vision

in which the old woman reappears, promising to return about the fifth hour in order to explain the revelation. Whereupon Hermas betook himself into the country to the appointed place, where he found a couch of ivory, set with a pillow and a cover of fine linen.

As I beheld these things lying there, I was sore amazed, and a quaking fell upon me and my hair stood on end, and a dreadful fear befell me, because I was alone in that place. But when I came once more to myself, I remembered the glory of God and took new courage; I knelt down and again confessed my sins unto God, as I had done before. Then she drew near with six young men, the which also I had seen before, and stood beside me and listened while I prayed and confessed my sins unto God. And she touched me and said: "Hermas, have done with all thy prayers and the reciting of thy sins. Pray also for righteousness, whereby thou mayest bear some of it with thee to thy house." And she raised me up by the hand and led me to the couch, and said unto the young men: "Go and build!" And when the youths were gone and we were alone, she said unto me: "Sit thee here!" I said unto her: "Mistress, let the aged first be seated." She said: "Do as I said unto thee and be thou seated." But, when I made as though to seat myself upon her right hand, she motioned me with a gesture of the hand to be seated upon her left.

As I wondered thereat, and was troubled, that I might not sit upon the right side, she said unto me: "Why art thou grieved, Hermas? The seat upon the right is for those who are already well-pleasing to God and have suffered for the Name. But to thee there lacketh much before thou canst sit with them. Yet remain as heretofore in thy simplicity, and thou shalt surely sit with them, and thus shall it be for all who shall have accomplished the work which those wrought, and endured what they suffered."[129]

89 In this situation, it would have been very easy for Hermas to give way to an erotic misunderstanding. The rendezvous has about it the feeling of a trysting-place in a "beautiful and sequestered spot," as he puts it. The rich couch waiting there is a fatal reminder of Eros, so that the terror which overcame Hermas at the sight of it is quite understandable. Clearly he must fight vigorously against these erotic associations lest he fall into a mood far from holy. He does not appear to have recognized the temptation for what it was, unless perhaps it is

[129] Cf. ibid., pp. 27ff.

tacitly admitted in the description of his terror, a touch of honesty that came more easily to the man of that time than to the man of today. For in that age man was more closely in touch with his own nature than we are, and was therefore in a position to perceive his natural reactions directly and to recognize what they were. In the case of Hermas, the confession of his sins may very well have been prompted by unholy sensations. At all events, the ensuing question as to whether he shall sit on the right hand or the left leads to a moral reprimand from his mistress. For although signs coming from the left were regarded as favourable in the Roman auguries, the left side, for both the Greeks and the Romans, was on the whole inauspicious, as the double meaning of the word "sinister" shows. But the question raised here of left and right has nothing to do with popular superstitions and is clearly of Biblical origin, referring to Matthew 25:33: "And he shall set the sheep on his right hand, but the goats on the left." Because of their guileless and gentle nature, sheep are an allegory of the good, while the unruly and lascivious nature of goats makes them an image of evil. By assigning him a seat on the left, his mistress tactfully reveals to him her understanding of his psychology.

390 When Hermas has taken his seat on her left, rather sadly, as he records, his mistress shows him a visionary scene which unrolls itself before his eyes. He beholds how the youths, assisted by ten thousand other men, build a mighty tower whose stones fit together without seams. This seamless tower, of indestructible solidity, signifies the Church, so Hermas is given to understand. *His mistress is the Church, and so is the tower.* We have seen already in the Litany of Loreto that the Virgin is named "tower of David" and "tower of ivory." The same or a similar association seems to be made here. The tower undoubtedly has the meaning of something solid and secure, as in Psalm 61:4: "For thou hast been a shelter for me, and a strong tower from the enemy." Any resemblance to the tower of Babel would involve an intense inner contradiction and must be excluded, but there may nevertheless be echoes of it, since Hermas, in company with every other thoughtful mind of that epoch, must have suffered much from the depressing spectacle of the ceaseless schisms and heretical disputes of the early Church. Such an impression may even have been his

main reason for writing these confessions, an inference supported by the fact that the mysterious book that was revealed to him inveighed against heathens and apostates. The same confusion of tongues that frustrated the building of the tower of Babel almost completely dominated the Church in the early centuries, demanding desperate efforts on the part of the faithful to overcome the chaos. Since Christendom at that time was far from being one flock under one shepherd, it was only natural that Hermas should long for the "shepherd," the *poimen,* as well as for some solid and stable structure, the "tower," that would unite in one inviolable whole the elements gathered from the four winds, the mountains and seas.

91 Earth-bound desire, sensuality in all its forms, attachment to the lures of this world, and the incessant dissipation of psychic energy in the world's prodigal variety, are the main obstacle to the development of a coherent and purposive attitude. Hence the elimination of this obstacle must have been one of the most important tasks of the time. It is therefore not surprising that, in the *Shepherd* of Hermas, it is the mastering of this task that is unfolded before our eyes. We have already seen how the original erotic stimulus and the energy it released were canalized into the personification of the unconscious complex, becoming the figure of Ecclesia, the old woman, whose visionary appearance demonstrates the spontaneity of the underlying complex. We learn, moreover, that the old woman now turns into a tower, since the tower is also the Church. This transformation is unexpected, because the connection between the tower and the old woman is not immediately apparent. But the attributes of the Virgin in the Litany of Loreto will put us on the right track, for there we find, as already mentioned, the tower associated with the Virgin Mother. This attribute has its source in the Song of Songs 4:4: "Thy neck is like the tower of David builded for an armoury," and 7:4: "Thy neck is a tower of ivory." Similarly 8:10: "I am a wall, and my breasts like towers."

92 The Song of Songs, as we know, was originally a love poem, perhaps a wedding song, which was denied canonical recognition even by Jewish scholars until very late. Mystical interpretation, however, has always loved to conceive the bride as Israel and the bridegroom as Jehovah, impelled by a sound

instinct to turn even erotic feelings into a relationship between God and the chosen people. Christianity appropriated the Song of Songs for the same reason, interpreting the bridegroom as Christ and the bride as the Church. To the psychology of the Middle Ages this analogy had an extraordinary appeal, and it inspired the quite unabashed Christ-eroticism of the Christian mystics, some of the best examples of which are supplied by Mechtild of Magdeburg. The Litany of Loreto was conceived in this spirit. It derived certain attributes of the Virgin directly from the Song of Songs, as in the case of the tower symbol. The rose, too, was used as one of her attributes even at the time of the Greek Fathers, together with the lily, which likewise appear in the Song of Songs (2:1): "I am the rose of Sharon, and the lily of the valleys." Images much used in the medieval hymns are the "enclosed garden" and the "sealed fountain" (Song of Songs 4:12: "A garden inclosed is my sister, my spouse; a spring shut up, a fountain sealed"). The unmistakably erotic nature of these images was explicitly accepted as such by the Fathers. Thus St. Ambrose interprets the "enclosed garden" as virginity.[130] In the same way, he[131] compares Mary with the ark of bulrushes in which Moses was found:

> By the ark of bulrushes is meant the Blessed Virgin. Therefore his mother prepared the ark of bulrushes wherein Moses was placed, because the wisdom of God, which is the Son of God, chose blessed Mary the virgin and formed in her womb a man to whom he might become joined in unity of person.[132]

393 St. Augustine employs the simile (frequently used by later writers) of the *thalamus*, bridal chamber, for Mary, again in an expressly anatomical sense: "He chose for himself a chaste bridal chamber, where the bridegroom was joined to the bride,"[133] and: "He issued forth from the bridal chamber, that is from the virginal womb."[134]

[130] *De institutione virginis*, cap. 9 (Migne, *P.L.*, vol. 16, col. 321).

[131] [A. S. B. Glover, who made the following translation, points out that this *Sermo* is by *pseudo*-Ambrose. See bibliography *s.v.* Ambrose.—EDITORS.]

[132] *Expositio beati Ambrosii Episcopi super Apocalypsin*, Visio III, cap. 6, p. 38.

[133] [A. S. B. Glover was unable to locate this quotation.—EDITORS.]

[134] *Sermo* 192 (Migne, *P.L.*, vol. 38, col. 1013).

94 The interpretation of *vas* as the womb may therefore be taken as certain when St. Ambrose says in confirmation of St. Augustine: "Not of earth but of heaven did he choose for himself this vessel, through which he should descend to sanctify the temple of shame."[135] The designation σκεῦος (vessel) is not uncommon with the Greek Fathers. Here again there is probably an allusion to the Song of Songs, for although the designation *vas* does not appear in the Vulgate text, we find instead the image of the goblet and of drinking (7:2): "Thy navel is like a round goblet, which wanteth not liquor; thy belly is like a heap of wheat set about with lilies." The meaning of the first sentence has a parallel in the *Meisterlieder der Kolmarer Handschrift,* where Mary is compared with the widow's cruse of oil (I Kings: 17:9ff.): ". . . Zarephath in the land of Zidon, whither Elijah was sent to a widow who should feed him; my body is fitly compared with hers, for God sent the prophet unto me, to change for us our time of famine."[136] With regard to the second, St. Ambrose says: "In the womb of the virgin grace increased like a heap of wheat and the flowers of the lily, even as it generated the grain of wheat and the lily."[137] In Catholic sources[138] very far-fetched passages are drawn into this vessel symbolism, as for instance Song of Songs 1:1 (DV): "Let him kiss me with the kiss of his mouth: for thy *breasts* are better than wine," and even Exodus 16:33: "Take a *pot,* and put an omer full of manna therein, and lay it up before the Lord, to be kept for your generations."

95 These associations are so contrived that they argue against rather than for the Biblical origin of the vessel symbolism. In favour of an extra-Biblical source is the fact that the medieval hymns to Mary brazenly borrowed their imagery from everywhere, so that everything that was in any way precious became associated with her. The fact that the vessel symbol is very old —it stems from the third to fourth century—is no argument against its secular origin, since even the Fathers had a weakness for non-Biblical, pagan imagery; for instance Tertullian,[139]

135 *De institutione virginis,* cap. 5 (Migne, *P.L.*, vol. 16, col. 313).

136 Ed. Bartsch, p. 216.

137 *De institutione virginis,* cap. 14 (Migne, *P.L.*, vol. 16, col. 327).

138 E.g., Salzer, *Sinnbilder und Beiworte Mariens.*

139 *Adversus Judaeos,* XIII (Migne, *P.L.*, vol. 2, col. 635): "That virgin earth, not yet watered by the rains nor fecundated by showers."

Augustine,[140] and others compared the Virgin with the undefiled earth and the unploughed field, not without a sidelong glance at the Kore of the mysteries.[141] Such comparisons were based on pagan models, as Cumont has shown to be the case with the ascension of Elijah in the early medieval illustrated manuscripts, which keep closely to the Mithraic prototype. In many of its rites the Church followed the pagan model, not least in making the birth of Christ coincide with the birth of the *sol invictus*, the invincible sun. St. Jerome compares the Virgin with the sun as the mother of the light.

396 These non-Biblical allegories can have their source only in pagan conceptions still current at that time. It is therefore only just, when considering the vessel symbol, to call to mind the well-known and widespread Gnostic symbolism of the vessel. A great many incised gems have been preserved from that time which bear the symbol of a pitcher with remarkable winged bands, at once recalling the uterus with the *ligamenta lata*. This vessel is called the "vase of sins,"[142] in contrast with the hymns to Mary in which she is extolled as the "vessel of virtue." King[143] contests the former interpretation as arbitrary and agrees with Köhler[144] that the cameo-image (principally Egyptian) refers to the pots on the water-wheels that drew up water from the Nile to irrigate the fields; this would also explain the peculiar bands which clearly served for fastening the pot to the water-wheel. The fertilizing function of the pot was, as King notes, expressed as the "fecundation of Isis by the seed of Osiris." Often there is on the vessel a winnowing basket, probably with reference to the "mystical winnowing basket of Iakchos," or *λῖκνον*, the figurative birthplace of the grain of wheat, symbolizing fertility.[145] There used to be a Greek marriage ceremony in which a winnowing basket filled with

140 *Sermones*, 189, II (Migne, *P.L.*, vol. 38, col. 1006): "Truth is arisen from the earth, because Christ is born of a virgin."

141 Cf. Jung, "The Psychological Aspects of the Kore."

142 Jacques Matter, *Histoire critique du gnosticisme*. [As cited by King, *The Gnostics and Their Remains*, p. 111.]

143 King, ibid.

144 [Possibly H.K.E. von Köhler, "Einleitung über die Gemmen mit dem Namen der Künstler."—EDITORS.]

145 *Symbols of Transformation*, pars. 528ff.

fruit was placed on the head of the bride, an obvious fertility charm.

97 This interpretation of the vessel is supported by the ancient Egyptian view that everything originated from the primal water, Nu or Nut, who was also identified with the Nile or the ocean. Nu is written with three pots, three water signs, and the sign for heaven. A hymn to Ptah-Tenen says: "Maker of grain, which cometh forth from him in his name Nu the Aged, who maketh fertile the watery mass of heaven, and maketh to come forth the water on the mountains to give life to men and women."[146] Wallis Budge drew my attention to the fact that the uterus symbolism exists today in the southern hinterland of Egypt in the form of rain and fertility charms. Occasionally it still happens that the natives in the bush kill a woman and take out her uterus for use in magical rites.[147]

98 When one considers how strongly the Church Fathers were influenced by Gnostic ideas in spite of their resistance to these heresies,[148] it is not inconceivable that we have in the symbolism of the vessel a pagan relic that proved adaptable to Christianity, and this is all the more likely as the worship of Mary was itself a vestige of paganism which secured for the Christian Church the heritage of the Magna Mater, Isis, and other mother goddesses. The image of the *vas Sapientiae*, vessel of wisdom, likewise recalls its Gnostic prototype, Sophia.

99 Official Christianity, therefore, absorbed certain Gnostic elements that manifested themselves in the worship of woman and found a place for them in an intensified worship of Mary. I have selected the Litany of Loreto as an example of this process of assimilation from a wealth of equally interesting material. The assimilation of these elements to the Christian symbol nipped in the bud the psychic culture of the man; for his soul, previously reflected in the image of the chosen mistress, lost its individual form of expression through this absorption. Consequently, any possibility of an individual differentiation of the soul was lost when it became repressed in the collective worship. Such losses generally have unfortunate

146 Budge, *The Gods of the Egyptians*, I, p. 511.

147 Talbot, *In the Shadow of the Bush*, pp. 67, 74ff.

148 [Jung, *Aion*, chs. V and XIII.—EDITORS.]

consequences, and in this case they soon made themselves felt. Since the psychic relation to woman was expressed in the collective worship of Mary, the image of woman lost a value to which human beings had a natural right. This value could find its natural expression only through individual choice, and it sank into the unconscious when the individual form of expression was replaced by a collective one. In the unconscious the image of woman received an energy charge that activated the archaic and infantile dominants. And since all unconscious contents, when activated by dissociated libido, are projected upon external objects, the devaluation of the real woman was compensated by daemonic traits. She no longer appeared as an object of love, but as a persecutor or witch. The consequence of increasing Mariolatry was the witch hunt, that indelible blot on the later Middle Ages.

400 But this was not the only consequence. The splitting off and repression of a valuable progressive tendency resulted in a quite general activation of the unconscious. This activation could find no satisfying expression in collective Christian symbols, for an adequate expression always takes an individual form. Thus the way was paved for heresies and schisms, against which the only defence available to the Christian consciousness was fanaticism. The frenzied horror of the Inquisition was the product of over-compensated doubt, which came surging up from the unconscious and finally gave rise to one of the greatest schisms of the Church—the Reformation.

401 If I have dwelt rather longer on the symbolism of the vessel than my readers might have expected, I have done so for a definite reason, because I wanted to elucidate the psychological relations between the worship of woman and the legend of the Grail, which was so essentially characteristic of the early Middle Ages. The central religious idea in this legend, of which there are numerous variants, is the holy vessel, which, it must be obvious to everyone, is a thoroughly non-Christian image, whose origin is to be sought in extra-canonical sources.[149] From the material I have cited, it seems to me a

149 Further evidence of the pagan root of the vessel symbolism is the "magic cauldron" of Celtic mythology. Dagda, one of the benevolent gods of ancient Ireland, possesses such a cauldron, which supplies everybody with food according to his needs or merits. The Celtic god Bran likewise possesses a cauldron of renewal. It has even been suggested that the name Brons, one of the figures in the

genuine relic of Gnosticism, which either survived the extermination of heresies because of a secret tradition, or owed its revival to an unconscious reaction against the domination of official Christianity. The survival or unconscious revivification of the vessel symbol is indicative of a strengthening of the feminine principle in the masculine psychology of that time. Its symbolization in an enigmatic image must be interpreted as a spiritualization of the eroticism aroused by the worship of woman. But spiritualization always means the retention of a certain amount of libido, which would otherwise be immediately squandered in sexuality. Experience shows that when the libido is retained, one part of it flows into the spiritualized expression, while the remainder sinks into the unconscious and activates images that correspond to it, in this case the vessel symbol. The symbol lives through the restraint imposed upon certain forms of libido, and in turn serves to restrain these forms. The dissolution of the symbol means a streaming off of libido along the direct path, or at any rate an almost irresistible urge for its direct application. But the living symbol exorcises this danger. A symbol loses its magical or, if you prefer, its redeeming power as soon as its liability to dissolve is recognized. To be effective, a symbol must be by its very nature unassailable. It must be the best possible expression of the prevailing world-view, an unsurpassed container of meaning; it must also be sufficiently remote from comprehension to resist all attempts of the critical intellect to break it down; and finally, its aesthetic form must appeal so convincingly to our feelings that no argument can be raised against it on that score. For a certain time the Grail symbol clearly fulfilled these requirements, and to this fact it owed its vitality, which, as the example of Wagner shows, is still not exhausted today, even though our age and our psychology strive unceasingly for its dissolution.[150]

Grail legend, is derived from Bran. Alfred Nutt considers that Bran, lord of the cauldron, and Brons are steps in the transformation of the Celtic Peredur Saga into the quest of the Holy Grail. It would seem, therefore, that Grail motifs already existed in Celtic mythology. I am indebted to Dr. Maurice Nicoll, of London, for this information.

150 [Pars. 399–400 = *Ges. Werke* 6, par. 447, which there follows our par. 401.—EDITORS.]

402 Let us now recapitulate this rather lengthy discussion and see what insights have been gained. We began with the vision of Hermas, in which he saw a tower being built. The old woman, who at first had declared herself to be the Church, now explains that the tower is a symbol of the Church. Her significance is thus transferred to the tower, and it is with this that the whole remaining part of the text is concerned. For Hermas it is only the tower that matters, and no longer the old woman, let alone Rhoda. The detachment of libido from the real object, its concentration on the symbol and canalization into a symbolic function, is complete. The idea of a universal and undivided Church, expressed in the symbol of a seamless and impregnable tower, has become an unshakable reality in the mind of Hermas. The detachment of libido from the object transfers it into the subject, where it activates the images lying dormant in the unconscious. These images are archaic forms of expression which become symbols, and these appear in their turn as equivalents of the devalued objects. This process is as old as mankind, for symbols may be found among the relics of prehistoric man as well as among the most primitive human types living today. Symbol-formation, therefore, must obviously be an extremely important biological function. As the symbol can come alive only through the devaluation of the object, it is evident that the purpose it serves is to deprive the object of its value. If the object had an absolute value, it would be an absolute determining factor for the subject and would abolish his freedom of action absolutely, since even a relative freedom could not coexist with absolute determination by the object. Absolute relation to the object is equivalent to a complete exteriorization of the conscious processes; it amounts to an identity of subject and object which would render all cognition impossible. In a milder form this state still exists today among primitives. The projections we so often encounter in practical analysis are only residues of this original identity of subject and object.

403 The elimination of cognition and conscious experience resulting from such a state means a considerable impairment of the capacity for adaptation, and this weights the scales heavily against man, who is already handicapped by his nat-

ural defencelessness and the helplessness of his young. But it also produces a dangerous inferiority in the realm of affect, because an identity of feeling with the object means, firstly, that any object whatsoever can affect the subject to any degree, and secondly, any affect on the part of the subject immediately includes and violates the object. An incident in the life of a bushman may illustrate what I mean. A bushman had a little son whom he loved with the tender monkey-love characteristic of primitives. Psychologically, this love is completely auto-erotic—that is to say, the subject loves himself in the object. The object serves as a sort of erotic mirror. One day the bushman came home in a rage; he had been fishing, and had caught nothing. As usual the little fellow came running to meet him, but his father seized hold of him and wrung his neck on the spot. Afterwards, of course, he mourned for the dead child with the same unthinking abandon that had brought about his death.

404 This is a good example of the object's identity with a passing affect. Obviously this kind of mentality is inimical to any protective tribal organization and to the propagation of the species, and must therefore be repressed and transformed. This is the purpose the symbol serves, and to this end it came into being. It draws libido away from the object, devalues it, and bestows the surplus libido on the subject. This surplus exerts its effect upon the unconscious, so that the subject finds himself placed between an inner and an outer determinant, whence arises the possibility of choice and relative subjective freedom.

405 Symbols always derive from archaic residues, from racial engrams (imprints), about whose age and origin one can speculate much although nothing definite can be determined. It would be quite wrong to try to derive symbols from personal sources, for instance from repressed sexuality. Such a repression can at most supply the amount of libido required to activate the archaic engram. The engram, however, corresponds to an inherited mode of functioning which owes its existence not to centuries of sexual repression but to the differentiation of instinct in general. The differentiation of instinct was and still is a biological necessity; it is not peculiar to the human

species but manifests itself equally in the sexual atrophy of the worker-bee.

406 I have used the vessel symbolism as an illustration of the way symbols are derived from archaic conceptions. Just as we found the primitive notion of the uterus at the root of this symbol, we may conjecture a similar derivation in the case of the tower. The tower belongs in all probability to the category of phallic symbols in which the history of symbolism abounds. The fact that the tower, presumably symbolizing erection, appears at the very moment when Hermas has to repress his erotic fantasies at the sight of the alluring couch is not surprising. We have seen that other symbolic attributes of the Virgin and the Church are unquestionably erotic in origin, as already attested by their derivation from the Song of Songs, and that they were expressly so interpreted by the Church Fathers. The tower symbol in the Litany of Loreto has the same source and may therefore have a similar underlying meaning. The attribute "ivory" is undoubtedly erotic in origin, since it is an allusion to the tint and texture of the skin (Song of Songs 5:14: "His belly is as bright ivory"). But the tower itself is also found in an unmistakably erotic context in 8:10: "I am a wall, and my breasts like towers," which obviously refers to the jutting-out breasts with their full and elastic consistency. "His legs are as pillars of marble" (5:15), "thy neck is as a tower of ivory" (7:4), "thy nose is as the tower of Lebanon" (7:4), are equally obvious allusions to something slender and projecting. These attributes originate in tactile sensations which are transferred from the organ to the object. Just as a gloomy mood seems grey, and a joyous one bright and colourful, so also the sense of touch is influenced by subjective sexual sensations (in this case the sensation of erection) whose qualities are transferred to the object. The erotic psychology of the Song of Songs uses the images aroused in the subject for the purpose of enhancing the object's value. Ecclesiastical psychology employs these same images in order to guide the libido towards a figurative object, while the psychology of Hermas exalts the unconsciously activated image into an end in itself, using it to embody ideas that were of supreme importance for the minds of that time, namely, the consolidation and organization of the newly won Christian attitude and view of the world.

THE LOVE PROBLEM OF A STUDENT[1]

197 It is, I assure you, with no light heart that I undertake the task of opening your discussion of the love problem of a student by reading a general paper on this subject. Such a discussion is an unusual one, and presents difficulties if taken in a spirit of seriousness and with a fitting sense of responsibility.

198 Love is always a problem, whatever our age may be. In childhood, the love of one's parents is a problem, and for the old man the problem is what he has made of his love. Love is a force of destiny whose power reaches from heaven to hell. We must, I think, understand love in this way if we are to do any sort of justice to the problems it involves. They are of immense scope and complexity, not confined to any particular province but covering every aspect of human life. Love may be an ethical, a social, a psychological, a philosophical, an aesthetic, a religious, a medical, a legal, or a physiological problem, to name only a few aspects of this many-sided phenomenon. This invasion of love into all the collective spheres of life is, however, only a minor difficulty in comparison with the fact that love is also an intensely individual problem. For it means that every general criterion and rule loses its validity, in exactly the same way that religious beliefs, although constantly codified in the course of history, are always, in essence, an individual experience which bows to no traditional rule.

199 The very word "love" is itself an obstacle to our discussion. What, indeed, has not been called "love"! Beginning with the highest mystery of the Christian religion, we encounter, on the

[1] [A lecture to Zurich University students, probably in Dec., 1922. Originally published in English as "The Love Problem of the Student," trans. by C. F. and H. G. Baynes from the unpublished German ms., in *Contributions to Analytical Psychology* (London and New York, 1928). For the present trans. the Baynes version has been consulted.—EDITORS.]

next-lower stages, the *amor Dei* of Origen, the *amor intellectualis Dei* of Spinoza, Plato's love of the Idea, and the *Gottesminne* of the mystics. Goethe's words introduce us to the human sphere of love:

Let now the savage instincts sleep
And all the violence they do;
When human love stirs in the deep
The love of God is stirring too.

200 Here we find the love of one's neighbour, in the Christian sense as well as in the Buddhist sense of compassion, and the love of mankind as expressed in social service. Next there is love of one's country, and the love for ideal institutions such as the Church. Then comes parental love, above all mother-love, then filial love. When we come to conjugal love we leave the sphere of the spiritual and enter that intermediate realm between spirit and instinct. Here the pure flame of Eros sets fire to sexuality, and the ideal forms of love—love of parents, of country, of one's neighbour, etc.—are mingled with the lust for personal power and the desire to possess and to rule. This does not mean that all contact with instinct debases love. On the contrary, its beauty and truth and strength become the more perfect the more instinct it can absorb into itself. Only if instinct predominates does the animal come to the surface. Conjugal love can be of the kind of which Goethe says at the end of *Faust:*

Spirit by attraction draws
Elemental matter,
Forges bonds no man can force
And no angel shatter.
Double natures single grown,
Inwardly united,
By Eternal Love alone
Can it be divided.

201 But it need not necessarily be such a love. It may recall Nietzsche's words: "Two animals have lighted on each other." The love of the lover is again different. Even though the sacrament of marriage be lacking, and the pledge of a life together, this love may be transfigured by the power of fate or by its own

tragic nature. But as a rule instinct predominates, with its dark glow or its flickering fires.

2 Even this has not brought us to the limits of love. By "love" we also mean the sexual act on all levels, from officially sanctioned, wedded cohabitation to the physiological need which drives a man to prostitutes and to the mere business they make or are forced to make of love.

3 We also speak of "the love of boys," meaning homosexuality, which since classical times has lost its glamour as a social and educative institution, and now ekes out a miserable, terror-stricken existence as a so-called perversion and punishable offence, at least where men are concerned. In Anglo-Saxon countries it seems on the other hand that female homosexuality means rather more than Sapphic lyricism, since it somehow acts as a stimulus to the social and political organization of women, just as male homosexuality was an important factor in the rise of the Greek *polis*.

4 Finally, the word "love" must be stretched still further to cover all sexual perversions. There is incestuous love, and a masturbatory self-love that goes by the name of narcissism. The word "love" includes every kind of morbid sexual abomination as well as every kind of greed that has ever degraded man to the level of a beast or a machine.

05 Thus we find ourselves in the awkward position of beginning a discussion about a matter or concept whose outlines are of the vaguest and whose extent is well-nigh illimitable. At least for the purposes of the present discussion, one would like to restrict the concept of love to the problem of how a young student should come to terms with sex. But this just cannot be done, because all the meanings of the word "love" which I have already mentioned enter actively into the love problem of a student.

06 We can, however, agree to discuss the question of the way in which the average so-called normal person behaves under the conditions I have described. Disregarding the fact the "normal" person does not exist, we find, nevertheless, sufficient similarities even among individuals of the most varied types to warrant a discussion of the "average" problem. As always, the practical solution of the problem depends on two factors: the

demands and capacities of the individual, and the environmental conditions.

207 It is the duty of a speaker to present a general survey of the question under discussion. Naturally this can be done only if, as a doctor, I can give an objective account of things as they are, and abstain from that stale, moralizing talk which veils the subject with a mixture of bashfulness and hypocrisy. Moreover, I am not here to tell you what ought to be done. That must be left to those who always know what is better for other people.

208 Our theme is "The Love Problem of a Student," and I assume that "love problem" means the relation of the two sexes and is not to be construed as the "sexual problem" of a student. This provides a useful limitation of our theme, for the question of sex would need considering only so far as it is a love problem, or a problem of relationship. Hence we can exclude all those sexual phenomena that have nothing to do with relationship, such as sexual perversions (with the exception of homosexuality), masturbation, and intercourse with prostitutes. We cannot exclude homosexuality because very often it is a problem of relationship; but we can exclude prostitution because usually it does not involve a relationship, though there are exceptions which prove the rule.

209 The average solution of the love problem is, as you know, marriage. But experience shows that this statistical truth does not apply to the student. The immediate reason for this is that a student is generally not in a position to set up house. A further reason is the youthful age of most students, which, partly because of their unfinished studies, and partly because of their need for freedom to move from place to place, does not yet permit the social fixation entailed by marriage. Other factors to be considered are psychological immaturity, childish clinging to home and family, relatively undeveloped capacity for love and responsibility, lack of experience of life and the world, the typical illusions of youth, and so on. A reason that should not be underestimated is the sagacious reserve of the girl students. Their first aim is to complete their studies and take up a profession. They therefore abstain from marriage, especially from marriage with a student, who so long as he remains a student is not a desirable marriage partner for the reasons already mentioned. Another, very important, reason for the infrequency of

student marriages is the question of children. As a rule when a girl marries she wants a child, whereas a man can manage well enough for a time without children. A marriage without children has no special attraction for a woman; she prefers to wait.

10 In recent years, it is true, student marriages have become more frequent. This is due partly to the psychological changes in our modern outlook, and partly to the spread of contraceptive measures. The psychological changes that have produced, among other things, the phenomenon of the student marriage are probably the result of the spiritual upheavals of the last few decades, the total significance of which we are as yet unable to grasp. All we can say is that, as a consequence of the general dissemination of scientific knowledge and a more scientific way of thinking, a change in the very conception of the love problem has come about. Scientific objectivity has effected a rapprochement between the sacrosanct idea of man as a superior being and man as a natural being, and made it possible for *Homo sapiens* to take his place as part of the natural order. The change has an emotional as well as an intellectual aspect. Such a view works directly on the feelings of the individual. He feels released from the confines of a metaphysical system and from those moral categories which characterized the medieval outlook on the world. The taboos erected on man's exclusion from nature no longer prevail, and the moral judgments which in the last analysis always have their roots in the religious metaphysic of the age have lost their force. Within the traditional moral system everyone knows perfectly why marriage is "right" and why any other form of love is to be abhorred. But outside the system, on the playground and battlefield of nature, where man feels himself to be the most gifted member of the great family of animals, he must orient himself anew. The loss of the old standards and values amounts, at first, to moral chaos. All the hitherto accepted forms are doubted, people begin to discuss things that have long sheltered behind a moral prejudice. They boldly investigate the actual facts and feel an irresistible need to take stock of experience, to know and to understand. The eyes of science are fearless and clear; they do not flinch from gazing into moral darknesses and dirty corners. The man of today can no longer rest content with a traditional judg-

ment; he must know why. This search leads to the creation of new standards of value.

211 One of these is an evaluation of love in terms of hygiene. Through a franker and more objective discussion of sex a knowledge of the immense dangers of venereal disease has become much more widespread. The obligation to keep oneself healthy has superseded the guilty fears of the old morality. But this process of moral sanitation has not yet progressed to the point where public conscience would allow the same civic measures to be taken for dealing with venereal diseases as with other infectious diseases. Venereal diseases are still considered "indecent," unlike smallpox and cholera, which are morally acceptable in the drawing room. No doubt these fine distinctions will raise a smile in a more enlightened age.

212 The widespread discussion of the sexual question has brought the extraordinary importance of sexuality in all its psychic ramifications to the forefront of our social consciousness. A major contribution was made during the last twenty-five years by the much-decried psychoanalytic movement. Today it is no longer possible to brush aside the tremendous psychological importance of sex with a bad joke or a display of moral indignation. People are beginning to see the sexual question in the context of the great human problems and to discuss it with the seriousness it deserves. The natural result of this is that much that was formerly held to be beyond dispute is now open to doubt. There is, for instance, a doubt as to whether the officially sanctioned form of sexuality is the only one that is morally possible, and whether all other forms are to be condemned out of hand. The arguments for and against are gradually losing their moral acerbity, practical considerations force themselves into the discussion, and finally we are beginning to discover that legitimized sex is not *eo ipso* the equivalent of moral superiority.

213 In addition to this, the marriage problem with its usually sombre background has become a theme for romantic literature. Whereas the romance of the old style concluded with a happy betrothal or a wedding, the modern novel often begins after the marriage. In these novels, which get into everybody's hands, the most intimate problems are often treated with a lack of reticence that is positively painful. Of the veritable flood of

more or less undisguised pornographic writings we need hardly speak. A popular scientific book, Forel's *The Sexual Question,* not only had an enormous sale but found a good many imitators. In scientific literature, compilations have been produced which both in scope and in the dubious nature of their contents exceed anything found in Krafft-Ebing's *Psychopathia Sexualis,* in a way that would have been inconceivable thirty or forty years ago.

4 These widespread and widely known phenomena are a sign of the times. They make it possible for young people today to grasp the full importance of the problem of sex much earlier than they could have at any time during the last two decades. There are some who maintain that this early preoccupation with sex is unhealthy, a sign of urban degeneration. I remember reading an article fifteen years ago in Ostwald's *Annalen der Naturphilosophie,* which said, quite literally: "Primitive people like the Eskimos, Swiss, etc., have no sexual problem." It scarcely needs much reflection to see why primitives have no sexual problem; beyond the concerns of the stomach they have no other problems to worry about. Problems are the prerogative of civilized man. Here in Switzerland we have no great cities and yet such problems exist. I do not think that discussion of the sexual question is unhealthy or in the least degenerate; I see it rather as a symptom of the great psychological revolution of our time and the changes it has brought about. It seems to me that the more seriously and thoroughly we discuss this question, which is of such vital importance for man's health and happiness, the better it will be for all of us.

5 It is no doubt the serious interest shown in this question that has led to the hitherto unknown phenomenon of student marriages. Such a very recent phenomenon is difficult to judge for lack of sufficient data. In former times there were early marriages in abundance, also marriages that must have seemed socially very unstable. In itself, therefore, the student marriage is perfectly permissible. The question of children, however, is another matter. If both partners are studying, children must obviously be ruled out. But a marriage that remains artificially childless is always rather problematical. Children are the cement that holds it together as nothing else could. And it is the parents' concentration on the children which in innumera-

ble instances keeps alive the feeling of companionship so essential for the stability of a marriage. When there are no children the interest of each partner is directed to the other, which in itself might be a good thing. In practice, unfortunately, this mutual preoccupation is not always of an amiable kind. Each blames the other for the dissatisfaction felt by both. In these circumstances it is probably better for the wife to be studying, otherwise she is left without an object; for there are many women who cannot endure marriage without children and become unendurable themselves. If she is studying, she at least has a life outside her marriage that is sufficiently satisfying. A woman who is very set on children, and for whom children are more important than a husband, should certainly think twice before embarking on a student marriage. She should also realize that the urge to maternity often appears in imperative form only later, that is, after she is married.

216 As to whether student marriages are premature, we must take note of a fact that applies to all early marriages, namely, that a girl of twenty is usually older than a man of twenty-five, as far as maturity of judgment is concerned. With many men of twenty-five the period of psychological puberty is not yet over. Puberty is a period of illusion and only partial responsibility. The psychological difference is due to the fact that a boy, up to the time of sexual maturity, is as a rule quite childish, whereas a girl develops much earlier than he does the psychological subtleties that go hand in hand with adolescence. Into this childishness sexuality often breaks with brutal force, while, despite the onset of puberty, it often goes on slumbering in a girl until the passion of love awakens it. There are a surprising number of women whose real sexuality, even though they are married, remains virginal for years; they become conscious of it only when they fall in love with another man. That is the reason why very many women have no understanding at all of masculine sexuality—they are completely unconscious of their own. With men it is different. Sexuality bursts on them like a tempest, filling them with brute desires and needs, and there is scarcely one of them who escapes the painful problem of masturbation. But a girl can masturbate for years without knowing what she is doing.

217 The onrush of sexuality in a boy brings about a powerful

change in his psychology. He now has the sexuality of a grown man with the soul of a child. Often the flood of obscene fantasies and smutty talk with schoolfellows pours like a torrent of dirty water over all his delicate and childish feelings, sometimes smothering them for ever. Unexpected moral conflicts arise, temptations of every description lie in wait for him and weave themselves into his fantasies. The psychic assimilation of the sexual complex causes him the greatest difficulties even though he may not be conscious of its existence. The onset of puberty also brings about considerable changes in his metabolism, as can be seen from the pimples and acne that so often afflict adolescents. The psyche is disturbed in a similar manner and thrown off its balance. At this age the young man is full of illusions, which are always a sign of psychic disequilibrium. They make stability and maturity of judgment impossible. His tastes, his interests, his plans alter fitfully. He can suddenly fall head over heels in love with a girl, and a fortnight later he cannot conceive how anything of the sort could have happened to him. He is so riddled with illusions that he actually needs these mistakes to make him conscious of his own taste and individual judgment. He is still experimenting with life, and *must* experiment with it in order to learn how to judge things correctly. Hence there are very few men who have not had sexual experience of some kind before they are married. During puberty it is mostly homosexual experiences, and these are much more common than is generally admitted. Heterosexual experiences come later, not always of a very beautiful kind. For the less the sexual complex is assimilated to the whole of the personality, the more autonomous and instinctive it will be. Sexuality is then purely animal and recognizes no psychological distinctions. The most inferior woman will do; it is enough if she has the typical secondary sexual characteristics. A false step of this kind does not entitle us to draw conclusions about a man's character, as the act can easily occur at a time when the sexual complex is still split off from the psyche's influence. Nevertheless, too many experiences of this nature have a bad effect on the formation of the personality, as by force of habit they fix sexuality on too low a level and make it unacceptable to moral judgment. The result is that though the man in question is outwardly a respectable citizen, inwardly he is prey to sexual fantasies of the lowest kind, or else he represses them and on some festive occasion they come leaping to the surface in their primitive form, much to the astonishment of his unsuspecting wife—assuming, of course, that she notices what is going on. A frequent accompaniment is premature coldness towards the wife. Women are often frigid from the first day of marriage because their sensation function does not respond to this kind of sexuality in their husbands. The weakness of a man's judgment at the time of psychological puberty should prompt him to reflect very deeply on the premature choice of a wife.

218 Let us now turn to other forms of relationship between the sexes that are customary during the student period. There are, as you know, characteristic liaisons between students, chiefly in the great universities of other countries. These relationships are sometimes fairly stable and may even have a psychological value, as they do not consist entirely of sexuality but also, in part, of love. Occasionally the liaison is continued into marriage. The relationship stands, therefore, considerably higher than prostitution. But as a rule it is limited to those students who were careful in the choice of their parents. It is usually a question of money, for most of the girls are dependent on their lovers for financial help, though they could not be said to sell their love for money. Very often the relationship is a beautiful episode in the girl's life, otherwise poor and empty, while for the man it may be his first intimate acquaintance with a woman, and in later life a memory on which he looks back with emotion. Often, again, there is nothing valuable in these affairs, partly owing to the man's crude sensuality, thoughtlessness, and lack of feeling, and partly owing to the frivolity and fickleness of the girl.

219 Over all these relationships hangs the Damoclean sword of their transitoriness, which prevents the formation of real values. They are passing episodes, experiments of very limited validity. Their injurious effect on the personality is due to the fact that the man gets the girl too easily, so that the value of the love-object is depreciated. It is convenient for him to dispose of his sexual problem in such a simple and irresponsible way. He becomes spoilt. But even more, the fact that he is sexually satisfied robs him of a driving-force which no young man can do without. He becomes blasé and can afford to wait. Meanwhile he

can calmly review the massed femininity passing before him until the right party turns up. Then the wedding comes along and the latest date is thrown over. This procedure adds little of advantage to his character. The low level of relationship tends to keep sexuality on a correspondingly low level of development, and this can easily lead to difficulties in marriage. Or if his sexual fantasies are repressed, the result is only too likely to be a neurotic or, worse still, a moral zealot.

0 Homosexual relations between students of either sex are by no means uncommon. So far as I can judge of this phenomenon, I would say that these relationships are less common with us, and on the continent generally, than in certain other countries where boy and girl college students live in strict segregation. I am speaking here not of pathological homosexuals who are incapable of real friendship and meet with little sympathy among normal individuals, but of more or less normal youngsters who enjoy such a rapturous friendship that they also express their feelings in sexual form. With them it is not just a matter of mutual masturbation, which in all school and college life is the order of the day among the younger age groups, but of a higher and more spiritual form which deserves the name "friendship" in the classical sense of the word. When such a friendship exists between an older man and a younger its educative significance is undeniable. A slightly homosexual teacher, for example, often owes his brilliant educational gifts to his homosexual disposition. The homosexual relation between an older and a younger man can thus be of advantage to both sides and have a lasting value. An indispensable condition for the value of such a relation is the steadfastness of the friendship and their loyalty to it. But only too often this condition is lacking. The more homosexual a man is, the more prone he is to disloyalty and to the seduction of boys. Even when loyalty and true friendship prevail the results may be undesirable for the development of personality. A friendship of this kind naturally involves a special cult of feeling, of the feminine element in a man. He becomes gushing, soulful, aesthetic, over-sensitive, etc. —in a word, effeminate, and this womanish behaviour is detrimental to his character.

21 Similar advantages and disadvantages can be pointed out in friendships between women, only here the difference in age

and the educative factor are not so important. The main value lies in the exchange of tender feelings on the one hand and of intimate thoughts on the other. Generally they are high-spirited, intellectual, and rather masculine women who are seeking to maintain their superiority and to defend themselves against men. Their attitude to men is therefore one of disconcerting self-assurance, with a trace of defiance. Its effect on their character is to reinforce their masculine traits and to destroy their feminine charm. Often a man discovers their homosexuality only when he notices that these women leave him stone-cold.

222 Normally, the practice of homosexuality is not prejudicial to later heterosexual activity. Indeed, the two can even exist side by side. I know a very intelligent woman who spent her whole life as a homosexual and then at fifty entered into a normal relationship with a man.

223 Among the sexual relations of the student period we must mention yet another, which is quite normal even if rather peculiar. This is the attachment of a young man to an older woman, possibly married or at any rate widowed. You will perhaps remember Jean Jacques Rousseau and his connection with Mme de Warens; this is the kind of relationship I have in mind. The man is usually rather shy, unsure of himself, inwardly afraid, sometimes infantile. He naturally seeks a mother, perhaps because he has had too much or too little love in his own family. Many women like nothing better than a man who is rather helpless, especially when they are considerably older than he is; they do not love a man's strength, his virtues and his merits, but his weaknesses. They find his infantilisms charming. If he stammers a little, he is enchanting; or perhaps he has a limp, and this excites maternal compassion and a little more besides. As a rule the woman seduces him, and he willingly submits to her mothering.

224 Not always, however, does a timid youth remain half a child. It may be that this surfeit of maternal solicitude was just what was needed to bring his undeveloped masculinity to the surface. In this way the woman educates his feeling and brings it to full consciousness. He learns to understand a woman who has experience of life and the world, is sure of herself, and thus he has a rare opportunity for a glimpse behind the scenes. But he

can take advantage of it only if he quickly outgrows this relationship, for should he get stuck in it her mothering would ruin him. Maternal tenderness is the most pernicious poison for anyone who has to equip himself for the hard and pitiless struggle of life. If he cannot let go of her apron-strings he will become a spineless parasite—for most of these women have money—and sink to the level of a lap-dog or a pet cat.

225 We must now discuss those forms of relationship which offer no solution of the sexual question for the reason that they are asexual or "platonic." If there were any reliable statistics on this subject, I believe they would show that in Switzerland the majority of students prefer a platonic relationship. Naturally, this raises the question of sexual abstinence. One often hears that abstaining from sexual intercouse is injurious to health. This view is incorrect, at least for people of the student age. Abstinence is injurious to health only when a man has reached the age when he could win a woman for himself, and should do so according to his individual inclinations. The extraordinary intensification of the sexual need that is so often felt at this time has the biological aim of forcibly eliminating the man's scruples, misgivings, doubts, and hesitations. This is very necessary, because the very idea of marriage, with all its doubtful possibilities, often makes a man panicky. It is only to be expected, therefore, that nature will push him over the obstacle. Abstention from sexual intercourse may certainly have injurious effects under these conditions, but not when there is no urgent physical or psychological need for it.

226 This brings us to the very similar question concerning the injurious effects of masturbation. When for physical or psychological reasons normal intercouse is impossible, masturbation as a safety-valve has no ill effects. Young people who come to the doctor suffering from the harmful effects of masturbation are not by any means excessive masturbationists—these usually have no need of a doctor because they are not in any sense ill—rather, their masturbation has harmful effects because it shows psychic complications and is attended by pangs of conscience or by a riot of sexual fantasies. The latter are particularly common among women. Masturbation with psychic complications is harmful, but not the ordinary, uncomplicated kind. If, however, it is continued up to the age when normal intercourse

becomes physically, psychologically, and socially possible, and is indulged in merely in order to avoid the necessary tasks of life, then it is harmful.

227 Platonic relationships are very important during the student period. The form they most commonly take is flirting. Flirting is the expression of an experimental attitude which is altogether appropriate at this age. It is a voluntary activity which, by tacit agreement, puts neither side under an obligation. This is an advantage and at the same time a disadvantage. The experimental attitude enables both parties to get to know each other without any immediately undesirable results. Both exercise their judgment and their skill in self-expression, adaptation, and defence. An enormous variety of experiences which are uncommonly valuable in later life can be picked up from flirting. On the other hand, the absence of any obligation can easily lead to one's becoming an habitual flirt, shallow, frivolous, and heartless. The man turns into a drawing-room hero and professional heart-breaker, never dreaming what a boring figure he cuts; the girl a coquette, and a serious man instinctively feels that she is not to be taken seriously.

228 A phenomenon that is as rare as flirting is common is the conscious cultivation of a serious love. We might call this simply the ideal, without, however, identifying it with traditional romanticism. For the development of personality, there can be no doubt that the timely awakening and conscious cultivation of deeply serious and responsible feelings are of the utmost value. A relationship of this kind can be the most effective shield against the temptations that beset a young man, as well as being a powerful incentive to hard work, loyalty, and reliability. However, there is no value so great that it does not have its unfavourable side. A relationship that is too ideal easily becomes exclusive. Through his love the young man is too much cut off from the acquaintance of other women, and the girl does not learn the art of erotic conquest because she has got her man already. Woman's instinct for possession is a dangerous thing, and it may easily happen that the man will regret all the experiences he never had with women before marriage and will make up for them afterwards.

229 Hence it must not be concluded that every relationship of this kind is ideal. There are cases where the exact opposite is

true—when, for instance, a man or girl trails round with a school sweetheart for no intelligible reason, from mere force of habit. Whether from inertia, or lack of spirit, or helplessness they simply cannot get rid of each other. Perhaps the parents on both sides find the match suitable, and the affair, begun in a moment of thoughtlessness and prolonged by habit, is passively accepted as a *fait accompli*. Here the disadvantages pile up without a single advantage. For the development of personality, acquiescence and passivity are harmful because they are an obstacle to valuable experience and to the exercise of one's specific gifts and virtues. Moral qualities are won only in freedom and prove their worth only in morally dangerous situations. The thief who refrains from stealing merely because he is in prison is not a moral personality. Though the parents may gaze benignly on this touching marriage and add their children's respectability to the tale of their own virtues, it is all a sham and a delusion, lacking real strength, and sapped by moral inertia.

0 After this brief survey of the problems as we meet them in actual life, I will, in conclusion, turn to the land of heart's desire and utopian possibilities.

1 Nowadays we can hardly discuss the love problem without speaking of the utopia of free love, including trial marriage. I regard this idea as a wishful fantasy and an attempt to make light of a problem which in actual life is invariably very difficult. It is no more possible to make life easy than it is to grow a herb of immortality. The force of gravity can be overcome only by the requisite application of energy. Similarly, the solution of the love problem challenges all our resources. Anything else would be useless patchwork. Free love would be conceivable only if everyone were capable of the highest moral achievement. The idea of free love was not invented with this aim in view, but merely to make something difficult appear easy. Love requires depth and loyalty of feeling; without them it is not love but mere caprice. True love will always commit itself and engage in lasting ties; it needs freedom only to effect its choice, not for its accomplishment. Every true and deep love is a sacrifice. The lover sacrifices all other possibilities, or rather, the illusion that such possibilities exist. If this sacrifice is not made, his illusions prevent the growth of any deep and responsible

feeling, so that the very possibility of experiencing real love is denied him.

232 Love has more than one thing in common with religious faith. It demands unconditional trust and expects absolute surrender. Just as nobody but the believer who surrenders himself wholly to God can partake of divine grace, so love reveals its highest mysteries and its wonder only to those who are capable of unqualified devotion and loyalty of feeling. And because this is so difficult, few mortals can boast of such an achievement. But, precisely because the truest and most devoted love is also the most beautiful, let no man seek to make it easy. He is a sorry knight who shrinks from the difficulty of loving his lady. Love is like God: both give themselves only to their bravest knights.

233 I would offer the same criticism of trial marriages. The very fact that a man enters into a marriage on trial means that he is making a reservation; he wants to be sure of not burning his fingers, to risk nothing. But that is the most effective way of forestalling any real experience. You do not experience the terrors of the Polar ice by perusing a travel-book, or climb the Himalayas in a cinema.

234 Love is not cheap—let us therefore beware of cheapening it! All our bad qualities, our egotism, our cowardice, our worldly wisdom, our cupidity—all these would persuade us not to take love seriously. But love will reward us only when we do. I must even regard it as a misfortune that nowadays the sexual question is spoken of as something distinct from love. The two questions should not be separated, for when there is a sexual problem it can be solved only by love. Any other solution would be a harmful substitute. Sexuality dished out as sexuality is brutish; but sexuality as an expression of love is hallowed. Therefore, never ask what a man does, but how he does it. If he does it from love or in the spirit of love, then he serves a god; and whatever he may do is not ours to judge, for it is ennobled.

235 I trust that these remarks will have made it clear to you that I pass no sort of moral judgment on sexuality as a natural phenomenon, but prefer to make its moral evaluation dependent on the way it is expressed.

MARRIAGE AS A PSYCHOLOGICAL RELATIONSHIP [1]

4 Regarded as a psychological relationship, marriage is a highly complex structure made up of a whole series of subjective and objective factors, mostly of a very heterogeneous nature. As I wish to confine myself here to the purely psychological problems of marriage, I must disregard in the main the objective factors of a legal and social nature, although these cannot fail to have a pronounced influence on the psychological relationship between the marriage partners.

5 Whenever we speak of a "psychological relationship" we presuppose one that is *conscious,* for there is no such thing as a psychological relationship between two people who are in a state of unconsciousness. From the psychological point of view they would be wholly without relationship. From any other point of view, the physiological for example, they could be regarded as related, but one could not call their relationship psychological. It must be admitted that though such total unconsciousness as I have assumed does not occur, there is nevertheless a not inconsiderable degree of partial unconsciousness, and the psychological relationship is limited in the degree to which that unconsciousness exists.

[1] [First published as "Die Ehe als psychologische Beziehung," in *Das Ehebuch* (Celle, 1925), a volume edited by Count Hermann Keyserling; translated by Theresa Duerr in the English version, *The Book of Marriage* (New York, 1926). The original was reprinted in *Seelenprobleme der Gegenwart* (Zurich, 1931). The essay was again translated into English by H. G. and Cary F. Baynes in *Contributions to Analytical Psychology* (London and New York, 1928), and this version has been freely consulted in the present translation.—EDITORS.]

326 In the child, consciousness rises out of the depths of unconscious psychic life, at first like separate islands, which gradually unite to form a "continent," a continuous land-mass of consciousness. Progressive mental development means, in effect, extension of consciousness. With the rise of a continuous consciousness, and not before, psychological relationship becomes possible. So far as we know, consciousness is always ego-consciousness. In order to be conscious of myself, I must be able to distinguish myself from others. Relationship can only take place where this distinction exists. But although the distinction may be made in a general way, normally it is incomplete, because large areas of psychic life still remain unconscious. As no distinction can be made with regard to unconscious contents, on this terrain no relationship can be established; here there still reigns the original unconscious condition of the ego's primitive identity with others, in other words a complete absence of relationship.

327 The young person of marriageable age does, of course, possess an ego-consciousness (girls more than men, as a rule), but, since he has only recently emerged from the mists of original unconsciousness, he is certain to have wide areas which still lie in the shadow and which preclude to that extent the formation of psychological relationship. This means, in practice, that the young man (or woman) can have only an incomplete understanding of himself and others, and is therefore imperfectly informed as to his, and their, motives. As a rule the motives he acts from are largely unconscious. Subjectively, of course, he thinks himself very conscious and knowing, for we constantly overestimate the existing content of consciousness, and it is a great and surprising discovery when we find that what we had supposed to be the final peak is nothing but the first step in a very long climb. The greater the area of unconsciousness, the less is marriage a matter of free choice, as is shown subjectively in the fatal compulsion one feels so acutely when one is in love. The compulsion can exist even when one is not in love, though in less agreeable form.

328 Unconscious motivations are of a personal and of a general nature. First of all, there are the motives deriving from parental influence. The relationship of the young man to his mother, and of the girl to her father, is the determining factor in this respect.

It is the strength of the bond to the parents that unconsciously influences the choice of husband or wife, either positively or negatively. Conscious love for either parent favours the choice of a like mate, while an unconscious tie (which need not by any means express itself consciously as love) makes the choice difficult and imposes characteristic modifications. In order to understand them, one must know first of all the cause of the unconscious tie to the parents, and under what conditions it forcibly modifies, or even prevents, the conscious choice. Generally speaking, all the life which the parents could have lived, but of which they thwarted themselves for artificial motives, is passed on to the children in substitute form. That is to say, the children are driven unconsciously in a direction that is intended to compensate for everything that was left unfulfilled in the lives of their parents. Hence it is that excessively moral-minded parents have what are called "unmoral" children, or an irresponsible wastrel of a father has a son with a positively morbid amount of ambition, and so on. The worst results flow from parents who have kept themselves artificially unconscious. Take the case of a mother who deliberately keeps herself unconscious so as not to disturb the pretence of a "satisfactory" marriage. Unconsciously she will bind her son to her, more or less as a substitute for a husband. The son, if not forced directly into homosexuality, is compelled to modify his choice in a way that is contrary to his true nature. He may, for instance, marry a girl who is obviously inferior to his mother and therefore unable to compete with her; or he will fall for a woman of a tyrannical and overbearing disposition, who may perhaps succeed in tearing him away from his mother. The choice of a mate, if the instincts have not been vitiated, may remain free from these influences, but sooner or later they will make themselves felt as obstacles. A more or less instinctive choice might be considered the best from the point of view of maintaining the species, but it is not always fortunate psychologically, because there is often an uncommonly large difference between the purely instinctive personality and one that is individually differentiated. And though in such cases the race might be improved and invigorated by a purely instinctive choice, individual happiness would be bound to suffer. (The idea of "instinct" is of course nothing more than a collective term for all kinds of organic and psychic factors whose nature is for the most part unknown.)

329 If the individual is to be regarded solely as an instrument for maintaining the species, then the purely instinctive choice of a mate is by far the best. But since the foundations of such a choice are unconscious, only a kind of impersonal liaison can be built upon them, such as can be observed to perfection among primitives. If we can speak here of a "relationship" at all, it is, at best, only a pale reflection of what we mean, a very distant state of affairs with a decidedly impersonal character, wholly regulated by traditional customs and prejudices, the prototype of every conventional marriage.

330 So far as reason or calculation or the so-called loving care of the parents does not arrange the marriage, and the pristine instincts of the children are not vitiated either by false education or by the hidden influence of accumulated and neglected parental complexes, the marriage choice will normally follow the unconscious motivations of instinct. Unconsciousness results in non-differentiation, or unconscious identity. The practical consequence of this is that one person presupposes in the other a psychological structure similar to his own. Normal sex life, as a shared experience with apparently similar aims, further strengthens the feeling of unity and identity. This state is described as one of complete harmony, and is extolled as a great happiness ("one heart and one soul")—not without good reason, since the return to that original condition of unconscious oneness is like a return to childhood. Hence the childish gestures of all lovers. Even more is it a return to the mother's womb, into the teeming depths of an as yet unconscious creativity. It is, in truth, a genuine and incontestable experience of the Divine, whose transcendent force obliterates and consumes everything individual; a real communion with life and the impersonal power of fate. The individual will for self-possession is broken: the woman becomes the mother, the man the father, and thus both are robbed of their freedom and made instruments of the life urge.

331 Here the relationship remains within the bounds of the biological instinctive goal, the preservation of the species. Since this goal is of a collective nature, the psychological link between husband and wife will also be essentially collective, and cannot

be regarded as an individual relationship in the psychological sense. We can only speak of this when the nature of the unconscious motivations has been recognized and the original identity broken down. Seldom or never does a marriage develop into an individual relationship smoothly and without crises. There is no birth of consciousness without pain.

331a The ways that lead to conscious realization are many, but they follow definite laws. In general, the change begins with the onset of the second half of life. The middle period of life is a time of enormous psychological importance. The child begins its psychological life within very narrow limits, inside the magic circle of the mother and the family. With progressive maturation it widens its horizon and its own sphere of influence; its hopes and intentions are directed to extending the scope of personal power and possessions; desire reaches out to the world in ever-widening range; the will of the individual becomes more and more identical with the natural goals pursued by unconscious motivations. Thus man breathes his own life into things, until finally they begin to live of themselves and to multiply; and imperceptibly he is overgrown by them. Mothers are overtaken by their children, men by their own creations, and what was originally brought into being only with labour and the greatest effort can no longer be held in check. First it was passion, then it became duty, and finally an intolerable burden, a vampire that battens on the life of its creator. Middle life is the moment of greatest unfolding, when a man still gives himself to his work with his whole strength and his whole will. But in this very moment evening is born, and the second half of life begins. Passion now changes her face and is called duty; "I want" becomes the inexorable "I must," and the turnings of the pathway that once brought surprise and discovery become dulled by custom. The wine has fermented and begins to settle and clear. Conservative tendencies develop if all goes well; instead of looking forward one looks backward, most of the time involuntarily, and one begins to take stock, to see how one's life has developed up to this point. The real motivations are sought and real discoveries are made. The critical survey of himself and his fate enables a man to recognize his peculiarities. But these insights do not come to him easily; they are gained only through the severest shocks.

331b Since the aims of the second half of life are different from those of the first, to linger too long in the youthful attitude produces a division of the will. Consciousness still presses forward, in obedience, as it were, to its own inertia, but the unconscious lags behind, because the strength and inner resolve needed for further expansion have been sapped. This disunity with oneself begets discontent, and since one is not conscious of the real state of things one generally projects the reasons for it upon one's partner. A critical atmosphere thus develops, the necessary prelude to conscious realization. Usually this state does not begin simultaneously for both partners. Even the best of marriages cannot expunge individual differences so completely that the state of mind of the partners is absolutely identical. In most cases one of them will adapt to marriage more quickly than the other. The one who is grounded on a positive relationship to the parents will find little or no difficulty in adjusting to his or her partner, while the other may be hindered by a deep-seated unconscious tie to the parents. He will therefore achieve complete adaptation only later, and, because it is won with greater difficulty, it may even prove the more durable.

331c These differences in tempo, and in the degree of spiritual development, are the chief causes of a typical difficulty which makes its appearance at critical moments. In speaking of "the degree of spiritual development" of a personality, I do not wish to imply an especially rich or magnanimous nature. Such is not the case at all. I mean, rather, a certain complexity of mind or nature, comparable to a gem with many facets as opposed to the simple cube. There are many-sided and rather problematical natures burdened with hereditary traits that are sometimes very difficult to reconcile. Adaptation to such natures, or their adaptation to simpler personalities, is always a problem. These people, having a certain tendency to dissociation, generally have the capacity to split off irreconcilable traits of character for considerable periods, thus passing themselves off as much simpler than they are; or it may happen that their many-sidedness, their very versatility, lends them a peculiar charm. Their partners can easily lose themselves in such a labyrinthine nature, finding in it such an abundance of possible experiences that their personal interests are completely absorbed, sometimes in a not very agreeable way, since their sole occupation then consists in tracking the other through all the twists and turns of his character. There is always so much experience available that the simpler personality is surrounded, if not actually swamped, by it; he is swallowed up in his more complex partner and cannot see his way out. It is an almost regular occurrence for a woman to be wholly contained, spiritually, in her husband, and for a husband to be wholly contained, emotionally, in his wife. One could describe this as the problem of the "contained" and the "container."

332 The one who is contained feels himself to be living entirely within the confines of his marriage; his attitude to the marriage partner is undivided; outside the marriage there exist no essential obligations and no binding interests. The unpleasant side of this otherwise ideal partnership is the disquieting dependence upon a personality that can never be seen in its entirety, and is therefore not altogether credible or dependable. The great advantage lies in his own undividedness, and this is a factor not to be underrated in the psychic economy.

333 The container, on the other hand, who in accordance with his tendency to dissociation has an especial need to unify himself in undivided love for another, will be left far behind in this effort, which is naturally very difficult for him, by the simpler personality. While he is seeking in the latter all the subtleties and complexities that would complement and correspond to his own facets, he is disturbing the other's simplicity. Since in normal circumstances simplicity always has the advantage over complexity, he will very soon be obliged to abandon his efforts to arouse subtle and intricate reactions in a simpler nature. And soon enough his partner, who in accordance with her [2] simpler nature expects simple answers from him, will give him plenty to do by constellating his complexities with her everlasting insistence on simple answers. Willynilly, he must withdraw into himself before the suasions of simplicity. Any mental effort, like the conscious process itself, is so much of a strain for the ordinary man that he invariably prefers the simple, even when it does not

2 [In translating this and the following passages, I have, for the sake of clarity, assumed that the container is the man and the contained the woman. This assumption is due entirely to the exigencies of English grammar, and is not implied in the German text. Needless to say, the situation could just as easily be reversed.—TRANS.]

happen to be the truth. And when it represents at least a half-truth, then it is all up with him. The simpler nature works on the more complicated like a room that is too small, that does not allow him enough space. The complicated nature, on the other hand, gives the simpler one too many rooms with too much space, so that she never knows where she really belongs. So it comes about quite naturally that the more complicated contains the simpler. The former cannot be absorbed in the latter, but encompasses it without being itself contained. Yet, since the more complicated has perhaps a greater need of being contained than the other, he feels himself outside the marriage and accordingly always plays the problematical role. The more the contained clings, the more the container feels shut out of the relationship. The contained pushes into it by her clinging, and the more she pushes, the less the container is able to respond. He therefore tends to spy out of the window, no doubt unconsciously at first; but with the onset of middle age there awakens in him a more insistent longing for that unity and undividedness which is especially necessary to him on account of his dissociated nature. At this juncture things are apt to occur that bring the conflict to a head. He becomes conscious of the fact that he is seeking completion, seeking the contentedness and undividedness that have always been lacking. For the contained this is only a confirmation of the insecurity she has always felt so painfully; she discovers that in the rooms which apparently belonged to her there dwell other, unwished-for guests. The hope of security vanishes, and this disappointment drives her in on herself, unless by desperate and violent efforts she can succeed in forcing her partner to capitulate, and in extorting a confession that his longing for unity was nothing but a childish or morbid fantasy. If these tactics do not succeed, her acceptance of failure may do her a real good, by forcing her to recognize that the security she was so desperately seeking in the other is to be found in herself. In this way she finds herself and discovers in her own simpler nature all those complexities which the container had sought for in vain.

334 If the container does not break down in face of what we are wont to call "unfaithfulness," but goes on believing in the inner justification of his longing for unity, he will have to put up with his self-division for the time being. A dissociation is not healed

by being split off, but by more complete disintegration. All the powers that strive for unity, all healthy desire for selfhood, will resist the disintegration, and in this way he will become conscious of the possibility of an inner integration, which before he had always sought outside himself. He will then find his reward in an undivided self.

335 This is what happens very frequently about the midday of life, and in this wise our miraculous human nature enforces the transition that leads from the first half of life to the second. It is a metamorphosis from a state in which man is only a tool of instinctive nature, to another in which he is no longer a tool, but himself: a transformation of nature into culture, of instinct into spirit.

336 One should take great care not to interrupt this necessary development by acts of moral violence, for any attempt to create a spiritual attitude by splitting off and suppressing the instincts is a falsification. Nothing is more repulsive than a furtively prurient spirituality; it is just as unsavoury as gross sensuality. But the transition takes a long time, and the great majority of people get stuck in the first stages. If only we could, like the primitives, leave the unconscious to look after this whole psychological development which marriage entails, these transformations could be worked out more completely and without too much friction. So often among so-called "primitives" one comes across spiritual personalities who immediately inspire respect, as though they were the fully matured products of an undisturbed fate. I speak here from personal experience. But where among present-day Europeans can one find people not deformed by acts of moral violence? We are still barbarous enough to believe both in asceticism and its opposite. But the wheel of history cannot be put back; we can only strive towards an attitude that will allow us to live out our fate as undisturbedly as the primitive pagan in us really wants. Only on this condition can we be sure of not perverting spirituality into sensuality, and vice versa; for both must live, each drawing life from the other.

337 The transformation I have briefly described above is the very essence of the psychological marriage relationship. Much could be said about the illusions that serve the ends of nature and bring about the transformations that are characteristic of middle life. The peculiar harmony that characterizes mar-

riage during the first half of life—provided the adjustment is successful—is largely based on the projection of certain archetypal images, as the critical phase makes clear.

338 Every man carries within him the eternal image of woman, not the image of this or that particular woman, but a definite feminine image. This image is fundamentally unconscious, an hereditary factor of primordial origin engraved in the living organic system of the man, an imprint or "archetype" of all the ancestral experiences of the female, a deposit, as it were, of all the impressions ever made by woman—in short, an inherited system of psychic adaptation. Even if no women existed, it would still be possible, at any given time, to deduce from this unconscious image exactly how a woman would have to be constituted psychically. The same is true of the woman: she too has her inborn image of man. Actually, we know from experience that it would be more accurate to describe it as an image of *men,* whereas in the case of the man it is rather the image of *woman.* Since this image is unconscious, it is always unconsciously projected upon the person of the beloved, and is one of the chief reasons for passionate attraction or aversion. I have called this image the "anima," and I find the scholastic question *Habet mulier animam?* especially interesting, since in my view it is an intelligent one inasmuch as the doubt seems justified. Woman has no anima, no soul, but she has an *animus.* The anima has an erotic, emotional character, the animus a rationalizing one. Hence most of what men say about feminine eroticism, and particularly about the emotional life of women, is derived from their own anima projections and distorted accordingly. On the other hand, the astonishing assumptions and fantasies that women make about men come from the activity of the animus, who produces an inexhaustible supply of illogical arguments and false explanations.

339 Anima and animus are both characterized by an extraordinary many-sidedness. In a marriage it is always the contained who projects this image upon the container, while the latter is only partially able to project his unconscious image upon his partner. The more unified and simple this partner is, the less complete the projection. In which case, this highly fascinating image hangs as it were in mid air, as though waiting to be filled out by a living person. There are certain types of women who

seem to be made by nature to attract anima projections; indeed one could almost speak of a definite "anima type." The so-called "sphinx-like" character is an indispensable part of their equipment, also an equivocalness, an intriguing elusiveness—not an indefinite blur that offers nothing, but an indefiniteness that seems full of promises, like the speaking silence of a Mona Lisa. A woman of this kind is both old and young, mother and daughter, of more than doubtful chastity, childlike, and yet endowed with a naïve cunning that is extremely disarming to men.[3] Not every man of real intellectual power can be an animus, for the animus must be a master not so much of fine ideas as of fine words—words seemingly full of meaning which purport to leave a great deal unsaid. He must also belong to the "misunderstood" class, or be in some way at odds with his environment, so that the idea of self-sacrifice can insinuate itself. He must be a rather questionable hero, a man with possibilities, which is not to say that an animus projection may not discover a real hero long before he has become perceptible to the sluggish wits of the man of "average intelligence."[4]

340 For man as well as for woman, in so far as they are "containers," the filling out of this image is an experience fraught with consequences, for it holds the possibility of finding one's own complexities answered by a corresponding diversity. Wide vistas seem to open up in which one feels oneself embraced and contained. I say "seem" advisedly, because the experience may be two-faced. Just as the animus projection of a woman can often pick on a man of real significance who is not recognized by the mass, and can actually help him to achieve his true destiny with her moral support, so a man can create for himself a *femme inspiratrice* by his anima projection. But more often it turns out to be an illusion with destructive consequences, a failure because his faith was not sufficiently strong. To the pessimists I would say that these primordial psychic images have an extraordinarily positive value, but I must warn the optimists against

3 There are excellent descriptions of this type in H. Rider Haggard's *She* (London, 1887) and Pierre Benoît's *L'Atlantide* (Paris, 1920; trans. by Mary C. Tongue and Mary Ross as *Atlantida,* New York, 1920).

4 A passably good account of the animus is to be found in Marie Hay's book *The Evil Vineyard* (New York, 1923), also in Elinor Wylie's *Jennifer Lorn* (New York, 1923) and Selma Lagerlöf's *Gösta Berlings Saga* (1891; English trans. by P. B. Flach, *The Story of Gösta Berling,* 1898).

blinding fantasies and the likelihood of the most absurd aberrations.

341 One should on no account take this projection for an individual and conscious relationship. In its first stages it is far from that, for it creates a compulsive dependence based on unconscious motives other than the biological ones. Rider Haggard's *She* gives some indication of the curious world of ideas that underlies the anima projection. They are in essence spiritual contents, often in erotic disguise, obvious fragments of a primitive mythological mentality that consists of archetypes, and whose totality constitutes the collective unconscious. Accordingly, such a relationship is at bottom collective and not individual. (Benoît, who created in *L'Atlantide* a fantasy figure similar even in details to "She," denies having plagiarized Rider Haggard.)

342 If such a projection fastens on to one of the marriage partners, a collective spiritual relationship conflicts with the collective biological one and produces in the container the division or disintegration I have described above. If he is able to hold his head above water, he will find himself through this very conflict. In that case the projection, though dangerous in itself, will have helped him to pass from a collective to an individual relationship. This amounts to full conscious realization of the relationship that marriage brings. Since the aim of this paper is a discussion of the psychology of marriage, the psychology of projection cannot concern us here. It is sufficient to mention it as a fact.

343 One can hardly deal with the psychological marriage relationship without mentioning, even at the risk of misunderstanding, the nature of its critical transitions. As is well known, one understands nothing psychological unless one has experienced it oneself. Not that this ever prevents anyone from feeling convinced that his own judgment is the only true and competent one. This disconcerting fact comes from the necessary overvaluation of the momentary content of consciousness, for without this concentration of attention one could not be conscious at all. Thus it is that every period of life has its own psychological truth, and the same applies to every stage of psychological development. There are even stages which only the few can reach, it being a question of race, family, education, talent, and passion. Nature is aristocratic. The normal man is a fiction, al-

though certain generally valid laws do exist. Psychic life is a development that can easily be arrested on the lowest levels. It is as though every individual had a specific gravity, in accordance with which he either rises, or sinks down, to the level where he reaches his limit. His views and convictions will be determined accordingly. No wonder, then, that by far the greater number of marriages reach their upper psychological limit in fulfilment of the biological aim, without injury to spiritual or moral health. Relatively few people fall into deeper disharmony with themselves. Where there is a great deal of pressure from outside, the conflict is unable to develop much dramatic tension for sheer lack of energy. Psychological insecurity, however, increases in proportion to social security, unconsciously at first, causing neuroses, then consciously, bringing with it separations, discord, divorces, and other marital disorders. On still higher levels, new possibilities of psychological development are discerned, touching on the sphere of religion where critical judgment comes to a halt.

344 Progress may be permanently arrested on any of these levels, with complete unconsciousness of what might have followed at the next stage of development. As a rule graduation to the next stage is barred by violent prejudices and superstitious fears. This, however, serves a most useful purpose, since a man who is compelled by accident to live at a level too high for him becomes a fool and a menace.

345 Nature is not only aristocratic, she is also esoteric. Yet no man of understanding will thereby be induced to make a secret of what he knows, for he realizes only too well that the secret of psychic development can never be betrayed, simply because that development is a question of individual capacity.

WOMAN IN EUROPE [1]

> You call yourself free? Your dominant thought I would hear, and not that you have escaped from a yoke. Are you one of those who had the right to escape from a yoke? There are some who threw away their last value when they threw away their servitude.
>
> *Thus Spake Zarathustra*

236 To write about woman in Europe today is such a hazardous undertaking that I would scarcely have ventured to do so without a pressing invitation. Have we anything of fundamental importance to say about Europe? Is anyone sufficiently detached? Are we not all involved in some programme or experiment, or caught in some critical retrospect that clouds our judgment? And in regard to woman, cannot the same questions be asked? Moreover, what can a man say about woman, his own opposite? I mean of course something sensible, that is outside the sexual programme, free of resentment, illusion, and theory. Where is the man to be found capable of such superiority? Woman always stands just where the man's shadow falls, so that he is only too liable to confuse the two. Then, when he tries to repair this misunderstanding, he overvalues her and

1 [Originally published as "Die Frau in Europa," *Europäische Revue* (Berlin), III: 7 (Oct., 1927); republished by the *Neue Schweizer Rundschau* as a pamphlet (Zurich, 1929), which was reprinted by Rascher Verlag in 1932, 1948, and 1959 (cf. n. 2, infra). Trans. by C. F. and H. G. Baynes in *Contributions to Analytical Psychology* (London and New York, 1928), pp. 164–88, which version has been consulted here. The motto is from the trans. of Nietzsche by Common.—EDITORS.]

believes her the most desirable thing in the world. Thus it is with the greatest misgivings that I set out to treat of this theme.

237 One thing, however, is beyond doubt: that woman today is in the same process of transition as man. Whether this transition is a historical turning-point or not remains to be seen. Sometimes, when we look back at history, it seems as though the present time had analogies with certain periods in the past, when great empires and civilizations had passed their zenith and were hastening irresistibly towards decay. But these analogies are deceptive, for there are always renaissances. What *does* move more clearly into the foreground is Europe's position midway between the Asiatic East and the Anglo-Saxon—or shall we say American?—West. Europe now stands between two colossi, both uncouth in their form but implacably opposed to one another in their nature. They are profoundly different not only racially but in their ideals. In the West there is the maximum political freedom with the minimum personal freedom; in the East it is just the opposite. We see in the West a tremendous development of Europe's technological and scientific tendencies, and in the Far East an awakening of all those spiritual forces which, in Europe, these tendencies hold in check. The power of the West is material, that of the East ideal.[2] The struggle between these opposites, which in the world of the European man takes place in the realm of the scientifically applied intellect and finds expression on the battlefield and in the state of his bank balance, is, in woman, a psychic conflict.

238 What makes it so uncommonly difficult to discuss the problem of the modern European woman is that we are necessarily writing about a minority. There is no "modern European woman" properly speaking. Or is the peasant's wife of today different from her forbears of a hundred years ago? There is, in fact, a large body of the population that only to a very limited extent lives in the present and participates in present-day problems. We speak of a "woman's problem," but how many women have problems? In proportion to the sum-total of European women only a dwindling minority really live in the Europe of

2 In the thirty years since this essay was written the significance of the "East" has changed and has largely assumed the form of the "Russian Empire." This already reaches as far as central Germany, but it has lost nothing of its Asiatic character. [Author's footnote in 1959 pamphlet edition.—EDITORS.]

today; and these are city dwellers and belong—to put it cautiously—to the more complicated of their kind. This must always be so, for it is only the few who clearly express the spirit of the present in any age. In the fourth and fifth centuries of our era there were only a very few Christians who in any way understood the spirit of Christianity, the rest were still practically pagan. The cultural process that is characteristic of an epoch operates most intensely in cities, for it needs large agglomerations of men to make civilization possible, and from these agglomerations culture gradually spreads to the smaller, backward groups. Thus we find the present only in the large centres, and there alone do we encounter the "European woman," the woman who expresses the social and spiritual aspect of contemporary Europe. The further we go from the influence of the great centres, the more we find ourselves receding into history. In the remote Alpine valleys we can meet people who have never seen a railway, and in Spain, which is also a part of Europe, we plunge to a dark medieval age lacking even an alphabet. The people of those regions, or of the corresponding social strata, do not live in our Europe but in the Europe of 1400, and their problems are those of the bygone age in which they dwell. I have analysed such people, and have found myself carried back into an ambience that was not wanting in historical romance.

239 The "present" is a thin surface stratum that is laid down in the great centres of civilization. If it is very thin, as in Tsarist Russia, it has no meaning, as events have shown. But once it has attained a certain strength, we can speak of civilization and progress, and then problems arise that are characteristic of an epoch. In this sense Europe has a present, and there are women who live in it and suffer its problems. About these, and these only, are we entitled to speak. Those who are satisfied with a medieval life have no need of the present and its experiments. But the man of the present cannot—no matter what the reason—turn back again to the past without suffering an essential loss. Often this turning back is altogether impossible, even if he were prepared to make the sacrifice. The man of the present must work for the future and leave others to conserve the past. He is therefore not only a builder but also a destroyer. He and his world have both become questionable and ambiguous. The

ways that the past shows him and the answers it gives to his questions are insufficient for the needs of the present. All the old, comfortable ways are blocked, new paths have been opened up, and new dangers have arisen of which the past knew nothing. It is proverbial that one never learns anything from history, and in regard to present-day problems it usually teaches us nothing. The new path has to be made through untrodden regions, without presuppositions and often, unfortunately, without piety. The only thing that cannot be improved upon is morality, for every alteration of traditional morality is by definition an immorality. This *bon mot* has an edge to it, against which many an innovator has barked his shins.

240 All the problems of the present form a tangled knot, and it is hardly possible to single out one particular problem and treat it independently of the others. Thus there is no problem of "woman in Europe" without man and his world. If she is married, she usually has to depend economically on her husband; if she is unmarried and earning a living, she is working in some profession designed by a man. Unless she is prepared to sacrifice her whole erotic life, she again stands in some essential relationship to man. In numerous ways woman is indissolubly bound up with man's world and is therefore just as exposed as he is to all the shocks of his world. The war, for instance, has affected woman just as profoundly as it has man, and she has to adapt to its consequences as he must. What the upheavals of the last twenty or thirty years mean for man's world is apparent to everyone; we can read about it every day in the newspapers. But what it means for woman is not so evident. Neither politically, nor economically, nor spiritually is she a factor of visible importance. If she were, she would loom more largely in man's field of vision and would have to be considered a rival. Sometimes she is seen in this role, but only as a man, so to speak, who is accidentally a woman. But since as a rule her place is on man's intimate side, the side of him that merely feels and has no eyes and does not want to see, woman appears as an impenetrable mask behind which everything possible and impossible can be conjectured—and actually seen!—without his getting anywhere near the mark. The elementary fact that a person always thinks another's psychology is identical with his own effectively prevents a correct understanding of feminine psychology. This is

abetted by woman's own unconsciousness and passivity, useful though these may be from the biological point of view: she allows herself to be convinced by the man's projected feelings. Of course this is a general human characteristic, but in woman it is given a particularly dangerous twist, because in this respect she is not naïve and it is only too often her *intention* to let herself be convinced by them. It fits in with her nature to keep her ego and her will in the background, so as not to hinder the man in any way, and to invite him to realize his intentions with regard to her person. This is a sexual pattern, but it has far-reaching ramifications in the feminine psyche. By maintaining a passive attitude with an ulterior purpose, she helps the man to realize his ends and in that way holds him. At the same time she is caught in her own toils, for whoever digs a pit for others falls into it himself.

241 I admit that this is a rather unkind description of a process which might well be sung in more lyrical strains. But all natural things have two sides, and when something has to be made conscious we must see the shadow side as well as the light.

242 When we observe the way in which women, since the second half of the nineteenth century, have begun to take up masculine professions, to become active in politics, to sit on committees, etc., we can see that woman is in the process of breaking with the purely feminine sexual pattern of unconsciousness and passivity, and has made a concession to masculine psychology by establishing herself as a visible member of society. She no longer hides behind the mask of Mrs. So-and-so, with the obliging intention of having all her wishes fulfilled by the man, or to make him pay for it if things do not go as she wishes.

243 This step towards social independence is a necessary response to economic and other factors, but in itself it is only a symptom and not the thing about which we are most concerned. Certainly the courage and capacity for self-sacrifice of such women is admirable, and only the blind could fail to see the good that has come out of all these efforts. But no one can get round the fact that by taking up a masculine profession, studying and working like a man, woman is doing something not wholly in accord with, if not directly injurious to, her feminine nature. She is doing something that would scarcely be possible for a man to do, unless he were a Chinese. Could he, for instance, be

a nursemaid or run a kindergarten? When I speak of injury, I do not mean merely physiological injury but above all psychic injury. It is a woman's outstanding characteristic that she can do anything for the love of a man. But those women who can achieve something important for the love of a *thing* are most exceptional, because this does not really agree with their nature. Love for a thing is a man's prerogative. But since masculine and feminine elements are united in our human nature, a man can live in the feminine part of himself, and a woman in her masculine part. None the less the feminine element in man is only something in the background, as is the masculine element in woman. If one lives out the opposite sex in oneself one is living in one's own background, and one's real individuality suffers. A man should live as a man and a woman as a woman. The contrasexual element in either sex is always dangerously close to the unconscious. It is even typical that the effects of the unconscious upon the conscious mind have a contrasexual character. For instance the soul (anima, psyche) has a feminine character which compensates the masculine consciousness. (Mystical instruction among primitives is exclusively a masculine concern, corresponding to the function of the Catholic priest.)

244 The immediate presence of the unconscious exerts a magnetic influence on the conscious processes. This explains the fear or even horror we have of the unconscious. It is a purposeful defence-reaction of the conscious mind. The contrasexual element has a mysterious charm tinged with fear, perhaps even with disgust. For this reason its charm is particularly attractive and fascinating, even when it comes to us not directly from outside, in the guise of a woman, but from within, as a psychic influence—for instance in the form of a temptation to abandon oneself to a mood or an affect. This example is not characteristic of women, for a woman's moods and emotions do not come to her directly from the unconscious but are peculiar to her feminine nature. They are therefore never naïve, but are mixed with an unacknowledged purpose. What comes to a woman from the unconscious is a sort of *opinion,* which spoils her mood only secondarily. These opinions lay claim to being absolute truths, and they prove to be the more fixed and incorrigible the less they are subjected to conscious criticism. Like the moods and feelings of a man, they are somewhat hazy and often

totally unconscious, and are seldom recognized for what they are. They are in fact collective, having the character of the opposite sex, as though a man—the father, for example—had thought of them.

45 Thus it can happen—indeed it is almost the rule—that the mind of a woman who takes up a masculine profession is influenced by her unconscious masculinity in a way not noticeable to herself but quite obvious to everybody in her environment. She develops a kind of rigid intellectuality based on so-called principles, and backs them up with a whole host of arguments which always just miss the mark in the most irritating way, and always inject a little something into the problem that is not really there. Unconscious assumptions or opinions are the worst enemy of woman; they can even grow into a positively demonic passion that exasperates and disgusts men, and does the woman herself the greatest injury by gradually smothering the charm and meaning of her femininity and driving it into the background. Such a development naturally ends in profound psychological disunion, in short, in a neurosis.

46 Naturally, things need not go to this length, but long before this point is reached the mental masculinization of the woman has unwelcome results. She may perhaps be a good comrade to a man without having any access to his feelings. The reason is that her animus (that is, her masculine rationalism, assuredly not true reasonableness!) has stopped up the approaches to her own feeling. She may even become frigid, as a defence against the masculine type of sexuality that corresponds to her masculine type of mind. Or, if the defence-reaction is not successful, she develops, instead of the receptive sexuality of woman, an aggressive, urgent form of sexuality that is more characteristic of a man. This reaction is likewise a purposeful phenomenon, intended to throw a bridge across by main force to the slowly vanishing man. A third possibility, especially favoured in Anglo-Saxon countries, is optional homosexuality in the masculine role.

47 It may therefore be said that, whenever the attraction of the animus becomes noticeable, there is a quite special need for the woman to have an intimate relationship with the other sex. Many women in this situation are fully aware of this necessity and proceed—*faute de mieux*—to stir up another of those

present-day problems that is no less painful, namely, the marriage problem.

248 Traditionally, man is regarded as the marriage breaker. This legend comes from times long past, when men still had leisure to pursue all sorts of pastimes. But today life makes so many demands on men that the noble hidalgo, Don Juan, is to be seen nowhere save in the theatre. More than ever man loves his comfort, for ours is an age of neurasthenia, impotence, and easy chairs. There is no energy left for window-climbing and duels. If anything is to happen in the way of adultery it must not be too difficult. In no respect must it cost too much, hence the adventure can only be of a transitory kind. The man of today is thoroughly scared of jeopardizing marriage as an institution. He is a firm believer in doing things on the quiet, and therefore supports prostitution. I would wager that in the Middle Ages, with its notorious bagnios and unrestricted prostitution, adultery was relatively more frequent than it is today. In this respect marriage should be safer now than it ever was. But in reality it is beginning to be discussed. It is a bad sign when doctors begin writing books of advice on how to achieve the "perfect marriage." Healthy people need no doctors. Marriage today has indeed become rather precarious. In America about a quarter of the marriages end in divorce. And the remarkable thing is that this time the scapegoat is not the man but the woman. She is the one who doubts and feels uncertain. It is not surprising that this is so, for in post-war Europe there is such an alarming surplus of unmarried women that it would be inconceivable if there were no reaction from that quarter. Such a piling up of misery has inescapable consequences. It is no longer a question of a few dozen voluntary or involuntary old maids here and there, but of millions. Our legislation and our social morality give no answer to this question. Or can the Church provide a satisfactory answer? Should we build gigantic nunneries to accommodate all these women? Or should tolerated prostitution be increased? Obviously this is impossible, since we are dealing neither with saints nor sinners but with ordinary women who cannot register their spiritual requirements with the police. They are decent women who want to marry, and if this is not possible, well—the next best thing. When it comes to the question of love, laws and institutions and ideals mean less to

woman than ever before. If things cannot go straight they will have to go crooked.

9 At the beginning of our era, three-fifths of the population of Italy consisted of slaves—human chattels without rights. Every Roman was surrounded by slaves. The slave and his psychology flooded ancient Italy, and every Roman became inwardly a slave. Living constantly in the atmosphere of slaves, he became infected with their psychology. No one can shield himself from this unconscious influence. Even today the European, however highly developed, cannot live with impunity among the Negroes in Africa; their psychology gets into him unnoticed and unconsciously he becomes a Negro. There is no fighting against it. In Africa there is a well-known technical expression for this: "going black." It is no mere snobbery that the English should consider anyone born in the colonies, even though the best blood may run in his veins, "slightly inferior." There are facts to support this view.

0 A direct result of slave influence was the strange melancholy and longing for deliverance that pervaded imperial Rome and found striking expression in Virgil's Fourth Eclogue. The explosive spread of Christianity, a religion which might be said to have risen from the sewers of Rome—Nietzsche called it a "slave insurrection in morals"—was a sudden reaction that set the soul of the lowest slave on a par with that of the divine Caesar. Similar though perhaps less momentous processes of psychological compensation have repeatedly occurred in the history of the world. Whenever some social or psychological monstrosity is created, a compensation comes along in defiance of all legislation and all expectation.

1 Something similar is happening to women in present-day Europe. Too much that is inadmissible, that has not been lived, is accumulating in the unconscious, and this is bound to have an effect. Secretaries, typists, shop-girls, all are agents of this process, and through a million subterranean channels creeps the influence that is undermining marriage. For the desire of all these women is not to have sexual adventures—only the stupid could believe that—but to get married. The possessors of that bliss must be ousted, not as a rule by naked force, but by that silent, obstinate desire which, as we know, has magical effects, like the fixed stare of a snake. This was ever the way of women.

252 What is the attitude of the married woman to all this? She clings to the old idea that man is the scapegoat, that he switches from one love-affair to another as he pleases, and so on. On the strength of these outworn conceptions she can wrap herself still more deeply in her jealousies. But all this is only on the surface. Neither the pride of the Roman patrician nor the thick walls of the imperial palace availed to keep out the slave infection. In the same way, no woman can escape the secret, compelling atmosphere with which her own sister, perhaps, is enveloping her, the stifling atmosphere of a life that has never been lived. Unlived life is a destructive, irresistible force that works softly but inexorably. The result is that the married woman begins to have doubts about marriage. The unmarried believe in it because they want it. Equally, the man believes in marriage because of his love of comfort and a sentimental belief in institutions, which for him always tend to become objects of feeling.

253 Since women have to be down to earth in matters of feeling, a certain fact should not escape our notice. This is the possibility of contraceptive measures. Children are one of the main reasons for maintaining a responsible attitude towards marriage. If this reason disappears, then the things that are "not done" happen easily enough. This applies primarily to unmarried women, who thus have an opportunity to contract an "approximate" marriage. But it is a consideration that counts also with all those married women who, as I have shown in my essay "Marriage as a Psychological Relationship," [3] are the "containers." By this I mean women whose demands as individuals are not satisfied, or not wholly satisfied, by their husbands. Finally, contraception is a fact of enormous importance to women in general, because it does away with the constant fear of pregnancy and the care of an ever-increasing number of children. This deliverance from bondage to nature brings a release of psychic energies that inevitably seek an outlet. Whenever a sum of energy finds no congenial goal it causes a disturbance of the psychic equilibrium. Lacking a conscious goal, it reinforces the unconscious and gives rise to uncertainty and doubt.

254 Another factor of great importance is the more or less open

[3] In *The Development of Personality, Coll. Works,* Vol. 17.

discussion of the sexual problem. This territory, once so obscure, has now become a focus of scientific and other interests. Things can be heard and said in society that formerly would have been quite impossible. Large numbers of people have learned to think more freely and honestly, and have come to realize how important these matters are. The discussion of the sexual problem is, however, only a somewhat crude prelude to a far deeper question, and that is the question of the psychological relationship between the sexes. In comparison with this the other pales into insignificance, and with it we enter the real domain of woman.

5 Woman's psychology is founded on the principle of Eros, the great binder and loosener, whereas from ancient times the ruling principle ascribed to man is Logos. The concept of Eros could be expressed in modern terms as psychic relatedness, and that of Logos as objective interest. In the eyes of the ordinary man, love in its true sense coincides with the institution of marriage, and outside marriage there is only adultery or "platonic" friendship. For woman, marriage is not an institution at all but a human love-relationship—at least that is what she would like to believe. (Since her Eros is not naïve but is mixed with other, unavowed motives—marriage as a ladder to social position, etc.—the principle cannot be applied in any absolute sense.) Marriage means to her an exclusive relationship. She can endure its exclusiveness all the more easily, without dying of ennui, inasmuch as she has children or near relatives with whom she has a no less intimate relationship than with her husband. The fact that she has no sexual relationship with these others means nothing, for the sexual relationship is of far less importance to her than the psychic relationship. It is enough that she and her husband both believe their relationship to be unique and exclusive. If he happens to be the "container" he feels suffocated by this exclusiveness, especially if he fails to notice that the exclusiveness of his wife is nothing but a pious fraud. In reality she is distributed among the children and among as many members of the family as possible, thus maintaining any number of intimate relationships. If her husband had anything like as many relationships with other people she would be mad with jealousy. Most men, though, are erotically blinded—they commit the unpardonable mistake of confusing

Eros with sex. A man thinks he possesses a woman if he has her sexually. He never possesses her less, for to a woman the Eros-relationship is the real and decisive one. For her, marriage is a relationship with sex thrown in as an accompaniment. Since sex is a formidable thing on account of its consequences, it is useful to have it in a safe place. But when it is less of a danger it also becomes less relevant, and then the question of relationship moves into the foreground.

256 It is just here that the woman runs into great difficulties with her husband, for the question of relationship borders on a region that for him is dark and painful. He can face this question only when the woman carries the burden of suffering, that is, when he is the "contained"—in other words, when she can imagine herself having a relationship with another man, and as a consequence suffering disunion within herself. Then it is she who has the painful problem, and he is not obliged to see his own, which is a great relief to him. In this situation he is not unlike a thief who, quite undeservedly, finds himself in the enviable position of having been forestalled by another thief who has been caught by the police. Suddenly he becomes an honourable, impartial onlooker. In any other situation a man always finds the discussion of personal relations painful and boring, just as his wife would find it boring if he examined her on the *Critique of Pure Reason*. For him, Eros is a shadow-land which entangles him in his feminine unconscious, in something "psychic," while for woman Logos is a deadly boring kind of sophistry if she is not actually repelled and frightened by it.

257 Just as woman began, towards the end of the nineteenth century, to make a concession to masculinity by taking her place as an independent factor in the social world, so man has made, somewhat hesitantly, a concession to femininity by creating a new psychology of complex phenomena, inaugurated by the sexual psychology of Freud. What this psychology owes to the direct influence of women—psychiatrists' consulting-rooms are packed with women—is a theme that would fill a large volume. I am speaking here not only of analytical psychology but of the beginnings of psychopathology in general. By far the greatest number of "classic" cases, beginning with the "Seeress of Prevorst," were women, who, perhaps unconsciously, took enor-

mous trouble to put their own psychology on view in the most dramatic fashion, and thus demonstrated to the world the whole question of psychic relationship. Women like Frau Hauffe and Hélène Smith [4] and Miss Beauchamp have assured for themselves a kind of immortality, rather like those worthy folk whose miraculous cures brought fame and prosperity to the wonder-working spot.

8 An astonishingly high percentage of this material comes from women. This is not as remarkable as it might seem, for women are far more "psychological" than men. A man is usually satisfied with "logic" alone. Everything "psychic," "unconscious" etc., is repugnant to him; he considers it vague, nebulous, and morbid. He is interested in things, in facts, and not in the feelings and fantasies that cluster round them or have nothing to do with them. To a woman it is generally more important to know how a man feels about a thing than to know the thing itself. All those things which are merely futile impedimenta to a man are important to her. So it is naturally woman who is the most direct exponent of psychology and gives it its richest content. Very many things can be perceived in her with the utmost distinctness which in a man are mere shadowy processes in the background, whose very existence he is unwilling to admit. But, unlike the objective discussion and verification of facts, a human relationship leads into the world of the psyche, into that intermediate realm between sense and spirit, which contains something of both and yet forfeits nothing of its own unique character.

9 Into this territory a man must venture if he wishes to meet woman half way. Circumstances have forced her to acquire a number of masculine traits, so that she shall not remain caught in an antiquated, purely instinctual femininity, lost and alone in the world of men. So, too, man will be forced to develop his feminine side, to open his eyes to the psyche and to Eros. It is a task he cannot avoid, unless he prefers to go trailing after woman in a hopelessly boyish fashion, worshipping from afar but always in danger of being stowed away in her pocket.

60 For those in love with masculinity or femininity *per se* the traditional medieval marriage is enough—and a thoroughly

4 [See *Psychiatric Studies, Coll. Works,* Vol. 1, index, s. vv.—Editors.]

praiseworthy, well-tried, useful institution it is. But the man of today finds it extremely difficult to return to it, and for many the way back is simply impossible, because this sort of marriage can exist only by shutting out all contemporary problems. Doubtless there were many Romans who could shut their eyes to the slave problem and to Christianity, and spend their days in a more or less pleasant unconsciousness. They could do this because they had no relation to the present, only to the past. All those for whom marriage contains no problem are not living in the present, and who shall say they are not blessed! Modern man finds marriage only too problematical. I recently heard a German scholar exclaim before an audience of several hundred people: "Our marriages are sham marriages!" I admired his courage and sincerity. Usually we express ourselves less directly, cautiously offering good advice as to what might be done—in order not to tarnish the ideal. But for the modern woman—let men take note of this—the medieval marriage is an ideal no longer. True, she keeps her doubts to herself, and hides her rebelliousness; one woman because she is married and finds it highly inconvenient if the door of the safe is not hermetically sealed, another because she is unmarried and too virtuous to look her own tendencies squarely in the face. Nevertheless, their newly-won masculinity makes it impossible for either of them to believe in marriage in its traditional form ("He shall be thy master"). Masculinity means knowing what one wants and doing what is necessary to achieve it. Once this lesson has been learned it is so obvious that it can never again be forgotten without tremendous psychic loss. The independence and critical judgment she acquires through this knowledge are positive values and are felt as such by the woman. She can never part with them again. The same is true of the man who, with great efforts, wins that needful feminine insight into his own psyche, often at the cost of much suffering. He will never let it go again, because he is thoroughly aware of the importance of what he has won.

261 At first glance it might be thought that such a man and woman would be especially likely to make the "perfect marriage." In reality this is not so; on the contrary, a conflict begins immediately. What the woman, in her new-found self-assurance, wants to do is not at all pleasing to the man, while the feelings

he has discovered in himself are far from agreeable to the woman. What both have discovered in themselves is not a virtue or anything of intrinsic value; it is something comparatively inferior, and it might justly be condemned if it were understood as the outcome of a personal choice or mood. And that, indeed, is what usually happens. The masculinity of the woman and the femininity of the man *are* inferior, and it is regrettable that the full value of their personalities should be contaminated by something that is less valuable. On the other hand, the shadow belongs to the wholeness of the personality: the strong man must somewhere be weak, somewhere the clever man must be stupid, otherwise he is too good to be true and falls back on pose and bluff. Is it not an old truth that woman loves the weaknesses of the strong man more than his strength, and the stupidity of the clever man more than his cleverness? Her love wants the whole man—not mere masculinity as such but also its negation. The love of woman is not sentiment, as is a man's, but a will that is at times terrifyingly unsentimental and can even force her to self-sacrifice. A man who is loved in this way cannot escape his inferior side, for he can only respond to the reality of her love with his own reality. And this reality is no fair semblance, but a faithful reflection of that eternal human nature which links together all humanity, a reflection of the heights and depths of human life which are common to us all. In this reality we are no longer differentiated persons (*persona* means a mask), but are conscious of our common human bonds. Here I strip off the distinctiveness of my own personality, social or otherwise, and reach down to the problems of the present day, problems which do not arise out of myself—or so at least I like to imagine. Here I can no longer deny them; I feel and know myself to be one of many, and what moves the many moves me. In our strength we are independent and isolated, and are masters of our own fate; in our weakness we are dependent and bound, and become unwilling instruments of fate, for here it is not the individual will that counts but the will of the species.

262 What the two sexes have won through mutual assimilation is an inferiority when viewed from the two-dimensional, personal world of appearances, and an immoral pretension if regarded as a personal claim. But in its truest meaning for life

and society it is an overcoming of personal isolation and selfish reserve in order to take an active part in the solution of present-day problems. If, therefore, the woman of today consciously or unconsciously loosens the cohesion of the marriage bond by her spiritual or economic independence, this is not the expression of her personal will, but of the will of the species, which makes her, the individual woman, its tool.

263 The institution of marriage is such a valuable thing, both socially and morally—religious people even regard it as a sacrament—that it is quite understandable that any weakening of it should be felt as undesirable, indeed scandalous. Human imperfection is always a discord in the harmony of our ideals. Unfortunately, no one lives in the world as we desire it, but in the world of actuality where good and evil clash and destroy one another, where no creating or building can be done without dirtying one's hands. Whenever things get really bad, there is always some one to assure us amid great applause that nothing has happened and everything is in order. I repeat, anyone who lives and thinks like this is not living in the present. If we examine any marriage with a really critical eye, we shall find—unless acute pressure of circumstances has completely extinguished all signs of "psychological" trouble—symptoms of its weakening and clandestine disruption, "marriage problems" ranging from unbearable moods to neurosis and adultery. Unfortunately, those who can still bear to remain unconscious cannot be imitated; their example is not infectious enough to induce more conscious people to descend again to the level of mere unconsciousness.

264 As to all those—and they are many—who are not obliged to live in the present, it is extremely important that they should believe in the ideal of marriage and hold fast to it. Nothing is gained if a valuable ideal is merely destroyed and not replaced by something better. Therefore even the women hesitate, whether they are married or not, to go over openly to the side of rebellion. But at least they do not follow the lead of that well-known authoress who, after trying out all sorts of experiments, ended up in the secure haven of matrimony, whereupon marriage became the best solution, and all those who did not achieve it could brood on their mistakes and end their days in pious renunciation. For the modern woman marriage is not as

easy as that. Her husband would have something to say on this score.

5 So long as there are legalistic clauses that lay down exactly what adultery is, women will have to remain with their doubts. But do our legislators really know what "adultery" is? Is their definition of it the final embodiment of the truth? From the psychological standpoint, the only one that counts for a woman, it is a wretched piece of bungling, like everything else contrived by men for the purpose of codifying love. For a woman, love has nothing to do with "marital misconduct," "extramarital intercourse," "deception of the husband," or any of the less savoury formulas invented by the erotically blind masculine intellect and echoed by the self-opinionated demon in woman. Nobody but the absolute believer in the inviolability of traditional marriage could perpetrate such breaches of good taste, just as only the believer in God can really blaspheme. Whoever doubts marriage in the first place cannot infringe against it; for him the legal definition is invalid because, like St. Paul, he feels himself beyond the law, on the higher plane of love. But because the believers in the law so frequently trespass against their own laws, whether from stupidity, temptation, or mere viciousness, the modern woman begins to wonder whether she too may not belong to the same category. From the traditional standpoint she does, and she has to realize this in order to smash the idol of her own respectability. To be "respectable" means, as the word tells us, to allow oneself to be seen; a respectable person is one who comes up to public expectations, who wears an ideal mask—in short, is a fraud. "Good form" is not a fraud, but when respectability represses the psyche, the God-given essence of man, then one becomes what Christ called a whited sepulchre.

6 The modern woman has become conscious of the undeniable fact that only in the state of love can she attain the highest and best of which she is capable, and this knowledge drives her to the other realization that love is beyond the law. Her respectability revolts against this, and one is inclined to identify this reaction with public opinion. That would be the lesser evil; what is worse is that public opinion is in her blood. It comes to her like a voice from within, a sort of conscience, and this is the power that holds her in check. She is unaware that love, her most personal, most prized possession, could bring her into

conflict with history. Such a thing would seem to her most unexpected and absurd. But who, if it comes to that, has fully realized that history is not contained in thick books but lives in our very blood?

267 So long as a woman lives the life of the past she can never come into conflict with history. But no sooner does she begin to deviate, however slightly, from a cultural trend that has dominated the past than she encounters the full weight of historical inertia, and this unexpected shock may injure her, perhaps fatally. Her hesitation and her doubt are understandable enough, for, if she submits to the law of love, she finds that she is not only in a highly disagreeable and dubious situation, where every kind of lewdness and depravity abounds, but actually caught between two universal forces—historical inertia and the divine urge to create.

268 Who, then, will blame her for hesitating? Do not most men prefer to rest on their laurels rather than get into a hopeless conflict as to whether they shall or shall not make history? In the end it boils down to this: is one prepared to break with tradition, to be "unhistorical" in order to make history, or not? No one can make history who is not willing to risk everything for it, to carry the experiment with his own life through to the bitter end, and to declare that his life is not a continuation of the past, but a new beginning. Mere continuation can be left to the animals, but inauguration is the prerogative of man, the one thing he can boast of that lifts him above the beasts.

269 There is no doubt that the woman of today is deeply concerned with this problem. She gives expression to one of the cultural tendencies of our time: the urge to live a completer life, a longing for meaning and fulfilment, a growing disgust with senseless one-sidedness, with unconscious instinctuality and blind contingency. The psyche of the modern European has not forgotten the lesson of the last war, however much it has been banished from his consciousness. Women are increasingly aware that love alone can give them full stature, just as men are beginning to divine that only the spirit can give life its highest meaning. Both seek a psychic relationship, because love needs the spirit, and the spirit love, for its completion.

270 Woman nowadays feels that there is no real security in marriage, for what does her husband's faithfulness mean when she

knows that his feelings and thoughts are running after others and that he is merely too calculating or too cowardly to follow them? What does her own faithfulness mean when she knows that she is simply using it to exploit her legal right of possession, and warping her own soul? She has intimations of a higher fidelity to the spirit and to a love beyond human weakness and imperfection. Perhaps she will yet discover that what seems like weakness and imperfection, a painful disturbance, or an alarming deviation, must be interpreted in accordance with its dual nature. These are steps that lead down to the lowest human level and finally end in the morass of unconsciousness if the individual lets go of his personal distinctiveness. But if he can hold on to it, he will experience for the first time the meaning of selfhood, provided that he can simultaneously descend below himself into the undifferentiated mass of humanity. What else can free him from the inner isolation of his personal differentiation? And how else can he establish a psychic bridge to the rest of mankind? The man who stands on high and distributes his goods to the poor is separated from mankind by the height of his own virtue, and the more he forgets himself and sacrifices himself for others the more he is inwardly estranged from them.

71 The word "human" sounds very beautiful, but properly understood it does not mean anything particularly beautiful, or virtuous, or intelligent, but just a low average. This is the step which Zarathustra could not take, the step to the "Ugliest Man," who is real man. Our resistance to taking this step, and our fear of it, show how great is the attraction and seductive power of our own depths. To cut oneself off from them is no solution; it is a mere sham, an essential misunderstanding of their meaning and value. For where is a height without depth, and how can there be light that throws no shadow? There is no good that is not opposed by evil. "No man can be redeemed from a sin he has not committed," says Carpocrates; a deep saying for all who wish to understand, and a golden opportunity for all those who prefer to draw false conclusions. What is down below is not just an excuse for more pleasure, but something we fear because it demands to play its part in the life of the more conscious and more complete man.

272 What I am saying here is not for the young—it is precisely what they ought not to know—but for the more mature man whose consciousness has been widened by experience of life. No man can begin with the present; he must slowly grow into it, for there would be no present but for the past. A young person has not yet acquired a past, therefore he has no present either. He does not create culture, he merely exists. It is the privilege and the task of maturer people, who have passed the meridian of life, to create culture.

273 The European psyche has been torn to shreds by the hellish barbarism of the war. While man turns his hand to repairing the outer damage, woman—unconsciously as ever—sets about healing the inner wounds, and for this she needs, as her most important instrument, a psychic relationship. But nothing hampers this more than the exclusiveness of the medieval marriage, for it makes relationship altogether superfluous. Relationship is possible only if there is a psychic distance between people, in the same way that morality presupposes freedom. For this reason the unconscious tendency of woman aims at loosening the marriage structure, but not at the destruction of marriage and the family. That would be not only immoral but a thoroughly pathological misuse of her powers.

274 It would take volumes of case-material to describe the innumerable ways in which this goal is achieved. It is the way of woman, as of nature, to work indirectly, without naming her goal. To anything unsatisfactory she reacts purposively, with moods, outbursts of affects, opinions, and actions that all have the same end in view, and their apparent senselessness, virulence, and cold-blooded ruthlessness are infinitely distressing to the man who is blind to Eros.

275 The indirect method of woman is dangerous, for it can hopelessly compromise her aim. That is why she longs for greater consciousness, which would enable her to name her goal and give it meaning, and thus escape the blind dynamism of nature. In any other age it would have been the prevailing religion that showed her where her ultimate goal lay; but today religion leads back to the Middle Ages, back to that soul-destroying unrelatedness from which came all the fearful barbarities of war. Too much soul is reserved for God, too little for man. But God

himself cannot flourish if man's soul is starved. The feminine psyche responds to this hunger, for it is the function of Eros to unite what Logos has sundered. The woman of today is faced with a tremendous cultural task—perhaps it will be the dawn of a new era.

ANIMA AND ANIMUS

296 Among all possible spirits the spirits of the parents are in practice the most important; hence the universal incidence of the ancestor cult. In its original form it served to conciliate the *revenants,* but on a higher level of culture it became an essentially moral and educational institution, as in China. For the child, the parents are his closest and most influential relations. But as he grows older this influence is split off; consequently the parental imagos become increasingly shut away from consciousness, and on account of the restrictive influence they sometimes continue to exert, they easily acquire a negative aspect. In this way the parental imagos remain as alien elements somewhere "outside" the psyche. In place of the parents, woman now takes up her position as the most immediate environmental influence in the life of the adult man. She becomes his companion, she belongs to him in so far as she shares his life and is more or less of the same age. She is not of a superior order, either by virtue of age, authority, or physical strength. She is, however, a very influential factor and, like the parents, she produces an imago of a relatively autonomous nature—not an imago to be split off like that of the parents, but one that has to be kept associated with consciousness. Woman, with her very dissimilar psychology, is and always has been a source of information about things for which a man has no eyes. She can be his inspiration; her intuitive capacity, often superior to man's, can give him timely warning, and her feeling, always directed towards the personal, can show him ways which his own less personally accented feeling would never have discovered. What Tacitus says about the Germanic women is exactly to the point in this respect.[1]

297 Here, without a doubt, is one of the main sources for the feminine quality of the soul. But it does not seem to be the only

1 *Germania* (Loeb edn.), pars. 18, 19.

source. No man is so entirely masculine that he has nothing feminine in him. The fact is, rather, that very masculine men have—carefully guarded and hidden—a very soft emotional life, often incorrectly described as "feminine." A man counts it a virtue to repress his feminine traits as much as possible, just as a woman, at least until recently, considered it unbecoming to be "mannish." The repression of feminine traits and inclinations naturally causes these contrasexual demands to accumulate in the unconscious. No less naturally, the imago of woman (the soul-image) becomes a receptacle for these demands, which is why a man, in his love-choice, is strongly tempted to win the woman who best corresponds to his own unconscious femininity—a woman, in short, who can unhesitatingly receive the projection of his soul. Although such a choice is often regarded and felt as altogether ideal, it may turn out that the man has manifestly married his own worst weakness. This would explain some highly remarkable conjunctions.

298 It seems to me, therefore, that apart from the influence of woman there is also the man's own femininity to explain the feminine nature of the soul-complex. There is no question here of any linguistic "accident," of the kind that makes the sun feminine in German and masculine in other languages. We have, in this matter, the testimony of art from all ages, and besides that the famous question: *habet mulier animam?* Most men, probably, who have any psychological insight at all will know what Rider Haggard means by "She-who-must-be-obeyed," and will also recognize the chord that is struck when they read Benoît's description of Antinéa.[2] Moreover they know at once the kind of woman who most readily embodies this mysterious factor, of which they have so vivid a premonition.

299 The wide recognition accorded to such books shows that there must be some supra-individual quality in this image of the anima,[3] something that does not owe a fleeting existence simply to its individual uniqueness, but is far more typical, with roots that go deeper than the obvious surface attachments I have pointed out. Both Rider Haggard and Benoît give unmistak-

2 Cf. Rider Haggard, *She;* Benoît, *L'Atlantide.*

3 Cf. *Psychological Types,* Def. 48, "Soul." [Also "Concerning the Archetypes, with Special Reference to the Anima Concept" and "The Psychological Aspects of the Kore."—EDITORS.]

able utterance to this supposition in the *historical* aspect of their anima figures.

300 As we know, there is no human experience, nor would experience be possible at all, without the intervention of a subjective aptitude. What is this subjective aptitude? Ultimately it consists in an innate psychic structure which allows man to have experiences of this kind. Thus the whole nature of man presupposes woman, both physically and spiritually. His system is tuned in to woman from the start, just as it is prepared for a quite definite world where there is water, light, air, salt, carbohydrates, etc. The form of the world into which he is born is already inborn in him as a virtual image. Likewise parents, wife, children, birth, and death are inborn in him as virtual images, as psychic aptitudes. These *a priori* categories have by nature a collective character; they are images of parents, wife, and children in general, and are not individual predestinations. We must therefore think of these images as lacking in solid content, hence as unconscious. They only acquire solidity, influence, and eventual consciousness in the encounter with empirical facts, which touch the unconscious aptitude and quicken it to life. They are in a sense the deposits of all our ancestral experiences, but they are not the experiences themselves. So at least it seems to us, in the present limited state of our knowledge. (I must confess that I have never yet found infallible evidence for the inheritance of memory images, but I do not regard it as positively precluded that in addition to these collective deposits which contain nothing specifically individual, there may also be inherited memories that are individually determined.)

301 An inherited collective image of woman exists in a man's unconscious, with the help of which he apprehends the nature of woman. This inherited image is the third important source for the femininity of the soul.

302 As the reader will have grasped, we are not concerned here with a philosophical, much less a religious, concept of the soul, but with the psychological recognition of the existence of a semiconscious psychic complex, having partial autonomy of function. Clearly, this recognition has as much or as little to do with philosophical or religious conceptions of the soul, as psychology has as much or as little to do with philosophy or religion. I have no wish to embark here on a "battle of the facul-

ties," nor do I seek to demonstrate either to the philosopher or to the theologian what exactly he means by "soul." I must, however, restrain both of them from prescribing what the psychologist *ought* to mean by "soul." The quality of personal immortality so fondly attributed to the soul by religion is, for science, no more than a psychological *indicium* which is already included in the idea of autonomy. The quality of personal immortality is by no means a constant attribute of the soul as the primitive sees it, nor even immortality as such. But setting this view aside as altogether inaccessible to science, the immediate meaning of "immortality" is simply a psychic activity that transcends the limits of consciousness. "Beyond the grave" or "on the other side of death" means, psychologically, "beyond consciousness." There is positively nothing else it could mean, since statements about immortality can only be made by the living, who, as such, are not exactly in a position to pontificate about conditions "beyond the grave."

303 The autonomy of the soul-complex naturally lends support to the notion of an invisible, personal entity that apparently lives in a world very different from ours. Consequently, once the activity of the soul is felt to be that of an autonomous entity having no ties with our mortal substance, it is but a step to imagining that this entity must lead an entirely independent existence, perhaps in a world of invisible things. Yet it is not immediately clear why the *invisibility* of this independent entity should simultaneously imply its *immortality*. The quality of immortality might easily derive from another fact to which I have already alluded, namely the characteristically historical aspect of the soul. Rider Haggard has given one of the best descriptions of this in *She*. When the Buddhists say that progressive perfection through meditation awakens memories of former incarnations, they are no doubt referring to the same psychological reality, the only difference being that they ascribe the historical factor not to the soul but to the Self (*atman*). It is altogether in keeping with the thoroughly extraverted attitude of the Western mind so far, that immortality should be ascribed, both by feeling and by tradition, to a soul which we distinguish more or less from our ego, and which also differs from the ego on account of its feminine qualities. It would be entirely logical if, by deepening that neglected, introverted side of our spiritual culture, there

were to take place in us a transformation more akin to the Eastern frame of mind, where the quality of immortality would transfer itself from the ambiguous figure of the soul (*anima*) to the self. For it is essentially the overvaluation of the material object without that constellates a spiritual and immortal figure within (obviously for the purpose of compensation and self-regulation). Fundamentally, the historical factor does not attach only to the archetype of the feminine, but to all archetypes whatsoever, i.e., to every inherited unit, mental as well as physical. Our life is indeed the same as it ever was. At all events, in our sense of the word it is not transitory; for the same physiological and psychological processes that have been man's for hundreds of thousands of years still endure, instilling into our inmost hearts this profound intuition of the "eternal" continuity of the living. But the self, as an inclusive term that embraces our whole living organism, not only contains the deposit and totality of all past life, but is also a point of departure, the fertile soil from which all future life will spring. This premonition of futurity is as clearly impressed upon our innermost feelings as is the historical aspect. The idea of immortality follows legitimately from these psychological premises.

04 In the Eastern view the concept of the anima, as we have stated it here, is lacking, and so, logically, is the concept of a persona. This is certainly no accident, for, as I have already indicated, a compensatory relationship exists between persona and anima.

05 The persona is a complicated system of relations between the individual consciousness and society, fittingly enough a kind of mask, designed on the one hand to make a definite impression upon others, and, on the other, to conceal the true nature of the individual. That the latter function is superfluous could be maintained only by one who is so identified with his persona that he no longer knows himself; and that the former is unnecessary could only occur to one who is quite unconscious of the true nature of his fellows. Society expects, and indeed must expect, every individual to play the part assigned to him as perfectly as possible, so that a man who is a parson must not only carry out his official functions objectively, but must at all times and in all circumstances play the role of parson in a flawless manner. Society demands this as a kind of surety; each must stand at his

post, here a cobbler, there a poet. No man is expected to be both. Nor is it advisable to be both, for that would be "odd." Such a man would be "different" from other people, not quite reliable. In the academic world he would be a dilettante, in politics an "unpredictable" quantity, in religion a free-thinker—in short, he would always be suspected of unreliability and incompetence, because society is persuaded that only the cobbler who is not a poet can supply workmanlike shoes. To present an unequivocal face to the world is a matter of practical importance: the average man—the only kind society knows anything about—must keep his nose to one thing in order to achieve anything worth while, two would be too much. Our society is undoubtedly set on such an ideal. It is therefore not surprising that everyone who wants to get on must take these expectations into account. Obviously no one could completely submerge his individuality in these expectations; hence the construction of an artificial personality becomes an unavoidable necessity. The demands of propriety and good manners are an added inducement to assume a becoming mask. What goes on behind the mask is then called "private life." This painfully familiar division of consciousness into two figures, often preposterously different, is an incisive psychological operation that is bound to have repercussions on the unconscious.

306 The construction of a collectively suitable persona means a formidable concession to the external world, a genuine self-sacrifice which drives the ego straight into identification with the persona, so that people really do exist who believe they are what they pretend to be. The "soullessness" of such an attitude is, however, only apparent, for under no circumstances will the unconscious tolerate this shifting of the centre of gravity. When we examine such cases critically, we find that the excellence of the mask is compensated by the "private life" going on behind it. The pious Drummond once lamented that "bad temper is the vice of the virtuous." Whoever builds up too good a persona for himself naturally has to pay for it with irritability. Bismarck had hysterical weeping fits, Wagner indulged in correspondence about the belts of silk dressing-gowns, Nietzsche wrote letters to his "dear lama," Goethe held conversations with Eckermann, etc. But there are subtler things than the banal lapses of heroes. I once made the acquaintance of a very venerable personage—in

fact, one might easily call him a saint. I stalked round him for three whole days, but never a mortal failing did I find in him. My feeling of inferiority grew ominous, and I was beginning to think seriously of how I might better myself. Then, on the fourth day, his wife came to consult me. . . . Well, nothing of the sort has ever happened to me since. But this I did learn: that any man who becomes one with his persona can cheerfully let all disturbances manifest themselves through his wife without her noticing it, though she pays for her self-sacrifice with a bad neurosis.

07 These identifications with a social role are a very fruitful source of neuroses. A man cannot get rid of himself in favour of an artificial personality without punishment. Even the attempt to do so brings on, in all ordinary cases, unconscious reactions in the form of bad moods, affects, phobias, obsessive ideas, backslidings, vices, etc. The social "strong man" is in his private life often a mere child where his own states of feeling are concerned; his discipline in public (which he demands quite particularly of others) goes miserably to pieces in private. His "happiness in his work" assumes a woeful countenance at home; his "spotless" public morality looks strange indeed behind the mask—we will not mention deeds, but only fantasies, and the wives of such men would have a pretty tale to tell. As to his selfless altruism, his children have decided views about that.

08 To the degree that the world invites the individual to identify with the mask, he is delivered over to influences from within. "High rests on low," says Lao-tzu. An opposite forces its way up from inside; it is exactly as though the unconscious suppressed the ego with the very same power which drew the ego into the persona. The absence of resistance outwardly against the lure of the persona means a similar weakness inwardly against the influence of the unconscious. Outwardly an effective and powerful role is played, while inwardly an effeminate weakness develops in face of every influence coming from the unconscious. Moods, vagaries, timidity, even a limp sexuality (culminating in impotence) gradually gain the upper hand.

09 The persona, the ideal picture of a man as he should be, is inwardly compensated by feminine weakness, and as the individual outwardly plays the strong man, so he becomes inwardly a woman, i.e., the anima, for it is the anima that reacts to the

persona. But because the inner world is dark and invisible to the extraverted consciousness, and because a man is all the less capable of conceiving his weaknesses the more he is identified with the persona, the persona's counterpart, the anima, remains completely in the dark and is at once projected, so that our hero comes under the heel of his wife's slipper. If this results in a considerable increase of her power, she will acquit herself none too well. She becomes inferior, thus providing her husband with the welcome proof that it is not he, the hero, who is inferior in private, but his wife. In return the wife can cherish the illusion, so attractive to many, that at least she has married a hero, unperturbed by her own uselessness. This little game of illusion is often taken to be the whole meaning of life.

310 Just as, for the purpose of individuation, or self-realization, it is essential for a man to distinguish between what he is and how he appears to himself and to others, so it is also necessary for the same purpose that he should become conscious of his invisible system of relations to the unconscious, and especially of the anima, so as to be able to distinguish himself from her. One cannot of course distinguish oneself from something unconscious. In the matter of the persona it is easy enough to make it clear to a man that he and his office are two different things. But it is very difficult for a man to distinguish himself from his anima, the more so because she is invisible. Indeed, he has first to contend with the prejudice that everything coming from inside him springs from the truest depths of his being. The "strong man" will perhaps concede that in private life he is singularly undisciplined, but that, he says, is just his "weakness" with which, as it were, he proclaims his solidarity. Now there is in this tendency a cultural legacy that is not to be despised; for when a man recognizes that his ideal persona is responsible for his anything but ideal anima, his ideals are shattered, the world becomes ambiguous, he becomes ambiguous even to himself. He is seized by doubts about goodness, and what is worse, he doubts his own good intentions. When one considers how much our private idea of good intentions is bound up with vast historical assumptions, it will readily be understood that it is pleasanter and more in keeping with our present view of the world to deplore a personal weakness than to shatter ideals.

311 But since the unconscious factors act as determinants no less

than the factors that regulate the life of society, and are no less collective, I might just as well learn to distinguish between what *I* want and what the unconscious thrusts upon me, as to see what my office demands of me and what I myself desire. At first the only thing that is at all clear is the incompatibility of the demands coming from without and from within, with the ego standing between them, as between hammer and anvil. But over against this ego, tossed like a shuttlecock between the outer and inner demands, there stands some scarcely definable arbiter, which I would on no account label with the deceptive name "conscience," although, taken in its best sense, the word fits that arbiter very aptly indeed. What we have made of this "conscience" Spitteler has described with unsurpassable humour.[4] Hence we should strenuously avoid this particular signification. We should do far better to realize that the tragic counterplay between inside and outside (depicted in Job and *Faust* as the wager with God) represents, at bottom, the energetics of the life process, the polar tension that is necessary for self-regulation. However different, to all intents and purposes, these opposing forces may be, their fundamental meaning and desire is the life of the individual: they always fluctuate round this centre of balance. Just because they are inseparably related through opposition, they also unite in a mediatory meaning, which, willingly or unwillingly, is born out of the individual and is therefore divined by him. He has a strong feeling of what should be and what could be. To depart from this divination means error, aberration, illness.

312 It is probably no accident that our modern notions of "personal" and "personality" derive from the word *persona*. I can assert that my ego is personal or a personality, and in exactly the same sense I can say that my persona is a personality with which I identify myself more or less. The fact that I then possess two personalities is not so remarkable, since every autonomous or even relatively autonomous complex has the peculiarity of appearing as a personality, i.e., of being personified. This can be observed most readily in the so-called spiritualistic manifestations of automatic writing and the like. The sentences produced are always personal statements and are propounded in the first person singular, as though behind every utterance there stood

4 *Psychological Types*, pars. 282ff.

an actual personality. A naïve intelligence at once thinks of spirits. The same sort of thing is also observable in the hallucinations of the insane, although these, more clearly than the first, can often be recognized as mere thoughts or fragments of thoughts whose connection with the conscious personality is immediately apparent to everyone.

3 The tendency of the relatively autonomous complex to direct personification also explains why the persona exercises such a "personal" effect that the ego is all too easily deceived as to which is the "true" personality.

4 Now, everything that is true of the persona and of all autonomous complexes in general also holds true of the anima. She likewise is a personality, and this is why she is so easily projected upon a woman. So long as the anima is unconscious she is always projected, for everything unconscious is projected. The first bearer of the soul-image is always the mother; later it is borne by those women who arouse the man's feelings, whether in a positive or a negative sense. Because the mother is the first bearer of the soul-image, separation from her is a delicate and important matter of the greatest educational significance. Accordingly among primitives we find a large number of rites designed to organize this separation. The mere fact of becoming adult, and of outward separation, is not enough; impressive initiations into the "men's house" and ceremonies of rebirth are still needed in order to make the separation from the mother (and hence from childhood) entirely effective.

15 Just as the father acts as a protection against the dangers of the external world and thus serves his son as a model persona, so the mother protects him against the dangers that threaten from the darkness of his psyche. In the puberty rites, therefore, the initiate receives instruction about these things of "the other side," so that he is put in a position to dispense with his mother's protection.

16 The modern civilized man has to forgo this primitive but nonetheless admirable system of education. The consequence is that the anima, in the form of the mother-imago, is transferred to the wife; and the man, as soon as he marries, becomes childish, sentimental, dependent, and subservient, or else truculent, tyrannical, hypersensitive, always thinking about the prestige of his superior masculinity. The last is of course merely the reverse

of the first. The safeguard against the unconscious, which is what his mother meant to him, is not replaced by anything in the modern man's education; unconsciously, therefore, his ideal of marriage is so arranged that his wife has to take over the magical role of the mother. Under the cloak of the ideally exclusive marriage he is really seeking his mother's protection, and thus he plays into the hands of his wife's possessive instincts. His fear of the dark incalculable power of the unconscious gives his wife an illegitimate authority over him, and forges such a dangerously close union that the marriage is permanently on the brink of explosion from internal tension—or else, out of protest, he flies to the other extreme, with the same results.

317 I am of the opinion that it is absolutely essential for a certain type of modern man to recognize his distinction not only from the persona, but from the anima as well. For the most part our consciousness, in true Western style, looks outwards, and the inner world remains in darkness. But this difficulty can be overcome easily enough, if only we will make the effort to apply the same concentration and criticism to the psychic material which manifests itself, not outside, but in our private lives. So accustomed are we to keep a shamefaced silence about this other side —we even tremble before our wives, lest they betray us!—and, if found out, to make rueful confessions of "weakness," that there would seem to be only one method of education, namely, to crush or repress the weaknesses as much as possible or at least hide them from the public. But that gets us nowhere.

318 Perhaps I can best explain what has to be done if I use the persona as an example. Here everything is plain and straightforward, whereas with the anima all is dark, to Western eyes anyway. When the anima continually thwarts the good intentions of the conscious mind, by contriving a private life that stands in sorry contrast to the dazzling persona, it is exactly the same as when a naive individual, who has not the ghost of a persona, encounters the most painful difficulties in his passage through the world. There are indeed people who lack a developed persona—"Canadians who know not Europe's sham politeness"—blundering from one social solecism to the next, perfectly harmless and innocent, soulful bores or appealing children, or, if they are women, spectral Cassandras dreaded for their tactlessness, eternally misunderstood, never knowing what they are about, al-

ways taking forgiveness for granted, blind to the world, hopeless dreamers. From them we can see how a neglected persona works, and what one must do to remedy the evil. Such people can avoid disappointments and an infinity of sufferings, scenes, and social catastrophes only by learning to see how men behave in the world. They must learn to understand what society expects of them; they must realize that there are factors and persons in the world far above them; they must know that what they do has a meaning for others, and so forth. Naturally all this is child's play for one who has a properly developed persona. But if we reverse the picture and confront the man who possesses a brilliant persona with the anima, and, for the sake of comparison, set him beside the man with no persona, then we shall see that the latter is just as well informed about the anima and her affairs as the former is about the world. The use which either makes of his knowledge can just as easily be abused, in fact it is more than likely that it will be.

319 The man with the persona is blind to the existence of inner realities, just as the other is blind to the reality of the world, which for him has merely the value of an amusing or fantastic playground. But the fact of inner realities and their unqualified recognition is obviously the *sine qua non* for a serious consideration of the anima problem. If the external world is, for me, simply a phantasm, how should I take the trouble to establish a complicated system of relationship and adaptation to it? Equally, the "nothing but fantasy" attitude will never persuade me to regard my anima manifestations as anything more than fatuous weakness. If, however, I take the line that the world is outside *and* inside, that reality falls to the share of both, I must logically accept the upsets and annoyances that come to me from inside as symptoms of faulty adaptation to the conditions of that inner world. No more than the blows rained on the innocent abroad can be healed by moral repression will it help him resignedly to catalogue his "weaknesses." Here are reasons, intentions, consequences, which can be tackled by will and understanding. Take, for example, the "spotless" man of honour and public benefactor, whose tantrums and explosive moodiness terrify his wife and children. What is the anima doing here?

320 We can see it at once if we just allow things to take their natural course. Wife and children will become estranged; a vac-

uum will form about him. At first he will bewail the hard-heartedness of his family, and will behave if possible even more vilely than before. That will make the estrangement absolute. If the good spirits have not utterly forsaken him, he will after a time notice his isolation, and in his loneliness he will begin to understand how he caused the estrangement. Perhaps, aghast at himself, he will ask, "What sort of devil has got into me?"—without of course seeing the meaning of this metaphor. Then follow remorse, reconciliation, oblivion, repression, and, in next to no time, a new explosion. Clearly, the anima is trying to enforce a separation. This tendency is in nobody's interest. The anima comes between them like a jealous mistress who tries to alienate the man from his family. An official post or any other advantageous social position can do the same thing, but there we can understand the force of the attraction. Whence does the anima obtain the power to wield such enchantment? On the analogy with the persona there must be values or some other important and influential factors lying in the background like seductive promises. In such matters we must guard against rationalizations. Our first thought is that the man of honour is on the lookout for another woman. That might be—it might even be arranged by the anima as the most effective means to the desired end. Such an arrangement should not be misconstrued as an end in itself, for the blameless gentleman who is correctly married according to the law can be just as correctly divorced according to the law, which does not alter his fundamental attitude one iota. The old picture has merely received a new frame.

321 As a matter of fact, this arrangement is a very common method of implementing a separation—and of hampering a final solution. Therefore it is more reasonable not to assume that such an obvious possibility is the end-purpose of the separation. We would be better advised to investigate what is behind the tendencies of the anima. The first step is what I would call the objectivation of the anima, that is, the strict refusal to regard the trend towards separation as a weakness of one's own. Only when this has been done can one face the anima with the question, "Why do you want this separation?" To put the question in this personal way has the great advantage of recognizing the anima as a personality, and of making a relationship possible. The more personally she is taken the better.

322 To anyone accustomed to proceed purely intellectually and rationally, this may seem altogether too ridiculous. It would indeed be the height of absurdity if a man tried to have a conversation with his persona, which he recognized merely as a psychological means of relationship. But it is absurd only for the man who *has* a persona. If he has none, he is in this point no different from the primitive who, as we know, has only one foot in what we commonly call reality. With the other foot he stands in a world of spirits, which is quite real to him. Our model case behaves, in the world, like a modern European; but in the world of spirits he is the child of a troglodyte. He must therefore submit to living in a kind of prehistoric kindergarten until he has got the right idea of the powers and factors which rule that other world. Hence he is quite right to treat the anima as an autonomous personality and to address personal questions to her.

323 I mean this as an actual technique. We know that practically every one has not only the peculiarity, but also the faculty, of holding a conversation with himself. Whenever we are in a predicament we ask ourselves (or whom else?), "What shall I do?" either aloud or beneath our breath, and we (or who else?) supply the answer. Since it is our intention to learn what we can about the foundations of our being, this little matter of living in a metaphor should not bother us. We have to accept it as a symbol of our primitive backwardness (or of such naturalness as is still, mercifully, left to us) that we can, like the Negro, discourse personally with our "snake." The psyche not being a unity but a contradictory multiplicity of complexes, the dissociation required for our dialectics with the anima is not so terribly difficult. The art of it consists only in allowing our invisible partner to make herself heard, in putting the mechanism of expression momentarily at her disposal, without being overcome by the distaste one naturally feels at playing such an apparently ludicrous game with oneself, or by doubts as to the genuineness of the voice of one's interlocutor. This latter point is technically very important: we are so in the habit of identifying ourselves with the thoughts that come to us that we invariably assume we have made them. Curiously enough, it is precisely the most impossible thoughts for which we feel the greatest subjective responsibility. If we were more conscious of the inflexible universal laws that govern even the wildest and most wanton fantasy, we

might perhaps be in a better position to see these thoughts above all others as objective occurrences, just as we see dreams, which nobody supposes to be deliberate or arbitrary inventions. It certainly requires the greatest objectivity and absence of prejudice to give the "other side" the opportunity for perceptible psychic activity. As a result of the repressive attitude of the conscious mind, the other side is driven into indirect and purely symptomatic manifestations, mostly of an emotional kind, and only in moments of overwhelming affectivity can fragments of the unconscious come to the surface in the form of thoughts or images. The inevitable accompanying symptom is that the ego momentarily identifies with these utterances, only to revoke them in the same breath. And, indeed, the things one says when in the grip of an affect sometimes seem very strange and daring. But they are easily forgotten, or wholly denied. This mechanism of deprecation and denial naturally has to be reckoned with if one wants to adopt an objective attitude. The habit of rushing in to correct and criticize is already strong enough in our tradition, and it is as a rule further reinforced by fear—a fear that can be confessed neither to oneself nor to others, a fear of insidious truths, of dangerous knowledge, of disagreeable verifications, in a word, fear of all those things that cause so many of us to flee from being alone with ourselves as from the plague. We say that it is egoistic or "morbid" to be preoccupied with oneself; one's own company is the worst, "it makes you melancholy"—such are the glowing testimonials accorded to our human make-up. They are evidently deeply ingrained in our Western minds. Whoever thinks in this way has obviously never asked himself what possible pleasure other people could find in the company of such a miserable coward. Starting from the fact that in a state of affect one often surrenders involuntarily to the truths of the other side, would it not be far better to make use of an affect so as to give the other side an opportunity to speak? It could therefore be said just as truly that one should cultivate the art of conversing with oneself in the setting provided by an affect, as though the affect itself were speaking without regard to our rational criticism. So long as the affect is speaking, criticism must be withheld. But once it has presented its case, we should begin criticizing as conscientiously as though a real person closely connected with us were our interlocutor. Nor should the matter rest there, but statement and answer must follow one another until a satisfactory end to the discussion is reached. Whether the result is satisfactory or not, only subjective feeling can decide. Any humbug is of course quite useless. Scrupulous honesty with oneself and no rash anticipation of what the other side might conceivably say are the indispensable conditions of this technique for educating the anima.

324 There is, however, something to be said for this characteristically Western fear of the other side. It is not entirely without justification, quite apart from the fact that it is real. We can understand at once the fear that the child and the primitive have of the great unknown. We have the same childish fear of our inner side, where we likewise touch upon a great unknown world. All we have is the affect, the fear, without knowing that this is a world-fear—for the world of affects is invisible. We have either purely theoretical prejudices against it, or superstitious ideas. One cannot even talk about the unconscious before many educated people without being accused of mysticism. The fear is legitimate in so far as our rational *Weltanschauung* with its scientific and moral certitudes—so hotly believed in because so deeply questionable—is shattered by the facts of the other side. If only one could avoid them, then the emphatic advice of the Philistine to "let sleeping dogs lie" would be the only truth worth advocating. And here I would expressly point out that I am not recommending the above technique as either necessary or even useful to any person not driven to it by necessity. The stages, as I said, are many, and there are greybeards who die as innocent as babes in arms, and in this year of grace troglodytes are still being born. There are truths which belong to the future, truths which belong to the past, and truths which belong to no time.

325 I can imagine someone using this technique out of a kind of holy inquisitiveness, some youth, perhaps, who would like to set wings to his feet, not because of lameness, but because he yearns for the sun. But a grown man, with too many illusions dissipated, will submit to this inner humiliation and surrender only if forced, for why should he let the terrors of childhood again have their way with him? It is no light matter to stand between a day-world of exploded ideals and discredited values, and a night-world of apparently senseless fantasy. The weirdness of this

standpoint is in fact so great that there is probably nobody who does not reach out for security, even though it be a reaching back to the mother who shielded his childhood from the terrors of night. Whoever is afraid must needs be dependent; a weak thing needs support. That is why the primitive mind, from deep psychological necessity, begot religious instruction and embodied it in magician and priest. *Extra ecclesiam nulla salus* is still a valid truth today—for those who can go back to it. For the few who cannot, there is only dependence upon a human being, a humbler and a prouder dependence, a weaker and a stronger support, so it seems to me, than any other. What can one say of the Protestant? He has neither church nor priest, but only God—and even God becomes doubtful.

26 The reader may ask in some consternation, "But what on earth does the anima do, that such double insurances are needed before one can come to terms with her?" I would recommend my reader to study the comparative history of religion so intently as to fill these dead chronicles with the emotional life of those who lived these religions. Then he will get some idea of what lives on the other side. The old religions with their sublime and ridiculous, their friendly and fiendish symbols did not drop from the blue, but were born of this human soul that dwells within us at this moment. All those things, their primal forms, live on in us and may at any time burst in upon us with annihilating force, in the guise of mass-suggestions against which the individual is defenceless. Our fearsome gods have only changed their names: they now rhyme with *ism*. Or has anyone the nerve to claim that the World War or Bolshevism was an ingenious invention? Just as outwardly we live in a world where a whole continent may be submerged at any moment, or a pole be shifted, or a new pestilence break out, so inwardly we live in a world where at any moment something similar may occur, albeit in the form of an idea, but no less dangerous and untrustworthy for that. Failure to adapt to this inner world is a negligence entailing just as serious consequences as ignorance and ineptitude in the outer world. It is after all only a tiny fraction of humanity, living mainly on that thickly populated peninsula of Asia which juts out into the Atlantic Ocean, and calling themselves "cultured," who, because they lack all contact with nature, have hit upon the idea that religion is a peculiar kind of

mental disturbance of undiscoverable purport. Viewed from a safe distance, say from central Africa or Tibet, it would certainly look as if this fraction had projected its own unconscious mental derangements upon nations still possessed of healthy instincts.

327 Because the things of the inner world influence us all the more powerfully for being unconscious, it is essential for anyone who intends to make progress in self-culture (and does not all culture begin with the individual?) to objectivate the effects of the anima and then try to understand what contents underlie those effects. In this way he adapts to, and is protected against, the invisible. No adaptation can result without concessions to both worlds. From a consideration of the claims of the inner and outer worlds, or rather, from the conflict between them, the possible and the necessary follows. Unfortunately our Western mind, lacking all culture in this respect, has never yet devised a concept, nor even a name, for the *union of opposites through the middle path,* that most fundamental item of inward experience, which could respectably be set against the Chinese concept of Tao. It is at once the most individual fact and the most universal, the most legitimate fulfilment of the meaning of the individual's life.

328 In the course of my exposition so far, I have kept exclusively to *masculine* psychology. The anima, being of feminine gender, is exclusively a figure that compensates the masculine consciousness. In woman the compensating figure is of a masculine character, and can therefore appropriately be termed the *animus.* If it was no easy task to describe what is meant by the anima, the difficulties become almost insuperable when we set out to describe the psychology of the animus.

329 The fact that a man naïvely ascribes his anima reactions to himself, without seeing that he really cannot identify himself with an autonomous complex, is repeated in feminine psychology, though if possible in even more marked form. This identification with an autonomous complex is the essential reason why it is so difficult to understand and describe the problem, quite apart from its inherent obscurity and strangeness. We always start with the naïve assumption that we are masters in our own house. Hence we must first accustom ourselves to the thought that, in our most intimate psychic life as well, we live in a kind of house which has doors and windows to the world, but that,

although the objects or contents of this world act upon us, they do not belong to us. For many people this hypothesis is by no means easy to conceive, just as they do not find it at all easy to understand and to accept the fact that their neighbour's psychology is not necessarily identical with their own. My reader may think that the last remark is something of an exaggeration, since in general one is aware of individual differences. But it must be remembered that our individual conscious psychology develops out of an original state of unconsciousness and therefore of non-differentiation (termed by Lévy-Bruhl *participation mystique*). Consequently, consciousness of differentiation is a relatively late achievement of mankind, and presumably but a relatively small sector of the indefinitely large field of original identity. Differentiation is the essence, the *sine qua non* of consciousness. Everything unconscious is undifferentiated, and everything that happens unconsciously proceeds on the basis of non-differentiation—that is to say, there is no determining whether it belongs or does not belong to oneself. It cannot be established *a priori* whether it concerns me, or another, or both. Nor does feeling give us any sure clues in this respect.

330 An inferior consciousness cannot *eo ipso* be ascribed to women; it is merely different from masculine consciousness. But, just as a woman is often clearly conscious of things which a man is still groping for in the dark, so there are naturally fields of experience in a man which, for woman, are still wrapped in the shadows of non-differentiation, chiefly things in which she has little interest. Personal relations are as a rule more important and interesting to her than objective facts and their interconnections. The wide fields of commerce, politics, technology, and science, the whole realm of the applied masculine mind, she relegates to the penumbra of consciousness; while, on the other hand, she develops a minute consciousness of personal relationships, the infinite nuances of which usually escape the man entirely.

331 We must therefore expect the unconscious of woman to show aspects essentially different from those found in man. If I were to attempt to put in a nutshell the difference between man and woman in this respect, i.e., what it is that characterizes the animus as opposed to the anima, I could only say this: as the anima produces *moods,* so the animus produces *opinions;* and as the

moods of a man issue from a shadowy background, so the opinions of a woman rest on equally unconscious prior assumptions. Animus opinions very often have the character of solid convictions that are not lightly shaken, or of principles whose validity is seemingly unassailable. If we analyse these opinions, we immediately come upon unconscious assumptions whose existence must first be inferred; that is to say, the opinions are apparently conceived *as though* such assumptions existed. But in reality the opinions are not thought out at all; they exist ready made, and they are held so positively and with so much conviction that the woman never has the shadow of a doubt about them.

332 One would be inclined to suppose that the animus, like the anima, personifies itself in a single figure. But this, as experience shows, is true only up to a point, because another factor unexpectedly makes its appearance, which brings about an essentially different situation from that existing in a man. The animus does not appear as one person, but as a plurality of persons. In H. G. Wells' novel *Christina Alberta's Father,* the heroine, in all that she does or does not do, is constantly under the surveillance of a supreme moral authority, which tells her with remorseless precision and dry matter-of-factness what she is doing and for what motives. Wells calls this authority a "Court of Conscience." This collection of condemnatory judges, a sort of College of Preceptors, corresponds to a personification of the animus. The animus is rather like an assembly of fathers or dignitaries of some kind who lay down incontestable, "rational," *ex cathedra* judgments. On closer examination these exacting judgments turn out to be largely sayings and opinions scraped together more or less unconsciously from childhood on, and compressed into a canon of average truth, justice, and reasonableness, a compendium of preconceptions which, whenever a conscious and competent judgment is lacking (as not infrequently happens), instantly obliges with an opinion. Sometimes these opinions take the form of so-called sound common sense, sometimes they appear as principles which are like a travesty of education: "People have always done it like this," or "Everybody says it is like that."

333 It goes without saying that the animus is just as often projected as the anima. The men who are particularly suited to these projections are either walking replicas of God himself, who know all about everything, or else they are misunderstood

word-addicts with a vast and windy vocabulary at their command, who translate common or garden reality into the terminology of the sublime. It would be insufficient to characterize the animus merely as a conservative, collective conscience; he is also a neologist who, in flagrant contradiction to his correct opinions, has an extraordinary weakness for difficult and unfamiliar words which act as a pleasant substitute for the odious task of reflection.

334 Like the anima, the animus is a jealous lover. He is an adept at putting, in place of the real man, an opinion about him, the exceedingly disputable grounds for which are never submitted to criticism. Animus opinions are invariably collective, and they override individuals and individual judgments in exactly the same way as the anima thrusts her emotional anticipations and projections between man and wife. If the woman happens to be pretty, these animus opinions have for the man something rather touching and childlike about them, which makes him adopt a benevolent, fatherly, professorial manner. But if the woman does not stir his sentimental side, and competence is expected of her rather than appealing helplessness and stupidity, then her animus opinions irritate the man to death, chiefly because they are based on nothing but opinion for opinion's sake, and "everybody has a right to his own opinions." Men can be pretty venomous here, for it is an inescapable fact that the animus always plays up the anima—and *vice versa,* of course—so that all further discussion becomes pointless.

335 In intellectual women the animus encourages a critical disputatiousness and would-be highbrowism, which, however, consists essentially in harping on some irrelevant weak point and nonsensically making it the main one. Or a perfectly lucid discussion gets tangled up in the most maddening way through the introduction of a quite different and if possible perverse point of view. Without knowing it, such women are solely intent upon exasperating the man and are, in consequence, the more completely at the mercy of the animus. "Unfortunately I am always right," one of these creatures once confessed to me.

336 However, all these traits, as familiar as they are unsavoury, are simply and solely due to the extraversion of the animus. The animus does not belong to the function of conscious relationship; his function is rather to facilitate relations with the uncon-

scious. Instead of the woman merely associating opinions with external situations—situations which she ought to think about consciously—the animus, as an associative function, should be directed inwards, where it could associate the contents of the unconscious. The technique of coming to terms with the animus is the same in principle as in the case of the anima; only here the woman must learn to criticize and hold her opinions at a distance; not in order to repress them, but, by investigating their origins, to penetrate more deeply into the background, where she will then discover the primordial images, just as the man does in his dealings with the anima. The animus is the deposit, as it were, of all woman's ancestral experiences of man—and not only that, he is also a creative and procreative being, not in the sense of masculine creativity, but in the sense that he brings forth something we might call the λόγος σπερματικός, the spermatic word. Just as a man brings forth his work as a complete creation out of his inner feminine nature, so the inner masculine side of a woman brings forth creative seeds which have the power to fertilize the feminine side of the man. This would be the *femme inspiratrice* who, if falsely cultivated, can turn into the worst kind of dogmatist and high-handed pedagogue—a regular "animus hound," as one of my women patients aptly expressed it.

337 A woman possessed by the animus is always in danger of losing her femininity, her adapted feminine persona, just as a man in like circumstances runs the risk of effeminacy. These psychic changes of sex are due entirely to the fact that a function which belongs inside has been turned outside. The reason for this perversion is clearly the failure to give adequate recognition to an inner world which stands autonomously opposed to the outer world, and makes just as serious demands on our capacity for adaptation.

338 With regard to the plurality of the animus as distinguished from what we might call the "uni-personality" of the anima, this remarkable fact seems to me to be a correlate of the conscious attitude. The conscious attitude of woman is in general far more exclusively personal than that of man. Her world is made up of fathers and mothers, brothers and sisters, husbands and children. The rest of the world consists likewise of families, who nod to each other but are, in the main, interested essentially in

themselves. The man's world is the nation, the state, business concerns, etc. His family is simply a means to an end, one of the foundations of the state, and his wife is not necessarily *the* woman for him (at any rate not as the woman means it when she says "my man"). The general means more to him than the personal; his world consists of a multitude of co-ordinated factors, whereas her world, outside her husband, terminates in a sort of cosmic mist. A passionate exclusiveness therefore attaches to the man's anima, and an indefinite variety to the woman's animus. Whereas the man has, floating before him, in clear outlines, the alluring form of a Circe or a Calypso, the animus is better expressed as a bevy of Flying Dutchmen or unknown wanderers from over the sea, never quite clearly grasped, protean, given to persistent and violent motion. These personifications appear especially in dreams, though in concrete reality they can be famous tenors, boxing champions, or great men in far-away, unknown cities.

339 These two crepuscular figures from the dark hinterland of the psyche—truly the semi-grotesque "guardians of the threshold," to use the pompous jargon of theosophy—can assume an almost inexhaustible number of shapes, enough to fill whole volumes. Their complicated transformations are as rich and strange as the world itself, as manifold as the limitless variety of their conscious correlate, the persona. They inhabit the twilight sphere, and we can just make out that the autonomous complex of anima and animus is essentially a psychological function that has usurped, or rather retained, a "personality" only because this function is itself autonomous and undeveloped. But already we can see how it is possible to break up the personifications, since by making them conscious we convert them into bridges to the unconscious. It is because we are not using them purposefully as functions that they remain personified complexes. So long as they are in this state they must be accepted as relatively independent personalities. They cannot be integrated into consciousness while their contents remain unknown. The purpose of the dialectical process is to bring these contents into the light; and only when this task has been completed, and the conscious mind has become sufficiently familiar with the unconscious processes reflected in the anima, will the anima be felt simply as a function.

340 I do not expect every reader to grasp right away what is meant by animus and anima. But I hope he will at least have gained the impression that it is not a question of anything "metaphysical," but far rather of empirical facts which could equally well be expressed in rational and abstract language. I have purposely avoided too abstract a terminology because, in matters of this kind, which hitherto have been so inaccessible to our experience, it is useless to present the reader with an intellectual formulation. It is far more to the point to give him some conception of what the actual possibilities of experience are. Nobody can really understand these things unless he has experienced them himself. I am therefore much more interested in pointing out the possible ways to such experience than in devising intellectual formulae which, for lack of experience, must necessarily remain an empty web of words. Unfortunately there are all too many who learn the words by heart and add the experiences in their heads, thereafter abandoning themselves, according to temperament, either to credulity or to criticism. We are concerned here with a new questioning, a new—and yet age-old—field of psychological experience. We shall be able to establish relatively valid theories about it only when the corresponding psychological facts are known to a sufficient number of people. The first things to be discovered are always facts, not theories. Theory-building is the outcome of discussion among many.

II

PSYCHOLOGICAL ASPECTS OF THE MOTHER ARCHETYPE

[First published as a lecture, "Die psychologischen Aspekte des Mutterarchetypus," in *Eranos-Jahrbuch 1938*. Later revised and published in *Von den Wurzeln des Bewusstseins* (Zurich, 1954). The present translation is of the latter, but it is also based partially on a translation of the 1938 version by Cary F. Baynes and Ximena de Angulo, privately issued in *Spring* (New York), 1943.—EDITORS.]

1. ON THE CONCEPT OF THE ARCHETYPE

148 The concept of the Great Mother belongs to the field of comparative religion and embraces widely varying types of mother-goddess. The concept itself is of no immediate concern to psychology, because the image of a Great Mother in this form is rarely encountered in practice, and then only under very special conditions. The symbol is obviously a derivative of the *mother archetype.* If we venture to investigate the background of the Great Mother image from the standpoint of psychology, then the mother archetype, as the more inclusive of the two, must form the basis of our discussion. Though lengthy discussion of the *concept* of an archetype is hardly necessary at this stage, some preliminary remarks of a general nature may not be out of place.

149 In former times, despite some dissenting opinion and the influence of Aristotle, it was not too difficult to understand Plato's conception of the Idea as supraordinate and pre-existent to all phenomena. "Archetype," far from being a modern term, was already in use before the time of St. Augustine, and was synonymous with "Idea" in the Platonic usage. When the *Corpus Hermeticum,* which probably dates from the third century, describes God as τὸ ἀρχέτυπον φῶς, the 'archetypal light,' it expresses the idea that he is the prototype of all light; that is to say, pre-existent and supraordinate to the phenomenon "light." Were I a philosopher, I should continue in this Platonic strain and say: Somewhere, in "a place beyond the skies," there is a prototype or primordial image of the mother that is pre-existent and supraordinate to all phenomena in which the "maternal," in the broadest sense of the term, is manifest. But I am an empiricist, not a philosopher; I cannot let myself presuppose that my peculiar temperament, my own attitude to intellectual problems, is universally valid. Apparently this is an assumption in which only the philosopher may indulge, who always takes it for granted that his own disposition and attitude are universal,

and will not recognize the fact, if he can avoid it, that his "personal equation" conditions his philosophy. As an empiricist, I must point out that there is a temperament which regards ideas as real entities and not merely as *nomina*. It so happens—by the merest accident, one might say—that for the past two hundred years we have been living in an age in which it has become unpopular or even unintelligible to suppose that ideas could be anything but *nomina*. Anyone who continues to think as Plato did must pay for his anachronism by seeing the "supracelestial," i.e., metaphysical, essence of the Idea relegated to the unverifiable realm of faith and superstition, or charitably left to the poet. Once again, in the age-old controversy over universals, the nominalistic standpoint has triumphed over the realistic, and the Idea has evaporated into a mere *flatus vocis*. This change was accompanied—and, indeed, to a considerable degree caused—by the marked rise of empiricism, the advantages of which were only too obvious to the intellect. Since that time the Idea is no longer something *a priori*, but is secondary and derived. Naturally, the new nominalism promptly claimed universal validity for itself in spite of the fact that it, too, is based on a definite and limited thesis coloured by temperament. This thesis runs as follows: we accept as valid anything that comes from outside and can be verified. The ideal instance is verification by experiment. The antithesis is: we accept as valid anything that comes from inside and cannot be verified. The hopelessness of this position is obvious. Greek natural philosophy with its interest in matter, together with Aristotelian reasoning, has achieved a belated but overwhelming victory over Plato.

150 Yet every victory contains the germ of future defeat. In our own day signs foreshadowing a change of attitude are rapidly increasing. Significantly enough, it is Kant's doctrine of categories, more than anything else, that destroys in embryo every attempt to revive metaphysics in the old sense of the word, but at the same time paves the way for a rebirth of the Platonic spirit. If it be true that there can be no metaphysics transcending human reason, it is no less true that there can be no empirical knowledge that is not already caught and limited by the *a priori* structure of cognition. During the century and a half that have elapsed since the appearance of the *Critique of Pure Reason,* the conviction has gradually gained ground that thinking, under-

standing, and reasoning cannot be regarded as independent processes subject only to the eternal laws of logic, but that they are *psychic functions* co-ordinated with the personality and subordinate to it. We no longer ask, "Has this or that been seen, heard, handled, weighed, counted, thought, and found to be logical?" We ask instead, "*Who* saw, heard, or thought?" Beginning with "the personal equation" in the observation and measurement of minimal processes, this critical attitude has gone on to the creation of an empirical psychology such as no time before ours has known. Today we are convinced that in all fields of knowledge psychological premises exist which exert a decisive influence upon the choice of material, the method of investigation, the nature of the conclusions, and the formulation of hypotheses and theories. We have even come to believe that Kant's personality was a decisive conditioning factor of his *Critique of Pure Reason.* Not only our philosophers, but our own predilections in philosophy, and even what we are fond of calling our "best" truths are affected, if not dangerously undermined, by this recognition of a personal premise. All creative freedom, we cry out, is taken away from us! What? Can it be possible that a man only thinks or says or does what he himself *is*?

151 Provided that we do not again exaggerate and so fall a victim to unrestrained "psychologizing," it seems to me that the critical standpoint here defined is inescapable. It constitutes the essence, origin, and method of modern psychology. There *is* an *a priori* factor in all human activities, namely the inborn, preconscious and unconscious individual structure of the psyche. The preconscious psyche—for example, that of a new-born infant—is not an empty vessel into which, under favourable conditions, practically anything can be poured. On the contrary, it is a tremendously complicated, sharply defined individual entity which appears indeterminate to us only because we cannot see it directly. But the moment the first visible manifestations of psychic life begin to appear, one would have to be blind not to recognize their individual character, that is, the unique personality behind them. It is hardly possible to suppose that all these details come into being only at the moment in which they appear. When it is a case of morbid predispositions already present in the parents, we infer hereditary transmission through

the germ-plasm; it would not occur to us to regard epilepsy in the child of an epileptic mother as an unaccountable mutation. Again, we explain by heredity the gifts and talents which can be traced back through whole generations. We explain in the same way the reappearance of complicated instinctive actions in animals that have never set eyes on their parents and therefore could not possibly have been "taught" by them.

152 Nowadays we have to start with the hypothesis that, so far as predisposition is concerned, there is no essential difference between man and all other creatures. Like every animal, he possesses a preformed psyche which breeds true to his species and which, on closer examination, reveals distinct features traceable to family antecedents. We have not the slightest reason to suppose that there are certain human activities or functions that could be exempted from this rule. We are unable to form any idea of what those dispositions or aptitudes are which make instinctive actions in animals possible. And it is just as impossible for us to know the nature of the preconscious psychic disposition that enables a child to react in a human manner. We can only suppose that his behaviour results from patterns of functioning, which I have described as *images*. The term "image" is intended to express not only the form of the activity taking place, but the typical situation in which the activity is released.[1] These images are "primordial" images in so far as they are peculiar to whole species, and if they ever "originated" their origin must have coincided at least with the beginning of the species. They are the "human quality" of the human being, the specifically human form his activities take. This specific form is hereditary and is already present in the germ-plasm. The idea that it is not inherited but comes into being in every child anew would be just as preposterous as the primitive belief that the sun which rises in the morning is a different sun from that which set the evening before.

153 Since everything psychic is preformed, this must also be true of the individual functions, especially those which derive directly from the unconscious predisposition. The most important of these is creative fantasy. In the products of fantasy the primordial images are made visible, and it is here that the concept of the archetype finds its specific application. I do not claim to

1 Cf. my "Instinct and the Unconscious," par. 277.

have been the first to point out this fact. The honour belongs to Plato. The first investigator in the field of ethnology to draw attention to the widespread occurrence of certain "elementary ideas" was Adolf Bastian. Two later investigators, Hubert and Mauss,[2] followers of Dürkheim, speak of "categories" of the imagination. And it was no less an authority than Hermann Usener [3] who first recognized unconscious preformation under the guise of "unconscious thinking." If I have any share in these discoveries, it consists in my having shown that archetypes are not disseminated only by tradition, language, and migration, but that they can rearise spontaneously, at any time, at any place, and without any outside influence.

154 The far-reaching implications of this statement must not be overlooked. For it means that there are present in every psyche forms which are unconscious but nonetheless active—living dispositions, ideas in the Platonic sense, that preform and continually influence our thoughts and feelings and actions.

155 Again and again I encounter the mistaken notion that an archetype is determined in regard to its content, in other words that it is a kind of unconscious idea (if such an expression be admissible). It is necessary to point out once more that archetypes are not determined as regards their content, but only as regards their form and then only to a very limited degree. A primordial image is determined as to its content only when it has become conscious and is therefore filled out with the material of conscious experience. Its form, however, as I have explained elsewhere, might perhaps be compared to the axial system of a crystal, which, as it were, preforms the crystalline structure in the mother liquid, although it has no material existence of its own. This first appears according to the specific way in which the ions and molecules aggregate. The archetype in itself is empty and purely formal, nothing but a *facultas praeformandi,* a possibility of representation which is given *a priori.* The representations themselves are not inherited, only the forms, and in that respect they correspond in every way to the instincts, which are also determined in form only. The existence of the instincts can no more be proved than the existence of the archetypes, so long as they do not manifest them-

2 [Cf. the previous paper, "Concerning the Archetypes," par. 137, n. 25.—EDITORS.]
3 Usener, *Das Weihnachtsfest,* p. 3.

selves concretely. With regard to the definiteness of the form, our comparison with the crystal is illuminating inasmuch as the axial system determines only the stereometric structure but not the concrete form of the individual crystal. This may be either large or small, and it may vary endlessly by reason of the different size of its planes or by the growing together of two crystals. The only thing that remains constant is the axial system, or rather, the invariable geometric proportions underlying it. The same is true of the archetype. In principle, it can be named and has an invariable nucleus of meaning—but always only in principle, never as regards its concrete manifestation. In the same way, the specific appearance of the mother-image at any given time cannot be deduced from the mother archetype alone, but depends on innumerable other factors.

2. THE MOTHER ARCHETYPE

156 Like any other archetype, the mother archetype appears under an almost infinite variety of aspects. I mention here only some of the more characteristic. First in importance are the personal mother and grandmother, stepmother and mother-in-law; then any woman with whom a relationship exists—for example, a nurse or governess or perhaps a remote ancestress. Then there are what might be termed mothers in a figurative sense. To this category belongs the goddess, and especially the Mother of God, the Virgin, and Sophia. Mythology offers many variations of the mother archetype, as for instance the mother who reappears as the maiden in the myth of Demeter and Kore; or the mother who is also the beloved, as in the Cybele-Attis myth. Other symbols of the mother in a figurative sense appear in things representing the goal of our longing for redemption, such as Paradise, the Kingdom of God, the Heavenly Jerusalem. Many things arousing devotion or feelings of awe, as for instance the Church, university, city or country, heaven, earth, the woods, the sea or any still waters, matter even, the underworld and the moon, can be mother-symbols. The archetype is often associated with things and places standing for fertility and fruitfulness: the cornucopia, a ploughed field, a garden. It can be attached to a rock, a cave, a tree, a spring, a deep well, or to various vessels such as the baptismal font, or to vessel-shaped flowers like the rose or the lotus. Because of the protection it implies, the magic circle or mandala can be a form of mother archetype. Hollow objects such as ovens and cooking vessels are associated with the mother archetype, and, of course, the uterus, *yoni,* and anything of a like shape. Added to this list there are many animals, such as the cow, hare, and helpful animals in general.

157 All these symbols can have a positive, favourable meaning or a negative, evil meaning. An ambivalent aspect is seen in the goddesses of fate (Moira, Graeae, Norns). Evil symbols are the

witch, the dragon (or any devouring and entwining animal, such as a large fish or a serpent), the grave, the sarcophagus, deep water, death, nightmares and bogies (Empusa, Lilith, etc.). This list is not, of course, complete; it presents only the most important features of the mother archetype.

158 The qualities associated with it are maternal solicitude and sympathy; the magic authority of the female; the wisdom and spiritual exaltation that transcend reason; any helpful instinct or impulse; all that is benign, all that cherishes and sustains, that fosters growth and fertility. The place of magic transformation and rebirth, together with the underworld and its inhabitants, are presided over by the mother. On the negative side the mother archetype may connote anything secret, hidden, dark; the abyss, the world of the dead, anything that devours, seduces, and poisons, that is terrifying and inescapable like fate. All these attributes of the mother archetype have been fully described and documented in my book *Symbols of Transformation*. There I formulated the ambivalence of these attributes as "the loving and the terrible mother." Perhaps the historical example of the dual nature of the mother most familiar to us is the Virgin Mary, who is not only the Lord's mother, but also, according to the medieval allegories, his cross. In India, "the loving and terrible mother" is the paradoxical Kali. Sankhya philosophy has elaborated the mother archetype into the concept of *prakṛti* (matter) and assigned to it the three *gunas* or fundamental attributes: *sattva, rajas, tamas:* goodness, passion, and darkness.[1] These are three essential aspects of the mother: her cherishing and nourishing goodness, her orgiastic emotionality, and her Stygian depths. The special feature of the philosophical myth, which shows Prakṛti dancing before Purusha in order to remind him of "discriminating knowledge," does not belong to the mother archetype but to the archetype of the anima, which in a man's psychology invariably appears, at first, mingled with the mother-image.

159 Although the figure of the mother as it appears in folklore is more or less universal, this image changes markedly when it appears in the individual psyche. In treating patients one is at

1 This is the etymological meaning of the three *gunas*. See Weckerling, *Anandaraya-makhi: Das Glück des Lebens,* pp. 21ff., and Garbe, *Die Samkhya Philosophie,* pp. 272ff. [Cf. also Zimmer, *Philosophies of India,* index, s.v.—EDITORS.]

first impressed, and indeed arrested, by the apparent significance of the personal mother. This figure of the personal mother looms so large in all personalistic psychologies that, as we know, they never got beyond it, even in theory, to other important aetiological factors. My own view differs from that of other medico-psychological theories principally in that I attribute to the personal mother only a limited aetiological significance. That is to say, all those influences which the literature describes as being exerted on the children do not come from the mother herself, but rather from the archetype projected upon her, which gives her a mythological background and invests her with authority and numinosity.[2] The aetiological and traumatic effects produced by the mother must be divided into two groups: (1) those corresponding to traits of character or attitudes actually present in the mother, and (2) those referring to traits which the mother only seems to possess, the reality being composed of more or less fantastic (i.e., archetypal) projections on the part of the child. Freud himself had already seen that the real aetiology of neuroses does not lie in traumatic effects, as he at first suspected, but in a peculiar development of infantile fantasy. This is not to deny that such a development can be traced back to disturbing influences emanating from the mother. I myself make it a rule to look first for the cause of infantile neuroses in the mother, as I know from experience that a child is much more likely to develop normally than neurotically, and that in the great majority of cases definite causes of disturbances can be found in the parents, especially in the mother. The contents of the child's abnormal fantasies can be referred to the personal mother only in part, since they often contain clear and unmistakable allusions which could not possibly have reference to human beings. This is especially true where definitely mythological products are concerned, as is frequently the case in infantile phobias where the mother may appear as a wild beast, a witch, a spectre, an ogre, a hermaphrodite, and so on. It must be borne in mind, however, that such fantasies are not always of unmistakably mythological origin, and even if they are, they may not always be rooted in the unconscious archetype but may have been occasioned by fairytales or accidental remarks. A

2 American psychology can supply us with any amount of examples. A blistering but instructive lampoon on this subject is Philip Wylie's *Generation of Vipers.*

thorough investigation is therefore indicated in each case. For practical reasons, such an investigation cannot be made so readily with children as with adults, who almost invariably transfer their fantasies to the physician during treatment—or, to be more precise, the fantasies are projected upon him automatically.

160 When that happens, nothing is gained by brushing them aside as ridiculous, for archetypes are among the inalienable assets of every psyche. They form the "treasure in the realm of shadowy thoughts" of which Kant spoke, and of which we have ample evidence in the countless treasure motifs of mythology. An archetype is in no sense just an annoying prejudice; it becomes so only when it is in the wrong place. In themselves, archetypal images are among the highest values of the human psyche; they have peopled the heavens of all races from time immemorial. To discard them as valueless would be a distinct loss. Our task is not, therefore, to deny the archetype, but to dissolve the projections, in order to restore their contents to the individual who has involuntarily lost them by projecting them outside himself.

3. THE MOTHER-COMPLEX

161 The mother archetype forms the foundation of the so-called mother-complex. It is an open question whether a mother-complex can develop without the mother having taken part in its formation as a demonstrable causal factor. My own experience leads me to believe that the mother always plays an active part in the origin of the disturbance, especially in infantile neuroses or in neuroses whose aetiology undoubtedly dates back to early childhood. In any event, the child's instincts are disturbed, and this constellates archetypes which, in their turn, produce fantasies that come between the child and its mother as an alien and often frightening element. Thus, if the children of an over-anxious mother regularly dream that she is a terrifying animal or a witch, these experiences point to a split in the child's psyche that predisposes it to a neurosis.

I. THE MOTHER-COMPLEX OF THE SON

162 The effects of the mother-complex differ according to whether it appears in a son or a daughter. Typical effects on the son are homosexuality and Don Juanism, and sometimes also impotence.[1] In homosexuality, the son's entire heterosexuality is tied to the mother in an unconscious form; in Don Juanism, he unconsciously seeks his mother in every woman he meets. The effects of a mother-complex on the son may be seen in the ideology of the Cybele and Attis type: self-castration, madness, and early death. Because of the difference in sex, a son's mother-complex does not appear in pure form. This is the reason why in every masculine mother-complex, side by side with the mother archetype, a significant role is played by the image of the man's sexual counterpart, the anima. The mother is the first feminine being with whom the man-to-be comes in contact, and

1 But the father-complex also plays a considerable part here.

she cannot help playing, overtly or covertly, consciously or unconsciously, upon the son's masculinity, just as the son in his turn grows increasingly aware of his mother's femininity, or unconsciously responds to it by instinct. In the case of the son, therefore, the simple relationships of identity or of resistance and differentiation are continually cut across by erotic attraction or repulsion, which complicates matters very considerably. I do not mean to say that for this reason the mother-complex of a son ought to be regarded as more serious than that of a daughter. The investigation of these complex psychic phenomena is still in the pioneer stage. Comparisons will not become feasible until we have some statistics at our disposal, and of these, so far, there is no sign.

163 Only in the daughter is the mother-complex clear and uncomplicated. Here we have to do either with an overdevelopment of feminine instincts indirectly caused by the mother, or with a weakening of them to the point of complete extinction. In the first case, the preponderance of instinct makes the daughter unconscious of her own personality; in the latter, the instincts are projected upon the mother. For the present we must content ourselves with the statement that in the daughter a mother-complex either unduly stimulates or else inhibits the feminine instinct, and that in the son it injures the masculine instinct through an unnatural sexualization.

164 Since a "mother-complex" is a concept borrowed from psychopathology, it is always associated with the idea of injury and illness. But if we take the concept out of its narrow psychopathological setting and give it a wider connotation, we can see that it has positive effects as well. Thus a man with a mother-complex may have a finely differentiated Eros [2] instead of, or in addition to, homosexuality. (Something of this sort is suggested by Plato in his *Symposium*.) This gives him a great capacity for friendship, which often creates ties of astonishing tenderness between men and may even rescue friendship between the sexes from the limbo of the impossible. He may have good taste and an aesthetic sense which are fostered by the presence of a feminine streak. Then he may be supremely gifted as a teacher because of his almost feminine insight and tact. He is likely to have a feeling for history, and to be conservative in the best

[2] [Cf. *Two Essays on Analytical Psychology*, pars. 16ff.—EDITORS.]

sense and cherish the values of the past. Often he is endowed with a wealth of religious feelings, which help to bring the *ecclesia spiritualis* into reality; and a spiritual receptivity which makes him responsive to revelation.

165 In the same way, what in its negative aspect is Don Juanism can appear positively as bold and resolute manliness; ambitious striving after the highest goals; opposition to all stupidity, narrow-mindedness, injustice, and laziness; willingness to make sacrifices for what is regarded as right, sometimes bordering on heroism; perseverance, inflexibility and toughness of will; a curiosity that does not shrink even from the riddles of the universe; and finally, a revolutionary spirit which strives to put a new face upon the world.

166 All these possibilities are reflected in the mythological motifs enumerated earlier as different aspects of the mother archetype. As I have already dealt with the mother-complex of the son, including the anima complication, elsewhere, and my present theme is the archetype of the mother, in the following discussion I shall relegate masculine psychology to the background.

II. THE MOTHER-COMPLEX OF THE DAUGHTER [3]

167 (a) *Hypertrophy of the Maternal Element.*—We have noted that in the daughter the mother-complex leads either to a hypertrophy of the feminine side or to its atrophy. The exaggeration of the feminine side means an intensification of all female instincts, above all the maternal instinct. The negative aspect is seen in the woman whose only goal is childbirth. To her the husband is obviously of secondary importance; he is first and foremost the instrument of procreation, and she regards him merely as an object to be looked after, along with children, poor relations, cats, dogs, and household furniture. Even her own

3 In the present section I propose to present a series of different "types" of mother-complex; in formulating them, I am drawing on my own therapeutic experiences. "Types" are not individual cases, neither are they freely invented schemata into which all individual cases have to be fitted. "Types" are ideal instances, or pictures of the average run of experience, with which no single individual can be identified. People whose experience is confined to books or psychological laboratories can form no proper idea of the cumulative experience of a practising psychologist.

personality is of secondary importance; she often remains entirely unconscious of it, for her life is lived in and through others, in more or less complete identification with all the objects of her care. First she gives birth to the children, and from then on she clings to them, for without them she has no existence whatsoever. Like Demeter, she compels the gods by her stubborn persistence to grant her the right of possession over her daughter. Her Eros develops exclusively as a maternal relationship while remaining unconscious as a personal one. An unconscious Eros always expresses itself as will to power.[4] Women of this type, though continually "living for others," are, as a matter of fact, unable to make any real sacrifice. Driven by ruthless will to power and a fanatical insistence on their own maternal rights, they often succeed in annihilating not only their own personality but also the personal lives of their children. The less conscious such a mother is of her own personality, the greater and the more violent is her unconscious will to power. For many such women Baubo rather than Demeter would be the appropriate symbol. The mind is not cultivated for its own sake but usually remains in its original condition, altogether primitive, unrelated, and ruthless, but also as true, and sometimes as profound, as Nature herself.[5] She herself does not know this and is therefore unable to appreciate the wittiness of her mind or to marvel philosophically at its profundity; like as not she will immediately forget what she has said.

168 (b) *Overdevelopment of Eros.*—It by no means follows that the complex induced in a daughter by such a mother must necessarily result in hypertrophy of the maternal instinct. Quite the contrary, this instinct may be wiped out altogether. As a substitute, an overdeveloped Eros results, and this almost invariably leads to an unconscious incestuous relationship with the father.[6] The intensified Eros places an abnormal emphasis on the personality of others. Jealousy of the mother and the desire to outdo her become the leitmotifs of subsequent undertakings, which

4 This statement is based on the repeated experience that, where love is lacking, power fills the vacuum.

5 In my English seminars [privately distributed] I have called this the "natural mind."

6 Here the initiative comes from the daughter. In other cases the father's psychology is responsible; his projection of the anima arouses an incestuous fixation in the daughter.

are often disastrous. A woman of this type loves romantic and sensational episodes for their own sake, and is interested in married men, less for themselves than for the fact that they are married and so give her an opportunity to wreck a marriage, that being the whole point of her manoeuvre. Once the goal is attained, her interest evaporates for lack of any maternal instinct, and then it will be someone else's turn.[7] This type is noted for its remarkable unconsciousness. Such women really seem to be utterly blind to what they are doing,[8] which is anything but advantageous either for themselves or for their victims. I need hardly point out that for men with a passive Eros this type offers an excellent hook for anima projections.

169 (c) *Identity with the Mother.*—If a mother-complex in a woman does not produce an overdeveloped Eros, it leads to identification with the mother and to paralysis of the daughter's feminine initiative. A complete projection of her personality on to the mother then takes place, owing to the fact that she is unconscious both of her maternal instinct and of her Eros. Everything which reminds her of motherhood, responsibility, personal relationships, and erotic demands arouses feelings of inferiority and compels her to run away—to her mother, naturally, who lives to perfection everything that seems unattainable to her daughter. As a sort of superwoman (admired involuntarily by the daughter), the mother lives out for her beforehand all that the girl might have lived for herself. She is content to cling to her mother in selfless devotion, while at the same time unconsciously striving, almost against her will, to tyrannize over her, naturally under the mask of complete loyalty and devotion. The daughter leads a shadow-existence, often visibly sucked dry by her mother, and she prolongs her mother's life by a sort of continuous blood transfusion. These bloodless maidens are by no means immune to marriage. On the contrary, despite their shadowiness and passivity, they command a high price on the marriage market. First, they are so empty that a man is free to impute to them anything he fancies. In addition, they are so unconscious that the unconscious puts out countless invisible

7 Herein lies the difference between this type of complex and the feminine father-complex related to it, where the "father" is mothered and coddled.

8 This does not mean that they are unconscious of the *facts*. It is only their *meaning* that escapes them.

feelers, veritable octopus-tentacles, that suck up all masculine projections; and this pleases men enormously. All that feminine indefiniteness is the longed-for counterpart of male decisiveness and single-mindedness, which can be satisfactorily achieved only if a man can get rid of everything doubtful, ambiguous, vague, and muddled by projecting it upon some charming example of feminine innocence.[9] Because of the woman's characteristic passivity, and the feelings of inferiority which make her continually play the injured innocent, the man finds himself cast in an attractive role: he has the privilege of putting up with the familiar feminine foibles with real superiority, and yet with forbearance, like a true knight. (Fortunately, he remains ignorant of the fact that these deficiencies consist largely of his own projections.) The girl's notorious helplessness is a special attraction. She is so much an appendage of her mother that she can only flutter confusedly when a man approaches. She just doesn't know a thing. She is so inexperienced, so terribly in need of help, that even the gentlest swain becomes a daring abductor who brutally robs a loving mother of her daughter. Such a marvellous opportunity to pass himself off as a gay Lothario does not occur every day and therefore acts as a strong incentive. This was how Pluto abducted Persephone from the inconsolable Demeter. But, by a decree of the gods, he had to surrender his wife every year to his mother-in-law for the summer season. (The attentive reader will note that such legends do not come about by chance!)

170 (d) *Resistance to the Mother.*—These three extreme types are linked together by many intermediate stages, of which I shall mention only one important example. In the particular intermediate type I have in mind, the problem is less an overdevelopment or an inhibition of the feminine instincts than an overwhelming resistance to maternal supremacy, often to the exclusion of all else. It is the supreme example of the negative mother-complex. The motto of this type is: Anything, so long as it is not like Mother! On one hand we have a fascination which never reaches the point of identification; on the other, an intensification of Eros which exhausts itself in jealous resist-

9 This type of woman has an oddly disarming effect on her husband, but only until he discovers that the person he has married and who shares his nuptial bed is his mother-in-law.

ance. This kind of daughter knows what she does *not* want, but is usually completely at sea as to what she would choose as her own fate. All her instincts are concentrated on the mother in the negative form of resistance and are therefore of no use to her in building her own life. Should she get as far as marrying, either the marriage will be used for the sole purpose of escaping from her mother, or else a diabolical fate will present her with a husband who shares all the essential traits of her mother's character. All instinctive processes meet with unexpected difficulties; either sexuality does not function properly, or the children are unwanted, or maternal duties seem unbearable, or the demands of marital life are responded to with impatience and irritation. This is quite natural, since none of it has anything to do with the realities of life when stubborn resistance to the power of the mother in every form has come to be life's dominating aim. In such cases one can often see the attributes of the mother archetype demonstrated in every detail. For example, the mother as representative of the family (or clan) causes either violent resistances or complete indifference to anything that comes under the head of family, community, society, convention, and the like. Resistance to the mother as *uterus* often manifests itself in menstrual disturbances, failure of conception, abhorrence of pregnancy, hemorrhages and excessive vomiting during pregnancy, miscarriages, and so on. The mother as *materia,* 'matter,' may be at the back of these women's impatience with objects, their clumsy handling of tools and crockery and bad taste in clothes.

171 Again, resistance to the mother can sometimes result in a spontaneous development of intellect for the purpose of creating a sphere of interest in which the mother has no place. This development springs from the daughter's own needs and not at all for the sake of a man whom she would like to impress or dazzle by a semblance of intellectual comradeship. Its real purpose is to break the mother's power by intellectual criticism and superior knowledge, so as to enumerate to her all her stupidities, mistakes in logic, and educational shortcomings. Intellectual development is often accompanied by the emergence of masculine traits in general.

4. POSITIVE ASPECTS OF THE MOTHER-COMPLEX

I. THE MOTHER

172 The positive aspect of the first type of complex, namely the overdevelopment of the maternal instinct, is identical with that well-known image of the mother which has been glorified in all ages and all tongues. This is the mother-love which is one of the most moving and unforgettable memories of our lives, the mysterious root of all growth and change; the love that means homecoming, shelter, and the long silence from which everything begins and in which everything ends. Intimately known and yet strange like Nature, lovingly tender and yet cruel like fate, joyous and untiring giver of life—*mater dolorosa* and mute implacable portal that closes upon the dead. Mother is mother-love, *my* experience and *my* secret. Why risk saying too much, too much that is false and inadequate and beside the point, about that human being who was our mother, the accidental carrier of that great experience which includes herself and myself and all mankind, and indeed the whole of created nature, the experience of life whose children we are? The attempt to say these things has always been made, and probably always will be; but a sensitive person cannot in all fairness load that enormous burden of meaning, responsibility, duty, heaven and hell, on to the shoulders of one frail and fallible human being—so deserving of love, indulgence, understanding, and forgiveness—who was our mother. He knows that the mother carries for us that inborn image of the *mater natura* and *mater spiritualis*, of the totality of life of which we are a small and helpless part. Nor should we hesitate for one moment to relieve the human mother of this appalling burden, for our own sakes as well as hers. It is just this massive weight of meaning that ties us to the mother and chains her to her child, to the physical and mental

detriment of both. A mother-complex is not got rid of by blindly reducing the mother to human proportions. Besides that we run the risk of dissolving the experience "Mother" into atoms, thus destroying something supremely valuable and throwing away the golden key which a good fairy laid in our cradle. That is why mankind has always instinctively added the pre-existent divine pair to the personal parents—the "god"-father and "god"-mother of the newborn child—so that, from sheer unconsciousness or shortsighted rationalism, he should never forget himself so far as to invest his own parents with divinity.

173 The archetype is really far less a scientific problem than an urgent question of psychic hygiene. Even if all proofs of the existence of archetypes were lacking, and all the clever people in the world succeeded in convincing us that such a thing could not possibly exist, we would have to invent them forthwith in order to keep our highest and most important values from disappearing into the unconscious. For when these fall into the unconscious the whole elemental force of the original experience is lost. What then appears in its place is fixation on the mother-imago; and when this has been sufficiently rationalized and "corrected," we are tied fast to human reason and condemned from then on to believe exclusively in what is rational. That is a virtue and an advantage on the one hand, but on the other a limitation and impoverishment, for it brings us nearer to the bleakness of doctrinairism and "enlightenment." This Déesse Raison emits a deceptive light which illuminates only what we know already, but spreads a darkness over all those things which it would be most needful for us to know and become conscious of. The more independent "reason" pretends to be, the more it turns into sheer intellectuality which puts doctrine in the place of reality and shows us man not as he is but how it wants him to be.

174 Whether he understands them or not, man must remain conscious of the world of the archetypes, because in it he is still a part of Nature and is connected with his own roots. A view of the world or a social order that cuts him off from the primordial images of life not only is no culture at all but, in increasing degree, is a prison or a stable. If the primordial images remain conscious in some form or other, the energy that belongs to

them can flow freely into man. But when it is no longer possible to maintain contact with them, then the tremendous sum of energy stored up in these images, which is also the source of the fascination underlying the infantile parental complex, falls back into the unconscious. The unconscious then becomes charged with a force that acts as an irresistible *vis a tergo* to whatever view or idea or tendency our intellect may choose to dangle enticingly before our desiring eyes. In this way man is delivered over to his conscious side, and reason becomes the arbiter of right and wrong, of good and evil. I am far from wishing to belittle the divine gift of reason, man's highest faculty. But in the role of absolute tyrant it has no meaning—no more than light would have in a world where its counterpart, darkness, was absent. Man would do well to heed the wise counsel of the mother and obey the inexorable law of nature which sets limits to every being. He ought never to forget that the world exists only because opposing forces are held in equilibrium. So, too, the rational is counterbalanced by the irrational, and what is planned and purposed by what *is*.

175 This excursion into the realm of generalities was unavoidable, because the mother is the first world of the child and the last world of the adult. We are all wrapped as her children in the mantle of this great Isis. But let us now return to the different types of feminine mother-complex. It may seem strange that I am devoting so much more time to the mother-complex in woman than to its counterpart in man. The reason for this has already been mentioned: in a man, the mother-complex is never "pure," it is always mixed with the anima archetype, and the consequence is that a man's statements about the mother are always emotionally prejudiced in the sense of showing "animosity." Only in women is it possible to examine the effects of the mother archetype without admixture of animosity, and even this has prospects of success only when no compensating animus has developed.

II. THE OVERDEVELOPED EROS

176 I drew a very unfavourable picture of this type as we encounter it in the field of psychopathology. But this type, uninviting

as it appears, also has positive aspects which society could ill afford to do without. Indeed, behind what is possibly the worst effect of this attitude, the unscrupulous wrecking of marriages, we can see an extremely significant and purposeful arrangement of nature. This type often develops in reaction to a mother who is wholly a thrall of nature, purely instinctive and therefore all-devouring. Such a mother is an anachronism, a throw-back to a primitive state of matriarchy where the man leads an insipid existence as a mere procreator and serf of the soil. The reactive intensification of the daughter's Eros is aimed at some man who ought to be rescued from the preponderance of the female-maternal element in his life. A woman of this type instinctively intervenes when provoked by the unconsciousness of the marriage partner. She will disturb that comfortable ease so dangerous to the personality of a man but frequently regarded by him as marital faithfulness. This complacency leads to blank unconsciousness of his own personality and to those supposedly ideal marriages where he is nothing but Dad and she is nothing but Mom, and they even call each other that. This is a slippery path that can easily degrade marriage to the level of a mere breeding-pen.

177 A woman of this type directs the burning ray of her Eros upon a man whose life is stifled by maternal solicitude, and by doing so she arouses a moral conflict. Yet without this there can be no consciousness of personality. "But why on earth," you may ask, "should it be necessary for man to achieve, by hook or by crook, a higher level of consciousness?" This is truly the crucial question, and I do not find the answer easy. Instead of a real answer I can only make a confession of faith: I believe that, after thousands and millions of years, someone had to realize that this wonderful world of mountains and oceans, suns and moons, galaxies and nebulae, plants and animals, *exists*. From a low hill in the Athi plains of East Africa I once watched the vast herds of wild animals grazing in soundless stillness, as they had done from time immemorial, touched only by the breath of a primeval world. I felt then as if I were the first man, the first creature, to know that all this *is*. The entire world round me was still in its primeval state; it did not know that it *was*. And then, in that one moment in which I came to know, the world sprang into being; without that moment it would never have

been. All Nature seeks this goal and finds it fulfilled in man, but only in the most highly developed and most fully conscious man. Every advance, even the smallest, along this path of conscious realization adds that much to the world.

178 There is no consciousness without discrimination of opposites. This is the paternal principle, the Logos, which eternally struggles to extricate itself from the primal warmth and primal darkness of the maternal womb; in a word, from unconsciousness. Divine curiosity yearns to be born and does not shrink from conflict, suffering, or sin. Unconsciousness is the primal sin, evil itself, for the Logos. Therefore its first creative act of liberation is matricide, and the spirit that dared all heights and all depths must, as Synesius says, suffer the divine punishment, enchainment on the rocks of the Caucasus. Nothing can exist without its opposite; the two were one in the beginning and will be one again in the end. Consciousness can only exist through continual recognition of the unconscious, just as everything that lives must pass through many deaths.

179 The stirring up of conflict is a Luciferian virtue in the true sense of the word. Conflict engenders fire, the fire of affects and emotions, and like every other fire it has two aspects, that of combustion and that of creating light. On the one hand, emotion is the alchemical fire whose warmth brings everything into existence and whose heat burns all superfluities to ashes (*omnes superfluitates comburit*). But on the other hand, emotion is the moment when steel meets flint and a spark is struck forth, for emotion is the chief source of consciousness. There is no change from darkness to light or from inertia to movement without emotion.

180 The woman whose fate it is to be a disturbing element is not solely destructive, except in pathological cases. Normally the disturber is herself caught in the disturbance; the worker of change is herself changed, and the glare of the fire she ignites both illuminates and enlightens all the victims of the entanglement. What seemed a senseless upheaval becomes a process of purification:

> So that all that is vain
> Might dwindle and wane.[1]

[1] *Faust,* Part II, Act 5.

181 If a woman of this type remains unconscious of the meaning of her function, if she does not know that she is

> Part of that power which would
> Ever work evil but engenders good,[2]

she will herself perish by the sword she brings. But consciousness transforms her into a deliverer and redeemer.

III. THE "NOTHING-BUT" DAUGHTER

182 The woman of the third type, who is so identified with the mother that her own instincts are paralysed through projection, need not on that account remain a hopeless nonentity forever. On the contrary, if she is at all normal, there is a good chance of the empty vessel being filled by a potent anima projection. Indeed, the fate of such a woman depends on this eventuality; she can never find herself at all, not even approximately, without a man's help; she has to be literally abducted or stolen from her mother. Moreover, she must play the role mapped out for her for a long time and with great effort, until she actually comes to loathe it. In this way she may perhaps discover who she really is. Such women may become devoted and self-sacrificing wives of husbands whose whole existence turns on their identification with a profession or a great talent, but who, for the rest, are unconscious and remain so. Since they are nothing but masks themselves, the wife, too, must be able to play the accompanying part with a semblance of naturalness. But these women sometimes have valuable gifts which remained undeveloped only because they were entirely unconscious of their own personality. They may project the gift or talent upon a husband who lacks it himself, and then we have the spectacle of a totally insignificant man who seemed to have no chance whatsoever suddenly soaring as if on a magic carpet to the highest summits of achievement. *Cherchez la femme,* and you have the secret of his success. These women remind me—if I may be forgiven the impolite comparison—of hefty great bitches who turn tail before the smallest cur simply because he is a terrible male and it never occurs to them to bite him.

2 Ibid., Part I, Act 1.

83 Finally, it should be remarked that *emptiness* is a great feminine secret. It is something absolutely alien to man; the chasm, the unplumbed depths, the *yin*. The pitifulness of this vacuous nonentity goes to his heart (I speak here as a man), and one is tempted to say that this constitutes the whole "mystery" of woman. Such a female is fate itself. A man may say what he likes about it; be for it or against it, or both at once; in the end he falls, absurdly happy, into this pit, or, if he doesn't, he has missed and bungled his only chance of making a man of himself. In the first case one cannot disprove his foolish good luck to him, and in the second one cannot make his misfortune seem plausible. "The Mothers, the Mothers, how eerily it sounds!" [3] With this sigh, which seals the capitulation of the male as he approaches the realm of the Mothers, we will turn to the fourth type.

IV. THE NEGATIVE MOTHER-COMPLEX

84 As a pathological phenomenon this type is an unpleasant, exacting, and anything but satisfactory partner for her husband, since she rebels in every fibre of her being against everything that springs from natural soil. However, there is no reason why increasing experience of life should not teach her a thing or two, so that for a start she gives up fighting the mother in the personal and restricted sense. But even at her best she will remain hostile to all that is dark, unclear, and ambiguous, and will cultivate and emphasize everything certain and clear and reasonable. Excelling her more feminine sister in her objectivity and coolness of judgment, she may become the friend, sister, and competent adviser of her husband. Her own masculine aspirations make it possible for her to have a human understanding of the individuality of her husband quite transcending the realm of the erotic. The woman with this type of mother-complex probably has the best chance of all to make her marriage an outstanding success during the second half of life. But this is true only if she succeeds in overcoming the hell of "nothing but femininity," the chaos of the maternal womb, which is her greatest danger because of her negative complex. As we know, a com-

[3] Ibid., Part II, Act 1.

plex can be really overcome only if it is lived out to the full. In other words, if we are to develop further we have to draw to us and drink down to the very dregs what, because of our complexes, we have held at a distance.

185 This type started out in the world with averted face, like Lot's wife looking back on Sodom and Gomorrah. And all the while the world and life pass by her like a dream—an annoying source of illusions, disappointments, and irritations, all of which are due solely to the fact that she cannot bring herself to look straight ahead for once. Because of her merely unconscious, reactive attitude toward reality, her life actually becomes dominated by what she fought hardest against—the exclusively maternal feminine aspect. But if she should later turn her face, she will see the world for the first time, so to speak, in the light of maturity, and see it embellished with all the colours and enchanting wonders of youth, and sometimes even of childhood. It is a vision that brings knowledge and discovery of truth, the indispensable prerequisite for consciousness. A part of life was lost, but the meaning of life has been salvaged for her.

186 The woman who fights against her father still has the possibility of leading an instinctive, feminine existence, because she rejects only what is alien to her. But when she fights against the mother she may, at the risk of injury to her instincts, attain to greater consciousness, because in repudiating the mother she repudiates all that is obscure, instinctive, ambiguous, and unconscious in her own nature. Thanks to her lucidity, objectivity, and masculinity, a woman of this type is frequently found in important positions in which her tardily discovered maternal quality, guided by a cool intelligence, exerts a most beneficial influence. This rare combination of womanliness and masculine understanding proves valuable in the realm of intimate relationships as well as in practical matters. As the spiritual guide and adviser of a man, such a woman, unknown to the world, may play a highly influential part. Owing to her qualities, the masculine mind finds this type easier to understand than women with other forms of mother-complex, and for this reason men often favour her with the projection of positive mother-complexes. The excessively feminine woman terrifies men who have a mother-complex characterized by great sensitivity. But this woman is not frightening to a man, because she builds bridges

for the masculine mind over which he can safely guide his feelings to the opposite shore. Her clarity of understanding inspires him with confidence, a factor not to be underrated and one that is absent from the relationship between a man and a woman much more often than one might think. The man's Eros does not lead upward only but downward into that uncanny dark world of Hecate and Kali, which is a horror to any intellectual man. The understanding possessed by this type of woman will be a guiding star to him in the darkness and seemingly unending mazes of life.

5. CONCLUSION

87 From what has been said it should be clear that in the last analysis all the statements of mythology on this subject as well as the observed effects of the mother-complex, when stripped of their confusing detail, point to the unconscious as their place of origin. How else could it have occurred to man to divide the cosmos, on the analogy of day and night, summer and winter, into a bright day-world and a dark night-world peopled with fabulous monsters, unless he had the prototype of such a division in himself, in the polarity between the conscious and the invisible and unknowable unconscious? Primitive man's perception of objects is conditioned only partly by the objective behaviour of the things themselves, whereas a much greater part is often played by intrapsychic facts which are not related to the external objects except by way of projection.[1] This is due to the simple fact that the primitive has not yet experienced that ascetic discipline of mind known to us as the critique of knowledge. To him the world is a more or less fluid phenomenon within the stream of his own fantasy, where subject and object are undifferentiated and in a state of mutual interpenetration. "All that is outside, also is inside," we could say with Goethe. But this "inside," which modern rationalism is so eager to derive from "outside," has an *a priori* structure of its own that antedates all conscious experience. It is quite impossible to conceive how "experience" in the widest sense, or, for that matter, anything psychic, could originate exclusively in the outside world. The psyche is part of the inmost mystery of life, and it has its own peculiar structure and form like every other organism. Whether this psychic structure and its elements, the archetypes, ever "originated" at all is a metaphysical question and therefore unanswerable. The structure is something given, the precondition that is found to be present in every case. And this is the *mother*, the matrix—the form into which all experience is

1 [Cf. above, "Archetypes of the Collective Unconscious," par. 7.—EDITORS.]

poured. The *father,* on the other hand, represents the *dynamism* of the archetype, for the archetype consists of both—form and energy.

188 The carrier of the archetype is in the first place the personal mother, because the child lives at first in complete participation with her, in a state of unconscious identity. She is the psychic as well as the physical precondition of the child. With the awakening of ego-consciousness the participation gradually weakens, and consciousness begins to enter into opposition to the unconscious, its own precondition. This leads to differentiation of the ego from the mother, whose personal peculiarities gradually become more distinct. All the fabulous and mysterious qualities attaching to her image begin to fall away and are transferred to the person closest to her, for instance the grandmother. As the mother of the mother, she is "greater" than the latter; she is in truth the "grand" or "Great Mother." Not infrequently she assumes the attributes of wisdom as well as those of a witch. For the further the archetype recedes from consciousness and the clearer the latter becomes, the more distinctly does the archetype assume mythological features. The transition from mother to grandmother means that the archetype is elevated to a higher rank. This is clearly demonstrated in a notion held by the Bataks. The funeral sacrifice in honour of a dead father is modest, consisting of ordinary food. But if the son has a son of his own, then the father has become a grandfather and has consequently attained a more dignified status in the Beyond, and very important offerings are made to him.[2]

189 As the distance between conscious and unconscious increases, the grandmother's more exalted rank transforms her into a "Great Mother," and it frequently happens that the opposites contained in this image split apart. We then get a good fairy and a wicked fairy, or a benevolent goddess and one who is malevolent and dangerous. In Western antiquity and especially in Eastern cultures the opposites often remain united in the same figure, though this paradox does not disturb the primitive mind in the least. The legends about the gods are as full of contradictions as are their moral characters. In the West, the paradoxical behaviour and moral ambivalence of the gods scandalized people even in antiquity and gave rise to criticism that led

2 Warnecke, *Die Religion der Batak.*

finally to a devaluation of the Olympians on the one hand and to their philosophical interpretation on the other. The clearest expression of this is the Christian reformation of the Jewish concept of the Deity: the morally ambiguous Yahweh became an exclusively good God, while everything evil was united in the devil. It seems as if the development of the feeling function in Western man forced a choice on him which led to the moral splitting of the divinity into two halves. In the East the predominantly intuitive intellectual attitude left no room for feeling values, and the gods—Kali is a case in point—could retain their original paradoxical morality undisturbed. Thus Kali is representative of the East and the Madonna of the West. The latter has entirely lost the shadow that still distantly followed her in the allegories of the Middle Ages. It was relegated to the hell of popular imagination, where it now leads an insignificant existence as the devil's grandmother.[3] Thanks to the development of feeling-values, the splendour of the "light" god has been enhanced beyond measure, but the darkness supposedly represented by the devil has localized itself in man. This strange development was precipitated chiefly by the fact that Christianity, terrified of Manichaean dualism, strove to preserve its monotheism by main force. But since the reality of darkness and evil could not be denied, there was no alternative but to make man responsible for it. Even the devil was largely, if not entirely, abolished, with the result that this metaphysical figure, who at one time was an integral part of the Deity, was introjected into man, who thereupon became the real carrier of the *mysterium iniquitatis:* "omne bonum a Deo, omne malum ab homine." In recent times this development has suffered a diabolical reverse, and the wolf in sheep's clothing now goes about whispering in our ear that evil is really nothing but a misunderstanding of good and an effective instrument of progress. We think that the world of darkness has thus been abolished for good and all, and nobody realizes what a poisoning this is of man's soul. In this way he turns himself into the devil, for the devil is half of the archetype whose irresistible power makes even unbelievers ejaculate "Oh God!" on every suitable and unsuitable occasion. If one can possibly avoid it, one ought never to identify with an archetype, for, as psychopathology

[3] [A familiar figure of speech in German.—EDITORS.]

and certain contemporary events show, the consequences are terrifying.

190 Western man has sunk to such a low level spiritually that he even has to deny the apotheosis of untamed and untameable psychic power—the divinity itself—so that, after swallowing evil, he may possess himself of the good as well. If you read Nietzsche's *Zarathustra* with attention and psychological understanding, you will see that he has described with rare consistency and with the passion of a truly religious person the psychology of the "Superman" for whom God is dead, and who is himself burst asunder because he tried to imprison the divine paradox within the narrow framework of the mortal man. Goethe has wisely said: "What terror then shall seize the Superman!"—and was rewarded with a supercilious smile from the Philistines. His glorification of the Mother who is great enough to include in herself both the Queen of Heaven and Maria Aegyptiaca is supreme wisdom and profoundly significant for anyone willing to reflect upon it. But what can one expect in an age when the official spokesmen of Christianity publicly announce their inability to understand the foundations of religious experience! I extract the following sentence from an article by a Protestant theologian: "We understand ourselves—whether naturalistically or idealistically—to be *homogeneous creatures who are not so peculiarly divided that alien forces can intervene in our inner life,* as the New Testament supposes." [4] (Italics mine.) The author is evidently unacquainted with the fact that science demonstrated the lability and dissociability of consciousness more than half a century ago and proved it by experiment. Our conscious intentions are continually disturbed and thwarted, to a greater or lesser degree, by unconscious intrusions whose causes are at first strange to us. The psyche is far from being a homogeneous unit—on the contrary, it is a boiling cauldron of contradictory impulses, inhibitions, and affects, and for many people the conflict between them is so insupportable that they even wish for the deliverance preached by theologians. Deliverance from what? Obviously, from a highly questionable psychic state. The unity of consciousness or of the so-called personality is not a reality at all but a desideratum. I still have a vivid memory of a certain philosopher who also raved about this unity and

[4] Buri, "Theologie und Philosophie," p. 117. [Quoting Rudolf Bultmann.—EDS.]

used to consult me about his neurosis: he was obsessed by the idea that he was suffering from cancer. I do not know how many specialists he had consulted already, and how many X-ray pictures he had had made. They all assured him that he had no cancer. He himself told me: "I know I have no cancer, but I still could have one." Who is responsible for this "imaginary" idea? He certainly did not make it himself; it was forced on him by an "alien" power. There is little to choose between this state and that of the man possessed in the New Testament. Now whether you believe in a demon of the air or in a factor in the unconscious that plays diabolical tricks on you is all one to me. The fact that man's imagined unity is menaced by alien powers remains the same in either case. Theologians would do better to take account for once of these psychological facts than to go on "demythologizing" them with rationalistic explanations that are a hundred years behind the times.

*

191 I have tried in the foregoing to give a survey of the psychic phenomena that may be attributed to the predominance of the mother-image. Although I have not always drawn attention to them, my reader will presumably have had no difficulty in recognizing those features which characterize the Great Mother mythologically, even when they appear under the guise of personalistic psychology. When we ask patients who are particularly influenced by the mother-image to express in words or pictures what "Mother" means to them—be it positive or negative—we invariably get symbolical figures which must be regarded as direct analogies of the mythological mother-image. These analogies take us into a field that still requires a great deal more work of elucidation. At any rate, I personally do not feel able to say anything definitive about it. If, nevertheless, I venture to offer a few suggestions, they should be regarded as altogether provisional and tentative.

192 Above all, I should like to point out that the mother-image in a man's psychology is entirely different in character from a woman's. For a woman, the mother typifies her own conscious life as conditioned by her sex. But for a man the mother typifies something alien, which he has yet to experience and which is filled with the imagery latent in the unconscious. For this

reason, if for no other, the mother-image of a man is essentially different from a woman's. The mother has from the outset a decidedly symbolical significance for a man, which probably accounts for his strong tendency to idealize her. Idealization is a hidden apotropaism; one idealizes whenever there is a secret fear to be exorcized. What is feared is the unconscious and its magical influence.[5]

193 Whereas for a man the mother is *ipso facto* symbolical, for a woman she becomes a symbol only in the course of her psychological development. Experience reveals the striking fact that the Urania type of mother-image predominates in masculine psychology, whereas in a woman the chthonic type, or Earth Mother, is the most frequent. During the manifest phase of the archetype an almost complete identification takes place. A woman can identify directly with the Earth Mother, but a man cannot (except in psychotic cases). As mythology shows, one of the peculiarities of the Great Mother is that she frequently appears paired with her male counterpart. Accordingly the man identifies with the son-lover on whom the grace of Sophia has descended, with a *puer aeternus* or a *filius sapientiae.* But the companion of the chthonic mother is the exact opposite: an ithyphallic Hermes (the Egyptian Bes) or a lingam. In India this symbol is of the highest spiritual significance, and in the West Hermes is one of the most contradictory figures of Hellenistic syncretism, which was the source of extremely important spiritual developments in Western civilization. He is also the god of revelation, and in the unofficial nature philosophy of the early Middle Ages he is nothing less than the world-creating Nous itself. This mystery has perhaps found its finest expression in the words of the *Tabula smaragdina:* "omne superius sicut inferius" (as it is above, so it is below).

194 It is a psychological fact that as soon as we touch on these identifications we enter the realm of the syzygies, the paired opposites, where the One is never separated from the Other, its antithesis. It is a field of personal experience which leads directly to the experience of individuation, the attainment of the self. A vast number of symbols for this process could be mustered from the medieval literature of the West and even more

5 Obviously a daughter can idealize her mother too, but for this special circumstances are needed, whereas in a man idealization is almost the normal thing.

from the storehouses of Oriental wisdom, but in this matter words and ideas count for little. Indeed, they may become dangerous bypaths and false trails. In this still very obscure field of psychological experience, where we are in direct contact, so to speak, with the archetype, its psychic power is felt in full force. This realm is so entirely one of immediate experience that it cannot be captured by any formula, but can only be hinted at to one who already knows. He will need no explanations to understand what was the tension of opposites expressed by Apuleius in his magnificent prayer to the Queen of Heaven, when he associates "heavenly Venus" with "Proserpina, who strikest terror with midnight ululations": [6] it was the terrifying paradox of the primordial mother-image.

*

95 When, in 1938, I originally wrote this paper, I naturally did not know that twelve years later the Christian version of the mother archetype would be elevated to the rank of a dogmatic truth. The Christian "Queen of Heaven" has, obviously, shed all her Olympian qualities except for her brightness, goodness, and eternality; and even her human body, the thing most prone to gross material corruption, has put on an ethereal incorruptibility. The richly varied allegories of the Mother of God have nevertheless retained some connection with her pagan prefigurations in Isis (Io) and Semele. Not only are Isis and the Horus-child iconological exemplars, but the ascension of Semele, the originally mortal mother of Dionysus, likewise anticipates the Assumption of the Blessed Virgin. Further, this son of Semele is a dying and resurgent god and the youngest of the Olympians. Semele herself seems to have been an earth-goddess, just as the Virgin Mary is the earth from which Christ was born. This being so, the question naturally arises for the psychologist: what has become of the characteristic relation of the mother-image to the earth, darkness, the abysmal side of the bodily man with his animal passions and instinctual nature, and to "matter" in general? The declaration of the dogma comes at a time when the achievements of science and technology, combined with a rationalistic and materialistic view of the world, threaten

[6] "Nocturnis ululatibus horrenda Proserpina." Cf. *Symbols of Transformation*, par. 148.

the spiritual and psychic heritage of man with instant annihilation. Humanity is arming itself, in dread and fascinated horror, for a stupendous crime. Circumstances might easily arise when the hydrogen bomb would have to be used and the unthinkably frightful deed became unavoidable in legitimate self-defence. In striking contrast to this disastrous turn of events, the Mother of God is now enthroned in heaven; indeed, her Assumption has actually been interpreted as a deliberate counterstroke to the materialistic doctrinairism that provoked the chthonic powers into revolt. Just as Christ's appearance in his own day created a real devil and adversary of God out of what was originally a son of God dwelling in heaven, so now, conversely, a heavenly figure has split off from her original chthonic realm and taken up a counter-position to the titanic forces of the earth and the underworld that have been unleashed. In the same way that the Mother of God was divested of all the essential qualities of materiality, matter became completely de-souled, and this at a time when physics is pushing forward to insights which, if they do not exactly "de-materialize" matter, at least endue it with properties of its own and make its relation to the psyche a problem that can no longer be shelved. For just as the tremendous advancement of science led at first to a premature dethronement of mind and to an equally ill-considered deification of matter, so it is this same urge for scientific knowledge that is now attempting to bridge the huge gulf that has opened out between the two *Weltanschauungen*. The psychologist inclines to see in the dogma of the Assumption a symbol which, in a sense, anticipates this whole development. For him the relationship to the earth and to matter is one of the inalienable qualities of the mother archetype. So that when a figure that is conditioned by this archetype is represented as having been taken up into heaven, the realm of the spirit, this indicates a union of earth and heaven, or of matter and spirit. The approach of natural science will almost certainly be from the other direction: it will see in matter itself the equivalent of spirit, but this "spirit" will appear divested of all, or at any rate most, of its known qualities, just as earthly matter was stripped of its specific characteristics when it staged its entry into heaven. Nevertheless, the way will gradually be cleared for a union of the two principles.

96 Understood concretely, the Assumption is the absolute opposite of materialism. Taken in this sense, it is a counterstroke that does nothing to diminish the tension between the opposites, but drives it to extremes.

97 Understood symbolically, however, the Assumption of the body is a recognition and acknowledgment of matter, which in the last resort was identified with evil only because of an overwhelmingly "pneumatic" tendency in man. In themselves, spirit and matter are neutral, or rather, "utriusque capax"—that is, capable of what man calls good or evil. Although as names they are exceedingly relative, underlying them are very real opposites that are part of the energic structure of the physical and of the psychic world, and without them no existence of any kind could be established. There is no position without its negation. In spite or just because of their extreme opposition, neither can exist without the other. It is exactly as formulated in classical Chinese philosophy: *yang* (the light, warm, dry, masculine principle) contains within it the seed of *yin* (the dark, cold, moist, feminine principle), and vice versa. Matter therefore would contain the seed of spirit and spirit the seed of matter. The long-known "synchronistic" phenomena that have now been statistically confirmed by Rhine's experiments [7] point, to all appearances, in this direction. The "psychization" of matter puts the absolute immateriality of spirit in question, since this would then have to be accorded a kind of substantiality. The dogma of the Assumption, proclaimed in an age suffering from the greatest political schism history has ever known, is a compensating symptom that reflects the strivings of science for a uniform world-picture. In a certain sense, both developments were anticipated by alchemy in the *hieros gamos* of opposites, but only in symbolic form. Nevertheless, the symbol has the great advantage of being able to unite heterogeneous or even incommensurable factors in a *single* image. With the decline of alchemy the symbolical unity of spirit and matter fell apart, with the result that modern man finds himself uprooted and alienated in a de-souled world.

98 The alchemist saw the union of opposites under the symbol of the tree, and it is therefore not surprising that the unconscious of present-day man, who no longer feels at home in his

[7] Cf. my "Synchronicity: An Acausal Connecting Principle."

world and can base his existence neither on the past that is no more nor on the future that is yet to be, should hark back to the symbol of the cosmic tree rooted in this world and growing up to heaven—the tree that is also man. In the history of symbols this tree is described as the way of life itself, a growing into that which eternally is and does not change; which springs from the union of opposites and, by its eternal presence, also makes that union possible. It seems as if it were only through an experience of symbolic reality that man, vainly seeking his own "existence" and making a philosophy out of it, can find his way back to a world in which he is no longer a stranger.

III

THE PSYCHOLOGICAL ASPECTS OF THE KORE

THE PSYCHOLOGICAL ASPECTS OF THE KORE

306 Not only is the figure of Demeter and the Kore in its threefold aspect as maiden, mother, and Hecate not unknown to the psychology of the unconscious, it is even something of a practical problem. The "Kore" has her psychological counterpart in those archetypes which I have called the *self* or *supraordinate personality* on the one hand, and the *anima* on the other. In order to explain these figures, with which I cannot assume all readers to be familiar, I must begin with some remarks of a general nature.

307 The psychologist has to contend with the same difficulties as the mythologist when an exact definition or clear and concise information is demanded of him. The picture is concrete, clear, and subject to no misunderstandings only when it is seen in its habitual context. In this form it tells us everything it contains. But as soon as one tries to abstract the "real essence" of the picture, the whole thing becomes cloudy and indistinct. In order to understand its living function, we must let it remain an organic thing in all its complexity and not try to examine the anatomy of its corpse in the manner of the scientist, or the archaeology of its ruins in the manner of the historian. Naturally this is not to deny the justification of such methods when applied in their proper place.

308 In view of the enormous complexity of psychic phenomena, a purely phenomenological point of view is, and will be for a long time, the only possible one and the only one with any prospect of success. "Whence" things come and "what" they are, these, particularly in the field of psychology, are questions which are apt to call forth untimely attempts at explanation. Such speculations are moreover based far more on unconscious philosophical premises than on the nature of the phenomena themselves. Psychic phenomena occasioned by unconscious processes are so rich and so multifarious that I prefer to *describe* my findings and observations and, where possible, to classify them—

that is, to arrange them under certain definite types. That is the method of natural science, and it is applied wherever we have to do with multifarious and still unorganized material. One may question the utility or the appropriateness of the categories or types used in the arrangement, but not the correctness of the method itself.

309 Since for years I have been observing and investigating the products of the unconscious in the widest sense of the word, namely dreams, fantasies, visions, and delusions of the insane, I have not been able to avoid recognizing certain regularities, that is, *types*. There are types of *situations* and types of *figures* that repeat themselves frequently and have a corresponding meaning. I therefore employ the term "motif" to designate these repetitions. Thus there are not only typical dreams but typical motifs in the dreams. These may, as we have said, be situations or figures. Among the latter there are human figures that can be arranged under a series of archetypes, the chief of them being, according to my suggestion,[1] the *shadow*, the *wise old man*, the *child* (including the child hero), the *mother* ("Primordial Mother" and "Earth Mother") as a supraordinate personality ("daemonic" because supraordinate), and her counterpart the *maiden*, and lastly the *anima* in man and the *animus* in woman.

310 The above types are far from exhausting all the statistical regularities in this respect. The figure of the Kore that interests us here belongs, when observed in a man, to the *anima* type; and when observed in a woman to the type of *supraordinate personality*. It is an essential characteristic of psychic figures that they are duplex or at least capable of duplication; at all events they are bipolar and oscillate between their positive and negative meanings. Thus the "supraordinate" personality can appear in a despicable and distorted form, like for instance Mephistopheles, who is really more positive as a personality than the vapid and unthinking careerist Faust. Another negative figure

1 To the best of my knowledge, no other suggestions have been made so far. Critics have contented themselves with asserting that no such archetypes exist. Certainly they do not exist, any more than a botanical system exists in nature! But will anyone deny the existence of natural plant-families on that account? Or will anyone deny the occurrence and continual repetition of certain morphological and functional similarities? It is much the same thing in principle with the typical figures of the unconscious. They are forms existing *a priori*, or biological norms of psychic activity.

is the Tom Thumb or Tom Dumb of the folktales. The figure corresponding to the Kore in a woman is generally a double one, i.e., a mother and a maiden, which is to say that she appears now as the one, now as the other. From this I would conclude, for a start, that in the formation of the Demeter-Kore myth the feminine influence so far outweighed the masculine that the latter had practically no significance. The man's role in the Demeter myth is really only that of seducer or conqueror.

311 As a matter of practical observation, the Kore often appears in woman as an *unknown young girl,* not infrequently as Gretchen or the unmarried mother.[2] Another frequent modulation is the *dancer,* who is often formed by borrowings from classical knowledge, in which case the "maiden" appears as the *corybant, maenad,* or *nymph.* An occasional variant is the nixie or water-sprite, who betrays her superhuman nature by her fish-tail. Sometimes the Kore- and mother-figures slither down altogether to the animal kingdom, the favourite representatives then being the *cat* or the *snake* or the *bear,* or else some black monster of the underworld like the crocodile, or other salamander-like, saurian creatures.[3] The maiden's helplessness exposes her to all sorts of *dangers,* for instance of being devoured by reptiles or ritually slaughtered like a beast of sacrifice. Often there are bloody, cruel, and even obscene *orgies* to which the innocent child falls victim. Sometimes it is a true *nekyia,* a descent into Hades and a quest for the "treasure hard to attain," occasionally connected with orgiastic sexual rites or offerings of menstrual blood to the moon. Oddly enough, the various tortures and obscenities are carried out by an "Earth Mother." There are *drinkings of blood* and *bathings in blood,*[4] also cruci-

2 The "personalistic" approach interprets such dreams as "wish-fulfilments." To many, this kind of interpretation seems the only possible one. These dreams, however, occur in the most varied circumstances, even in circumstances when the wish-fulfilment theory becomes entirely forced or arbitrary. The investigation of motifs in the field of dreams therefore seems to me the more cautious and the more appropriate procedure.

3 The double vision of a salamander, of which Benvenuto Cellini tells in his autobiography, would be an anima-projection caused by the music his father was playing.

4 One of my patients, whose principal difficulty was a negative mother-complex, developed a series of fantasies on a primitive mother-figure, an Indian woman,

fixions. The maiden who crops up in case histories differs not inconsiderably from the vaguely flower-like Kore in that the modern figure is more sharply delineated and not nearly so "unconscious," as the following examples will show.

312 The figures corresponding to Demeter and Hecate are supraordinate, not to say over-life-size "Mothers" ranging from the Pietà type to the Baubo type. The unconscious, which acts as a counterbalance to woman's conventional innocuousness, proves to be highly inventive in this latter respect. I can recall only very few cases where Demeter's own noble figure in its pure form breaks through as an image rising spontaneously from the unconscious. I remember a case, in fact, where a maiden-goddess appears clad all in purest white, but carrying a black monkey in her arms. The Earth Mother is always chthonic and is occasionally related to the moon, either through the blood-sacrifice already mentioned, or through a child-sacrifice, or else because she is adorned with a sickle moon.[5] In pictorial or plastic representations the Mother is dark deepening to *black,* or *red* (these being her principal colours), and with a primitive or animal expression of face; in form she not infrequently resembles the

who instructed her on the nature of woman in general. In these pronouncements a special paragraph is devoted to blood, running as follows: "A woman's life is close to the *blood.* Every month she is reminded of this, and birth is indeed a bloody business, destructive and creative. A woman is only *permitted* to give birth, but the new life is not *her* creation. In her heart of hearts she knows this and rejoices in the grace that has fallen to her. She is a little mother, not the *Great Mother.* But her little pattern is like the great pattern. If she understands this she is blessed by nature, because she has submitted in the right way and can thus partake of the nourishment of the Great Mother. . . ."

5 Often the moon is simply "there," as for instance in a fantasy of the chthonic mother in the shape of the "Woman of the Bees" (Josephine D. Bacon, *In the Border Country,* pp. 14ff.): "The path led to a tiny hut of the same colour as the *four great trees* that stood about it. Its door hung wide open, and in the middle of it, on a low stool, there sat an old woman wrapped in a long cloak, looking kindly at her. . . ." The hut was filled with the steady *humming of bees.* In the corner of the hut there was a deep cold *spring,* in which "a white moon and little stars" were reflected. The old woman exhorted the heroine to remember the duties of a woman's life. In Tantric yoga an "indistinct hum of swarms of love-mad bees" proceeds from the slumbering Shakti (*Shat-Chakra Nirupana,* in Avalon, *The Serpent Power,* p. 29). Cf. infra, the dancer who dissolves into a *swarm of bees.* Bees are also, as an allegory, connected with Mary, as the text for the consecration of the Easter candle shows. See Duchesne, *Christian Worship: Its Origin and Evolution,* p. 253.

neolithic ideal of the "Venus" of Brassempouy or that of Willendorf, or again the sleeper of Hal Saflieni.[6] Now and then I have come across *multiple breasts,* arranged like those of a sow. The Earth Mother plays an important part in the woman's unconscious, for all her manifestations are described as "powerful." This shows that in such cases the Earth Mother element in the conscious mind is abnormally weak and requires strengthening.

313 In view of all this it is, I admit, hardly understandable why such figures should be reckoned as belonging to the type of "supraordinate personality." In a scientific investigation, however, one has to disregard moral or aesthetic prejudices and let the facts speak for themselves. The *maiden* is often described as not altogether human in the usual sense; she is either of unknown or peculiar origin, or she looks strange or undergoes strange experiences, from which one is forced to infer the maiden's extraordinary, myth-like nature. Equally and still more strikingly, the Earth Mother is a divine being—in the classical sense. Moreover, she does not by any means always appear in the guise of Baubo, but, for instance, more like Queen Venus in the *Hypnerotomachia Poliphili,* though she is invariably heavy with destiny. The often unaesthetic forms of the Earth Mother are in keeping with a prejudice of the modern feminine unconscious; this prejudice was lacking in antiquity. The underworld nature of Hecate, who is closely connected with Demeter, and Persephone's fate both point nevertheless to the dark side of the human psyche, though not to the same extent as the modern material.

314 The "supraordinate personality" is the total man, i.e., man as he really is, not as he appears to himself. To this wholeness the unconscious psyche also belongs, which has its requirements and needs just as consciousness has. I do not want to interpret the unconscious personalistically and assert, for instance, that fantasy-images like those described above are the "wish-fulfilments" due to repression. These images were as such never conscious and consequently could never have been repressed. I understand the unconscious rather as an *impersonal* psyche common to all men, even though it expresses itself through a

6 [See Neumann, *The Great Mother,* Pls. 1a, 3. This entire work elucidates the present study.—EDITORS.]

personal consciousness. When anyone breathes, his breathing is not a phenomenon to be interpreted personally. The mythological images belong to the structure of the unconscious and are an impersonal possession; in fact, the great majority of men are far more *possessed by* them than possessing them. Images like those described above give rise under certain conditions to corresponding disturbances and symptoms, and it is then the task of medical therapy to find out whether and how and to what extent these impulses can be integrated with the conscious personality, or whether they are a secondary phenomenon which some defective orientation of consciousness has brought out of its normal potential state into actuality. Both possibilities exist in practice.

315 I usually describe the supraordinate personality as the "self," thus making a sharp distinction between the ego, which, as is well known, extends only as far as the conscious mind, and the *whole* of the personality, which includes the unconscious as well as the conscious component. The ego is thus related to the self as part to whole. To that extent the self is supraordinate. Moreover, the self is felt empirically not as subject but as object, and this by reason of its unconscious component, which can only come to consciousness indirectly, by way of projection. Because of its unconscious component the self is so far removed from the conscious mind that it can only be partially expressed by human figures; the other part of it has to be expressed by objective, abstract symbols. The human figures are father and son, mother and daughter, king and queen, god and goddess. Theriomorphic symbols are the dragon, snake, elephant, lion, bear, and other powerful animals, or again the spider, crab, butterfly, beetle, worm, etc. Plant symbols are generally flowers (lotus and rose). These lead on to geometrical figures like the circle, the sphere, the square, the quaternity, the clock, the firmament, and so on.[7] The indefinite extent of the unconscious component makes a comprehensive description of the human personality impossible. Accordingly, the unconscious supplements the picture with living figures ranging from the animal to the divine, as the two extremes outside man, and rounds out the animal extreme, through the addition of

[7] *Psychology and Alchemy,* Part II.

vegetable and inorganic abstractions, into a microcosm. These addenda have a high frequency in anthropomorphic divinities, where they appear as "attributes."

316 Demeter and Kore, mother and daughter, extend the feminine consciousness both upwards and downwards. They add an "older and younger," "stronger and weaker" dimension to it and widen out the narrowly limited conscious mind bound in space and time, giving it intimations of a greater and more comprehensive personality which has a share in the eternal course of things. We can hardly suppose that myth and mystery were invented for any conscious purpose; it seems much more likely that they were the involuntary revelation of a psychic, but unconscious, pre-condition. The psyche pre-existent to consciousness (e.g., in the child) participates in the maternal psyche on the one hand, while on the other it reaches across to the daughter psyche. We could therefore say that every mother contains her daughter in herself and every daughter her mother, and that every woman extends backwards into her mother and forwards into her daughter. This participation and intermingling give rise to that peculiar uncertainty as regards *time:* a woman lives earlier as a mother, later as a daughter. The conscious experience of these ties produces the feeling that her life is spread out over generations—the first step towards the immediate experience and conviction of being outside time, which brings with it a feeling of *immortality*. The individual's life is elevated into a type, indeed it becomes the archetype of woman's fate in general. This leads to a restoration or *apocatastasis* of the lives of her ancestors, who now, through the bridge of the momentary individual, pass down into the generations of the future. An experience of this kind gives the individual a place and a meaning in the life of the generations, so that all unnecessary obstacles are cleared out of the way of the life-stream that is to flow through her. At the same time the individual is rescued from her isolation and restored to wholeness. All ritual preoccupation with archetypes ultimately has this aim and this result.

317 It is immediately clear to the psychologist what cathartic and at the same rejuvenating effects must flow from the Demeter cult into the feminine psyche, and what a lack of psychic hygiene

characterizes our culture, which no longer knows the kind of wholesome experience afforded by Eleusinian emotions.

318 I take full account of the fact that not only the psychologically minded layman but the professional psychologist and psychiatrist as well, and even the psychotherapist, do not possess an adequate knowledge of their patients' archetypal material, in so far as they have not specially investigated this aspect of the phenomenology of the unconscious. For it is precisely in the field of psychiatric and psychotherapeutic observation that we frequently meet with cases characterized by a rich crop of archetypal symbols.[8] Since the necessary historical knowledge is lacking to the physician observing them, he is not in a position to perceive the parallelism between his observations and the findings of anthropology and the humane sciences in general. Conversely, an expert in mythology and comparative religion is as a rule no psychiatrist and consequently does not know that his mythologems are still fresh and living—for instance, in dreams and visions—in the hidden recesses of our most personal life, which we would on no account deliver up to scientific dissection. The archetypal material is therefore the great unknown, and it requires special study and preparation even to collect such material.

319 It does not seem to me superfluous to give a number of examples from my case histories which bring out the occurrence of archetypal images in dreams or fantasies. Time and again with my public I come across the difficulty that they imagine illustration by "a few examples" to be the simplest thing in the world. In actual fact it is almost impossible, with a few words and one or two images torn out of their context, to demonstrate anything. This only works when dealing with an expert. What Perseus has to do with the Gorgon's head would never occur to anyone who did not know the myth. So it is with the individual images: they need a context, and the context is not only a myth but an individual anamnesis. Such contexts, however, are of enormous extent. Anything like a complete series of images would require for its proper presentation a book of about two hundred pages. My own investigation of the Miller fantasies

8 I would refer to the thesis of my pupil Jan Nelken, "Analytische Beobachtungen über Phantasien eines Schizophrenen," as also to my own analysis of a series of fantasies in *Symbols of Transformation*.

gives some idea of this.[9] It is therefore with the greatest hesitation that I make the attempt to illustrate from case-histories. The material I shall use comes partly from normal, partly from slightly neurotic, persons. It is part dream, part vision, or dream mixed with vision. These "visions" are far from being hallucinations or ecstatic states; they are spontaneous, visual images of fantasy or so-called *active imagination.* The latter is a method (devised by myself) of introspection for observing the stream of interior images. One concentrates one's attention on some impressive but unintelligible dream-image, or on a spontaneous visual impression, and observes the changes taking place in it. Meanwhile, of course, all criticism must be suspended and the happenings observed and noted with absolute objectivity. Obviously, too, the objection that the whole thing is "arbitrary" or "thought up" must be set aside, since it springs from the anxiety of an ego-consciousness which brooks no master besides itself in its own house. In other words, it is the inhibition exerted by the conscious mind on the unconscious.

320 Under these conditions, long and often very dramatic series of fantasies ensue. The advantage of this method is that it brings a mass of unconscious material to light. Drawing, painting, and modelling can be used to the same end. Once a visual series has become dramatic, it can easily pass over into the auditive or linguistic sphere and give rise to dialogues and the like. With slightly pathological individuals, and particularly in the not infrequent cases of latent schizophrenia, the method may, in certain circumstances, prove to be rather dangerous and therefore requires medical control. It is based on a deliberate weakening of the conscious mind and its inhibiting effect, which either limits or suppresses the unconscious. The aim of the method is naturally therapeutic in the first place, while in the second it also furnishes rich empirical material. Some of our examples are taken from this. They differ from dreams only by reason of their better form, which comes from the fact that the contents were perceived not by a dreaming but by a waking consciousness. The examples are from women in middle life.

9 Cf. *Symbols of Transformation.* H. G. Baynes' book, *The Mythology of the Soul,* runs to 939 pages and endeavours to do justice to the material provided by only two cases.

1. *Case X (spontaneous visual impressions, in chronological order)*

321 i. *"I saw a white bird with outstretched wings. It alighted on the figure of a woman, clad in blue, who sat there like an* antique statue. *The bird perched on her hand, and in it she held a* grain of wheat. *The bird took it in its beak and flew into the sky again."*

322 For this X painted a picture: a blue-clad, archaically simple "Mother"-figure on a white marble base. Her maternity is emphasized by the large breasts.

323 ii. *A bull lifts a child up from the ground and carries it to the antique statue of a woman. A naked young girl with a wreath of flowers in her hair appears, riding on a white bull. She takes the child and throws it into the air like a ball and catches it again. The white bull carries them both to a temple. The girl lays the child on the ground, and so on (initiation follows).*

324 In this picture the *maiden* appears, rather in the form of Europa. (Here a certain school knowledge is being made use of.) Her nakedness and the wreath of flowers point to Dionysian abandonment. The game of ball with the child is the motif of some secret rite which always has to do with "child-sacrifice." (Cf. the accusations of ritual murder levelled by the pagans against the Christians and by the Christians against the Jews and Gnostics; also the Phoenician child-sacrifices, rumours about the Black Mass, etc., and "the ball-game in church.")[10]

325 iii. *"I saw a golden* pig *on a pedestal. Beast-like beings* danced *round it in a circle. We made haste to dig* a hole in the ground. *I reached in and found* water. *Then a man appeared* in a golden carriage. *He jumped into the hole and began swaying back and forth, as if dancing. . . . I swayed in rhythm with him. Then he suddenly leaped out of the hole, raped me, and got me with child."*

326 X is identical with the young girl, who often appears as a *youth,* too. This youth is an animus-figure, the embodiment of the masculine element in a woman. Youth and young girl together form a syzygy or *coniunctio* which symbolizes the essence

10 [Cf. infra, "On the Psychology of the Trickster-Figure."—EDITORS.]

of wholeness (as also does the Platonic hermaphrodite, who later became the symbol of perfected wholeness in alchemical philosophy). X evidently dances with the rest, hence "*we* made haste." The parallel with the motifs stressed by Kerényi seems to me remarkable.

327 iv. *"I saw a beautiful youth with golden cymbals, dancing and leaping in joy and abandonment. . . . Finally he fell to the ground and buried his face in the flowers. Then he sank into the lap of a* very old mother. *After a time he got up and jumped into the water, where he sported like a* dolphin. . . . *I saw that his hair was golden. Now we were leaping together, hand in hand. So we came to a* gorge. . . ." *In leaping the gorge the youth falls into the chasm. X is left alone and comes to a river where a white* sea-horse *is waiting for her with a golden boat.*

328 In this scene X is the youth; therefore he disappears later, leaving her the sole heroine of the story. She is the child of the "very old mother," and is also the dolphin, the youth lost in the gorge, and the bride evidently expected by Poseidon. The peculiar overlapping and displacement of motifs in all this individual material is about the same as in the mythological variants. X found the youth in the lap of the mother so impressive that she painted a picture of it. The figure is the same as in item i; only, instead of the grain of wheat in her hand, there is the body of the youth lying completely exhausted in the lap of the gigantic mother.

329 v. *There now follows a sacrifice of sheep, during which a game of ball is likewise played with the sacrificial animal. The participants* smear themselves with the sacrificial blood, *and afterwards bathe in the pulsing gore. X is thereupon transformed into a* plant.

330 vi. *After that X comes to a* den of snakes, *and the snakes wind all round her.*

331 vii. *In a den of snakes beneath the sea there is a* divine woman, *asleep.* (She is shown in the picture as much larger than the others.) *She is wearing a blood-red garment that covers only the lower half of her body. She has a dark skin, full red lips, and seems to be of great physical strength. She kisses X, who is obviously in the role of the young girl, and hands her as a present to the many men who are standing by, etc.*

332 This chthonic goddess is the typical Earth Mother as she appears in so many modern fantasies.

333 viii. *As X emerged from the depths and saw the light again, she experienced a kind of illumination: white flames played about her head as she walked through waving* fields of grain.

334 With this picture the Mother-episode ended. Although there is not the slightest trace of any known myth being repeated, the motifs and the connections between them are all familiar to us from mythology. These images present themselves spontaneously and are based on no conscious knowledge whatever. I have applied the method of active imagination to myself over a long time and have observed numerous symbols and symbolic associations which in many cases I was only able to verify years afterwards in texts of whose existence I was totally ignorant. It is the same with dreams. Some years ago I dreamed for example that: *I was climbing slowly and toilsomely up a mountain. When I had reached, as I imagined, the top, I found that I was standing on the edge of a plateau. The crest that represented the real top of the mountain only rose far off in the distance. Night was coming on, and I saw, on the dark slope opposite, a brook flowing down with a metallic shimmer, and two paths leading upwards, one to the left, the other to the right, winding like serpents. On the crest, to the right, there was a hotel. Down below, the brook ran to the left with a bridge leading across.*

335 Not long afterwards I discovered the following "allegory" in an obscure alchemical treatise. In his *Speculativae philosophiae* [11] the Frankfurt physician Gerard Dorn, who lived in the second half of the sixteenth century, describes the "Mundi peregrinatio, quam erroris viam appellamus" (Tour of the world, which we call the way of error) on the one hand and the "Via veritatis" on the other. Of the first way the author says:

> The human race, whose nature it is to resist God, does not cease to ask how it may, by its own efforts, escape the pitfalls which it has laid for itself. But it does not ask help from Him on whom alone depends every gift of mercy. Hence it has come about that men have built for themselves a great Workshop on the left-hand side of the road . . . presided over by Industry. After this has been attained, they turn aside from Industry and bend their steps towards the

[11] *Theatrum chemicum,* I (1602), pp. 286ff.

second region of the world, making their crossing *on the bridge of infirmity.* . . . But because the good God desires to draw them back, He allows their infirmities to rule over them; then, seeking as before a remedy in themselves [industry!], they flock *to the great Hospital likewise built on the left,* presided over by Medicine. Here there is a great multitude of apothecaries, surgeons, and physicians, [etc.].[12]

336 Of the "way of truth," which is the "right" way, our author says: ". . . you will come to the camp of Wisdom and on being received there, you will be refreshed with food far more powerful than before." Even the brook is there: ". . . a stream of living water flowing with such wonderful artifice from the mountain peak. (From the Fountain of Wisdom the waters gush forth.)" [13]

337 An important difference, compared with my dream, is that here, apart from the situation of the hotel being reversed, the river of Wisdom is on the right and not, as in my dream, in the middle of the picture.

338 It is evident that in my dream we are not dealing with any known "myth" but with a group of ideas which might easily have been regarded as "individual," i.e., unique. A thorough analysis, however, could show without difficulty that it is an archetypal image such as can be reproduced over and over again in any age and any place. But I must admit that the archetypal nature of the dream-image only became clear to me when I read Dorn. These and similar incidents I have observed repeatedly not only in myself but in my patients. But, as this

12 "Humanum genus, cui Deo resistere iam innatum est, non desistit media quaerere, quibus proprio conatu laqueos evadat, quos sibimet posuit, ab eo non petens auxilium, a quo solo dependet omnis misericordiae munus. Hinc factum est, ut in sinistram viae partem officinam sibi maximam exstruxerint . . . huic domui praeest industria, etc. Quod postquam adepti fuerint, ab industria recedentes *in secundam mundi regionem* tendunt: *per infirmitatis pontem* facientes transitum. . . . At quia bonus Deus retrahere vellet, infirmitates in ipsis dominari permittit, tum rursus ut prius remedium [industria!] a se quaerentes, *ad xenodochium etiam a sinistris constructum* et permaximum confluunt, cui medicina praeest. Ibi pharmacopolarum, chirurgorum et physicorum ingens est copia." (p. 288.)

13 ". . . pervenietis ad Sophiae castra, quibus excepti, longe vehementiori quam antea cibo reficiemini. . . . viventis aquae fluvius tam admirando fluens artificio de montis apice. (De Sophiae fonte scaturiunt aquae!)" [Slightly modified by Professor Jung. Cf. Dorn, pp. 279–80.—EDITORS.]

example shows, it needs special attention if such parallels are not to be missed.

339 The antique Mother-image is not exhausted with the figure of Demeter. It also expresses itself in Cybele-Artemis. The next case points in this direction.

2. *Case Y (dreams)*

340 i. *"I am wandering over a great mountain; the way is lonely, wild, and difficult. A woman comes down from the sky to accompany and help me. She is all bright with light hair and shining eyes. Now and then she vanishes. After going on for some time alone I notice that I have left my stick somewhere, and must turn back to fetch it. To do this I have to pass a terrible monster, an enormous bear. When I came this way the first time I had to pass it, but then the sky-woman protected me. Just as I am passing the beast and he is about to come at me, she stands beside me again, and at her look the bear lies down quietly and lets us pass. Then the sky-woman vanishes."*

341 Here we have a maternally protective goddess related to bears, a kind of Diana or the Gallo-Roman Dea Artio. The sky-woman is the positive, the bear the negative aspect of the "supraordinate personality," which extends the conscious human being upwards into the celestial and downwards into the animal regions.

342 ii. *"We go through a door into a tower-like room, where we climb a long flight of steps. On one of the topmost steps I read an inscription:* 'Vis ut sis.' *The steps end in a temple situated on the crest of a wooded mountain, and there is no other approach. It is the shrine of* Ursanna, *the bear-goddess and Mother of God in one. The temple is of red stone. Bloody sacrifices are offered there. Animals are standing about the altar. In order to enter the temple precincts one has to be transformed into an animal—a beast of the forest. The temple has the form of a cross with equal arms and a circular space in the middle, which is not roofed, so that one can look straight up at the sky and the constellation of the Bear. On the altar in the middle of the open space there stands the moon-bowl, from which smoke or vapour continually rises. There is also a huge image of the goddess, but it cannot be seen clearly. The worshippers, who*

have been changed into animals and to whom I also belong, have to touch the goddess's foot with their own foot, whereupon the image gives them a sign or an oracular utterance like 'Vis ut sis.' "

343 In this dream the bear-goddess emerges plainly, although her statue "cannot be seen clearly." The relationship to the self, the supraordinate personality, is indicated not only by the oracle "Vis ut sis" but by the quaternity and the circular central precinct of the temple. From ancient times any relationship to the stars has always symbolized eternity. The soul comes "from the stars" and returns to the stellar regions. "Ursanna's" relation to the moon is indicated by the "moon-bowl."

344 The moon-goddess also appears in children's dreams. A girl who grew up in peculiarly difficult psychic circumstances had a recurrent dream between her seventh and tenth years: *"The moon-lady was always waiting for me down by the water at the landing-stage, to take me to her island."* Unfortunately she could never remember what happened there, but it was so beautiful that she often prayed she might have this dream again. Although, as is evident, the two dreamers are not identical, the *island motif* also occurred in the previous dream as the inaccessible mountain crest.

345 Thirty years later, the dreamer of the moon-lady had a dramatic fantasy:

346 *"I am climbing a steep dark mountain, on top of which stands a domed castle. I enter and go up a winding stairway to the left. Arriving inside the dome, I find myself in the presence of a woman wearing a head-dress of cow's horns. I recognize her immediately as the* moon-lady *of my childhood dreams. At her behest I look to the* right *and see a dazzlingly bright sun shining on the other side of a deep chasm. Over the chasm stretches a narrow, transparent bridge, upon which I step, conscious of the fact that in no circumstances must I look down. An uncanny fear seizes me, and I hesitate. Treachery seems to be in the air, but at last I go across and stand before the sun. The sun speaks: 'If you can approach me nine times without being burned, all will be well.' But I grow more and more afraid, finally I do look down, and I see a black tentacle like that of an octopus groping towards me from underneath the sun. I step back in fright and plunge into the abyss. But instead of being dashed*

to pieces I lie in the arms of the Earth Mother. When I try to look into her face, she turns to clay, and I find myself lying on the earth."

347 It is remarkable how the beginning of this fantasy agrees with the dream. The moon-lady above is clearly distinguished from the Earth Mother below. The former urges the dreamer to her somewhat perilous adventure with the sun; the latter catches her protectively in her maternal arms. The dreamer, as the one in danger, would therefore seem to be in the role of the Kore.

348 Let us now turn back to our dream-series:

349 iii. *Y sees two pictures in a dream, painted by the Scandinavian painter Hermann Christian Lund.*

I. "*The first picture is of a Scandinavian peasant room. Peasant girls in gay costumes are walking about arm in arm (that is, in a row). The middle one is smaller than the rest and, besides this, has a hump and keeps turning her head back. This, together with her peculiar glance, gives her a witchlike look.*"

II. "*The second picture shows a dragon with its neck stretched out over the whole picture and especially over a girl, who is in the dragon's power and cannot move, for as soon as she moves, the dragon, which can make its body big or little at will, moves too; and when the girl wants to get away it simply stretches out its neck over her, and so catches her again. Strangely enough, the girl has no face, at least I couldn't see it.*"

350 The painter is an invention of the dream. The animus often appears as a painter or has some kind of projection apparatus, or is a cinema-operator or owner of a picture-gallery. All this refers to the animus as the function mediating between conscious and unconscious: the unconscious contains pictures which are transmitted, that is, made manifest, by the animus, either as fantasies or, unconsciously, in the patient's own life and actions. The animus-projection gives rise to fantasied relations of love and hatred for "heroes" or "demons." The favourite victims are tenors, artists, movie-stars, athletic champions, etc. In the first picture the maiden is characterized as demonic, with a hump and an evil look "over her shoulder." (Hence amulets against the evil eye are often worn by primitives on the nape of the neck, for the vulnerable spot is at the back, where you can't see.)

351 In the second picture the "maiden" is portrayed as the innocent victim of the monster. Just as before there was a relationship of identity between the sky-woman and the bear, so here between the young girl and the dragon—which in practical life is often rather more than just a bad joke. Here it signifies a widening of the conscious personality, i.e., through the helplessness of the victim on the one hand and the dangers of the humpback's evil eye and the dragon's might on the other.

352 iv (part dream, part visual imagination). *"A magician is demonstrating his tricks to an Indian prince. He produces a beautiful young girl from under a cloth. She is a dancer, who has the power to change her shape or at least hold her audience spell-bound by faultless illusion. During the dance she dissolves with the music into a swarm of bees. Then she changes into a leopard, then into a jet of water, then into an octopus that has twined itself about a young pearl-fisher. Between times, she takes human form again at the dramatic moment. She appears as a she-ass bearing two baskets of wonderful fruits. Then she becomes a many-coloured peacock. The prince is beside himself with delight and calls her to him. But she dances on, now naked, and even tears the skin from her body, and finally falls down—a naked skeleton. This is buried, but at night a lily grows out of the grave, and from its cup there rises a* white lady, *who floats slowly up to the sky."*

353 This piece describes the successive transformations of the illusionist (artistry in illusion being a specifically feminine talent) until she becomes a transfigured personality. The fantasy was not invented as a sort of allegory; it was part dream, part spontaneous imagery.

354 v. *"I am in a church made of grey sandstone. The apse is built rather high. Near the tabernacle a girl in a red dress is hanging on the stone cross of the window. (Suicide?)"*

355 Just as in the preceding cases the sacrifice of a child or a sheep played a part, so here the sacrifice of the maiden hanging on the "cross." The death of the dancer is also to be understood in this sense, for these maidens are always doomed to die, because their exclusive domination of the feminine psyche hinders the individuation process, that is, the maturation of personality. The "maiden" corresponds to the anima of the man and makes use of it to gain her natural ends, in which illusion plays the

greatest role imaginable. But as long as a woman is content to be a *femme à homme,* she has no feminine individuality. She is empty and merely glitters—a welcome vessel for masculine projections. Woman as a personality, however, is a very different thing: here illusion no longer works. So that when the question of personality arises, which is as a rule the painful fact of the second half of life, the childish form of the self disappears too.

356 All that remains for me now is to describe the Kore as observable in man, the *anima.* Since a man's wholeness, in so far as he is not constitutionally homosexual, can only be a masculine personality, the feminine figure of the anima cannot be catalogued as a type of supraordinate personality but requires a different evaluation and position. In the products of unconscious activity, the anima appears equally as maiden and mother, which is why a personalistic interpretation always reduces her to the personal mother or some other female person. The real meaning of the figure naturally gets lost in the process, as is inevitably the case with all these reductive interpretations whether in the sphere of the psychology of the unconscious or of mythology. The innumerable attempts that have been made in the sphere of mythology to interpret gods and heroes in a solar, lunar, astral, or meteorological sense contribute nothing of importance to the understanding of them; on the contrary, they all put us on a false track. When, therefore, in dreams and other spontaneous products, we meet with an unknown female figure whose significance oscillates between the extremes of goddess and whore, it is advisable to let her keep her independence and not reduce her arbitrarily to something known. If the unconscious shows her as an "unknown," this attribute should not be got rid of by main force with a view to arriving at a "rational" interpretation. Like the "supraordinate personality," the anima is bipolar and can therefore appear positive one moment and negative the next; now young, now old; now mother, now maiden; now a good fairy, now a witch; now a saint, now a whore. Besides this ambivalence, the anima also has "occult" connections with "mysteries," with the world of darkness in general, and for that reason she often has a religious tinge. Whenever she emerges with some degree of clarity, she always has a peculiar relationship to *time:* as a rule she is more or less immortal, because outside time. Writers who have tried

their hand at this figure have never failed to stress the anima's peculiarity in this respect. I would refer to the classic descriptions in Rider Haggard's *She* and *The Return of She,* in Pierre Benoît's *L'Atlantide,* and above all in the novel of the young American author, William M. Sloane, *To Walk the Night.* In all these accounts, the anima is outside time as we know it and consequently immensely old or a being who belongs to a different order of things.

357 Since we can no longer or only partially express the archetypes of the unconscious by means of figures in which we religiously believe, they lapse into unconsciousness again and hence are unconsciously projected upon more or less suitable human personalities. To the young boy a clearly discernible anima-form appears in his mother, and this lends her the radiance of power and superiority or else a daemonic aura of even greater fascination. But because of the anima's ambivalence, the projection can be entirely negative. Much of the fear which the female sex arouses in men is due to the projection of the anima-image. An infantile man generally has a maternal anima; an adult man, the figure of a younger woman. The senile man finds compensation in a very young girl, or even a child.

[3. *Case Z*]

358 The anima also has affinities with animals, which symbolize her characteristics. Thus she can appear as a snake or a tiger or a bird. I quote by way of example a dream-series that contains transformations of this kind: [14]

359 i. *A white bird perches on a table. Suddenly it changes into a fair-haired seven-year-old girl and just as suddenly back into a bird, which now speaks with a human voice.*

360 ii. *In an underground house, which is really the underworld, there lives an old magician and prophet with his "daughter." She is, however, not really his daughter; she is a dancer, a very loose person, but is blind and seeks healing.*

361 iii. *A lonely house in a wood, where an old scholar is living. Suddenly his daughter appears, a kind of ghost, complaining that people only look upon her as a figment of fancy.*

[14] Only extracts from the dreams are given, so far as they bear on the anima.

362 iv. *On the façade of a church there is a Gothic Madonna, who is alive and is the "unknown and yet known woman." Instead of a child, she holds in her arms a sort of flame or a snake or a dragon.*

363 v. *A black-clad "countess" kneels in a dark chapel. Her dress is hung with costly pearls. She has red hair, and there is something uncanny about her. Moreover, she is surrounded by the spirits of the dead.*

364 vi. *A female snake comports herself tenderly and insinuatingly, speaking with a human voice. She is only "accidentally" shaped like a snake.*

365 vii. *A bird speaks with the same voice, but shows herself helpful by trying to rescue the dreamer from a dangerous situation.*

366 viii. *The unknown woman sits, like the dreamer, on the tip of a church-spire and stares at him uncannily across the abyss.*

367 ix. *The unknown woman suddenly appears as an old female attendant in an underground public lavatory with a temperature of 40° below zero.*

368 x. *The unknown woman leaves the house as a* petite bourgeoise *with a female relation, and in her place there is suddenly an over-life-size goddess clad in blue, looking like Athene.*

369 xi. *Then she appears in a church, taking the place of the altar, still over-life-size but with veiled face.*

370 In all these dreams [15] the central figure is a mysterious feminine being with qualities like those of no woman known to the dreamer. The unknown is described as such in the dreams themselves, and reveals her extraordinary nature firstly by her power to change shape and secondly by her paradoxical ambivalence. Every conceivable shade of meaning glitters in her, from the highest to the lowest.

371 *Dream i* shows the anima as elflike, i.e., only partially human. She can just as well be a bird, which means that she may belong wholly to nature and can vanish (i.e., become unconscious) from the human sphere (i.e., consciousness).

372 *Dream ii* shows the unknown woman as a mythological figure from the beyond (the unconscious). She is the *soror* or *filia mystica* of a hierophant or "philosopher," evidently a parallel to

15 The following statements are not meant as "interpretations" of the dreams. They are intended only to sum up the various forms in which the anima appears.

those mystic syzygies which are to be met with in the figures of Simon Magus and Helen, Zosimus and Theosebeia, Comarius and Cleopatra, etc. Our dream-figure fits in best with Helen. A really admirable description of anima-psychology in a woman is to be found in Erskine's *Helen of Troy*.

373 *Dream iii* presents the same theme, but on a more "fairytale-like" plane. Here the anima is shown as rather spookish.

374 *Dream iv* brings the anima nearer to the Mother of God. The "child" refers to the mystic speculations on the subject of the redemptive serpent and the "fiery" nature of the redeemer.

375 In *dream v,* the anima is visualized somewhat romantically as the "distinguished" fascinating woman, who nevertheless has dealings with spirits.

376 *Dreams vi and vii* bring theriomorphic variations. The anima's identity is at once apparent to the dreamer because of the voice and what it says. The anima has "accidentally" taken the form of a snake, just as in *dream i* she changed with the greatest ease into a bird and back again. As a snake, she is playing the negative role, as a bird the positive.

377 *Dream viii* shows the dreamer confronted with his anima. This takes place high above the ground (i.e., above human reality). Obviously it is a case of dangerous fascination by the anima.

378 *Dream ix* signifies the anima's deep plunge into an extremely "subordinate" position, where the last trace of fascination has gone and only human sympathy is left.

379 *Dream x* shows the paradoxical double nature of the anima: banal mediocrity and Olympian divinity.

380 *Dream xi* restores the anima to the Christian church, not as an icon but as the altar itself. The altar is the place of sacrifice and also the receptacle for consecrated relics.

381 To throw even a moderate light on all these anima associations would require special and very extensive investigation, which would be out of place here because, as we have already said, the anima has only an indirect bearing on the interpretation of the Kore figure. I have presented this dream-series simply for the purpose of giving the reader some idea of the empirical material on which the idea of the anima is based.[16] From this series and others like it we get an average picture of that strange factor which has such an important part to play in the

16 Cf. the third paper in this volume.

masculine psyche, and which naïve presumption invariably identifies with certain women, imputing to them all the illusions that swarm in the male Eros.

382 It seems clear enough that the man's anima found occasion for projection in the Demeter cult. The Kore doomed to her subterranean fate, the two-faced mother, and the theriomorphic aspects of both afforded the anima ample opportunity to reflect herself, shimmering and equivocal, in the Eleusinian cult, or rather to experience herself there and fill the celebrants with her unearthly essence, to their lasting gain. For a man, anima experiences are always of immense and abiding significance.

383 But the Demeter-Kore myth is far too feminine to have been merely the result of an anima-projection. Although the anima can, as we have said, experience herself in Demeter-Kore, she is yet of a wholly different nature. She is in the highest degree *femme à homme,* whereas Demeter-Kore exists on the plane of mother-daughter experience, which is alien to man and shuts him out. In fact, the psychology of the Demeter cult bears all the features of a matriarchal order of society, where the man is an indispensable but on the whole disturbing factor.

THE SHADOW AND THE SYZYGY

1: THE SHADOW

13 Whereas the contents of the personal unconscious are acquired during the individual's lifetime, the contents of the collective unconscious are invariably archetypes that were present from the beginning. Their relation to the instincts has been discussed elsewhere.[1] The archetypes most clearly characterized from the empirical point of view are those which have the most frequent and the most disturbing influence on the ego. These are the *shadow*, the *anima*, and the *animus*.[2] The most accessible of these, and the easiest to experience, is the shadow, for its nature can in large measure be inferred from the contents of the personal unconscious. The only exceptions to this rule are those rather rare cases where the positive qualities of the personality are repressed, and the ego in consequence plays an essentially negative or unfavourable role.

14 The shadow is a moral problem that challenges the whole ego-personality, for no one can become conscious of the shadow without considerable moral effort. To become conscious of it involves recognizing the dark aspects of the personality as present and real. This act is the essential condition for any kind of self-knowledge, and it therefore, as a rule, meets with considerable resistance. Indeed, self-knowledge as a psychotherapeutic measure frequently requires much painstaking work extending over a long period.

15 Closer examination of the dark characteristics—that is, the inferiorities constituting the shadow—reveals that they have an *emotional* nature, a kind of autonomy, and accordingly an obsessive or, better, possessive quality. Emotion, incidentally, is

1 "Instinct and the Unconscious" and "On the Nature of the Psyche," pars. 397ff.

2 The contents of this and the following chapter are taken from a lecture delivered to the Swiss Society for Practical Psychology, in Zurich, 1948. The material was first published in the *Wiener Zeitschrift für Nervenheilkunde und deren Grenzgebiete*, I (1948) : 4.

not an activity of the individual but something that happens to him. Affects occur usually where adaptation is weakest, and at the same time they reveal the reason for its weakness, namely a certain degree of inferiority and the existence of a lower level of personality. On this lower level with its uncontrolled or scarcely controlled emotions one behaves more or less like a primitive, who is not only the passive victim of his affects but also singularly incapable of moral judgment.

16 Although, with insight and good will, the shadow can to some extent be assimilated into the conscious personality, experience shows that there are certain features which offer the most obstinate resistance to moral control and prove almost impossible to influence. These resistances are usually bound up with *projections,* which are not recognized as such, and their recognition is a moral achievement beyond the ordinary. While some traits peculiar to the shadow can be recognized without too much difficulty as one's own personal qualities, in this case both insight and good will are unavailing because the cause of the emotion appears to lie, beyond all possibility of doubt, in the *other person.* No matter how obvious it may be to the neutral observer that it is a matter of projections, there is little hope that the subject will perceive this himself. He must be convinced that he throws a very long shadow before he is willing to withdraw his emotionally-toned projections from their object.

17 Let us suppose that a certain individual shows no inclination whatever to recognize his projections. The projection-making factor then has a free hand and can realize its object—if it has one—or bring about some other situation characteristic of its power. As we know, it is not the conscious subject but the unconscious which does the projecting. Hence one meets with projections, one does not make them. The effect of projection is to isolate the subject from his environment, since instead of a real relation to it there is now only an illusory one. Projections change the world into the replica of one's own unknown face. In the last analysis, therefore, they lead to an autoerotic or autistic condition in which one dreams a world whose reality remains forever unattainable. The resultant *sentiment d'incomplétude* and the still worse feeling of sterility are in their turn explained by projection as the malevolence of the environment, and by means of this vicious circle the isolation is intensified. The more

projections are thrust in between the subject and the environment, the harder it is for the ego to see through its illusions. A forty-five-year-old patient who had suffered from a compulsion neurosis since he was twenty and had become completely cut off from the world once said to me: "But I can never admit to myself that I've wasted the best twenty-five years of my life!"

18 It is often tragic to see how blatantly a man bungles his own life and the lives of others yet remains totally incapable of seeing how much the whole tragedy originates in himself, and how he continually feeds it and keeps it going. Not *consciously,* of course—for consciously he is engaged in bewailing and cursing a faithless world that recedes further and further into the distance. Rather, it is an unconscious factor which spins the illusions that veil his world. And what is being spun is a cocoon, which in the end will completely envelop him.

19 One might assume that projections like these, which are so very difficult if not impossible to dissolve, would belong to the realm of the shadow—that is, to the negative side of the personality. This assumption becomes untenable after a certain point, because the symbols that then appear no longer refer to the same but to the opposite sex, in a man's case to a woman and vice versa. The source of projections is no longer the shadow—which is always of the same sex as the subject—but a contrasexual figure. Here we meet the animus of a woman and the anima of a man, two corresponding archetypes whose autonomy and unconsciousness explain the stubbornness of their projections. Though the shadow is a motif as well known to mythology as anima and animus, it represents first and foremost the personal unconscious, and its content can therefore be made conscious without too much difficulty. In this it differs from anima and animus, for whereas the shadow can be seen through and recognized fairly easily, the anima and animus are much further away from consciousness and in normal circumstances are seldom if ever realized. With a little self-criticism one can see through the shadow—so far as its nature is personal. But when it appears as an archetype, one encounters the same difficulties as with anima and animus. In other words, it is quite within the bounds of possibility for a man to recognize the relative evil of his nature, but it is a rare and shattering experience for him to gaze into the face of absolute evil.

20 What, then, is this projection-making factor? The East calls it the "Spinning Woman" [1]—Maya, who creates illusion by her dancing. Had we not long since known it from the symbolism of dreams, this hint from the Orient would put us on the right track: the enveloping, embracing, and devouring element points unmistakably to the mother,[2] that is, to the son's relation to the real mother, to her imago, and to the woman who is to become a mother for him. His Eros is passive like a child's; he hopes to be caught, sucked in, enveloped, and devoured. He seeks, as it were, the protecting, nourishing, charmed circle of the mother, the condition of the infant released from every care, in which the outside world bends over him and even forces happiness upon him. No wonder the real world vanishes from sight!

21 If this situation is dramatized, as the unconscious usually dramatizes it, then there appears before you on the psychological stage a man living regressively, seeking his childhood and his mother, fleeing from a cold cruel world which denies him understanding. Often a mother appears beside him who apparently shows not the slightest concern that her little son should become a man, but who, with tireless and self-immolating effort, neglects nothing that might hinder him from growing up and marrying. You behold the secret conspiracy between mother and son, and how each helps the other to betray life.

22 Where does the guilt lie? With the mother, or with the son? Probably with both. The unsatisfied longing of the son for life and the world ought to be taken seriously. There is in him a

1 Erwin Rousselle, "Seelische Führung im lebenden Taoismus," Pl. I, pp. 150, 170. Rousselle calls the spinning woman the "animal soul." There is a saying that runs, "The spinner sets in motion." I have defined the anima as a personification of the unconscious.

2 Here and in what follows, the word "mother" is not meant in the literal sense but as a symbol of everything that functions as a mother.

desire to touch reality, to embrace the earth and fructify the field of the world. But he makes no more than a series of fitful starts, for his initiative as well as his staying power are crippled by the secret memory that the world and happiness may be had as a gift—from the mother. The fragment of world which he, like every man, must encounter again and again is never quite the right one, since it does not fall into his lap, does not meet him half way, but remains resistant, has to be conquered, and submits only to force. It makes demands on the masculinity of a man, on his ardour, above all on his courage and resolution when it comes to throwing his whole being into the scales. For this he would need a faithless Eros, one capable of forgetting his mother and undergoing the pain of relinquishing the first love of his life. The mother, foreseeing this danger, has carefully inculcated into him the virtues of faithfulness, devotion, loyalty, so as to protect him from the moral disruption which is the risk of every life adventure. He has learnt these lessons only too well, and remains true to his mother. This naturally causes her the deepest anxiety (when, to her greater glory, he turns out to be a homosexual, for example) and at the same time affords her an unconscious satisfaction that is positively mythological. For, in the relationship now reigning between them, there is consummated the immemorial and most sacred archetype of the marriage of mother and son. What, after all, has commonplace reality to offer, with its registry offices, pay envelopes, and monthly rent, that could outweigh the mystic awe of the *hieros gamos*? Or the star-crowned woman whom the dragon pursues, or the pious obscurities veiling the marriage of the Lamb?

23 This myth, better than any other, illustrates the nature of the collective unconscious. At this level the mother is both old and young, Demeter and Persephone, and the son is spouse and sleeping suckling rolled into one. The imperfections of real life, with its laborious adaptations and manifold disappointments, naturally cannot compete with such a state of indescribable fulfilment.

24 In the case of the son, the projection-making factor is identical with the mother-imago, and this is consequently taken to be the real mother. The projection can only be dissolved when the son sees that in the realm of his psyche there is an imago not only of the mother but of the daughter, the sister, the beloved,

the heavenly goddess, and the chthonic Baubo. Every mother and every beloved is forced to become the carrier and embodiment of this omnipresent and ageless image, which corresponds to the deepest reality in a man. It belongs to him, this perilous image of Woman; she stands for the loyalty which in the interests of life he must sometimes forgo; she is the much needed compensation for the risks, struggles, sacrifices that all end in disappointment; she is the solace for all the bitterness of life. And, at the same time, she is the great illusionist, the seductress, who draws him into life with her Maya—and not only into life's reasonable and useful aspects, but into its frightful paradoxes and ambivalences where good and evil, success and ruin, hope and despair, counterbalance one another. Because she is his greatest danger she demands from a man his greatest, and if he has it in him she will receive it.

25 This image is "My Lady Soul," as Spitteler called her. I have suggested instead the term "anima," as indicating something specific, for which the expression "soul" is too general and too vague. The empirical reality summed up under the concept of the anima forms an extremely dramatic content of the unconscious. It is possible to describe this content in rational, scientific language, but in this way one entirely fails to express its living character. Therefore, in describing the living processes of the psyche, I deliberately and consciously give preference to a dramatic, mythological way of thinking and speaking, because this is not only more expressive but also more exact than an abstract scientific terminology, which is wont to toy with the notion that its theoretic formulations may one fine day be resolved into algebraic equations.

26 The projection-making factor is the anima, or rather the unconscious as represented by the anima. Whenever she appears, in dreams, visions, and fantasies, she takes on personified form, thus demonstrating that the factor she embodies possesses all the outstanding characteristics of a feminine being.[3] She is not an invention of the conscious, but a spontaneous product of the

[3] Naturally, she is a typical figure in *belles-lettres*. Recent publications on the subject of the anima include Linda Fierz-David, *The Dream of Poliphilo,* and my "Psychology of the Transference." The anima as a psychological idea first appears in the 16th-cent. humanist Richardus Vitus. Cf. my *Mysterium Coniunctionis,* pars. 91ff.

unconscious. Nor is she a substitute figure for the mother. On the contrary, there is every likelihood that the numinous qualities which make the mother-imago so dangerously powerful derive from the collective archetype of the anima, which is incarnated anew in every male child.

27 Since the anima is an archetype that is found in men, it is reasonable to suppose that an equivalent archetype must be present in women; for just as the man is compensated by a feminine element, so woman is compensated by a masculine one. I do not, however, wish this argument to give the impression that these compensatory relationships were arrived at by deduction. On the contrary, long and varied experience was needed in order to grasp the nature of anima and animus empirically. Whatever we have to say about these archetypes, therefore, is either directly verifiable or at least rendered probable by the facts. At the same time, I am fully aware that we are discussing pioneer work which by its very nature can only be provisional.

28 Just as the mother seems to be the first carrier of the projection-making factor for the son, so is the father for the daughter. Practical experience of these relationships is made up of many individual cases presenting all kinds of variations on the same basic theme. A concise description of them can, therefore, be no more than schematic.

29 Woman is compensated by a masculine element and therefore her unconscious has, so to speak, a masculine imprint. This results in a considerable psychological difference between men and women, and accordingly I have called the projection-making factor in women the animus, which means mind or spirit. The animus corresponds to the paternal Logos just as the anima corresponds to the maternal Eros. But I do not wish or intend to give these two intuitive concepts too specific a definition. I use Eros and Logos merely as conceptual aids to describe the fact that woman's consciousness is characterized more by the connective quality of Eros than by the discrimination and cognition associated with Logos. In men, Eros, the function of relationship, is usually less developed than Logos. In women, on the other hand, Eros is an expression of their true nature, while their Logos is often only a regrettable accident. It gives rise to misunderstandings and annoying interpretations in the family

circle and among friends. This is because it consists of *opinions* instead of reflections, and by opinions I mean *a priori* assumptions that lay claim to absolute truth. Such assumptions, as everyone knows, can be extremely irritating. As the animus is partial to argument, he can best be seen at work in disputes where both parties know they are right. Men can argue in a very womanish way, too, when they are anima-possessed and have thus been transformed into the animus of their own anima. With them the question becomes one of personal vanity and touchiness (as if they were females); with women it is a question of *power,* whether of truth or justice or some other "ism"—for the dressmaker and hairdresser have already taken care of their vanity. The "Father" (i.e., the sum of conventional opinions) always plays a great role in female argumentation. No matter how friendly and obliging a woman's Eros may be, no logic on earth can shake her if she is ridden by the animus. Often the man has the feeling—and he is not altogether wrong—that only seduction or a beating or rape would have the necessary power of persuasion. He is unaware that this highly dramatic situation would instantly come to a banal and unexciting end if he were to quit the field and let a second woman carry on the battle (his wife, for instance, if she herself is not the fiery war horse). This sound idea seldom or never occurs to him, because no man can converse with an animus for five minutes without becoming the victim of his own anima. Anyone who still had enough sense of humour to listen objectively to the ensuing dialogue would be staggered by the vast number of commonplaces, misapplied truisms, clichés from newspapers and novels, shopsoiled platitudes of every description interspersed with vulgar abuse and brain-splitting lack of logic. It is a dialogue which, irrespective of its participants, is repeated millions and millions of times in all the languages of the world and always remains essentially the same.

30 This singular fact is due to the following circumstance: when animus and anima meet, the animus draws his sword of power and the anima ejects her poison of illusion and seduction. The outcome need not always be negative, since the two are equally likely to fall in love (a special instance of love at first sight). The language of love is of astonishing uniformity, using the well-worn formulas with the utmost devotion and fidelity,

so that once again the two partners find themselves in a banal collective situation. Yet they live in the illusion that they are related to one another in a most individual way.

31 In both its positive and its negative aspects the anima/animus relationship is always full of "animosity," i.e., it is emotional, and hence collective. Affects lower the level of the relationship and bring it closer to the common instinctual basis, which no longer has anything individual about it. Very often the relationship runs its course heedless of its human performers, who afterwards do not know what happened to them.

32 Whereas the cloud of "animosity" surrounding the man is composed chiefly of sentimentality and resentment, in woman it expresses itself in the form of opinionated views, interpretations, insinuations, and misconstructions, which all have the purpose (sometimes attained) of severing the relation between two human beings. The woman, like the man, becomes wrapped in a veil of illusions by her demon-familiar, and, as the daughter who alone understands her father (that is, is eternally right in everything), she is translated to the land of sheep, where she is put to graze by the shepherd of her soul, the animus.

33 Like the anima, the animus too has a positive aspect. Through the figure of the father he expresses not only conventional opinion but—equally—what we call "spirit," philosophical or religious ideas in particular, or rather the attitude resulting from them. Thus the animus is a psychopomp, a mediator between the conscious and the unconscious and a personification of the latter. Just as the anima becomes, through integration, the Eros of consciousness, so the animus becomes a Logos; and in the same way that the anima gives relationship and relatedness to a man's consciousness, the animus gives to woman's consciousness a capacity for reflection, deliberation, and self-knowledge.

34 The effect of anima and animus on the ego is in principle the same. This effect is extremely difficult to eliminate because, in the first place, it is uncommonly strong and immediately fills the ego-personality with an unshakable feeling of rightness and righteousness. In the second place, the cause of the effect is projected and appears to lie in objects and objective situations. Both these characteristics can, I believe, be traced back to the peculiarities of the archetype. For the archetype, of course, exists

a priori. This may possibly explain the often totally irrational yet undisputed and indisputable existence of certain moods and opinions. Perhaps these are so notoriously difficult to influence because of the powerfully suggestive effect emanating from the archetype. Consciousness is fascinated by it, held captive, as if hypnotized. Very often the ego experiences a vague feeling of moral defeat and then behaves all the more defensively, defiantly, and self-righteously, thus setting up a vicious circle which only increases its feeling of inferiority. The bottom is then knocked out of the human relationship, for, like megalomania, a feeling of inferiority makes mutual recognition impossible, and without this there is no relationship.

35 As I said, it is easier to gain insight into the shadow than into the anima or animus. With the shadow, we have the advantage of being prepared in some sort by our education, which has always endeavoured to convince people that they are not one-hundred-per-cent pure gold. So everyone immediately understands what is meant by "shadow," "inferior personality," etc. And if he has forgotten, his memory can easily be refreshed by a Sunday sermon, his wife, or the tax collector. With the anima and animus, however, things are by no means so simple. Firstly, there is no moral education in this respect, and secondly, most people are content to be self-righteous and prefer mutual vilification (if nothing worse!) to the recognition of their projections. Indeed, it seems a very natural state of affairs for men to have irrational moods and women irrational opinions. Presumably this situation is grounded on instinct and must remain as it is to ensure that the Empedoclean game of the hate and love of the elements shall continue for all eternity. Nature is conservative and does not easily allow her courses to be altered; she defends in the most stubborn way the inviolability of the preserves where anima and animus roam, Hence it is much more difficult to become conscious of one's anima/animus projections than to acknowledge one's shadow side. One has, of course, to overcome certain moral obstacles, such as vanity, ambition, conceit, resentment, etc., but in the case of projections all sorts of purely intellectual difficulties are added, quite apart from the contents of the projection which one simply doesn't know how to cope with. And on top of all this there arises a profound doubt as to whether one is not meddling too much with nature's

business by prodding into consciousness things which it would have been better to leave asleep.

36 Although there are, in my experience, a fair number of people who can understand without special intellectual or moral difficulties what is meant by anima and animus, one finds very many more who have the greatest trouble in visualizing these empirical concepts as anything concrete. This shows that they fall a little outside the usual range of experience. They are unpopular precisely because they seem unfamiliar. The consequence is that they mobilize prejudice and become taboo like everything else that is unexpected.

37 So if we set it up as a kind of requirement that projections should be dissolved, because it is wholesomer that way and in every respect more advantageous, we are entering upon new ground. Up till now everybody has been convinced that the idea "my father," "my mother," etc., is nothing but a faithful reflection of the real parent, corresponding in every detail to the original, so that when someone says "my father" he means no more and no less than what his father is in reality. This is actually what he supposes he does mean, but a supposition of identity by no means brings that identity about. This is where the fallacy of the *enkekalymmenos* ('the veiled one') comes in.[4] If one includes in the psychological equation X's picture of his father, which he takes for the real father, the equation will not work out, because the unknown quantity he has introduced does not tally with reality. X has overlooked the fact that his idea of a person consists, in the first place, of the possibly very incomplete picture he has received of the real person and, in the second place, of the subjective modifications he has imposed upon this picture. X's idea of his father is a complex quantity for which the real father is only in part responsible, an indefinitely larger share falling to the son. So true is this that every time he criticizes or praises his father he is unconsciously hitting back at himself, thereby bringing about those psychic consequences that overtake people who habitually disparage or overpraise themselves. If, however, X carefully compares his reactions with reality, he stands a chance of noticing that he has miscalculated

[4] The fallacy, which stems from Eubulides the Megarian, runs: "Can you recognize your father?" Yes. "Can you recognize this veiled one?" No. "This veiled one is your father. Hence you can recognize your father and not recognize him."

somewhere by not realizing long ago from his father's behaviour that the picture he has of him is a false one. But as a rule X is convinced that he is right, and if anybody is wrong it must be the other fellow. Should X have a poorly developed Eros, he will be either indifferent to the inadequate relationship he has with his father or else annoyed by the inconsistency and general incomprehensibility of a father whose behaviour never really corresponds to the picture X has of him. Therefore X thinks he has every right to feel hurt, misunderstood, and even betrayed.

38 One can imagine how desirable it would be in such cases to dissolve the projection. And there are always optimists who believe that the golden age can be ushered in simply by telling people the right way to go. But just let them try to explain to these people that they are acting like a dog chasing its own tail. To make a person see the shortcomings of his attitude considerably more than mere "telling" is needed, for more is involved than ordinary common sense can allow. What one is up against here is the kind of fateful misunderstanding which, under ordinary conditions, remains forever inaccessible to insight. It is rather like expecting the average respectable citizen to recognize himself as a criminal.

39 I mention all this just to illustrate the order of magnitude to which the anima/animus projections belong, and the moral and intellectual exertions that are needed to dissolve them. Not all the contents of the anima and animus are projected, however. Many of them appear spontaneously in dreams and so on, and many more can be made conscious through active imagination. In this way we find that thoughts, feelings, and affects are alive in us which we would never have believed possible. Naturally, possibilities of this sort seem utterly fantastic to anyone who has not experienced them himself, for a normal person "knows what he thinks." Such a childish attitude on the part of the "normal person" is simply the rule, so that no one without experience in this field can be expected to understand the real nature of anima and animus. With these reflections one gets into an entirely new world of psychological experience, provided of course that one succeeds in realizing it in practice. Those who do succeed can hardly fail to be impressed by all that the ego does not know and never has known. This increase in self-knowledge is still very rare nowadays and is usually

paid for in advance with a neurosis, if not with something worse.

40 The autonomy of the collective unconscious expresses itself in the figures of anima and animus. They personify those of its contents which, when withdrawn from projection, can be integrated into consciousness. To this extent, both figures represent *functions* which filter the contents of the collective unconscious through to the conscious mind. They appear or behave as such, however, only so long as the tendencies of the conscious and unconscious do not diverge too greatly. Should any tension arise, these functions, harmless till then, confront the conscious mind in personified form and behave rather like systems split off from the personality, or like part souls. This comparison is inadequate in so far as nothing previously belonging to the ego-personality has split off from it; on the contrary, the two figures represent a disturbing accretion. The reason for their behaving in this way is that though the *contents* of anima and animus can be integrated they themselves cannot, since they are archetypes. As such they are the foundation stones of the psychic structure, which in its totality exceeds the limits of consciousness and therefore can never become the object of direct cognition. Though the effects of anima and animus can be made conscious, they themselves are factors transcending consciousness and beyond the reach of perception and volition. Hence they remain autonomous despite the integration of their contents, and for this reason they should be borne constantly in mind. This is extremely important from the therapeutic standpoint, because constant observation pays the unconscious a tribute that more or less guarantees its co-operation. The unconscious as we know can never be "done with" once and for all. It is, in fact, one of the most important tasks of psychic hygiene to pay continual attention to the symptomatology of unconscious contents and processes, for the good reason that the conscious mind is always in danger of becoming one-sided, of keeping to well-worn paths and getting stuck in blind alleys. The complementary and compensating function of the unconscious ensures that these dangers, which are especially great in neurosis, can in some measure be avoided. It is only under ideal conditions, when life is still simple and unconscious enough to follow the serpentine path of instinct without hesitation or misgiving, that the compensation works with entire success. The more civilized, the more con-

scious and complicated a man is, the less he is able to follow his instincts. His complicated living conditions and the influence of his environment are so strong that they drown the quiet voice of nature. Opinions, beliefs, theories, and collective tendencies appear in its stead and back up all the aberrations of the conscious mind. Deliberate attention should then be given to the unconscious so that the compensation can set to work. Hence it is especially important to picture the archetypes of the unconscious not as a rushing phantasmagoria of fugitive images but as constant, autonomous factors, which indeed they are.

41 Both these archetypes, as practical experience shows, possess a fatality that can on occasion produce tragic results. They are quite literally the father and mother of all the disastrous entanglements of fate and have long been recognized as such by the whole world. Together they form a divine pair,[5] one of whom, in accordance with his Logos nature, is characterized by *pneuma* and *nous,* rather like Hermes with his ever-shifting hues, while the other, in accordance with her Eros nature, wears the features of Aphrodite, Helen (Selene), Persephone, and Hecate. Both of them are unconscious powers, "gods" in fact, as the ancient world quite rightly conceived them to be. To call them by this name is to give them that central position in the scale of psychological values which has always been theirs whether consciously acknowledged or not; for their power grows in proportion to the degree that they remain unconscious. Those who do not see them are in their hands, just as a typhus epidemic flourishes best when its source is undiscovered. Even in Christianity the divine syzygy has not become obsolete, but occupies the highest place as Christ and his bride the Church.[6] Parallels like these prove extremely helpful in our attempts to find the right

[5] Naturally this is not meant as a psychological definition, let alone a metaphysical one. As I pointed out in "The Relations between the Ego and the Unconscious" (pars. 296ff.), the syzygy consists of three elements: the femininity pertaining to the man and the masculinity pertaining to the woman; the experience which man has of woman and vice versa; and, finally, the masculine and feminine archetypal image. The first element can be integrated into the personality by the process of conscious realization, but the last one cannot.

[6] "For the Scripture says, God made man male and female; the male is Christ, the female is the Church."—Second Epistle of Clement to the Corinthians, xiv, 2 (trans. by Lake, I, p. 151). In pictorial representations, Mary often takes the place of the Church.

criterion for gauging the significance of these two archetypes. What we can discover about them from the conscious side is so slight as to be almost imperceptible. It is only when we throw light into the dark depths of the psyche and explore the strange and tortuous paths of human fate that it gradually becomes clear to us how immense is the influence wielded by these two factors that complement our conscious life.

42 Recapitulating, I should like to emphasize that the integration of the shadow, or the realization of the personal unconscious, marks the first stage in the analytic process, and that without it a recognition of anima and animus is impossible. The shadow can be realized only through a relation to a partner, and anima and animus only through a relation to a partner of the opposite sex, because only in such a relation do their projections become operative. The recognition of the anima gives rise, in a man, to a triad, one third of which is transcendent: the masculine subject, the opposing feminine subject, and the transcendent anima. With a woman the situation is reversed. The missing fourth element that would make the triad a quaternity is, in a man, the archetype of the Wise Old Man, which I have not discussed here, and in a woman the Chthonic Mother. These four constitute a half immanent and half transcendent quaternity, an archetype which I have called the *marriage quaternio.*[7] The marriage quaternio provides a schema not only for the self but also for the structure of primitive society with its cross-cousin marriage, marriage classes, and division of settlements into quarters. The self, on the other hand, is a God-image, or at least cannot be distinguished from one. Of this the early Christian spirit was not ignorant, otherwise Clement of Alexandria could never have said that he who knows himself knows God.[8]

7 "The Psychology of the Transference," pars. 425ff. Cf. infra, pars. 358ff., the Naassene *quaternio.*

8 Cf. infra, par. 347.

THE COLLECTED WORKS OF

C. G. JUNG

EDITORS: SIR HERBERT READ, MICHAEL FORDHAM, AND GERHARD ADLER; *EXECUTIVE EDITOR*, WILLIAM McGUIRE. *TRANSLATED BY* R.F.C. HULL, EXCEPT WHERE NOTED.

IN THE FOLLOWING LIST, dates of original publication are given in parentheses (of original composition, in brackets). Multiple dates indicate revisions.

1. PSYCHIATRIC STUDIES (1957; 2nd edn., 1970)
   On the Psychology and Pathology of So-Called Occult Phenomena (1902)
   On Hysterical Misreading (1904)
   Cryptomnesia (1905)
   On Manic Mood Disorder (1903)
   A Case of Hysterical Stupor in a Prisoner in Detention (1902)
   On Simulated Insanity (1903)
   A Medical Opinion on a Case of Simulated Insanity (1904)
   A Third and Final Opinion on Two Contradictory Psychiatric Diagnoses (1906)
   On the Psychological Diagnosis of Facts (1905)

2. EXPERIMENTAL RESEARCHES (1973)
   Translated by Leopold Stein in collaboration with Diana Riviere

   STUDIES IN WORD ASSOCIATION (1904–7, 1910)
   The Associations of Normal Subjects (by Jung and F. Riklin)
   An Analysis of the Associations of an Epileptic
   The Reaction-Time Ratio in the Association Experiment

(*continued*)

2. (*continued*)

Experimental Observations on the Faculty of Memory
Psychoanalysis and Association Experiments
The Psychological Diagnosis of Evidence
Association, Dream, and Hysterical Symptom
The Psychopathological Significance of the Association Experiment
Disturbances in Reproduction in the Association Experiment
The Association Method
The Family Constellation

PSYCHOPHYSICAL RESEARCHES (1907–8)

On the Psychophysical Relations of the Association Experiment
Psychophysical Investigations with the Galvanometer and Pneumograph in Normal and Insane Individuals (by F. Peterson and Jung)
Further Investigations on the Galvanic Phenomenon and Respiration in Normal and Insane Individuals (by C. Ricksher and Jung)
Appendix: Statistical Details of Enlistment (1906); New Aspects of Criminal Psychology (1908); The Psychological Methods of Investigation Used in the Psychiatric Clinic of the University of Zurich (1910); On the Doctrine of Complexes ([1911] 1913); On the Psychological Diagnosis of Evidence (1937)

3. THE PSYCHOGENESIS OF MENTAL DISEASE (1960)

The Psychology of Dementia Praecox (1907)
The Content of the Psychoses (1908/1914)
On Psychological Understanding (1914)
A Criticism of Bleuler's Theory of Schizophrenic Negativism (1911)
On the Importance of the Unconscious in Psychopathology (1914)
On the Problem of Psychogenesis in Mental Disease (1919)
Mental Disease and the Psyche (1928)
On the Psychogenesis of Schizophrenia (1939)
Recent Thoughts on Schizophrenia (1957)
Schizophrenia (1958)

4. FREUD AND PSYCHOANALYSIS (1967)

Freud's Theory of Hysteria: A Reply to Aschaffenburg (1906)
The Freudian Theory of Hysteria (1908)
The Analysis of Dreams (1909)
A Contribution to the Psychology of Rumour (1910–11)
On the Significance of Number Dreams (1910–11)
Morton Prince, "The Mechanism and Interpretation of Dreams": A Critical Review (1911)
On the Criticism of Psychoanalysis (1910)
Concerning Psychoanalysis (1912)

The Theory of Psychoanalysis (1913)
General Aspects of Psychoanalysis (1913)
Psychoanalysis and Neurosis (1916)
Some Crucial Points in Psychoanalysis: A Correspondence between Dr. Jung and Dr. Loÿ (1914)
Prefaces to "Collected Papers on Analytical Psychology" (1916, 1917)
The Significance of the Father in the Destiny of the Individual (1909/1949)
Introduction to Kranefeldt's "Secret Ways of the Mind" (1930)
Freud and Jung: Contrasts (1929)

5. SYMBOLS OF TRANSFORMATION ([1911–12/1952] 1956; 2nd edn., 1967)

PART I
Introduction
Two Kinds of Thinking
The Miller Fantasies: Anamnesis
The Hymn of Creation
The Song of the Moth

PART II
Introduction
The Concept of Libido
The Transformation of Libido
The Origin of the Hero
Symbols of the Mother and of Rebirth
The Battle for Deliverance from the Mother
The Dual Mother
The Sacrifice
Epilogue
Appendix: The Miller Fantasies

6. PSYCHOLOGICAL TYPES ([1921] 1971)

A revision by R.F.C. Hull of the translation by H. G. Baynes

Introduction
The Problem of Types in the History of Classical and Medieval Thought
Schiller's Ideas on the Type Problem
The Apollinian and the Dionysian
The Type Problem in Human Character
The Type Problem in Poetry
The Type Problem in Psychopathology

(*continued*)

6. (*continued*)

The Type Problem in Aesthetics
The Type Problem in Modern Philosophy
The Type Problem in Biography
General Description of the Types
Definitions
Epilogue
Four Papers on Psychological Typology (1913, 1925, 1931, 1936)

7. TWO ESSAYS ON ANALYTICAL PSYCHOLOGY (1953; 2nd edn., 1966)
On the Psychology of the Unconscious (1917/1926/1943)
The Relations between the Ego and the Unconscious (1928)
Appendix: New Paths in Psychology (1912); The Structure of the Unconscious (1916) (new versions, with variants, 1966)

8. THE STRUCTURE AND DYNAMICS OF THE PSYCHE (1960; 2nd edn., 1969)
On Psychic Energy (1928)
The Transcendent Function ([1916] 1957)
A Review of the Complex Theory (1934)
The Significance of Constitution and Heredity in Psychology (1929)
Psychological Factors Determining Human Behavior (1937)
Instinct and the Unconscious (1919)
The Structure of the Psyche (1927/1931)
On the Nature of the Psyche (1947/1954)
General Aspects of Dream Psychology (1916/1948)
On the Nature of Dreams (1945/1948)
The Psychological Foundations of Belief in Spirits (1920/1948)
Spirit and Life (1926)
Basic Postulates of Analytical Psychology (1931)
Analytical Psychology and *Weltanschauung* (1928/1931)
The Real and the Surreal (1933)
The Stages of Life (1930–1931)
The Soul and Death (1934)
Synchronicity: An Acausal Connecting Principle (1952)
Appendix: On Synchronicity (1951)

9. PART I. THE ARCHETYPES AND THE COLLECTIVE UNCONSCIOUS (1959; 2nd ed., 1968)
Archetypes of the Collective Unconscious (1934/1954)
The Concept of the Collective Unconscious (1936)
Concerning the Archetypes, with Special Reference to the Anima Concept (1936/1954)

Psychological Aspects of the Mother Archetype (1938/1954)
Concerning Rebirth (1940/1950)
The Psychology of the Child Archetype (1940)
The Psychological Aspects of the Kore (1941)
The Phenomenology of the Spirit in Fairytales (1945/1948)
On the Psychology of the Trickster-Figure (1954)
Conscious, Unconscious, and Individuation (1939)
A Study in the Process of Individuation (1934/1950)
Concerning Mandala Symbolism (1950)
Appendix: Mandalas (1955)

9. PART II. AION ([1951] 1959; 2nd ed., 1968)

RESEARCHES INTO THE PHENOMENOLOGY OF THE SELF

The Ego
The Shadow
The Syzygy: Anima and Animus
The Self
Christ, a Symbol of the Self
The Sign of the Fishes
The Prophecies of Nostradamus
The Historical Significance of the Fish
The Ambivalence of the Fish Symbol
The Fish in Alchemy
The Alchemical Interpretation of the Fish
Background to the Psychology of Christian Alchemical Symbolism
Gnostic Symbols of the Self
The Structure and Dynamics of the Self
Conclusion

10. CIVILIZATION IN TRANSITION (1964; 2nd edn., 1970)
The Role of the Unconscious (1918)
Mind and Earth (1927/1931)
Archaic Man (1931)
The Spiritual Problem of Modern Man (1928/1931)
The Love Problem of a Student (1928)
Woman in Europe (1927)
The Meaning of Psychology for Modern Man (1933/1934)
The State of Psychotherapy Today (1934)
Preface and Epilogue to "Essays on Contemporary Events" (1946)
Wotan (1936)
After the Catastrophe (1945)
The Fight with the Shadow (1946)

(continued)

10. (*continued*)

The Undiscovered Self (Present and Future) (1957)
Flying Saucers: A Modern Myth (1958)
A Psychological View of Conscience (1958)
Good and Evil in Analytical Psychology (1959)
Introduction to Wolff's "Studies in Jungian Psychology" (1959)
The Swiss Line in the European Spectrum (1928)
Reviews of Keyserling's "America Set Free" (1930) and "La Révolution Mondiale" (1934)
The Complications of American Psychology (1930)
The Dreamlike World of India (1939)
What India Can Teach Us (1939)
Appendix: Documents (1933–1938)

11. PSYCHOLOGY AND RELIGION: WEST AND EAST (1958; 2nd edn., 1969)

WESTERN RELIGION

Psychology and Religion (The Terry Lectures) (1938/1940)
A Psychological Approach to the Dogma of the Trinity (1942/1948)
Transformation Symbolism in the Mass (1942/1954)
Forewords to White's "God and the Unconscious" and Werblowsky's "Lucifer and Prometheus" (1952)
Brother Klaus (1933)
Psychotherapists or the Clergy (1932)
Psychoanalysis and the Cure of Souls (1928)
Answer to Job (1952)

EASTERN RELIGION

Psychological Commentaries on "The Tibetan Book of the Great Liberation" (1939/1954) and "The Tibetan Book of the Dead" (1935/1953)
Yoga and the West (1936)
Foreword to Suzuki's "Introduction to Zen Buddhism" (1939)
The Psychology of Eastern Meditation (1943)
The Holy Men of India: Introduction to Zimmer's "Der Weg zum Selbst" (1944)
Foreword to the "I Ching" (1950)

12. PSYCHOLOGY AND ALCHEMY ([1944] 1953; 2nd edn., 1968)

Prefatory note to the English Edition ([1951?] added 1967)
Introduction to the Religious and Psychological Problems of Alchemy
Individual Dream Symbolism in Relation to Alchemy (1936)
Religious Ideas in Alchemy (1937)
Epilogue

13. ALCHEMICAL STUDIES (1968)
Commentary on "The Secret of the Golden Flower" (1929)
The Visions of Zosimos (1938/1954)
Paracelsus as a Spiritual Phenomenon (1942)
The Spirit Mercurius (1943/1948)
The Philosophical Tree (1945/1954)

14. MYSTERIUM CONIUNCTIONIS ([1955–56] 1963; 2nd edn., 1970)

AN INQUIRY INTO THE SEPARATION AND
SYNTHESIS OF PSYCHIC OPPOSITES IN ALCHEMY
The Components of the Coniunctio
The Paradoxa
The Personification of the Opposites
Rex and Regina
Adam and Eve
The Conjunction

15. THE SPIRIT IN MAN, ART, AND LITERATURE (1966)
Paracelsus (1929)
Paracelsus the Physician (1941)
Sigmund Freud in His Historical Setting (1932)
In Memory of Sigmund Freud (1939)
Richard Wilhelm: In Memoriam (1930)
On the Relation of Analytical Psychology to Poetry (1922)
Psychology and Literature (1930/1950)
"Ulysses": A Monologue (1932)
Picasso (1932)

16. THE PRACTICE OF PSYCHOTHERAPY (1954; 2nd edn., 1966)

GENERAL PROBLEMS OF PSYCHOTHERAPY
Principles of Practical Psychotherapy (1935)
What Is Psychotherapy? (1935)
Some Aspects of Modern Psychotherapy (1930)
The Aims of Psychotherapy (1931)
Problems of Modern Psychotherapy (1929)
Psychotherapy and a Philosophy of Life (1943)
Medicine and Psychotherapy (1945)
Psychotherapy Today (1945)
Fundamental Questions of Psychotherapy (1951)

SPECIFIC PROBLEMS OF PSYCHOTHERAPY
The Therapeutic Value of Abreaction (1921/1928)
The Practical Use of Dream-Analysis (1934)

(*continued*)

16. (*continued*)

The Psychology of the Transference (1946)
Appendix: The Realities of Practical Psychotherapy ([1937] added 1966)

17. THE DEVELOPMENT OF PERSONALITY (1954)
Psychic Conflicts in a Child (1910/1946)
Introduction to Wickes's "Analyses der Kinderseele" (1927/1931)
Child Development and Education (1928)
Analytical Psychology and Education: Three Lectures (1926/1946)
The Gifted Child (1943)
The Significance of the Unconscious in Individual Education (1928)
The Development of Personality (1934)
Marriage as a Psychological Relationship (1925)

18. THE SYMBOLIC LIFE (1954)
Translated by R.F.C. Hull and others

Miscellaneous writings

19. COMPLETE BIBLIOGRAPHY OF C. G. JUNG'S WRITINGS (1976; 2nd edn., 1992)

20. GENERAL INDEX TO THE COLLECTED WORKS (1979)

THE ZOFINGIA LECTURES (1983)
Supplementary Volume A to The Collected Works. Edited by William McGuire, translated by Jan van Heurck, introduction by Marie-Louise von Franz

PSYCHOLOGY OF THE UNCONSCIOUS ([1912] 1992)

A STUDY OF THE TRANSFORMATIONS AND SYMBOLISMS OF THE LIBIDO.
A CONTRIBUTION TO THE HISTORY OF THE EVOLUTION OF THOUGHT

Supplementary Volume B to the Collected Works. Translated by Beatrice M. Hinkle, introduction by William McGuire

Related publications:

THE BASIC WRITINGS OF C. G. JUNG
Selected and introduced by Violet S. de Laszlo

C. G. JUNG: LETTERS
Selected and edited by Gerhard Adler, in collaboration with Aniela Jaffé.
Translations from the German by R.F.C. Hull.

VOL. 1: 1906–1950
VOL. 2: 1951–1961

C. G. JUNG SPEAKING: Interviews and Encounters
Edited by William McGuire and R.F.C. Hull

C. G. JUNG: Word and Image
Edited by Aniela Jaffé

THE ESSENTIAL JUNG
Selected and introduced by Anthony Storr

THE GNOSTIC JUNG
Selected and introduced by Robert A. Segal

PSYCHE AND SYMBOL
Selected and introduced by Violet S. de Laszlo

Notes of C. G. Jung's Seminars:

DREAM ANALYSIS ([1928–30] 1984)
Edited by William McGuire

NIETZSCHE'S *ZARATHUSTRA* ([1934–39] 1988)
Edited by James L. Jarrett (2 vols.)

ANALYTICAL PSYCHOLOGY ([1925] 1989)
Edited by William McGuire